Tourism in the New South Africa

Tourism, Retailing and Consumption series

Edited by:
Professor Gareth Shaw, University of Exeter
Dr Dimitri Ioannides, Southwest Missouri State University

Consumption has become an important theme in geography and the social sciences and within this broad debate two key areas of concern are tourism and retailing. To date there is no series that brings together these closely related topics under a unifying perspective. Tourism, Retailing and Consumption will provide such a perspective.

The series will provide core texts for students of geography and related disciplines at first degree level. It will be wide-ranging in scope and cover both historical and contemporary debates in tourism, retailing and consumption. A number of more specialised texts suited to postgraduate study will also be included.

Also in the series:
Tourism in Transition:
Economic Change in Central Europe
Allan M. Williams and Aladimir Balaz

Understanding Urban Tourism:
Image, Culture and Experience
Martin Selby

Tourism in the New South Africa

Social Responsibility and the Tourist Experience

Garth Allen
&
Frank Brennan

I.B. TAURIS

LONDON · NEW YORK

Published in 2004 by I.B.Tauris & Co Ltd
6 Salem Road, London W2 4BU
175 Fifth Avenue, New York NY 10010
www.ibtauris.com

In the United States and Canada distributed by Palgrave Macmillan,
a division of St. Martin's Press
175 Fifth Avenue, New York NY 10010

ISBN   hardback 1 86064 793 6
       paperback 1 86064 794 4
EAN   hardback 978 1 86064 793 2
       paperback 978 1 86064 794 9

A full CIP record for this book is available from the British Library
A full CIP record for this book is available from the Library of Congress

Typeset in Bodoni Book by Dexter Haven Associates Ltd, London
Printed and bound in Great Britain by TJ International Ltd, Padstow, Cornwall

Contents

Figures and tables

Figures

Tables

Map

Acknowledgements

Throughout the time spent in KwaZulu-Natal many South Africans were generous with their time and their encouragement, and many of them kindly provided helpful advice and further contacts. We cannot name them all but we hope we have acknowledged those whose interest and support were particularly significant. We have indicated below the nature of the contribution and have described the position they held at the time of their engagement with the project.

Professor Eleanor Preston-Whyte, formerly Deputy Vice Chancellor, at the University of Natal, provided office space and facilities, introduced helpful contacts, and offered warm hospitality, as did Professor Lynn Dalrymple of the University of Zululand. Professor Robert Preston-Whyte, formerly Dean of the Faculty of Social Sciences at the University of Natal and author of three excellent articles cited in this paper, also introduced researchers and organisations interested in eco-tourism development in KwaZulu-Natal and generally offered a sophisticated orientation to issues in tourism development in South Africa. Christopher Proctor, author of an important report on tourism in the province was particularly generous in talking through the economics of development in the South Africa context, as was Professor Mike Morris, an economist at the University of Natal. Two lengthy meetings with Andrew Zaloumis were held, a busy, dedicated member of the Community Resources Optimisation Programme (CROP), an NGO active in sustainable development in Maputaland. During these interviews, Andrew was highly informative on the politics of rural development in KwaZulu-Natal, and on the possible role of NGOs in that process.

Officers of the KwaZulu-Natal Nature Conservation Service, a public conservation authority responsible for the stewardship of many beautiful protected areas of KwaZulu-Natal, were most welcoming and generous with their time. Among those interviewed, David Hibbs, Director of Tourism, and Geert Creemers, a resource economist, outlined the history of the KwaZulu-Natal Conservation Service (formerly the Natal Parks Board and now also known as KZN-Wildlife), its excellent record of conservation work, and its plans for eco-tourism development in the future. Martin Brooks, Head of Scientific Services, Trevor Sandwith, Head of Planning, Michael Haynes, an Environmental Planner, and numerous officers at St Lucia, Hluhluwe, and other parks, spent valuable time with us.

Eddie Koch, journalist and author on eco-tourism, through correspondence convinced us of the need to visit South Africa, and has recently (2001) published his own account of domestic tourism in South Africa. Professor John

Argyle, Justin Barnes, Mary de Haas and Jim Kieranan, all at the University of Natal, Karen Kohler, Research Co-ordinator at the KwaZulu-Natal Tourist Board and Julian Baskin, Peter Derman and Eddie Russell all made numerous reports and papers available. Karen Kohler also generously read the first five chapters of the book in order to try and ensure that we are as up-to-date as possible with changes in the names of South African authorities and organisations. Of course, we are solely responsible for any remaining mistakes and failures.

Les Carlisle, Community Development Officer, Phinda Resource Reserve made sure we did not intrude on the Spice Girls' vacation at Phinda when we visited to talk with him. Jacob Luvumbo, Director of Community Development, Satour, briefed us on Satour's policy position on community-led tourism development; Isaiah Mahlangu and Steve Collins of Interface Africa, an NGO active in conflict resolution and community development in KwaZulu-Natal, set up meetings in St Lucia and Kosi Bay, and Aka Stavrou of Database Africa and formerly with LAPC, author of many papers on rural development, gave us a background to tourism development in Kosi Bay. Nicky Barker (now Moore) of St Lucia, journalist, activist and hotelier, offered a vivid account of the history of and alternative futures for Dukuduku and its peoples.

Tim Foggin, of the Natal Technicon at Pietermaritzburg, shared a visit to Phinda Game Reserve, accompanied us on a visit to Kosi Bay, and helped sustain our enthusiasm for the project. Carolyn Bolton, of British Airways Assisting Conservation, granted us complimentary stand-by tickets for two of our journeys to South Africa and Tony Reilly, Director of the British Council in Durban, sanctioned a grant to meet some of the travel and subsistence costs in South Africa for our first joint visit in 1996.

Finally, thanks to the Research Committee and the Social Sciences Department of The College of St Mark and St John, Plymouth, England, which part-funded Frank Brennan's initial visit to KwaZulu-Natal in 1995.

These acknowledgements illustrate the pragmatism that shaped our choice of respondents. No attempt was made nor could have been made, given the logistics and limited resources available to us, to gather 'evidence' from all those agencies, groups and key individuals, who will significantly determine the future for South Africa tourism. The closest we get to methodological rigour is through the 'snowballing' approach to gathering respondents, always asking people who we talked with who they thought we should talk with next – and we tried to do that, with all the obvious limitations of such an approach. Many significant 'voices' were not able to be sought out and the book may be significantly different because of that. We are particularly conscious of our enforced partiality given the political emphasis in South African politics on the value of diverse voices and inclusion.

Acronyms and abbreviations

ACTSA	Action for Southern Africa
ANC	African National Congress
BEE	Black Economic Empowerment
CBO	Community-based organisation
CGE	Commission on Gender Equality
CORD	Centre for Community Organisation, Research and Development
COSATU	Congress of South African Trade Unions
CROP	Community Resources Optimisation Programme
DACST	Department of Arts, Culture, Science and Technology
DDTA	Dukuduku Development and Tourism Association
DEAT	Department of Environmental Affairs and Tourism
DLA	Department of Land Affairs
EIA	Environmental Impact Assessment
EIU	Economist Intelligence Unit
EOC	Education Opportunities Council
GEAR	Growth, Employment and Reconstruction
GNU	Government of National Unity
GSLWP	Greater St Lucia Wetland Park
ICDP	Integrated Conservation and Development Project
IFP	Inkatha Freedom Party
IMF	International Monetary Fund
KDNC	KwaZulu Department of Nature Conservation
KEN	KwaDapha eMalangeni Nkovokeni
KNCS	KwaZulu-Natal Conservation Service
KZNNCS	KwaZulu-Natal Nature Conservation Service
KZNTA	KwaZulu-Natal Tourism Authority
LAPC	Land and Agriculture Policy Centre
MICE	Meetings, Incentives, Conventions and Exhibitions
NGOs	Non-government organisations
NOW	Natal Organisation of Women
NPA	Natal Provincial Administration
NPB	Natal Parks Board
NTF	National Tourism Forum
RBM	Richard's Bay Minerals
RDP	Reconstruction and Development Programme
RDS	Rural Development Strategy

RENAMO	Resistência Nacional Moçambicana
RETOSA	Regional Tourism Organisation of Southern Africa
SACP	South African Communist Party
SADC	Southern African Development Community
SADF	South African Defence Force
SANCO	South African National Civic Organisation
SAPS	South African Police Service
Satour	South African Tourism Authority
SDI	Spatial Development Initiative
SMDF	Southern Maputaland Development Forum
TANK	Tourism Association of KwaZulu-Natal
THETA	Tourism, Hospitality, Education and Training Authority
TRC	Truth and Reconciliation Commission
TSA	Tourism South Africa
UDF	United Democratic Front
UWO	United Women's Organisation
WESSA	Wildlife and Environmental Society of South Africa
WTO	World Tourism Organisation

Introduction

Origins

This book evolved in the first instance from Frank Brennan's account of his visit to South Africa in 1995. The decision to focus on Kosi Bay, Phinda and St Lucia, all in the province of KwaZulu-Natal in the sub-tropical north east of the country, was prompted by his original work in those areas, and also through long and detailed discussions he had with members of influential development groups, such as the Community Resources Optimisation Programme and Interface Africa, and with officers of the then Natal Parks Board. Frank was concerned to write up the visit within an overlapping academic framework of tourism studies, development studies and social anthropology. Chapters 1–4 of the book owe their shape and focus to Frank's first attempts at setting pen to paper and discussing the process and outcome with Garth Allen. The project itself, any mention of Durban in the text, and the other chapters have their origins in Garth Allen's first visit in October, 1994, when the need for a study became apparent and the logistics and pragmatics of a study were explored both *in situ* and through subsequent institutional arrangements and fund-raising activity in the UK. The presumptive decision to write the study up as a book was taken following Frank Brennan's initial report in 1995 and the warm response to his work from academics in the UK and South Africa who were asked to read the material.

Tensions

The satisfaction we both experience from working in South Africa on issues of importance to poor people, both arises from and is tempered by the discomforts of privilege, and we have tried to offer a feel in the text for the origins and significance of personal moral dilemmas as we experienced them. People we talked to in the UK about our work had usually absorbed the message from others, notably the UK media, that South Africa was simply too dangerous to visit as a tourist. We were also told by many white South Africans, particularly during the early years of our research, that the province of KwaZulu-Natal was a particularly violent region of the country. One director of a research institute at the University of Natal told Frank Brennan to take his work to any other part of the country rather than KwaZulu-Natal. During those early visits, violence was a regular and frequent topic of conversation with respondents, many of whom had personal stories to tell of criminal attacks against themselves or family members. The South African media at the time seemed to be besotted with murders, rapes, and hijacking. It has to be said that the frequent warnings about the risks of travelling in South Africa did alarm us. Much of our time in the country involved the juggling of fears for personal safety with anger at the continuing and stark injustices of South African society and we discuss selected personal experiences of being tourists in South Africa in the second part of the book, from chapter 5 onwards.

The difficulties we came across were of a much less dramatic order than being the victims of violent crime. These included personal discomfort during openly racist exchanges between white employers and black staff; the profoundly institutionalised spatial segregation of the races in places of work, residence and leisure, hindering genuine intercourse across the races; witnessing the harshest deprivations of black villages and illegal settlements, where hunger and AIDS leave many children orphaned; and the immediate promotion to elite status just by being white or black and the awkwardness of dealing with that imposed privilege.

On one visit in 1996, Frank Brennan returned to a laundry in Durban to collect the clothes he had left there two days earlier. Finding himself at the back of an orderly and silent queue of black South Africans was fine until the white owner of the business addressed him over the heads of the customers in front and served him first. Walking to the front of the queue to collect his laundry, perfectly washed, pressed and folded by black staff, was a confusing moment. None of the other customers complained or even spoke. It was normal. Nobody wanted a painful fuss.

We have had many such experiences during the past eight years, and they remain as difficult as ever to negotiate. Nevertheless, and in spite of the social divisions, South Africa is an exciting place to visit as a tourist. Neither of us is a trained moral or social philosopher, but the need to address the moral dimension in tourism development could not be avoided as the shape of the project emerged. An implicit concern throughout the book will hopefully be evident, where we try to offer the reader not only a text that meets academic conventions, but that also gives a more generalised, tentative feel for the intellectual riches possible from reflecting on the experience of being a tourist in South Africa. We have tried to write a book that will be enjoyable to read and useful to consult.

Tourism and tourist studies

Commentaries on tourism, on its developmental potential, on its casual exploitation of local peoples, on its negative demonstration effect and on its destructive impact on the environment, have often been marked by a predetermined, even supercilious hostility. The literature on tourism, at its worst, amounts to little more than a cluttered landscape of vapid moralising and unconvincing theory, focusing on the demerits of developing tourism, rarely on the demerits of not doing so. The literature is characterised by a series of anguished reflections on tourism's advance, in that miseries multiply without end, and where the course of things is profoundly troubled. We are invited to conclude that the Good Tourist, like Doris Lessing's 'Good Terrorist', is a contradiction in terms.

More recently, however, a novel trend in tourism theory has emerged that also leaps to essences and generalities but does not view the industry as a cataclysmic eventuality. This model of a new, community-based eco-tourism, although equally culpable in the simplification and reduction of vast complexities into easy currency, claims the high ground of an apolitical development that resolves all of the dilemmas of tourism development and its social and environmental impacts.

The gospel according to eco-tourism

Theories of eco-tourism have taken shape out of a widening and acute concern for the environment, out of a repeatedly stated need for a more ethical and democratic form of development, and as a particular elaboration of the notion of sustainability. In their enthusiasm, advocates of this awkward melding of philosophy, ethics, embryonic economic theory and environmentalism, often assume away the tangles of vested interests and the political factors involved in any allocation of resources towards one form of development (that has yet to prove itself) and away from other more conventional forms of rural or urban economic development.

For proponents of eco-tourism, small-scale, and dispersed sites of tourism activity are felt to be less environmentally threatening and more emotionally appealing than the ribbon developments that characterise major tourism

locations in so many parts of the world. They also facilitate the direct participation of local people in all aspects of development, including decision-making.
This proactive involvement, along with a more equitable distribution of costs
and benefits is commonly argued to be critical to sustainability (de Kadt, 1990).

Huge claims are made for this model of eco-tourism development, that
has many sub-forms and is variously called 'alternative tourism' (de Kadt,
1990), 'low impact tourism' (Lillywhite, 1991), 'responsible tourism'
(Wheeler, 1991), 'progressive tourism' (Wheeller, 1992) and 'new tourism'
(Poon, 1994). Some go so far as to argue that not only can eco-tourism protect
the environment, generate satisfying and sustainable employment, empower
local communities, provide authentic and quality host–tourist encounters,
treasure cultures and traditions, it can also play a major role in promoting
world peace (Spivack, 1991).

Such utopian visions are not without their critics. Perhaps the most trenchant
criticism of the notion of socially responsible tourism comes from Brian
Wheeller, who emphasises what he sees as the irresistible flow from small-
scale to mass tourism, that can only have devastating repercussions for the
environment and for impoverished rural peoples. Wheeller irritably argues
that the costs and benefits of tourism can never be evenly distributed, and that
the literature on responsible tourism is merely a distraction and offers at best a
short-lived micro-solution to the problems caused everywhere by mass tourism.
As Wheeller (1992) contends, the fundamental contradiction is simply stated:
for tourism to be sustainable, it has to be economically viable. Small-scale
localised trade cannot possibly offer the same level and distribution of economic
benefits as mass tourism, that is by definition, market driven and otherwise
uncontrollable. Eco-tourism is, for Wheeller, a middle-class preoccupation, that
offers no real alternative to mass tourism, and that, in any case, only serves as
the vanguard for the latter. For Duffy (2002), it is a 'Trip Too Far', the title of her
recent book based on fieldwork in Belize, where she argues that eco-tourism
is simply a new sub-sector of global capitalism, predictably (as opposed to the
radical claims made by eco-tourism's proponents) putting individual consumer
decisions at the heart of the cause of unfair income and wealth inequalities.

Tourist benefits

We have written this book in the conviction that, despite limitations, eco-tourism
can make significant contributions to the welfare of many impoverished rural
communities. But the book is also intended as a cautionary note; emphasising
the need to take account of the prevailing political and economic circumstances
in every case. Only by contextualising tourism research and development in

this way, can the heuristic value of the concept or paradigm of eco-tourism be helpfully tested and evaluated. We ask: does this new model of tourism development offer virtuous and realistic guidelines for decision-making, or does it amount to little more than a discourse of good intentions (Butler, 1994)? This question is of immense importance in that decisions made in the allocation of precious resources with the goal of sustainable development have had, and will continue to have, direct and crucial repercussions in the lives of many deprived rural people. Whether or not eco-tourism works in South Africa will affect the health, education and happiness of many chronically excluded and vulnerable members of South African society. Having witnessed the awful social consequences of apartheid in a remote but highly populated region of the country, in KwaZulu-Natal, in the north-east of South Africa, we are keenly aware of the need for fairness, efficiency and effectiveness in the allocation of public funds and community resources.

As a developmental strategy, tourism has been often criticised for the extent of leakages from the local economy (Dunning and McQueen, 1982; Gamble, 1989). Minimising such leakages is argued to be contingent upon the intensity of linkages with the wider tourism sector and with other sectors of the host economy (Mathieson and Wall, 1982). The necessity, and difficulties of integrating small-scale, community-led tourism initiatives into the predominantly white and upmarket international tourism industry in South Africa is a recurring theme of this book.

Tourism has also been criticised widely in the literature for its adverse impact upon the natural environment (Farrell and Runyan, 1991; Mader, 1985; Shaw and Williams, 1994). In response, other observers have argued that the tourist industry, fully aware of the importance of the natural surroundings for its success, can and should enter into a desirably symbiotic relationship with the environment (Ryan, 1994). Indeed, against the background of a striking growth in public concern for the protection of biodiversity, the case for environmental sustainability in tourism development, sometimes marginalised as naive evangelism, has in recent years been attributed an increasing degree of academic credibility and, for many now constitutes a serious agenda (de Kadt, 1990). The discourse of the environment is highly charged, authoritative, and almost unimpeachable. Cater (1993, p.85) suggests that the prefix 'eco' confers an aura of respectability that is 'only marginally less admirable than motherhood'.

However, 'the environment' and 'sustainability' are profoundly problematic notions. Differing views of the environment are discussed by Farrell and McLellan (1987), who argue that perceptions of the natural surroundings are informed by the latter's function. That is, the same piece of land will have very different meanings for, say, a farmer, a developer, a botanist, an environmentalist, or a tourist. Moreover, those respective valorisations are not fixed. Shaw

5

and Williams (1994) offer an account of how state environmental policy can be informed by changes in economic circumstances. For example, if unemployment increases rapidly, conservation strategies may be ignored in order to encourage tourism development and provide jobs in areas that had been formerly protected from such expansion.

The economic potential of eco-tourism development has also been recognised by private entrepreneurs, and one location drawn on in this book is concerned with an upmarket project, that attracts investors and tourists alike with high-quality services and accommodation, by emphasising its ethos of environmental sustainability, and by highlighting the economic and social benefits enjoyed by locals as a direct result of its tourism activities. This and other eco-tourism initiatives in South Africa are still in their infancy, and provide a rich opportunity for extensive and longitudinal research into the efficacy of efforts to marry conservation with rural upliftment, and into the changes necessary to engage the most disadvantaged sectors of rural communities in their own development.

Much of the literature on eco-tourism is preoccupied with the debilitating and ultimately frustrating search for a comprehensive and once-and-for-all definition. In this book, we address this problem, in part, by accepting as guidelines the broad framework for community-based eco-tourism development outlined in the Reconstruction and Development Programme (RDP) of the African National Congress (ANC, 1994), and in the Rural Development Strategy (Government of National Unity, or GNU, 1995). The RDP advocates sustainable development in South Africa, and highlights the social and environmental benefits anticipated from synergistic strategies that focus on the quality of growth, rather than on quantitative indicators of national economic expansion (Munslow et al., 1995). The ANC clearly states its support for the philosophical, humanitarian and environmental principles of proactive and sustainable development: 'Development is not about the delivery of goods to a passive citizenry. It is about active involvement and growing empowerment. In taking this approach we are building on the many forums, peace structures and negotiations that our people are involved in throughout the land' (ANC, 1994, p.5).

For the authors of the RDP, it is axiomatic that development of the human-resource base cannot be achieved without establishing appropriate and enabling democratic institutions to facilitate participation at all levels of South African society. This particular governmental model, with its emphasis on the humanitarian elements of democracy, empowerment and communal upliftment, provides the conceptual backdrop to the comparative analysis of the eco-tourism initiatives outlined in this chapter.

In the Rural Development Strategy, the authors are unencumbered by the definitional entanglements of academic literature, and broadly interpret eco-tourism as travel to protected areas that does not cause irreparable damage to the environment, and that benefits local people in terms of jobs and improvements in social services, such as schools, clinics, improved water supply and infrastructure. These improvements are to be funded by the proceeds of the eco-tourism initiatives themselves. Moreover, and most importantly, development will arise from the empowerment of local communities through their proactive involvement in all aspects of these projects, including any decision-making. This empowerment will be facilitated by the creation of a framework of democratic institutions, and by open and transparent relationships between political groups and civil society.

Eco-tourism is expected to contribute to the transfer of wealth from the urban sector to the agrarian economy, as well as to the nation's earnings of foreign exchange. It must be developed on a non-racial basis, and the needs of the most vulnerable, including women, must be given priority (GNU, 1995). Eco-tourism ventures should be integrated into the wider economy, and assistance given to small-scale enterprises. Where possible, local communities should come to own their eco-tourism initiatives.

As will be seen, these guidelines constitute something of an ideal type and, like earlier definitions, are open to interpretation. However, given the importance of both documents in terms of policy, this albeit wordy description will serve as a useful point of departure for the comparative discussion of eco-tourism development in KwaZulu-Natal, and for the speculative excursion into ways of making sense of the tourist experience.

In Europe, public knowledge of KwaZulu-Natal, in so far as it reaches the public gaze, has been dominated by vivid images of widespread violence, which, in the media, is commonly associated with the resurgence in Zulu ethnicity, and with bitter rivalries between the IFP and supporters of the ANC. The political reality (both local and provincial) is, of course, much more complex, but fears for personal safety among visitors are undoubtedly one of the most powerfully inhibiting factors in the development of a vibrant tourism culture (George, 1998). Moreover, the violence and political venality in the province act as obstacles to the establishment of a democratic system of local governance, a factor that has important implications for the development of community-based eco-tourism initiatives. Because of this, the violent clashes will be discussed at some length in relation to the historical struggle over scarce resources and also through the vehicle of recent and analytically powerful social theory.

The shape and focus of the book

One of the central academic goals for tourism studies is to create a programme of empirical research and theory building that will develop frameworks to enable the comparison and evaluation of eco-tourism initiatives. Until now there has been a marked lack of empirical material to substantiate or refute eco-tourism theories that, as indicated above, range from the evangelical to the contemptuous in tenor, with few intermediate evaluations (Pearce, 1992). We hope that the accounts of the travelling we offer in this book, together with the theoretical speculation that accompanies the detail of places and encounters, will contribute to the debate, and will lead to a sense of realism in assessments of the potential role of eco-tourism as a vehicle for sustainable development in the poorest regions of the world.

The various concepts of eco-tourism have been frequently referred to as constituting a new paradigm. In a seminal paper on important changes in the policies and practices in the development industry, Chambers (1986, p.1) defines a paradigm as: 'a coherent and mutually supporting pattern of concepts, values, methods and action, amenable to wide application'.

In this book we argue that the building blocks for developing a new paradigm for eco-tourism development are available. However, their potential contribution has been largely unrecognised by academics in the embryonic state of the contemporary study of the political economy of tourism development.

In search of pro-poor tourism

Although the empowerment of the disadvantaged through their proactive participation in their own development initiatives is commonly regarded as a prerequisite for sustainability, eliciting such commitment is not as straight-forward as might be expected. In rural KwaZulu-Natal, the enforced removal of African communities during the setting up of national parks and other game reserves from the late nineteenth century and through most of the twentieth century, has left a legacy of embittered relationships between conservation authorities and their neighbours. Moreover, among African communities, there exists a profound mistrust of elitist concepts of environmentalism, and of conservation itself. Overcoming the suspicions of local people, and dispelling their understandable apprehensions of the claimed intentions of state and other agencies will be critical in these efforts to reconcile the protection of biodiversity with rural development.

In the new South Africa, sustainable development, with all its implications of eternal well-being and justice, is argued to be contingent upon a 'paradigmatic shift' in institutional practices and policies that have their origins in the *de facto* survival of apartheid (Picard and Garrity, 1995; Schutte, 1995). This point will be shown to be critical, and important ideological and other impediments to that shift will be identified. While examining the notion of participation as an essential component of sustainability, we also hope to address the following questions: Given that democratic involvement of local people in eco-tourism initiatives has a powerful and moral appeal, what evidence is there to argue that it constitutes best practice in attempts to improve the living conditions of the poor rural communities in KwaZulu-Natal? What guarantees are there that the material and other benefits of eco-tourism will be enjoyed by the most vulnerable, including women, the elderly and the uneducated? Is 'empowerment' itself an indication of development, or should the value of eco-tourism be measured wholly in terms of income and improved services? Finally, is good governance, so sought after by the ANC through the establishment of democratic political and civil institutions, a crucial factor in development? In other words, in the twenty-first century, is democracy a prerequisite for development, and if so, what are the obstacles to the construction of that democracy?

> Responsible tourism...means the responsibility of government and business to involve the local communities that are in close proximity to the tourism plant and attractions through the development of meaningful economic linkages. It implies the responsibility to respect, invest in and develop local cultures and to protect them from over-commercialisation and over-exploitation [Department of Environmental Affairs and Tourism, DEAT, 1996, p.19, quoted in Koch and Massyn, 2001, p.151].

The next chapter will provide a background discussion of the role of tourism in the South African economy, and of national and provincial government determination to promote eco-tourism as part of its plans for the democratic development of chronically deprived rural communities. Some of the important factors that are informing the progress of eco-tourism in the country, and the main stakeholders involved, are identified, and a brief account of one such initiative is provided. Chapter 2 looks at the political economy in general, and more specifically at tourism and eco-tourism in KwaZulu-Natal, the province where we have been most active in our research during the past eight years. The larger part of the chapter is dedicated to a history and comparison of the two conservation authorities that were functioning during the apartheid era, and that have now combined to become the KwaZulu-Natal Nature Conservation Service (KZNNCS). The relationships between these organisations and their impoverished neighbouring African communities are examined, and their involvement in integrated conservation and eco-tourism projects is discussed at length.

Experimental eco-tourism projects in KwaZulu-Natal are manifold, involving various partnerships between rural communities, conservation authorities, the private sector, NGOs and local government. These projects differ in important ways, and three contrasting initiatives are discussed in chapter 3. We have focused on these particular initiatives from the early days of our visits to KwaZulu-Natal. Each of these examples of eco-tourism development high-lights specific issues and problems, and these are given full attention in chapter 4. Here the whole basis of the government's thrust for good governance and democratic participatory development is questioned in the light of the descriptive analysis of the four main places we visited in KwaZulu-Natal.

Another book?

This book reports on the travels together, and singly, of two academics, the one a social anthropologist, the other a political economist, to South Africa during the mid-1990s until April 2002. The travelling and subsequent discussion, analysis and writing was done on a shoe-string. The book is impoverished by that. We do not offer the detail a social anthropologist would wish for, and nor is this a full blown 'political economy of tourism in South Africa', or of KwaZulu-Natal for that matter.

The book is about the tourist experience in South Africa; in relation to selected aspects of the social and political context of place and about the morality of state, organisation and individual behaviour. We have not felt obliged to try and 'solve' the problems of tourism development in South Africa, nor to offer advice on the exploitation of current and projected strengths. The book is about aspects of the South African tourism experience and is neither a textbook for students of South African tourism nor a manual for policy analysts and policy makers. Crucial issues, for these texts, are ignored because we felt, in any case, that the nature of our work and our expertise and skills did not allow us to tackle policy issues that are contentious, not yet resolved, and possibly intractable. The example of South Africa's heroic attempts to introduce and sustain participatory democratic methods for identifying the direction and priorities of social development is a case in point.

What becomes apparent is that something of an orthodoxy has emerged in South Africa, in that local political bodies are expected to work closely with civil society organisations such as community-based organisations (CBOs) and non-governmental organisations (NGOs), who are deemed to be representative of the grassroots needs and aspirations of local communities. However, our work has shown that community life presents a plurality of changing realities in contests over resources and power. Local organisations may be led by powerful individuals or elites and for this and other reasons may not be able to reflect that plurality. There exist exclusions within exclusions, and voluntary bodies or NGOs may not be able to support the most severely marginalised sectors of rural society. Development is always messy and fitful, and a nuanced approach is necessary in building theories of community participation, in particular, in the context of the behaviour of the international tourist from the North. We continue the search for a *modus operandi* for this goal from chapter 5 onwards, where we select a small number of analytically powerful, social scientific constructs to inform an account of the tourist experience in South Africa. This approach is the defining feature of our project, and the attention we give to this theme leads, as said, to the necessary exclusion of other worthy themes and issues.

Tourists and tourism in South Africa: a snapshot

Tourism, perhaps more than any other sector, has the potential to achieve the objectives of the Reconstruction and Development Programme (RDP) of the new government ... Tourism development in South Africa has largely been a missed opportunity. Had its history been different, South Africa would probably have been one of the most visited places in the world [DEAT, 1996, p.4].

In 1994, the Land and Agriculture Policy Centre (LAPC) estimated that 5 per cent of economically active people in South Africa were directly or indirectly employed in the tourism sector, similar to the proportions employed in agriculture and mining. Anticipated growth in the tourism sector was expected to increase the numbers employed from 810,000 to 1,060,000 by the beginning of the new millennium.

South Africa is determined to become a major destination for international tourists, as well as to sustain the economic significance of domestic tourism. International tourists from Africa currently make up over 70 per cent of South Africa's international tourists, but this book says little about them, nor about domestic tourism. The 'tourist' in this book means at least two people (the authors) and others from the North, especially the UK. The country is now 'sold' as a 'safe-haven', following 11 September 2001 (ironic given the international perceptions of South African crime, as we shall see) and as a 'bargain', given the relative weakness of the rand against other currencies. From Europe, there is no jet-lag for the 90 per cent and more of visitors who come by air, and they are promised an 'all-year' climate and a dazzling array of sights and sounds and other sensations, wrapped up in a modern infrastructure (roads, hospitals, banks) and often, friends and family and business visits.

These features of South African tourism, and many other facets, are tracked by Satour, the South Africa Tourism Authority, that provides regular promotional material and annual and monthly data. Statistics South Africa also monitors economic trends and developments and offers an annual report. Both sources are drawn on in this section for data on tourist flows and economic indicators.

The 'rebirth' of South Africa is a promotional campaign, in part, promising oceans and landscapes, exotic people and animals, with the risky magnetism of an 'unexplored land', 'different' from anywhere else. The country now boasts four World Heritage Sites, bearing the rare Unesco recognition, and one of these, the Greater St Lucia Wetland Park (GSLWP) is one of the places reported on throughout the text. The other three sites are the uKahlamba-Drakensberg Park, Robben Island and the Cradle of Humankind at Sterkfontein. A further four sites have been presented to Unesco for recognition in 2003 (www.mintel.com/countrysurvey, 2002). As we shall see, social divisions and persecutions from the past are being turned into attractions of the present and future. 'Township Tourism', an example for us, of 'Dark Tourism', is growing, fuelled by day-tours into the townships with itineraries that include visits to schools, 'shebeens' (unlicensed bars) and 'sangoma' (faith healers). It is now also possible to book into township B&Bs using the internet.

International visitors, as we have noted, are mainly from neighbouring African countries (Lesotho, Botswana, Mozambique and Zimbabwe) and tourist figures here are notoriously unreliable because of the difficulty of distinguishing tourists, workers and migrants. One quarter of all international tourists come from the UK, and the latter numbers grew by 3.7 per cent, in 2000–2001 compared to 1990–2000. In the first year of the new millennium, 362,508 visitors left the UK for South Africa (part of just over a million from Europe and just under four million from Africa). North American tourists are the third largest market (202,959 recorded visitors), after Africa and Europe, and there are small numbers but showing significant growth from Australia and Asia (China has accredited South Africa with 'approved destination' status).

We shall discuss the significance of 'family and friends' tourism later, but over half of the UK visitors during 1998–99 report combining holidays with visiting family or with business, and over 75 per cent of visitors reported, in the same year, that 'word of mouth' was the prime influence on the decision to choose to travel to South Africa (South African Tourism, UK). The pattern of visits was multi-destination for an average period of almost three weeks. Tourists arriving by air to South Africa spent, on average, R834 while MICE visitors spent R1450 per day (about £100.00) and contributed about R457 (£30 million) per day to the economy (8.5 per cent of Gross Domestic Product).

Visitors from the North are induced by the climate, the chance to visit friends, and the scenic beauty; by the wildlife and value for money; by the opportunity to experience different cultures, to see the country after political change, to promote business interests, through curiosity and because of a diversity of attractions, in descending order of importance (the first three amount to over 70 per cent of the claimed attraction). On leaving the country, visitors upgraded the 'value for money' attraction to 40 per cent, from 21 per cent, and the 'scenic beauty' factor from 32 per cent to 50 per cent (South African Tourism, UK, 2001).

South Africa is currently in the second year of a government-led 'South Africa Welcome Campaign' (www.mintel.com/countrysurvey, 2002). This aims to encourage South Africans to believe that international tourists hold the key to prosperity and all citizens must act so as to make visitors 'feel safe and welcome'. The government's National Business Initiative has funded yet another new agency, the Tourism, Hospitality, Education and Training Authority (THETA) whose core ('flagship') programme is the 'Ubuntu We Care' programme, for people whose work is likely to bring them in contact with international tourists (discussed further in chapter 8).

To stimulate the international tourism market, in November 2000, South Africa Tourism began an eighteen month, global marketing campaign, that went through a number of transformations in its short life but ended up, in 2002, with the slogan 'Discover South Africa, Rediscover Yourself' (www.mintel.com/country profile, 2002). UK agents and operators selling South African tourism can register for 'Fundi' (the Nguni word for expert), recognition of their knowledge of South Africa, and taxis in London, Manchester and Birmingham, with the South African flag as coachwork, are testimony to the innovative and energetic government efforts to sustain and develop British visitors to South Africa.

The government has been no less creative and innovative inside the country. In 1996, for example, following the White Paper on Tourism in July, South Africa initiated a series of interlocking policies designed to promote the controlled expansion of the important domestic tourism market (Koch and Massyn, 2001). 'Responsible tourism' was to be practised and encouraged by government tourism agencies, rural economies were to be strengthened, joint ventures between public and private providers were idealised and financed (South Africa having caught the Northern public policy infection of 'partnership-working'). The 1996 White Paper was preceded in KwaZulu-Natal by a provincial Strategic Framework for the Implementation of the Tourism Policy of KwaZulu-Natal. This initiative coincided with the beginnings of our visits to KwaZulu-Natal, and the themes of the strategy, that include an evaluation of the province's tourism capital, of establishing focus points for development in the province, and for finding new roles for the key agencies (to become 'partners') recur through the chapters in the first part of the book.

In 1997, the Department of Arts, Culture, Science and Technology (DACST) took responsibility for putting a cultural dimension into the Lubombo Spatial Development Initiative (SDI), a developmental, regional (Southern Africa) focus point or node. This cultural dimension could include, for tourists, history and heritage, dance, music, and the visual arts, and the general rituals and symbols of everyday life that characterise a 'place' and its peoples. Cultural projects are alleged to have the twin beneficial capacity to promote tourism revenues and sustain local cultures.

In November 2000, ministers from Mozambique, Zimbabwe and South Africa agreed to form the Great Limpopo Transfrontier Park (formerly the Gaza-Kruger-Gonarezhou Transfrontiers Park), and the Park formally opened in December 2002, inaugurated Xai-Xai, Mozambique, in the presence of a Presidential triumvirate from South Africa, Mozambique and Zimbabwe. This Southern Africa agreement is indicative of a rash of recent treaties and projected regional (Southern Africa) partnerships, one of which involves land we will discuss later, in northern KwaZulu-Natal, the Lubombo Transfrontier Conservation Area, following a Protocol established between Mozambique, Swaziland and South Africa. Such regional agencies as the Southern African Development Community (SADC) and the Regional Tourism Organisation of Southern Africa (RETOSA) will be significant forces in reshaping the future tourist experience in South Africa. The particular significance of spatial development initiatives (SDIs) is discussed later but these programmes, in concert with other regional consortia and projects, are a major part of South Africa's macro-economic growth strategy (known as GEAR – Growth, Employment and Reconstruction).

The neo-liberal policies of GEAR are congruent with contemporary World Bank ideology and associated control mechanisms. Black empowerment consortiums, that have mushroomed since the 1994 elections (Koch and Massyn, 2001), have bought into this economic framework; in particular, they have invested heavily in the tourism sector. Koch and Massyn, in the most useful part of their work on 'South Africa's Domestic Tourism Sector: Promises and Problems' (in Ghimire, 2001) quote the examples of the Congress of South African Trade Unions (COSATU), South Africa's largest labour federation, and the South African National Civic Organisation (SANCO) both forming investment companies. Indeed, they are now bidding against each other, as part of the routine of business practice, taking and shedding private foreign partners, for a dominant stake in tourism development (one investment company set up this way is called Kipano ke Matla, or 'Unity is Strength').

The interest by organisations that once encouraged a boycott of South African tourism in order to weaken the apartheid state in direct investment in tourism plant is a barometer of the new-found fascination with tourism as a mechanism for social and economic development in the country. The same popular opinion is reflected in a wave of enthusiasm by rural people, previously excluded from the mainstream of the apartheid economy, in exploiting tourism as a form of business and entrepreneurship [Koch and Massyn, 2001, p.143].

South Africa is the first country outside of Europe to achieve Blue Flag status for some of its beaches (www.mintel.com/countrysurvey, 2002). The government's White Paper for Sustainable Coastal Development aims to manage marine resources through, for example, extending bans on off road vehicles on beaches, and through banning the use of thick plastic bags by supermarkets (that seem, like lemmings, to be drawn seaward). The White Paper recognises the contribution that the Department of Environmental Affairs and Tourism (DEAT) must make to tourism development through funding bodies such as the Wildlife and Environmental Society of South Africa (WESSA).

Race, gender and income

The racial composition of the workforce in South Africa has changed little in the time we have been carrying out this study (data sources for the annual picture are from South Africa's Central Statistical Services, Pretoria): currently, about half of all employees in the tourism and related sectors are black, a third white, one tenth coloured and one twentieth Asian. The gender split is even, though it varies between the various sub-sectors, with global features of depressingly stereotypical employment patterns (females dominate the poorest paid jobs inside the industry). The data offers no evidence that the tourism industry is a 'pro-poor' industry, benefiting past or current members of the poorest paid social groups. Racial inequalities in income persist, white employees earning three times on average as much as black employees, who dominate the lowest skilled jobs). The informal sector of the tourism industry is also gendered and coloured: black females dominate in street craft markets and the like, black and coloured males in taxi services, white and coloured males dominate in the hotel/entertainment business, and similar income inequalities are found. The main point, again, is that there is no evidence that tourism has in any general sense had a major income and wealth redistribution effect on the economy, although the economic status of some individuals and their families have been fundamentally altered.

Culture and violence

We describe a visit to Shakaland, a Zulu Cultural Village in KwaZulu-Natal, in the second part of the book but we have been unable to comment at length on cultural tourism and the role of cultural villages inside this sector of the tourism industry (important studies under the direction of Professor Keyan Tomaselli, Director of the Centre for Cultural and Media Studies at the University of Natal, are beginning to emerge in a variety of publications, as part of an ongoing research and publication programme (www.und.ac.za/und/ccms/intro). The main demand for cultural tourism (we have no definitive study yet) may come from organised groups of international tourists, where the cultural village is part of a local 'package' of attractions. For example, people off the cruise ships that come into Durban can opt to visit Shakaland.

However, even if it is the case that organised groups of international tourists drive the demand for this tourist 'product', secondary impacts on the indigenous population may be significant in a variety of ways (Ndleia, 2002). In Ndleia's study, for example, the evolution of personal and business relationships between Zulu performers and the hotel owners and management that 'housed' the cultural villages she studied, form a fascinating and significant backdrop to the 'front stage' tourist experience of the 'traditional Zulu at home' (described and analysed in this unique research degree study, by a Zulu woman, at the Centre for Cultural and Media Studies at the University of Natal).

KwaZulu-Natal was destabilised in the years immediately prior to our first visits in 1994 and 1995, by what Koch and Massyn euphemistically call a 'low-intensity civil war' (2001, p.164) between 'militant' ANC supporters and 'traditionalist' supporters of the IFP. This conflict was also divided on generational grounds, ANC supporters being largely young and also in sympathy with the South African Communist Party (SACP) and older influential men (chiefs and elders) who valued the IFP reification of long-standing Zulu custom and practice. Perversely, this conflict about the essential nature of 'Zulu-ness', couched here as traditional versus progressive Zulu identities, becomes simultaneously an international tourism product. The KwaZulu-Natal Tourism Authority (KZNTA) website opens with the slogan 'South Africa's Kingdom of the Zulu–KwaZulu-Natal!' and has a Zulu address (www.zulu.org.za).

Whether this KZNTA penchant for tradition and heritage (see their 'Battlefields' tour, for example) trickles out and into Zulu communities and acts as a bridge between generations remains to be seen (Anson and Allen, 2003). We discuss the notion of 'healing', arising from this context of the political quest for the South African identity, in chapter 5.

We end this introduction by leaving the last word to Satour, the South African Tourism Authority, now re-badged as Tourism South Africa (www.satour.org). In a passage headed 'Why South Africa is unique', we read:

> But there really is more to us than beasts and bush and beach. When you visit, do take the time to find out how we live and who we are. Visit our museums and villages, listen to our stories and dance to our music.
>
> When you visit South Africa, you're not just visiting a place, you're visiting a people.

And that is what we did and how we found it.

Chapter 1

The new South Africa and the promotion of new tourism: the emergence of evangelism

South Africa's tourism resource base is enormous; with professionally managed national and provincial parks holding accessible wildlife so attractive to Europeans and North Americans, and diverse and dramatic scenery with large areas seemingly untouched by modern society. The country enjoys dependable sunshine and hot summers, and has long beaches, a well-developed transportation system, and offers opportunities for all kinds of special interest tourism, such as whale watching, white water rafting, deep-sea fishing, bird-watching and water sports. In addition there are the internationally well known attractions such as Cape Town, Table Mountain, the Garden Route, Kruger National Park, Sun City and opportunities to visit other attractions in neighbouring countries including Victoria Falls in Zimbabwe. Many tourism bodies such as the World Tourism Organisation have described South Africa as one of the most outstanding tourist destinations in Africa.

In spite of these climatic and environmental advantages, from the mid-1970s to the late 1980s there occurred a long-term loss of interest in South Africa on the part of overseas tourists. This stagnation in demand happened at a time when there was marked growth in long-haul tourism elsewhere in the world. During those decades, the annual numbers of overseas arrivals in South Africa were low, and fluctuated between 250,000 and 500,000; figures that reflected the unfavourable and widely held perceptions of the apartheid regime (Economist Intelligence Unit (EIU), 2000). Also contributing to the persistently low demand was the high cost of flights to the country. South African Airways and other airlines using the country's airports had successfully resisted the move to deregulation that had characterised the more market-oriented policies of similar companies in other parts of the world. South Africa was one of the few major tourism destinations that prioritised the protection of its national airline over the expansion of its tourism sector. Meanwhile, growth in South African domestic tourism was restricted by the severe economic and social imbalances caused by apartheid. Tourism in South Africa was monopolised almost entirely by a white minority elite, many of whom were experiencing economic difficulties themselves as a result of the international sanctions imposed by a substantial number of important trading partners.

Comparisons of the performance of the national tourism sector prior to and following the first multi-racial elections in 1994 are problematic. Under apartheid, political factors had led to tourism data being inconsistently compiled and interpreted in South Africa. Statistical analyses varied in whether or not the bantustans were regarded as sources of foreign tourists. Similarly, under apartheid, arrivals from Namibia, Botswana, Lesotho and Swaziland were often ignored or discounted (EIU, 1995). These ambiguities, along with an overall tendency not to regard visitors from most African countries as 'real tourists', confirm the need for caution when estimating the economic significance of the South African tourism sector during the apartheid era. Unfortunately, the inauguration of the new political dispensation has not led to the provision of more reliable tourism data. The failure of the government to dedicate sufficient resources to the collection of economic data has led to a deterioration in the reliability of statistics generally within South Africa (EIU, 2000). Satour, one of the key sources of data and interpretations of tourism trends has suffered severe cutbacks in its budget since 1994, and has been forced to decrease its research output.

In 1994, there was a sharp rise of 18.6 per cent in tourist arrivals over the previous year, and this was followed in 1995 by a larger jump of 22.3 per cent (Department of Environmental Affairs and Tourism (DEAT), 2000). However, as impressive as these growth rates appear, it should be noted that the absolute numbers of overseas arrivals remained small in comparison with other major tourism destination countries. The bulk of foreign tourists continued to come from neighbouring African countries. At the time it was clear that the chronic violence within the country's borders created a powerful deterrent to tourists planning their vacations. Images of shockingly brutal and seemingly chaotic violence between black groups, but also increasingly against members of the white minority and tourists, have dominated the western media coverage of the transition from apartheid to majority rule (du Toit, 1993). It was certainly our experience that, in KwaZulu-Natal, many commentators on economic development regard the frequent occurrence of public violence as a huge obstacle to successful long-term planning. Press coverage of violence committed against tourists in the province has been seen to have an immediate and serious impact upon the numbers of visitors to particular sites we have visited. We develop this theme in chapter 5. In 1995, the South African government openly recognised that the hoped-for boom in tourism would not materialise until the debilitating problems of political instability and communal hostility were seen to be resolved.

Table 1: Trends in international tourist arrivals in South Africa, 1993–99

Market	1993	1994	1995	1996	1997	1998	1999
Europe	412,800	444,767	697,539	771,178	854,657	950,270	998,218
N. America	75,190	89,793	124,354	137,178	157,957	193,616	193,225
C. and S. America	11,760	19,585	29,037	32,362	41,421	45,397	42,284
Australasia	29,297	35,749	59,951	62,261	62,601	68,485	68,467
Middle East	13,982	15,162	18,546	23,978	24,067	27,385	28,506
Asia	67,814	91,263	131,339	133,979	130,752	130,198	147,405
Indian Ocean Islands	7,715	8,265	10,894	11,419	11,529	13,056	12,959
Africa	2,474,625	2,964,372	3,416,612	3,772,036	3,702,313	4,303,632	4,292,421
Total	**3,093,183**	**3,668,956**	**4,488,272**	**4,944,430**	**4,976,349**	**5,732,039**	**5,890,507**

Source: Department of Environmental Affairs and Tourism, South Africa

During the first four years of the 1990s, the prospects of radical political change and the creation of a multi-racial democracy did not lead to a massive turn-around in the performance of tourism. Within the sector, there were high expectations of a boom in overseas tourism demand. It was felt by the South African Tourism Authority (Satour) that the ending of apartheid, and the arrival of democracy with a government headed by the internationally admired Nelson Mandela, would together prompt an immediate and enormous rise in inter-national arrivals. But the political violence and social disturbance of the period leading up to the first multi-racial elections in 1994 caused a distinct slowdown in overseas arrivals in South Africa. Since then, the deregulation of the air traffic to the country, and the repeated depreciation of the rand have made holidays in South Africa much cheaper in real terms. But while there has occurred significant growth in the numbers of foreign tourists to South Africa, these increases have failed to reach the levels of the more optimistic forecasts made by Satour (EIU, 2000). In 1999, Africa continued to be the dominant market, with 72 per cent of foreign arrivals coming from the continent. The closely neighbouring countries of Lesotho (36.8 per cent), Swaziland (18 per cent), Botswana (13 per cent) and Zimbabwe (11 per cent) were the most important African markets of that year. In the same year, arrivals from Europe made up 62 per cent of the overseas market. Within that market, the United Kingdom was the most important country of origin, sending 33 per cent of overseas tourists, followed by Germany (21 per cent) and France (8 per cent). The USA provided 15 per cent of overseas arrivals. The Asian market, although small, showed two emerging contributors of India and Japan, with growth rates of 21 per cent and 8 per cent respectively (DEAT, 2000).

Table 2: Comparison of world's top tourism earners (1998)

	International tourism receipts ($ millions)	Ranks	Change 1998/97 (percentage)	Percentage of world total receipts 1998
United States	71,116	1	−2.9	16.2
Italy	30,427	2	2.4	6.9
France	29,700	3	6.0	6.8
Spain	29,585	4	11.0	6.7
United Kingdom	21,233	5	6.0	4.8
Germany	15,859	6	−3.9	3.6
Netherlands	6,806	16	7.6	1.5
Australia	5,694	19	−36.7	1.3
South Africa	2,366	42	3.0	0.5

Sources: World Tourism Organisation; Department of Environmental Affairs and Tourism, South Africa

Domestic tourism plays a far greater economic role than the overseas sector in South Africa. Satour estimates that 16 million South Africans undertook at least one leisure trip involving at least one night away from home in 1996, generating more than 30 million trips in total (EIU, 2000). Eighty-two per cent of the white population were thought to have made such trips. Although 60 per cent of blacks and Asians claimed to have made similar trips, this figure is probably explained by the practice of labour migrants returning periodically to home rural areas from urban places of work. KwaZulu-Natal was the most popular destination for domestic tourists, accounting for 26 per cent of domestic leisure trips. The Western Cape was the second most frequently visited with 22 per cent of the domestic market. Domestic travel is heavily concentrated around the Christmas period, the warmest time of the year.

Table 3: Value of the rand, 1993–99

Currency	1993	1994	1995	1996	1997	1998	1999
Rand/$US1	3.3	3.5	3.6	4.3	4.6	5.5	6.6
Rand/£1	4.9	5.4	5.7	6.7	7.6	9.2	10.4
Rand/DM1	2.0	2.2	2.5	2.9	2.7	3.2	3.7

Source: Reserve Bank of South Africa

As a result of the historical impediments to tourism growth in South Africa, tourism continues to occupy an unusually low place in the national economy. Although by 1999 foreign tourism had grown by 38 per cent over figures for 1994, the sector as a whole contributed less than 5 per cent to the South African economy, compared with the world average of 11 per cent. The disappointing figures for tourism development have led to a general reluctance by politicians to take the sector seriously as a growth area for employment. In spite of upbeat claims by politicians both before and after the 1994 elections, tourism remains undervalued by decision-makers in comparison with agriculture and other industrial sectors. By 1996, even though it was clear that tourism was not generating the awaited kick-start to the economy, the new Department of Environmental Affairs and Tourism (DEAT) was of the opinion that with a programme of aggressive marketing and improvements in levels of service and security, the sector could be contributing 10 per cent to the GDP by 2001. Given that the vast majority of South Africans are totally inexperienced in leisure travel, it is predicted by DEAT that now that many of the restrictions previously placed on travel by Africans have been removed, a growth in domestic tourism among black South Africans could, in time, enhance income in some of the tourist-receiving areas of the country.

Table 4: Employment in South Africa's tourism industry

Year	Direct tourism jobs	Indirect tourism jobs	Total tourism jobs	Growth in total tourism jobs (percentage)	Tourism as percentage of total employment
1990	223,539	277,745	501,284	–3.6	5.02
1991	220,356	290,447	510,803	1.9	5.17
1992	205,260	260,682	465,942	–8.8	4.71
1993	204,825	258,368	463,193	–0.6	4.69
1994	206,306	256,504	462,810	–0.1	4.65
1995	248,448	302,004	550,451	18.9	5.42
1996	289,763	338,149	627,912	14.1	6.16
1997	309,499	363,360	672,860	7.2	6.54
1998	341,932	395,685	737,617	9.6	7.02

Sources: WTO; Satour; Department of Environmental Affairs and Tourism, South Africa

DEAT (1996), noting the disappointing returns from overseas tourism, contends that an integrated strategy is needed to attract more foreigners, paying particular attention to the lucrative European and North American markets. The tourism sector has been sadly neglected historically, with limited international investment in tourism facilities. As such, the industry has not spawned entrepreneurship, nor has it created new services. It has also failed to stimulate other sectors of the economy, such as the growing of food for tourists on South African farms, or the manufacture of furniture and fittings for hotels and guesthouses. Further, tourism has not played its role in strengthening the economies of communities by providing better employment prospects (DEAT, 1996).

In its White Paper on Tourism (1992), prior to the political triumph of the ANC, the Ministry for Administration and Tourism appeared to be unequivocal in its wholehearted support for the tourism sector in South Africa's development planning. The Ministry had argued that tourism was already served by a sophisticated infrastructure, and employed over 300,000 full-time staff. Tourism, it had claimed, was regarded by the state as a possible kick-start for the flagging economy. The government's commitment to the industry was made clear in a number of proposals including: the creation of a single body responsible for the training of highly qualified staff; interest subsidies, and write-off programmes for work on the improvement of tourist facilities, particularly in the vicinity of game reserves. Moreover, in line with its now wider policies of deregulation, the government emphasised the need for decentralised planning and localised decision-making in order to encourage community involvement (Ministry for Administration and Tourism, 1992).

Table 5: Purpose of visit for all South African domestic leisure trips in 1996 (percentages)

Year	VFR	Holiday	Business/ holiday	Sports spectator	Sports participant	Excursion	Other
1996	53	37	1	3	1	2	3

Source: Department of Environmental Affairs and Tourism, South Africa

According to the White Paper (1992), scenery and wildlife are the most important attractions for over 90 per cent of foreign visitors, especially those from the highly developed world looking for contrasts to their home environments. Therefore, the conservation of biodiversity within South Africa's national parks and other protected areas would remain under the supervision of statutory bodies. It would also be the responsibility of those authorities to solve the problem of shortages of accommodation in the parks at times of peak demand. Shortfalls in capacity had acted as constraints on tourism income in earlier years (Ministry of Administration and Tourism, 1992). Satour would carry out the marketing of the country as a single destination, and the major focus of that marketing plan was to promote the country as the world's top eco-destination in terms of its wildlife, scenic beauty and cultural attractions.

Satour is energetically pursuing its objectives of marketing South Africa as the world's top eco-destination in terms of its wildlife, scenic beauty and cultural/hospitality attractions. In December 1999, the agency launched its nationwide Welcome Campaign, in that it was hoping to convince overseas travellers that South Africa is a safe holiday destination, by educating the host population in the needs of visitors to the country. By this time, Satour was stating its vision to be marketing the country for the sustainable, economic and social empowerment of all South Africans (Satour, 2001). In much earlier statements, Dr Ernie Heath (1994), the former Chief Director of Tourism Promotion, argues the case for a 'new tourism'. He predicts, tourism will have been transformed into a wholly new phenomenon by the early years of the twenty-first century. Growing environmental awareness and concern, along with the evolution of more sophisticated consumer expectations, are driving changes in the global tourism market. A 'new wave' of tourism activity is emerging, he argues, and the South African tourism sector must adapt its tourism products to meet the demands of the more individual and discerning visitor. Competition in this field is expected to be severe, and those agencies closest to the source areas of tourist demand must be vigorous in their support of the quality and value of the South African experience. Success in the new marketplace will be contingent upon the demonstrably sustainable use of the environment, and upon the construction of a dynamic private sector (Heath, 1994).

Table 6: Domestic and foreign tourism arrivals in South Africa (1996)

Type of Tourism	Percentage	Arrivals
Domestic Leisure	77.28	30,430,400
Domestic Business	10.16	4,002,531
Foreign Total	12.56	4,944,430
Total	**100.00**	**39,377,361**

Source: Department of Environmental Affairs and Tourism, South Africa

Satour (1994) argues that South Africa finds itself in a position of huge responsibility in the stewardship of its natural resources. Socially responsible tourism, however, is not simply concerned with the experience of nature by tourists; it should also entail improvements in the welfare of local people. In fact, Satour's definition of eco-tourism suggests a near perfect form of development:

> Eco-tourism implies tourism practices that would benefit all concerned parties rather than benefit some concerns and neglect others. The term 'eco-tourism' has therefore come to include concepts such as planning before development; sustainability of resources; economic viability of a tourism product; no negative impact on either the environment or local communities; responsibility for the environment from both developers, the tourism industry and tourists; environmentally friendly practices by all parties concerned; and economic benefits flowing to local communities [Satour Fact Sheet, 1994, p.6].

Somewhat typical of the discussion of eco-tourism in other Satour publications, no indication is given of how, and by whom these measures are to be implemented. All tourism has an impact of some form or other on the environment, and given the fact that the South African state is now committed to the deregulation of the tourism industry, the definition pays surprisingly little attention to how all parties are to be compelled to face their environmental and social responsibilities. Equally slippery is the image of economic benefits 'flowing' to local communities, with no apparent recognition of the fact that, within resident groups, entrepreneurial individuals, or importantly in South Africa, those in positions of traditional authority are quite likely to direct the benefits towards themselves. Moreover, there is no reference to what form these benefits will take, nor on what basis they are to be distributed.

In a more analytical report, Grossman and Koch (1995) assess the aims and achievements of eco-tourism initiatives in South Africa, paying more attention to the context-specific constraints and limitations on its development. The authors suggest that the commercial incentive to capitalise on the expected wave of new tourism is leading to innovative partnerships between the private sector, state agencies, NGOs and local communities. Integrated conservation development initiatives, although still few in number, have been undertaken during the period of political transition in the country, and have helped local people not only in their economic struggle, but also in the re-evaluation of their natural environment, now that the days of enforced removals are said to be over.

There exists a basket of key constraints on tourism growth in South Africa. These include a history of under-funding (arising from its poor performance during the apartheid era), and a private sector unwilling to take a proactive role in the sector with hotels failing to take responsibility for the safety of their guests (Stavrou, 9/12/98). DEAT (1996) acknowledges that although there are some socially responsible tourism operators, their number remains small. The South African tourism trade suffers from a near absence of community involvement, and from a lack of understanding of the sector among large sections of the population. The South African tourism sector is characterised by poor levels of service, by poor infrastructure in many rural areas, and by an internal transport system that does not serve tourist needs. There is a need for a well formed and effective national network of structures designed to promote the industry. On top of all these, and a recurrent theme of this book, tourism suffers from the growing level of violence on tourists, and the international perceptions of South Africa as a dangerous place to take a holiday (DEAT, 1996).

It is likely that had South Africa's history been different, it would have been a major tourist-receiving country before now. Political oppression, and social turmoil within the country in the second half of the twentieth century have discouraged international investment in the sector, and have deterred overseas visitors who tend to spend far more than domestic tourists or visitors from other African countries. Within the country, the sector has been satisfied by merely catering for a privileged minority. Because of this, the industry has not touched the lives of impoverished communities desperate for development. In spite of these past failings, tourism would appear to still have the potential to meet the objectives of the Reconstruction and Development Programme (ANC, 1994). In other developing countries, tourism has been seen to offer opportunities for small businesses, to encourage inter-ethnic mixing, and to enable people to participate in the informal sector opportunities. It is argued that responsible tourism can protect the environment, create linkages with agriculture and other sectors, and provide employment for untrained members of the population (DEAT, 1996). Most importantly here, it could provide employment opportunities in remote rural areas, such as those previously neglected by the apartheid regime.

The apartheid government made it very difficult for communities to become involved in the sector, and the years of racial exclusion have left Africans in ignorance of the potential benefits of the trade. Communities could contribute in a range of ways: small guesthouses, restaurants, taxi services, entertainment and craft shops. African communities could be trained to act as tour guides, and as travel agents. They could also become active in laundry services, the building of tourism infrastructure, traditional hunting and the production of foodstuffs for tourists (DEAT, 1996). Advocates of sustainability highlighted the social and environmental benefits anticipated from developmental strategies that focus on the quality of growth, and on the distribution of benefits, rather than predominantly on quantitative indicators of national economic expansion. The task ahead for the government was to establish long-term fiscal policies and developmental strategies that would address the issues of intergenerational justice and the meeting of basic needs, while continuing to attract foreign investment.

The ANC tried to meet that challenge by means of its Reconstruction and Development Programme (RDP). While the overwhelming emphasis of the programme was on democratically based, people-driven development and self-help, it also comprised a more conservatively orthodox economic approach than many of the more radical members of the ANC would have liked. Drawn up by the ANC in negotiation with other members of its alliance of mass organisations and NGOs, and after consultations with the private sector of society in South Africa, the programme paid limited attention to tourism development. Local communities have had little or no training and inadequate finances to become investors in tourism. Compounding the problem has been an unwillingness by the white elite sector to become involved with African communities in tourism-based business initiatives. This reluctance has persisted, in part, because there have been few incentives offered for them to do so.

In its White Paper on the Development and Promotion of Tourism (1996), DEAT addresses the needs to meet the requirements of the Reconstruction and Development Programme (RDP) by promoting responsible tourism that directly involves the previously excluded, as the guiding principle for the development of the sector. Responsible tourism entails protection of the environment through the promotion of sustainable tourism activities (such as game-viewing and water sports). It also necessitates the meaningful participation of those communities living in the vicinity of the tourist attractions. Further, responsible tourism respects those cultures that have been ignored in the past. Responsibility is also demanded of the communities, in that they must operate in an environmentally sustainable way, and must protect the tourists in their care. Modern trade union practices must be accepted by employers, and tourists themselves must behave responsibly, particularly when among hosts of a different culture from their own.

The White Paper is dedicated to arguing that responsible tourism is the way to develop the sector in South Africa because it acknowledges the obligation of the government and the private sector to include the disadvantaged, because environmentally sensitive tourism is the growing trend in the trade, and because it provides the country with the opportunity to act as a leader in this field of new tourism. It involves all agencies, including government, NGOs and the private sector in inclusive development. The government must accept important roles in tourism development, and these include making every effort to ensure the safety of all tourists, committing itself to the training of businesses and individuals in tourism skills, and the financing of tourism development through a dedicated tourism development fund and through the provision of investment incentives to encourage the involvement of the private sector (DEAT, 1996).

The deregulation of the aviation industry in South Africa has expanded the number of companies using its airports to over 50, and has resulted in a drop in real terms of the price of flights from Europe and the other major sending areas. The bulk of South African tourist activity at the time, however, remained domestic, with the country receiving only 0.6 per cent of world foreign arrivals in 1993 (Satour, 1994). Foreign exchange earnings as a percentage of the world tourism total were of the same order, yet tourism is still regarded as a significant potential contributor in economic growth and social development.

South Africa's economy, in spite of its mineral resources, is in a parlous condition. Population growth easily outstrips growth in GNP. The country's manufacturing sector is out of date and under-funded. It also lacks a skilled labour force; a consequence of job segregation under apartheid. The persistent current account deficit compels state planners to concentrate on strategies for growth to finance more redistributive basic-needs programmes in the future. In response, some observers have accused the alliance of the African National Congress (ANC); the Congress of South African Trade Unions (COSATU) and the South African Communist Party (SACP) of abandoning former socialist principles for the opportunity to take charge of a capitalist economy (Munck, 1994). While acknowledging the need for increased democracy in economic strategies, the ANC leadership has shown a reluctance to adopt popular support-gathering programmes, such as ambitious schemes to satisfy the urgent cries for better housing in the townships, arguing that, in the absence of the necessary capital-base, well-intentioned projects of this nature would aggravate the nation's debt problems, and would attract adverse criticism from the providers of concessionary aid.

Prior to 1990, Nelson Mandela had been convinced of the need to nationalise key industries and the banks to ensure a more just and economically efficient society in South Africa. But during that year, his public pronouncements to that effect caused considerable panic in the stock exchanges. ANC economic planning evolved out of the fundamental notion of 'growth through redistribution' through which the meeting of basic needs was to rejuvenate production, encourage consumption and stimulate growth. But by 1992, when ANC economic policy was eventually ratified, there had been a subtle but critical shift in emphasis; 'growth through redistribution' had faded as a guiding principle within the party leadership (Munck, 1994). Now the attention of the electorate was being directed towards the 'apartheid dividend'; the benefits that would accrue from the dismantling of the inarguably wasteful, and duplicative public sector resource management system of the National Party. Further, it was emphasised that the ending of international sanctions and economic isolation would boost the national economy as a whole.

The black population, that forms the huge majority of the electorate as well as the bedrock of ANC support, continues to be faced with the conspicuous prosperity of the white minority in times of acute hardship among the poorest members of South African society. The ANC is fully aware of the political imperatives of addressing economic injustice, but it also recognises that attempts to make amends must not jeopardise the foreign-exchange earning capacity of the white, rural and urban sectors. Moreover, the actual mechanisms of redistribution are not easy to implement. Given that the country is already a high-tax nation, new or higher taxes would have only a limited impact, and would act as disincentives to the already apprehensive decision-makers in private industry. Hard economic and fiscal facts such as these have tempered former socialist aspirations within the ANC. The discourse of nationalism and desegregation as the road to development has diluted the calls for public ownership of the means of production and for radical land restitution programmes. Development planning in South Africa now reflects a collective ambivalence towards these more traditionally socialist principles. As elsewhere on the continent of Africa, current trends in political thought in the country are parting company with the variety of African socialisms that have automatically assumed that a 'Third Worldist' route is the only alternative to total exploitation by a predatory, white, capitalist system.

Studies of political and economic change in modern Africa, often written in the idiom of dependency/underdevelopment theory, have come under criticism for their predictable and simplistic determinism, and for their failure to consider the range of developmental possibilities. They have effectively reified and demonised capitalism, rather than acknowledged it as a fitful and erratic process, and they have reduced the complexity of internal imperatives and manoeuvres to a condition of peripheral and unremitting dependency. In post-colonial Africa, socialist experiments of whatever indigenous variety have not, in the main, been marked by significant improvements in the welfare of the most needy. The often catastrophic consequences of hastily imposed, socialist models of development have led to a general despondency and lack of direction among African political thinkers (Kitching, 1982). The neighbouring countries of Mozambique and Zimbabwe have provided the state leadership of South Africa with clear examples of the socio-economic collapse and/or political oppression that have characterised so many attempts at constructing a vibrant economy on principles of state ownership and redistribution, prior to the accumulation of a sufficiently healthy capital base.

The political leadership of the new South Africa is fully aware of the scale and complexity of the task that is set in the RDP and has undergone what Said (1986, p.70) has, somewhat wistfully, called 'an historical contraction of horizons', where grand notions of egalitarianism and a return to old African ways of doing things have been allowed to fall away. Calls for emancipation through African socialism have lost much of their appeal, and now appear lacklustre in the context of recurrent food crises and tragically disappointing experiments with collectivisation in many parts of Africa during recent decades.

In South Africa, built-in conflicts in the administration of economic development are legion. The old apartheid system was heavily overstaffed, but now there are intense pressures on the government to provide even more public sector jobs to rectify the racial imbalance of power in the administrative and state service system. The cost of providing these new jobs appears folly to many observers, especially so in the context of a global process of reducing state wage bills. Founding ideologies are being compromised and interpreted in novel ways. As a result, a dualist approach is taking shape, in that growth through expanded exports is being energetically supported, while measures to generate an internal economy based on community-led, sustainable initiatives are being implemented for the upliftment of deprived urban and rural regions in the country (Munck, 1994). The empowerment of communities through the development of grassroots democratic organisations, sufficiently resourced and tuned into local needs, is argued to be the only way of remedying the historical sense of alienation commonly felt by the formerly disenfranchised members of South African society (Munslow and Fitzgerald, 1994).

The 'new South Africa' was born at a time when old certainties in development theory had lost much of their authority. Now, sustainable development seemed to offer, confidently and simultaneously, an ethos and economic policy that would transcend old divisions and heal and the National Party, the RDP was essentially a compromise, written in the hope of avoiding a continuing bloodbath. The period of transition had provided four years of learning to consult and to construct such a compromise with the encouragement of such outside bodies as the Organisation for Economic Cooperation and Development (Munslow and Fitzgerald, 1995). To sustain the consensus, the National Economic Development and Labour Council was established to provide a forum for government, business, labour and other groups to voice their needs, and to consider those of other sectors.

The authors of the RDP stated that the prime function of the programme was to correct the unrepresentative, undemocratic, highly oppressive, secretive and militaristic nature of government prior to 1994. Apartheid, it argued, was wasteful, corrupt and hopelessly hobbled by debts. As a result every aspect of South African society was marked by minority domination and privilege. Only by giving black South Africans the opportunities to achieve their potential would the country develop. To implement the goals of the RDP, a deepening democracy was required that would ensure that elected bodies were answerable and transparent in their conduct. Moreover, the empowerment of women necessitated their inclusion at all levels of government and on all RDP People's Forums. Attacking poverty, injustice and deprivation were its priorities in a programme of achievable and sustainable goals in a peaceful and stable country. But hard choices had to be made. Resources were scarce, and not all problems would be solved in the near future. Many decisions would be unpopular with large sectors of the population. The authors of the RDP claimed that the RDP constituted the framework for making these very difficult decisions (ANC, 1994).

The political and economic philosophy of the RDP was based on six core principles:

- An integrated and sustainable programme to overcome the piecemeal and unco-ordinated policies of the apartheid regime, to be implemented at all levels, by public organisations and civil society.
- A people-driven process focusing on immediate needs, regardless of race or sex, and the development to be about active involvement and increasing empowerment, building on the many forums already in place.
- Peace and security for all; reconstruction depends upon a security force that reflects the racial mix of the country, and must be non-partisan. The judicial system must be seen to be fair.

- Nation building, that helps correct the economic imbalances between white and black, and is not based on theories of trickle-down development.
- Links between reconstruction and development that demonstrate that there are no contradictions between growth and distribution.
- The democratisation of South Africa that will, above all, involve the active participation of all affected parties.

All of these principles were to form the ideological foundations of the five key programmes of action that were to be: meeting basic needs; developing human resources; building the economy; democratising the state and society; and implementing the RDP. Among its early targets were plans to build one million low-cost homes, to redistribute 30 per cent of the cultivable land, to provide free healthcare to all young children and pregnant women, and to introduce compulsory ten-year education (ANC, 1994).

In essence, the RDP amounts to a concise statement of the ANC's developmental vision, entailing a profound rebuilding of the country's institutional framework that, under the National Party, had been guided almost entirely by the needs of the white economy. Within this vision, it was regarded as axiomatic that the necessary development of the human-resource base could not be achieved without establishing appropriate and democratic institutions at all levels of South African society. People must feel themselves able to take active, decision-making roles in locally elected democratic bodies, if they were to take their own development in hand; good governance being the first step to development.

The authors of the programme are equally conscious of the fact that the plans to devolve power to locally elected authorities are fraught with obstacles. In the drafting of the Local Government Transition Act (1995), it is openly acknowledged that, in South Africa, factional rivalries and traditional chiefs jealous of their powers, can cause acute difficulties in the transfer of democratic authority to rural and urban communities. A commitment to conflict resolution and negotiation is essential if old power bases are to be diminished in the construction of democracy in South Africa. RDP forums are to be established in the more acutely marginalised communities, forging links between community-based organisations (CBOs), non-governmental organisations (NGOs), political parties and other local bodies concerned with development leading to self-reliance. The central responsibility of these forums is to identify and prioritise local needs, and to allocate resources accordingly.

The funding for this programme of ethical and developmental goals was not to come from a seizure of assets from the mainly white, commercial economy, nor would the RDP be paid for with loans from external agencies. The ANC leadership was fully aware that large-scale borrowing to fund social programmes could lead very quickly to inflationary pressures, that would cause enormous problems for those disadvantaged groups the RDP was designed to help. Instead, the short-term financing would come in the main from a reallocation of the existing departmental budgets. In the long term, the programme's efforts would be supported by the anticipated growth in the nation's economy, following the resumption of normal international trading relationships. Other sources of funding would include the selling of oil stocks accumulated during the period of international sanctions. In a truly innovative fashion, the ANC had tackled the compromises necessary to allay the fears of the markets, while making positive signals to the impoverished majority that their need for land, jobs, education and other resources was being taken seriously by the new government.

The RDP placed sustainability at its heart, and attempted to combine macro-economic and fiscal prudence with efforts to redress the injustices of the apartheid era. There is no doubt that, during the tumultuous period around the elections in 1994, it helped to consolidate the movement to form the Government of National Unity. But many difficulties remained, including the *de facto* apartheid that persisted in the commercial sector and in public institutions. Many members of the black unemployed were looking to the government for secure positions but were being told that they must recognise that there were limits to the numbers of jobs that could be created, without threatening the economy. In addition, even among apparent supporters of the Government of National Unity, there was a substantial number who would have welcomed the collapse and abandonment of the RDP.

The drafting of the RDP followed a great deal of consultation with key stakeholders, and at the time of the elections in 1994, there appeared to be a broad consensus accepting its principles. This consensus may have arrived in part from the fact that, while the goals were commendable and morally inarguable, the harsh means that would be necessary to achieve them were not always apparent or clearly stated. Major problems needed urgent attention, including the rise in unemployment, the drop in real wages, and the particular levels of exclusion suffered in the rural areas. It was also becoming clear that the proportions of the problems suffered in South Africa had been underestimated, because of the undercounting of the black population in the 1991 census. During its first year in power, the ANC faced the threat of a widespread rent boycott that, if it were to become a protracted and widespread protest, would rob the government of funds needed to improve the housing stock. It soon became apparent that even the cautious ambitions of the RDP would prove to be far more costly than had been estimated. Only months after the elections, and in contrast with the much earlier nationalisation policies of the ANC, the privatisation of public services was being considered as a fund-raiser.

In 1995, a Green Paper was published by the Central Economic Advisory Services, a national body, that made its job the identification of clearly stated mechanisms and timetables for achieving the goals outlined in the RDP. The Green Paper was more specific in estimated costs, and took a much stronger line than the original RDP on the government wage bill. It was argued that strong fiscal discipline was essential to generate private sector confidence in the South African economy. The Green Paper, in turn, was not warmly welcomed by the unions who saw its central thrust as a return to 'trickle-down' economics that the RDP had rejected. In support of their case, the National Institute for Economic Policy, that had consulted widely with unions and other bodies, argued for a demand-led economy, on the basis that a distribution of resources would lead to an increase in demand and a subsequent growth of the national economy (Munslow and Fitzgerald, 1995). Ultimately the government, faced by debts accrued during the period of transition, was unable to meet its predicted funding levels for the RDP, causing considerable concern among the unions who foresaw public sector redundancies as a result. In the first year of its implementation, the financing of RDP projects was severely restricted, and was directed in the main towards the school nutrition scheme, the public works programme, and urban renewal.

In a similar vein to the RDP, the Rural Development Strategy (Government of National Unity, 1995) makes plain the government's determination to incorporate local development with larger national goals. The subtitle of the document, 'Putting Rural People in Charge', reinforces the central development thrust of future rural development policy that is to be based on capacity building, and on utilising labour as the key resource (GNU, 1995). Particular attention is given to the need for women and other marginalised groups to take responsibility for their own development. While the Rural Development Strategy reflects the RDP in its view that many of the inhibiting factors on rural development have emerged from a history of racial discrimination in landholding patterns and forced removals, the former goes further by specifying the precise measures to be taken in the facilitation of rural development at a local level. Among other changes, the newly formed rural district councils will employ trained mediators, who have experience in conflict resolution and project management, and who are competent in business skills such as book-keeping. These facilitators will inform local authorities of the development options open to them. Strategies will be market-oriented, small and medium-scale enterprises that will benefit from planned land reforms (GNU, 1995). The strategy contains a huge raft of goals and mechanisms for implementing change in areas such as environmental resource management, water and sanitation, managing drought, gender issues and the role of NGOs. As in the RDP, emphasis is placed on the long-term aim of human capacity building, through improved rural education services and the training of adults for future economic possibilities.

Eco-tourism projects in areas with appropriate natural resource bases are identified as having strong possibilities in this context. The Rural Development Strategy argues that, now that the violent struggle against apartheid is over, new opportunities exist for attracting tourists to the rural areas of the country. But efforts must be made to redirect the benefits of tourism away from the usual beneficiaries, hotel chains and tour operators, and towards rural communities. Moreover, the communities themselves must be educated and encouraged to lessen their understandable hostility towards the protected areas and their conservation authorities. It is hoped that regions of the country that have been previously avoided by tourists, will attract visitors keen to learn more about the natural resources of South Africa, and about the history and culture of the African people.

The general principles of the Rural Development Strategy are supported and reinforced by the Rural Development Framework compiled by the Rural Development Task Team and the Department of Land Affairs (1997). In this later document, the means of creating the structure of local democracy in the rural areas is made much more explicit. The emphasis here is on the crucial requirement for democracy as a prerequisite for development. Novel relationships between the state and civil society are proposed to facilitate the empowerment and participation of the most vulnerable and excluded, including women and the elderly in South Africa's neglected rural communities. Good governance and political transparency are argued to be both worthy goals in themselves, and essential in the upliftment of impoverished rural populations. Along with the establishment of sound and efficient local government bodies, every encouragement is to be given to community-based organisations (CBOs), such as civics, community development forums and trusts that are not as widespread in rural areas as they are in the towns and cities of South Africa. Also, a special role for non-governmental organisations (NGOs) is foreseen, and these groups will be supported by the funding provided to the CBOs. A multitude of NGOs were active during the apartheid era, and many of them have developed trusting relationships with rural communities. However, the actual activities and responsibilities of local government and civil society will become clearer with time (the Rural Development Task Team and the Department of Land Affairs, 1997).

Poverty and conservation in South Africa

South Africa remains one of the most unequal societies in the world, and access to employment, education, land, housing, health services and other essential resources is still divided more or less clearly along lines of race. The spatial distribution of the population has also been determined by skin colour. During the apartheid era, rural areas were officially designated as either white dominated areas of the four provinces of the Republic of South Africa, or artificially created 'homelands' (bantustans), where 85 per cent of the black population lived on 13 per cent of the land (Meer, 1997). At the time of writing, 70 per cent of the population of the former homelands were classified as living below the poverty line (Motteux et al., 1999). In homelands such as KwaZulu, land-hunger is keenly felt and autocratic dictatorships have denied rural populations any genuine political voice (Motteux et al., 1999). The often oppressive and corrupt leadership of the homelands creates special problems for the implementation of the RDP in the new South Africa. Of particular interest here is the homeland of KwaZulu, where Chief Buthelezi has headed an often brutal political regime throughout the period of apartheid and after.

The homelands have their origins in the usually small areas of land left to the African peoples, following the colonial and settler conquests of the nineteenth century. During the early decades of the twentieth century, these 'native reserves' were expanded as sources of cheap labour for the rapidly expanding mines and factories of white South Africa. On the reserves, black families struggled to supplement their meagre incomes by subsistence farming on poor soils. From 1948 to 1994, under the apartheid regime, millions of black South Africans were removed from cities and farms, and forced to live in the ten 'homelands' designated for the various linguistic groups. Of the ten homelands, Transkei, Ciskei, Bophuthatswana and Venda were granted the dubious status of independent republics.

In the homelands, land was held almost entirely under communal tenure, and controlled by traditional chiefs and their headmen. This communal land system has had serious repercussions for the new political dispensation in South Africa, which has committed itself to a programme of land redistribution based largely on a system of claims made by individual households. Similarly, the political isolation of the homelands during the apartheid years led to environmental management practices that, if they existed at all, were very different from those followed elsewhere in South Africa. This places an extra burden on the post-apartheid state that has pledged to improve environmental protection throughout all the rural areas.

A far-reaching programme of land restitution has been prepared to ameliorate the plight of the historically disadvantaged, but there are major obstacles to its successful implementation. Along with the political and economic strength of the landed classes, who can be expected to resist changes in the landholding pattern of South Africa, there are constitutional constraints surrounding property rights. Moreover, land reform is hampered by the same crisis in funding that affects other government actions. Rural communities are often inexperienced in representing their own interests, and there are frequently conflicting claims among communities or individuals for the same piece of land. The government itself is inexperienced in dealing with problems of such magnitude and complexity, and the actual amount of cultivable land available is insufficient to meet all claims and needs.

The dangers to many of the world's conservation areas arise primarily from the poverty of their surrounding populations (Ghimire, 1994; Barrett and Arcese, 1995). In the past, managers of protected areas have focused on security and rigorously excluded local people, a militaristic approach that in some countries has led to severe sanctions, fines, prison sentences, and even the death of poachers. Not surprisingly, local residents have reacted with hostility, seeing themselves excluded from economic opportunities in hunting, farming and tourism (Wells and Brandon, 1992).

Conservation in South Africa has a reputation for professional management and scientific success. The white middle classes tend to support conservation enthusiastically, seeing it as a wholly worthy cause having no connection with politics or issues of race. However, conservation in the country has always been highly politicised, and has demonstrated strong links with the political economy. In South African black agrarian society there is a deep mistrust of the con-servation movement (Koch, 1994), which has its roots in the evictions of African families throughout the twentieth century. During the colonial period, with the movements of white settlers from the Cape to the Transvaal in the seventeenth and eighteenth centuries, there was a marked decline in game populations. Native African states were also using wildlife resources at this time, and fluctuating patterns of conflict and co-operation over game became common between the two societies. When diamonds were discovered in the Cape, and then gold in the Transvaal, the sudden influx of European settlers and the spread of ranching accelerated the drop in wildlife numbers.

During the early part of the twentieth century, governments in various parts of the country began proclaiming reserves; the Pongola Game Reserve, established in July 1889 by the government of Transvaal, was one of the first (Koch, 1994). The warden of this reserve immediately expelled all Africans living in the area. Africans were denied access to game, and were even prohibited from killing animals that were damaging their crops. Such restrictions were particularly advantageous to the white population, generating a dispossessed labour force for the mines and for commercial farming, thereby creating a black proletariat (Koch, 1994).

The best-known of South Africa's protected areas, the Kruger National Park, was established during the last years of the nineteenth century, and entailed the removal of more than 3000 Tsonga people. These inhabitants of the area were finally removed altogether, in 1969, to the homeland of Gazankulu.

Removals, forced labour and poll taxes became a feature of wildlife protection throughout South Africa during the twentieth century. Moreover, it was during the 1920s, with the creation of the Kruger National Park that the link was made between conservation and tourism (Koch, 1994). At the time, the Kruger authorities were resisting attempts by the mining industry to be granted permission to enter the Sabi reserve area, and tourism suddenly presented itself as an alternative and less destructive means of developing the economy of the region. The Park was restocked with game, and the now familiar system of fences and armed patrols was put in place. Africans who had previously hunted and gathered wood and grasses in the reserves were severely punished with fines and or hard labour if they encroached upon the Park. Acrimonious relationships between conservation agencies and their neighbours developed, and many of the latter came to hold wholly hostile views of both conservation and tourism.

Frequently illegal and sometimes destructive encroachments were the result. More recently, however, it has been recognised by environmentalists that conservation goals can be achieved only with support from and the direct involvement of local populations, and that environmental issues are indeed political. In fact, concern for environmental protection has highlighted the necessity to meet communities' basic needs and provide real alternatives to illegal land invasions and poaching.

The goal of integrating small and medium-sized enterprises into the established commercial sector has attracted attention in the literature (Baskin, 1995). But not all observers are optimistic of its chances of success (Munck, 1994). In 1994, the existing tourism associations and semi-official agencies remained largely in the hands of white South Africans, and continued to target white elites in their marketing operations. Within the sector, there was a marked reluctance to take on the role of development agency, and the personnel profile of these various bodies remained white and middle class. The tourism industry in South Africa was characterised by rivalry at the highest levels. The relationship between the South African Tourist Authority (Satour) and the National Tourism Forum (NTF), set up by the ANC, was an uneasy one. At the time, the former was concerned primarily with the more outward looking remit of promoting South Africa as a safe and exciting location for high-spending tourists from overseas. The latter had been set the goal of establishing tourism's role in community development (EIU, 1995).

Surprisingly, following the elections in April 1994, the post of Minister for the Environment and Tourism was offered to a member of the National Party, who had been responsible for the formation of Satour during the later years of the apartheid era. Consequently, Satour now felt less threatened by the NTF. However, Satour's lack of interest in developing a more modestly priced, and smaller scale domestic tourism product left it open to further criticism from the ANC-supported NTF (EIU, 1995). This tendency on the part of Satour to focus on the marketing of the country as a sophisticated venue for nature tourism was unhelpful in implementing a strategy of integrating small tourism operations into the larger tourism network.

Engaging African communities with development projects will not be achieved by goodwill alone. For many black South Africans, the sense of security needed to participate in developmental initiatives will only arise when the crucial issue of land redistribution is settled. During the years of apartheid, approximately 3.5 million people lost their rights to property through forced removals (Department of Land Affairs, 1995). A far-reaching programme of land reform is currently being implemented to ameliorate the plight of the histor- ically disadvantaged. However, there are innumerable problems hindering the progress of land redistribution. There is the political and economic strength of the landed classes in South Africa. There are constitutional constraints surrounding property. Land reform is hampered by the same funding constraints affecting other governmental activities. Rural communities are inexperienced in representing themselves in their own interests, and their lack of political voice impairs their ability to make forceful claims. Government inexperience in such matters also impedes land reform, and the actual amount of cultivable land available, insufficient to satisfy all claims, forces planners to make difficult and often unpopular decisions (Department of Land Affairs, 1995).

Land reform programmes elsewhere in Africa have had limited success in achieving either of their twin aims of a more equitable distribution of land and an energising of the rural economy. For nature-based, socially responsible tourism development in South Africa, the issue of land rights has a particularly strong resonance among rural people. The conservation of those protected areas likely to attract eco-tourists has, in the past, involved the forced, and often violent removal of African farmers from their land (Smith, 1992; Worden, 1994). Eco-tourism is now discussed as a mechanism for empowering local people who have suffered under apartheid, and who are looking for better things following the elections in which they were allowed to vote for the first time. But the restoration of land rights, and the imaginative creation of new forms of land tenure will not be well received everywhere. Economic and political changes rarely satisfy all stakeholders on anything like an equitable basis. In South Africa, complex and delicate trade-offs are being made between the conditions felt necessary to secure economic growth, and the demands of impoverished peoples looking for signs that their difficulties are being taken seriously by the government.

So far, the benefits to local communities from the expansion of eco-tourism have been slight, often taking the form of rights to gather thatch grass, herbs and some game meat from the protected areas. The state has made some low interest credit available for small-scale community reserves, with the proviso that indigenous people must enjoy the gains from these initiatives. Whether or not these projects prove to be economically viable remains to be seen. It has been noted, however, that many of these schemes are foundering on the mismanagement of funds officially bound for local inhabitants. It has become clear that community participatory programmes can lead to bitter feuding within villages and settlements (Koch, 1994). Shared geography does not imply shared economic or political interests (Harvey, 1996). In addition, experience has shown that even the most prestigious and high-profile game parks are heavily subsidised and fail to run at a profit. The only financially successful protected areas are those completely in the hands of private entrepreneurs. The capacity of eco-tourism to provide tangible improvements in the income of local inhabitants is still in question.

It was, ironically, in the impoverished homeland of Bophuthatswana, that eco-tourism involving novel relationships between communities and conservation authorities found its roots. In 1979, the dictatorial leader of this particularly repressive homeland, Chief Lucas Mangope, announced his plans to promote conservation in tandem with tourism in the newly formed Pilanesberg National Park, in an area where the grazing of domestic animals had had serious consequences for local biodiversity (Grossman and Koch, 1995). Although the Park is situated close to the mining areas of Gauteng, the local tribes are generally poor and dependent upon subsistence farming. Initially, the creation of the Pilanesberg Park followed the accepted model of removals, fines and fences. Villages were razed, water and tourism infrastructure were brought in. With funding from wildlife societies and private investors the Park was restocked. By the 1990s, the well-built and tastefully furnished facilities that characterise many of the protected areas in South Africa had been constructed there. The small Park is surrounded by a complex of casinos and luxurious hotels, including Sun City, and receives tourists on gambling holidays looking for entertainment during the day. Infrastructure and services within the Park are of a high standard. Two upmarket lodges were built in partnership with private companies. A chalet camp was also built, with plans to construct another in the future. The Park is estimated to add R25 million to the regional economy each year (Grossman and Koch, 1995).

However, the Park has become known for its innovative partnerships with local Africans (Honey, 1999). It represents the first attempt in South Africa to integrate conservation with the developmental needs of the local communities (Grossman and Koch, 1995). Popular free environmental education programmes have been provided for local people, and surplus stock animals are made available for communal areas. Better salaries offered by the Park have attracted talented staff, including a number of highly placed black officers. Also attracted to the Park were members of the white conservation movement who were troubled by the apartheid-based ethos of the National Parks system. However, not all of its revenue-generating schemes were welcomed by environmentalists. The facility to hunt endangered species using tranquilliser darts was viewed with great suspicion by many environmentalist observers.

During the 1980s, the Park commissioned anthropological research among its African neighbours to discover their views of the protected area. The research revealed that local people held very negative opinions of the way the Park was run, and were angry about the removals carried out to establish it in the first place. Their anger was made all the worse by the knowledge that corrupt tribal authorities had plundered the funds made available as compensation for the loss of territory (Koch, 1994). Having considered the findings of the research, the Park initiated a number of schemes to improve relationships with the communities living in the vicinity. Local people were allowed into the Park to gather firewood and herbs, and to visit the graves of their ancestors (Honey, 1999). Several hundred local Tswana people now work there, some of them filling senior positions. Construction work in the Park, although supervised by professional engineers, is often divided into smaller contracts so that local African builders can participate.

Perhaps most innovative of all, was the Park's approach to settling the most serious complaint of the local people; that they had never been properly compensated for the removals at the time of the Park's creation. In 1992, the Park and the local BaKGATLA people set up a Community Development Organisation; an elected body to oversee the operations of the protected area. The Park agreed to invest 10 per cent of gate revenues, and a proportion of earnings from other tourism ventures into the funds of the organisation. Some of the funds have been invested in improved facilities in the villages, but the major investment has been in a community-owned game park and cultural village. The Park stocked the game reserve, and the communities paid to have it fenced.

The community reserve has run into serious difficulties. Marketing was costly and generally unsuccessful. The road leading to it was in a poor state, and there have been serious disagreements between community leaders and officers at Pilanesberg. The response from tourists has been very slow. Surprisingly, even though there are suspicions that officers at Pilanesberg are not completely open about the workings of the Park, and in spite of the disappointing early returns from the game reserve, local opinions of the Pilanesberg Park have improved, in part because of the number of jobs it has provided for its neighbours. Like all the National Parks in South Africa, Pilanesberg is heavily dependent upon government subsidies to fund its operations and for infrastructural maintenance. During the years following the elections of 1994, increased government expenditure on social programmes has led to restrictions in the financial support given to conservation authorities. The full impact of the reduction in subsidies has yet to be revealed at Pilanesberg, but consequential cut-backs in its community projects are to be expected (Grossman and Koch, 1995).

As the earliest example of such an initiative in South Africa, the Pilanesberg experiment has acted as something of a template for integrated conservation and participatory community development in other projects elsewhere in the country. Of great significance is the recognition by stakeholders in the venture that conservation has little future without the support of neighbouring communities. The range of contractual arrangements between various agencies involved in such initiatives, and the degree to which local people enjoy the income from them, is discussed in chapter 3. For the moment, it should be noted that in South Africa a conflation of factors, including political change, restrictions on public resources, the desperate needs of poor rural communities, and growing public concern for the environment leading to a new kind of tourism demand, has resulted in an enthusiastic endorsement of the need to develop eco-tourism along socially responsible and environmentally sound principles. But there exist important inhibiting factors in its development, and the intersectoral integration of tourism requires the establishment of an effective institutional framework at all levels. This will in turn require the directing of scarce public resources away from other developmental options, and towards a sector that has yet to prove that it can deliver. Nevertheless, in March 2001, DEAT announced that, through the Tourism Enterprise Development Programme, it was about to invest R66 million to establish 200 small eco-tourism enterprises that would ultimately be owned by historically disadvantaged groups and individuals. Further, DEAT proposed to table a motion that would oblige government departments to make use of such enterprises in the future. Moreover, the 200 new initiatives will be monitored closely to develop the means of integrating small tourism businesses in the wider economy (DEAT, 2001).

A satisfactory settlement of land claims, always a contentious and politically difficult issue, is essential if resident people living in the vicinity of reserves and other protected areas are to feel secure in their commitment to eco-tourism partnerships. Africans have for long suffered at the hands of conservationists, and will be looking for evidence that past injustices are being remedied, and that conservation authorities can be trusted. An entirely different but equally significant constraint on tourism development in South Africa, as we have indicated, is the continuing violence that has preoccupied the foreign press in the coverage of current affairs in the country. Overseas

41

tourists need to be reassured that they will be safe in South Africa. But solving the issue of factional fighting is a long-term task, and likely to be contingent upon, among other things, noticeable improvements in the material well-being and political standing of the rival groups and individuals themselves.

The White Paper on the Conservation and Sustainable Use of South Africa's Biological Diversity (DEAT, 1997) looks particularly closely at the wealth of protected areas in South Africa and at their role in rural development strategies. Conservation is seen as both a resource and a burden for the developing countries that contain two-thirds of the world's biodiversity, and that so far have been expected to bear the cost of environmental protection, while the industrial sectors of countries in the developed world enjoy the economic benefits of access to plant genetic resources. South Africa, as a result of its mix of tropical and temperate climates and habitats, ranks as the third most biologically diverse country in the world. However, human activity has had enormous impact upon the range of ecosystems within the country. Agriculture, urban developments, deforestation, mining and dams have all contributed to the transformation of much of South Africa's natural habitats. In addition, the overexploitation of certain species, the introduction of alien exotic species, and the toxification of the soil and atmosphere have all had major effects on terrestrial and marine biodiversity. Fifteen per cent of South Africa's plant species, 14 per cent of bird species and 37 per cent of its mammal species are listed in the South African Red Data Books, that record the conservation status of threatened species.

The increasing exploitation of natural resources threatens far worse in the near future. This has particularly serious implications for the very large proportion of South Africa's population who are directly dependent upon natural resources for subsistence, medicine, shelter, fuel and building materials. The use of natural resources for this large number of people acts as a buffer against dire poverty, and as an opportunity for various forms of self-employment in the informal sector. Further, environmental degradation also threatens long-term economic planning, in that such sectors as eco-tourism, commercial fishing, and hunting are adversely affected.

New responsibilities for conservation authorities

South Africa possesses a well-developed system of protected areas, where the efforts towards biodiversity conservation have been focused. Four hundred and twenty-two formally protected areas constitute six per cent of the land surface area of the country, and high proportions of the various species are represented within their boundaries. However, in the past, conservation has operated on a piecemeal and *ad hoc* basis, with the protected areas being managed as separate islands of biodiversity, without an overall strategy, and there are many important habitats in the country that are not protected.

Although the central thrust of rural development planning in South Africa is for sustainable development for all sectors of society, DEAT (1997) argues that there is a particular need to pay attention to those communities living in the vicinity of protected areas, some of which are found within the most populous and deprived areas of the country. These reserves are often nodes of economic activity, and contrast starkly with conditions immediately outside their well-guarded fences. In order to improve the lives of the neighbours of the protected areas, and thereby to reduce the obvious threat to natural resources within them, the Department established plans for collaborative activities with conservation authorities, local communities, the private sector and other agencies. The government will introduce strategies, mechanisms and incentives to integrate protected areas within the broader social landscape, and encourage conservation in adjacent private and tribal land areas (DEAT, 1997). This could entail the setting up of buffer zones, multi-use areas within tourism projects, and the possible introduction of conservation grants. Activities adjacent to protected areas must be compatible with conservation goals, and must involve sustainable land-use planning. Going further, those neighbouring communities must enjoy access to decision-making roles within the fences of the protected areas themselves. Conservation authorities have had their roles greatly extended, in that now they must see themselves as agents of development as well as conservation.

The Tourism White Paper (ANC, 1996) is unambiguous in its expectations of public conservation bodies. They must, of course, ensure the protection of biodiversity in the country. They must also learn to proactively integrate areas under their authority into the national and local tourism base by providing access to those areas to communities and to the commercial tourism sector, and provide appropriate facilities. Further, conservation authorities should promote a range of attractive experiences for tourists that are not beyond the financial reach of the average South African citizen. Most importantly for this discussion, they are obliged by the government to facilitate and promote partnerships in eco-tourism ventures between communities and representatives of the private sector, also allowing local entrepreneurs to integrate their operations outside the gates of the protected areas with the activities of tourists within them. They should also assist local people to come to understand the value of conservation by providing educational programmes. Finally they should actively participate in drawing up plans and policies for the future development of tourism in South Africa (DEAT, 1996).

As state subsidised organisations, conservation authorities find themselves vulnerable to changes in government policies and developmental strategies. South Africa has suffered at the hands of foreign currency speculators on at least two occasions since 1996. In both cases about 30 per cent of the value of the rand disappeared. On the first occasion the government responded with the Growth, Employment and Reconstruction (GEAR) strategy, that described the major challenges facing the country in the face of globalisation and increased international competition. Arguing for more openness of the national economy, GEAR posited among other things that the labour force must be prepared to accept lower wages or face increased levels of unemployment. GEAR was met with great hostility by an alliance of unions and other mass organisations, questioning the wisdom of abandoning earlier principles of sustainable, people-centred development, and arguing that the overall aims of GEAR would make the country defenceless in the face of the volatile and unstable global economy. In fact, it was not long before even the most fervent advocates of GEAR had to accept its failure in many of its goals. GEAR had claimed that, between 1996 and 1998, 650,000 jobs would be created in the formal sector. In reality, about 300,000 jobs were lost.

The alliance of organisations opposed to GEAR disputed the orthodox model of the ever expanding global market in that developing countries had merely to adopt policies of liberalisation, privatisation, deregulation, and reduced government spending on services to enjoy the benefits of the consequential growth. However, even the strongest critics of GEAR within the ANC ultimately accepted a poorly defined compromise in that the South African economy would be made much more open to speculative financial flows, while attempting to forge new partnerships with other developing countries with significant and expanding economies, such as India and Brazil.

Many of the same organisations who voiced disapproval of GEAR were also very critical of any intervention in South Africa's affairs by outside institutions like the World Bank and the IMF. During a brief and low-profile visit to the country in 1997, the World Bank President, James Wolfensohn, gave a nod of approval to GEAR, and was impressed by the government's efforts to keep the budget deficit at 5.1 per cent of GDP (Mutume, 1997). He was also pleased by the South African government's determination to accelerate economic growth from three per cent in 1996 to six per cent in 2000. Although in the years since the end of apartheid, the Bank had only been acting in an advisory capacity within South Africa, many union leaders and politicians from the left were concerned by the government's application for a loan of $70 million to boost the small business sector. Leaders of the protest movement against the Bank were angry that it had already influenced decision-making in the country by advocating lower subsidies and more reliance on commercial banking in housing provision. South Africa had followed this advice and was still struggling to deliver 100,000 housing units, nearly three years after promising to build 1 million by 1999 (Mutume, 1997). Moreover, in the eyes of the opponents of any World Bank intervention in South Africa, pledges in the RDP to conduct relationships with the Bank in such a way as to protect the integrity of domestic policy formulation had been abandoned. The overall impact of this retreat from the former high principles and goals of the RDP upon conservation agencies, has been a severe reduction of state support, leading to radical schemes of rationalisation, including reductions in staffing.

The complexities of the changing relationships between conservation agencies and their impoverished African neighbours are discussed in the following chapter on eco-tourism development and conservation in the province of KwaZulu-Natal, where we have focused our research on eco-tourism initiatives in the north of the province. This terribly impoverished region has missed out on the modernisation and industrialisation that has characterised many other parts of South Africa, and the large protected areas there are sites of highly charged disputes over land use and land ownership. In KwaZulu-Natal, as in the other provinces of South Africa, local communities are being asked to go through a major sea change in political outlook. From a culture of resistance, where compliance could be seen as collusion with apartheid, local communities are being asked to see themselves as partners in development initiatives involving greatly mistrusted institutions. Conservation agencies, in turn, have difficult processes to undergo, in that a developmental role is to be adopted alongside their more familiar one of conservation. Any increased tourism activity will have impacts upon the environment, and it remains to be seen if it is at all possible to reconcile the needs of conservation with the imperatives of development (Barrett and Arcese, 1995). The trust that is needed before people will commit resources to any initiative, takes a great deal of time to generate. Very thorny trade-offs have to be negotiated where power in decision-making is at stake, resources are scarce, the environment is attributed with wholly incommensurate values, and where the processes are not smooth ones.

Summary

In spite of its huge natural resource base, the tourism sector in South Africa has yet to fill the economic role that it does in many other countries. Apartheid, and now seemingly endemic violence and crime, have effectively hobbled the development of tourism in the country. Against the background of the almost iconic RDP and the emphasis placed on the overwhelming need for good governance, a model for community-based eco-tourism has emerged in post-apartheid South Africa, requiring the development of new partnerships between conservation agencies and their impoverished African neighbours. But a history of removals and oppression has led to chronic hostility and mutual distrust.

At the same time, dwindling public resources available to conservation authorities place extra pressure on these agencies struggling to fulfil their traditional role of conservators of South Africa's biodiversity. Those eco-tourism initiatives discussed in this chapter have yet to prove that they can deliver sufficient economic benefits to radically improve the lives of excluded African communities. Moreover, not everyone accepts that conservation can ever be linked with rural development.

Chapter 2

Community-based eco-tourism and conservation in KwaZulu-Natal: conflict over nature

The newly established Province of KwaZulu-Natal, which comprises the former homeland of KwaZulu in amalgamation with the former province of Natal, is the third smallest in South Africa but, in 1995 it had the highest population, estimated to be 9.4 million people, of whom the majority were living in rural areas. The province had the third highest incidence of poverty, and some 74 per cent of the rural population existed below the poverty line (Data Research Africa, 1995). The poor of KwaZulu-Natal are vulnerable to TB, to environmental health problems such as malaria, and in 2000 there was a serious outbreak of cholera in the northern regions of the province. As in other parts of South Africa, AIDS has become a major killer in KwaZulu-Natal. The province has one of the highest HIV/AIDS infection rates in the country.

The homeland of KwaZulu came into being in March 1972 and at that time consisted of 44 diminutive and separate pockets of land. During the years of apartheid, the homeland was dependent on the state for more than 70 per cent of its revenue; a factor that informed relationships between itself and the South African leadership. These scattered and sometimes diminutive areas were characterised by overcrowding, poverty, and by a near absence of men; many of whom were away working in the mines and urban sectors, such as Durban. Migratory labour began to replace traditional military service and tribute to the chief as far back as 1888, when the colonial authorities implemented hut taxation and cash demands following the annexation of Zululand the previous year. During the years of apartheid, the mainly English-speaking administration of Natal was unpopular with the ruling National Party, and partly as a result of that discordant relationship, Natal received a less than generous proportion of central government expenditure. As a consequence, there is an acute lack of trained and skilled personnel throughout the province.

KwaZulu-Natal is a traditional holiday destination for domestic tourists in South Africa. The province contains some major scenic attractions as well as year-round sunshine, long beaches and the warm Indian Ocean. There are huge protected areas with substantial holdings of the 'big five': elephants, rhinos, buffaloes, leopards and lions. The Drakensberg Mountains and the rolling countryside of the Midlands attract walkers and climbers. Perhaps most importantly, the northern regions of the province are rich in wetlands and other special ecosystems that are recognised internationally and where biodiversity is protected by official conservation agencies.

During the early years of our research, the analysis of the economic importance of tourism in KwaZulu-Natal was bedevilled by the near absence of reliable data. The quantitative material provided by Satour (now South African Tourism) was compiled primarily for marketing purposes, not for economic planning. In the past, estimates of the size and relative significance of the tourism sector have been based on the not entirely safe calculations that tourism comprises 2–3 per cent of the South African economy as a whole, and that the province is one of the top four tourist destinations in South Africa (Proctor, 1995). What could be stated with a fair degree of confidence was that, during the final years of apartheid, tourism demand in KwaZulu-Natal had dropped in relation to demand in other locations in the country, and that the prime cause of that decline was the widely publicised, political, communal and criminal violence, including violent acts against tourists (Baskin, 16/11/95).

Table 7: Foreign tourism in KwaZulu-Natal (1998)

Number of tourists	500,000
Average spend per visitor	R4,015
Spend: total market value	R2–3bn
Average length of stay (days)	11
Main overseas source markets	UK, Germany, USA, France, Netherlands

Source: KwaZulu-Natal Tourism Authority

Prior to the period of transition and the elections of April 1994, tourism had not been regarded as a major developmental strategy in the province. Other than the marketing of South Africa as a single destination by Satour, the promotion of the sector was left entirely in the hands of commercial interests, which had concentrated almost exclusively on the lucrative white leisure market. Tourism's articulation with the black population of KwaZulu-Natal generally took the form of informal spin-offs, such as the selling of curios, or low-skilled and poorly paid jobs as porters or kitchen staff. Under apartheid, tourism development in Natal was not designated as a provincial respons-ibility by the national government. In contrast, the homeland of KwaZulu, like the other homelands, did have its own governmental tourism department.

However, establishing a tourism authority did not lead to the emergence of any genuinely long-term planning of the sector. The tourism department in fact devoted much of its resources to the expansion of the casino system. At the same time, the KwaZulu tourism administration gained a rather poor public image because of the apparent low levels of professionalism among its staff (Baskin, 16/11/95).

Following the elections of 1994, the KwaZulu Department of Tourism was subsumed within the newly created Department of Economic Affairs. The latter, having had little experience of tourism administration, absorbed many of the problems of the former. With the new political dispensation, the Natal Parks Board (NPB), a statutory body, remained responsible for the tourism facilities and services within the protected areas under its authority. Its counterpart in the former homeland of KwaZulu, the KwaZulu Department of Nature Conservation (KDNC), continued its management of tourism affairs within its parks. The lack of provincial tourism institutions in Natal arose as a consequence of the central government's reluctance to devolve the necessary powers to the Natal Provincial Administration (NPA) during the apartheid era. The highly fragmented character of the tourism sector, and the sometimes acrimonious rivalry between the two conservation authorities, had led to the formation of a feeble institutional framework for the planning and co-ordinating of tourism development in the province, and to an *ad hoc* and erratic style of project promotion.

In an exhaustive report prepared for the Government of KwaZulu-Natal, Proctor (1995) assesses the potential role of tourism in the developmental trajectory of the province. The author argues the need for an integrated strategy that would reflect the interests and aspirations of the public and private sectors, NGOs, labour organisations, and above all the communities themselves (Proctor, 1995). As part of that proposed strategy, and in the face of fierce competition in the tourism market, a positive marketing of the province's nature-based tourism products must be confidently promoted. It should be finely tuned into the growing trend and global growth in eco-tourism. Given the importance of the tourist–host encounter in the evaluation of the tourist experience, it is essential that communities are prepared to participate enthusiastically, and to welcome tourists into the province. The potential for conflict – over land rights, political allegiance, biodiversity conservation, and the use of public resources – is always a concern. Programmes of conflict resolution and education must be integral to future tourism planning in KwaZulu-Natal. The only prominent organisation working towards these goals in 1995, the Tourism Association of KwaZulu-Natal (TANK), was not supported by public authorities, and had relied almost entirely on funding from commercial sources (Proctor, 20/11/95). Although TANK had managed to include the interests and contributions of some parochial agencies, the apathy shown by trade unions, and the often overt hostility felt by the private sector towards those unions, had diminished the legitimacy of the organisation in the eyes of some concerned observers (Baskin, 16/11/95).

The institutional environment or any field of economic development consists of more than a simple list of the relevant commercial and public sector organisations. An institutional framework reflects, and is informed by, wider political and cultural values and assumptions. In KwaZulu-Natal in 1995, the cluster of organisations involved directly or indirectly in tourism development constituted a structural legacy of the apartheid era, expressing relationships of power between a minority white elite and the disempowered black majority. The problem was not confined to the tourism sector alone. Although the National Party did, in its later years, set up a small number of co-ordinating official bodies to rationalise developmental activities, and to overcome the problem of institutional overlap arising from policies of racial segregation, these moves were counteracted by the introduction of the tri-cameral constitution. In KwaZulu-Natal, with its already clearly divided societies, the creation of three 'own affairs' administrations, and the development of separate local authorities, seriously aggravated problems of bureaucratic complexity, corruption and inefficiency.

This multiplication of agencies concerned with development within the province led to a seriously wasteful duplication of responsibilities. At the same time, central government had maintained strict control over development planning and approval, thereby causing a marked degree of inflexibility in funding, and had also nurtured an even larger bureaucracy to administer its policies (Barnes, 15/11/95). It has been noted elsewhere (Chambers, 1985; Meyer and Zucker, 1989) that obviously ineffective and inefficient organisations often survive because their primary objective is not to maximise efficiency, but rather to maintain existing organisational patterns and structures. In KwaZulu-Natal, the prioritisation of apartheid over developmental goals had contributed to the proliferation and survival of a considerable number of unproductive agencies.

The historically disappointing performance of the fragmented and direction-less tourism sector, led the new provincial government in 1997 to establish the Interim Provincial Tourism Steering Committee, now the KwaZulu-Natal Tourism Authority (KZNTA), an overarching and publicly funded agency, to advise on policy and legislative issues, and to serve as both a co-ordinator and regulator of tourism in KwaZulu-Natal. This new agency is to act as the central forum where all major stakeholders will be represented. Among its many responsibilities, the KZNTA is required by the KwaZulu-Natal Tourism Act (1996) to broaden ownership in tourism, particularly among the previously disenfranchised, an unthinkable objective during the years of apartheid. The agency is also obliged to pay particular attention to the needs and promotion of small-scale, sustainable rural tourism initiatives. By 2001, the Provincial Minister for Economic Development was able to announce the opening of a number of such projects, and was optimistic over the contribution they might make to the betterment of life for poor rural communities (KZNTA, 2001). In tandem with these developments, a major turn in the branding of the province has led to KwaZulu-Natal now being marketed as the Kingdom of the Zulu, an equally unthinkable strategy only a few years ago.

The KZNTA estimates that the tourism sector of KwaZulu-Natal provides employment to some 200,000 people, and generates over R8 billion per annum; 10 per cent of the provincial GDP (KZNTA, 2001). Approximately 8 million domestic tourists visit the province each year, and the major attraction for them is to visit friends and relatives. The core market for such tourists are the residents of KwaZulu-Natal itself. The province of Gauteng is the major external source of tourists. The key destinations for domestic tourists are Durban, the coastal resorts to the north and south of Durban, and the Natal Midlands.

Surveys carried out by the KZNTA show that 500,000 foreign tourists – 30 per cent of all overseas and African air travel arrivals in South Africa – visit KwaZulu-Natal, and that the most important sending country is the UK. Foreign tourists tend to visit Durban, Zululand and Maputaland, and the North Coast resorts. Visits to beaches and to nature reserves are their most popular activities. The foreign tourism market is worth some R3 billion each year (KZNTA, 2001). The KZNTA identifies crime and grime as the factors most central in deterring larger numbers of tourists from visiting the province.

Table 8: Activities undertaken in KwaZulu-Natal by foreign visitors (1998)

Activity	percentage
Beach	36
Nature reserve	32
Art/craft venture	21
Cultural village	20
Hiking	19

Source: KwaZulu-Natal Tourism Authority

Along with the other developmental, tourism resource auditing, information and marketing responsibilities of the KZNTA is the key task of transforming the widely held image of the province as a dangerous and scruffy holiday venue. In several interviews with senior members of staff at Tourist Junction, the central offices of the organisation in Durban, the huge potential for the tourism sector within the province was eagerly emphasised. This optimism was frequently reflected in the media with jubilant reports of the gigantic economic boom that was about to hit the province through the coming expansion of the tourism sector. However, the task of transforming the institutional and social profile of the tourism sector in KwaZulu-Natal is an enormous and costly one, and even though the KwaZulu-Natal government has increased the funding of the agency to R40 million in 2002, the budget is not large. Various stakeholders in tourism throughout the province expressed deep scepticism to us about the ability of the KZNTA to achieve its ambitious goals, and feared that the KZNTA would ever have sufficient resources and commercial dynamism to radically increase the economic importance of the sector in KwaZulu-Natal.

Table 9: Length of stay of domestic holiday tourists (1996)

Province visited	Average length of stay (days)
Western Cape	9.5
Northern Cape	8.7
Eastern Cape	7.8
Gauteng	6.1
Mpumalanga	5.9
Free State	5.8
Northern Province	5.3
KwaZulu-Natal	5.1
North West	3.5
Overall average	**6.2**

Source: Department of Environmental Affairs and Tourism, South Africa

The sustainable development of eco-tourism in the province was discussed at great length at the Tourism Development Summit, called in March 1995 by the Minister of Economic Affairs and Tourism, Jacob Zuma. At the Summit it was agreed that the tourism industry has the potential to become the most important economic sector in KwaZulu-Natal (Department of Economic Affairs and Tourism, KwaZulu-Natal, 1995). But the enthusiasm for the earning capacity of the trade must be tempered by measures to ensure that old injustices and imbalances are corrected. The previously excluded groups must now be granted the opportunity to participate either as entrepreneurs or as tourists themselves. The following four guiding principles for tourism development quoted in full, were proposed and accepted at the Summit.

Tourism must:

- be a concept to which all can aspire in terms of contributing to the uplift-ment and socio-economic well-being of all the people of KwaZulu-Natal;

- provide a means of strengthening community pride;
- make a significant contribution to safeguarding environmental, historical and cultural resources;
- contribute to the creation of 'goodwill, peace, understanding and friendship between the people of KwaZulu-Natal and others from elsewhere in Southern Africa and around the world'

(Department of Economic Development and Tourism, 1995, p.4).

Clearly, a great deal is being asked of tourism. According to the Summit, the development of tourism must ensure that no citizen is worse off than they were before the promotion of the sector in the province, and that special attention should be paid to improving the opportunities for women. Government's responsibilities include the setting of tourism policy, the drafting of legislation, and the creating of institutional frameworks. For much of the capital and expertise essential for establishing and running a vibrant tourism economy, the government will look to the private sector, but will ensure that the aims of the RDP are met. To this end, sustainability must be the priority in planning. The natural resources of the province will be protected by directing a percentage of tourism profits towards conservation work in KwaZulu-Natal. Tourism development in rural areas must be small scale, and constitutional representatives of rural communities must be consulted prior to seeking government approval.

It was strongly argued at the Summit that the allocation of land that is suitable for tourism development should accord with the wishes of the local people concerned. Guidelines for such allocation are to be drawn up by the provincial government. Those people who have been unable to secure loans to establish tourism ventures should have access to a fund of low-interest loans guaranteed by government, and free vocational training should be provided for individuals hoping to build careers within the tourism trade. Small business development is one of the most effective means of creating jobs, and the government should actively encourage and support the participation of small enterprises (Ministry of Economic Affairs and Tourism, 1995). It is the government's task to foster a 'culture of tourism' among the communities. This entails making plain the potential rewards of the industry, particularly in those areas where there are few alternative means of earning a livelihood. Only by highlighting potential benefits will agrarian societies recognise the importance of providing a friendly welcome to those tourists who arrive in their localities.

The racial and class partiality of the institutional structure of the tourism sector in KwaZulu-Natal has contributed enormously to its lack of legitimacy in the eyes of the black population. Another significant structural bias is the disproportionate distribution of land rights between the racial communities. Between 1960 and 1983, approximately 750,000 Africans were removed from their land in KwaZulu-Natal, and towards the end of that period over 619,000 Africans were still under threat of enforced eviction (Khosa, 1994).

Contrary to the often repeated protestations of the white landholding community, research (Khosa, 1994) has demonstrated unequivocally that most of the land area of the province was occupied by Africans prior to white settlement during the nineteenth century. The Land Acts of the early twentieth century took away the land rights of the African occupiers and placed legal obstacles in the way of those black farmers who had sufficient capital to buy land in their own name. Labour tenants generally suffered the most from those programmes of dispossession and, until 1988, many of those removed under the National Party's land policies were receiving minimal compensation (Khosa, 1994). The common practice was to take families from areas of prime cultivable land to locations where there was overcrowding, and where soil conditions were not conducive to sustainable farming. In the former homeland of KwaZulu, these conditions prevail today, and widespread soil erosion has had a calamitous impact upon agricultural productivity.

The situation on land rights is made hopelessly complex by layer upon layer of claims and counter-claims of earlier individual or tribal control of sometimes violently contested areas of land. The national leadership contends that land reform programmes offer an efficient mechanism for restructuring power relationships in agrarian society (GNU, 1995). In accordance with the principles of the RDP, namely the strategies of sustainable, community-centred development, and the empowerment of the landless poor, in 1995 the government was trying to create and deliver novel forms of landholding to generate acceptable compromises. The authors of the 'Restitution of Land Rights Bill' (1994) estimate that almost 1.5 million South Africans are entitled to make claims to land formerly owned by their ancestors. In the setting up of the Land Claims Commission, central government hoped to expedite the process of redistribution while defusing this potentially disastrous social and political problem. Not all commentators on the land issue in KwaZulu-Natal were wholly convinced of the wisdom of establishing a new system of communal land rights. The recent history of political change among South Africa's neighbouring countries has revealed the often inherent weaknesses of a rural economy based on principles other than the commercialisation of agriculture and the centrality of market forces. Nieuvoudt (1994) reasons that if the economy of the new South Africa is to have the most auspicious launching, then those farmers struggling to establish themselves in the commercial sector should be given preferential treatment in any programme of land resettlement. Experience elsewhere in Africa has demonstrated that when land is held under state or communal ownership, individual cultivators lose the incentive to make best use of that land, and the agrarian economy stumbles into decline (Gowans,

1994). The political, cultural and economic significance of land in efforts to establish community-based eco-tourism projects in the province is discussed in more detail in the following chapters.

Political strife in KwaZulu-Natal

The general exclusion of the impoverished and vulnerable from decision-making processes in Zulu society is linked to the prevalence of criminal and communal violence in the province. During the period of transition, when state violence showed signs of abating and the politics of negotiation were emerging, seemingly pointless massacres and atrocities, many of them committed in KwaZulu-Natal, dominated media coverage (du Toit, 1993). The frequent and often fatal clashes between rival groups, which led to more than 500,000 people being displaced in KwaZulu-Natal (Carver, 1996), were often supported and sometimes led by key personnel in the Inkatha Freedom Party (IFP) in collusion with right-wing groups comprising a third force (Gwala, 1992). The leader of the IFP, Chief Mangosuthu Gatsha Buthelezi, who before the 1994 elections headed the repressive administration of the homeland of KwaZulu, and afterwards the Provincial Administration of KwaZulu-Natal, certainly exploited his relationships with the police and security forces in his political and territorial struggles with the supporters of the United Democratic Front and the ANC (S. Taylor, 1995). Moreover, Buthelezi's links with powerful organisations and individuals allowed a dangerous culture of impunity to flourish within the province. Unsurprisingly, public perceptions of KwaZulu-Natal as a dangerous destination led to disappointing growth rates in tourism demand in the province.

The Inkatha Freedom Party (IFP) was formed in 1975 by Buthelezi at a time when black political parties and related organisations of any kind were severely restricted. The Party was based on the ethnic movement, Inkatha, which was originally established by Buthelezi's grandfather during the 1920s, in response to the perceived threat from the growth in radical trade unionism among Zulus (Worden, 1994). Chiefs and the Zulu royal family were becoming increasingly anxious over the trend away from traditional political systems, particularly among the young. The segregation policies of Jan Smuts suited this section of Zulu society who were trying to rejuvenate old ways, at a time when urbanisation was accelerating. Later, under the Bantu Authorities Act 1951, chiefs were again rewarded for carrying out government policies, and in doing so were compromised even further in the eyes of the more modernising and often missionary-educated Zulus (S. Taylor, 1995). The IFP has always found its strongest support in the rural areas. The Party is conservative in ideology, referring to Zulu traditions, and stressing patriarchal discipline. The founding tenets of Inkatha were the maintenance of tribal hierarchical values, which were argued to be the quintessence of African political life. It quickly became the ruling political party in the homeland of KwaZulu, taking the vast majority of seats in the 1978 KwaZulu Legislative Assembly Elections and, by 1980, bearing in mind that the ANC was banned at that time, Inkatha was the largest political organisation in South Africa.

During the late 1970s, Buthelezi, a complex political figure, was regarded by many Africans as the most high-profile voice for ANC interests, and he was respected for his rejection of independence for KwaZulu. However, by the early 1980s he had moved away from black radicalism and from calls for international sanctions, helping him to build strong relationships with the business sector. His continuing appeals for federalism were welcomed by white political leaders, and, for a while, the National Party believed that a combination of its own supporters and those of Inkatha would form a considerable counterforce to the popularity of the ANC (Worden, 1994). Widespread public criticism of his relationship with Pretoria and the South African police, forced Buthelezi into an even more traditionalist corner to secure his power base in KwaZulu. Following the unbanning of the ANC, and the recognition by the government of that party's central role in negotiations, the IFP and Buthelezi were unceremoniously dumped by the National Party's leadership. Throughout the period of transition, Buthelezi, as chief powerbroker for the Zulus, campaigned for regional autonomy and frequently walked out of cross-party talks. This campaign has continued until today, and has led to some odd linkages with the far right Afrikaner movement, looking for an alternative to perennial ANC domination. The ANC, in an effort to weaken the patron–client bonds between Buthelezi and the Zulu chiefs, infuriated the Chief Minister by proposing a system of government payments to those chiefs, directly from the state rather than through the province's administration.

The ANC condemned the IFP for collaborating with the National Party, and the two parties became bitter opponents. The violence that ensued resulted in thousands of deaths throughout the 1980s and early 1990s. The IFP came under widespread criticism in 1991, when it was discovered that the South African government had been financing the party from secret funds. A 1994 inquiry revealed that the South African police had been providing weapons to the IFP and training guerrilla squads to heighten the violence between the ANC and the IFP and to destabilise the country to disrupt the first multi-racial elections.

Buthelezi announced that he intended to boycott the elections of 1994, but shortly before polling day he was persuaded to take part. Inkatha won 10.5 per cent of the national vote, winning 43 seats in the new 400-seat National Assembly. As Minister for Home Affairs he demanded more autonomy for the province than the ANC was prepared to allow and, in 1995, the IFP withdrew from parliament. During the first year of majority rule, violence between the IFP and ANC cost an estimated 1500 deaths in KwaZulu-Natal. A further consequence of the violence and political chaos was the plight of the estimated 500,000 internal refugees in the province, displaced from their villages by the armed gangs. At that time, militias from the IFP and self-defence units from the ANC were terrorising the population of the province, murdering opponents, burning houses and openly carrying guns even in the centre of Durban (Koch, Stober and Edmonds, 1995). The national government was unable to form a coherent strategy for dealing with the chaos in the KwaZulu-Natal, and even the sending of a thousand soldiers to deal with the problem failed to have any effect on the death rate from murders. Within the IFP there were also serious and acrimonious divisions between hardline conservative traditionalists, and moderates looking for a political future for the party in the federal system. The moderates were claiming that negotiations with the ANC leadership would result in favourable terms for the Zulus within the South African federation. The hardliners, led by Buthelezi, were pushing for an autonomous Zulu kingdom, to be ruled without interference from the ANC. The IFP rejoined parliament in 1996 and in the June 1999 elections, won 34 seats in the legislature, by which time there had occurred a considerable drop in the levels of violence in the province.

Our research interests took us to northern KwaZulu-Natal and to Maputaland, where there are many protected areas amid a population suffering the most awful hardships. Their economic choices are severely limited, and attempts to establish community-based eco-tourism projects, often involving the statutory conservation authorities, have met with varying degrees of success. Much of the literature concerned with the welfare of African communities in northern KwaZulu-Natal focuses, reasonably enough, on the debilitating and chronic poverty that characterises the region's tribal life. However, this does not always convey the tangle of processes and institutional factors that sustain extremely vulnerable communities. The concept of social exclusion, often used in the study of European and North American politics, is preferred here because of its usefulness in analysing social processes that block progress of the deprived and marginalised (Evans, 1998). These may include restricted access to land, unemployment, low incomes, little or no welfare support, gender inequalities, ethnic rivalries and social monopolies (Evans, 1998; Gaventa, 1998).

In northern KwaZulu-Natal, violence and the fear of it, the resurgence of chieftainship, political venality, the slow development of an appropriate institutional framework to support communal empowerment, and a shared memory of apartheid's injustices, also prevent the black rural population from progressing. With few property rights, and a weakened identity with place (itself the product of forced migration under apartheid) black rural communities in KwaZulu-Natal generally display low self-esteem, and an intensified sense of social exclusion. Such social anomie is a major challenge to developmental initiatives among remote and disempowered tribal groups in the northern regions of the province. Moreover, the democratising influence of developmental planning, framed in the language of the RDP and based on notions of social empowerment, is not always well received by traditional power holders such as Zulu chiefs. The sometimes evangelical support for community-based eco-tourism and democratic participation ignores these concerns, and in doing so encourages naive speculation on an approach which has yet to prove it can deliver.

It is not the intention here to provide another tidy developmental narrative. Instead, the next section focuses on conflicting needs and aspirations of the various stakeholders, and on the tangle of factors in the local and national political economy that inform the development of eco-tourism in KwaZulu-Natal. For concerned white South Africans, the discourse of sustainability is compelling, but the immediacies of rural African life deny many Zulus the privilege of adopting such considered and long-term assessments of their own economic opportunities.

Conservation, eco-tourism, and rural development in KwaZulu-Natal

At the beginning of our period of research, biodiversity in KwaZulu-Natal was protected by two official conservation agencies, the internationally well known Natal Parks Board (NPB) and the poorer and smaller KwaZulu Department of Nature Conservation (KDNC), which was responsible for protected areas within the former homeland. On 1 April 1998, the KwaZulu-Natal Conservation Service (KNCS) was formed by the long-planned amalgamation of these two authorities. A parastatal organisation, it was responsible to the provincial cabinet via the KwaZulu-Natal Conservation Board, which reports, in turn, to the Minister of Traditional and Environmental Affairs (Münster, 31/3/99). However, in November 2000 the authority changed its name again, and is now known as KwaZulu-Natal Wildlife (KZN-Wildlife). In this and following chapters, where discussion focuses on developments or events prior to April 1998, the conservation agencies will be referred to as the NPB and the KDNC respectively, whereas for later dates they will be referred to as the KNCS, and finally as KZN-Wildlife, or the KwaZulu-Natal Nature Conservation Service (KNNCS).

The Natal Parks Board was established in 1947, and by 1995 was responsible for the management of 80 protected areas totalling 694,753 hectares; about 11 per cent of the surface area of KwaZulu-Natal. In addition, the Board managed 28 per cent of the coastline in the form of maritime reserves (NPB, 1995a). Within its protected areas, there were 24 camps providing 2421 beds per night in various types of accommodation units, and there was room for close on 10,000 people in campsites. The NPB employed over 3200 staff including nature conservators, guards, scientists, builders and mechanics and management staff. Among its central responsibilities was the enforcement of legislation relating to flora and fauna throughout the province. In its Mission Statement, the goals of the NPB were to:

- conserve the wildlife resources of KwaZulu-Natal and the ecosystems and processes upon which they depend, and to assist all other public and private groups in ensuring the wise use of the biosphere.

Moreover, and among other concerns, the Board had to:

- prevent the man-induced extinction of any species indigenous to KwaZulu-Natal;
- promote the utilisation of wildlife resources in KwaZulu-Natal and exercise control in order to ensure that all forms of utilisation are sustainable;
- support the eco-tourism industry in KwaZulu-Natal by providing, on a self-funding basis, visitor facilities and experiences which are compatible with the conservation mission of the Board (NPB, 1994).

In its 1995 Annual Report, the NPB repeatedly emphasises its commitment to the upliftment of neighbouring communities through the provision of social services and other benefits. The NPB was a statutory body, and relied almost entirely on state funding. Tourism receipts were, in the main, reinvested in the conservation management and eco-tourism projects. The NPB was also active in environmental education programmes throughout the province. The Board considered such programmes as critical to the long-term protection of the natural resources of KwaZulu-Natal (Creemers, 15/11/95). Research into the sustainable use of natural resources within the province was a priority, and the NPB launched a Resource Economics Programme to take full advantage of the extensive academic and practical experience of its staff. As one of the best known and most successful conservation agencies in Africa, the NPB gained numerous international awards for its innovatory work in the protection of wildlife and the environment. However, under the new political dispensation of 1994 and within the parameters of the RDP, a profound personality change was required. Those neighbouring people whom the Board had regarded as a serious threat to the security of its parks for the past 49 years were now to be consulted on their views of the future role of the parks in rural development.

The NPB made much of the work of the Resource Economics Programme dedicated to eco-tourism as a key contributor to sustainable development; to the role of local communities in protected area management; to the pricing of nature conservation and eco-tourism services; and to intangible values derived from nature conservation (NPB, 1995b). Social responsibility became a new criterion by which the success of NPB operations was to be assessed. Eco-tourism was argued to offer opportunities to black South Africans to make a living, and by so doing, to come to understand the value of biodiversity. The Neighbour Relations Policy was developed in an effort to eliminate the rancour that had characterised the relationships between the Board and those communities who had suffered most from its activities in KwaZulu-Natal. Going beyond the traditional but *ad hoc* and tokenistic practice of periodically allowing neighbouring people into the parks to collect thatch or herbs, advocates within the Board of the Neighbour Relations Policy claimed that Zulu inhabitants were now able to negotiate over their utilisation of natural resources on an empowered and genuinely equitable basis (Dale, 26/3/98).

Through Neighbour Liaison Forums, issues such as the codification of boundaries, damage to crops caused by problem animals, and *controlled free access*, were discussed by NPB field staff, chiefs and community members at Board stations. In a more concrete sense, the Board, with funds supplied by a growing list of donors – South African and international – made demonstrable improvements in the standards of living among the deprived rural groups in the vicinity of the conservation areas (Creemers, 15/11/95). Having helped to identify and prioritise social needs, and by involving local African entre-preneurs and tradesmen, the NPB assisted in the delivery of infrastructural, medical, educational and environmental benefits to people often living in conditions as desperate and hopeless as those experienced in the poorest regions of the developing world. The NPB was very proud of its achievements in these endeavours to make life more bearable for its neighbours, whose voices had been muted during and before the era of apartheid. Accomplishments lauded in its literature included:

- the construction of simple technology toilets at a village school in the Drakensberg Mountains;
- a small block-making enterprise in the Mkesi reserve (profits pay for electricity in the village, a much-needed source of power for operating wells);
- a market garden, staffed and managed by women near St Lucia;
- school buildings and water projects (NPB, 1995a and b).

Awkward adjustments to its self-image were necessary as the Board squared up to meet its obligations to its neighbours as stipulated by government policy and the RDP. In response to those challenges, the NPB adopted a model of conservation of biodiversity that contained at least elements of socio-economic development. It saw itself as taking a proactive role in enhancing the tourism industry in KwaZulu-Natal by convincing people living close to its protected areas of the long-term benefits of environmental protection (Hibbs, 20/11/95).

However, it was apparent that the concept of eco-tourism development held by the NPB and the current KZN-Wildlife, did not include the degree of community participation deemed necessary by Wells and Brandon (1992), and by many other commentators on sustainable development (Cook, 1995; Munslow and Fitzgerald, 1995; Picard and Garrity, 1995). During interviews between 1997 and 1999, it was evident that several senior officers of the conservation authority were sceptical about the abilities of untrained Africans to fill decision-making roles in conservation/development programmes. Clearly there are professional boundaries in question that were and are being jealously guarded. In personal communications with members of 'Interface Africa', a small NGO active in conflict-resolution and community development in KwaZulu-Natal, it was stated that many of the socio-economic projects embarked upon by the NPB were bolted onto – rather than integrated with – the other business (and prime concern) of the organisation, the conservation of biodiversity (Mahlangu, 14/11/95). Indeed, in 1998, more than one senior officer working for the NPB told us that much of the interest shown by the Board in community-based eco-tourism had been primarily a public relations exercise.

Among communities living near the parks, there is little sense of 'ownership' of development projects, and rural people remain suspicious of the stated intentions of the Board. The efforts of the organisation to establish buffer zones of community development have to be seen in the context of the pending land claims and the threats of premature and illegal encroachments. African people are demanding secure rights to land, and are questioning the agenda of conservation-based development programmes, especially those informed by 'white' notions of environmentalism and eco-tourism. The NPB was staffed at managerial level entirely by whites, and there were no blacks in positions of authority at the headquarters in Pietermaritzburg (Hibbs, 15/11/95) during this difficult period in the history of the Board.

Eco-tourism is generally regarded as a white preoccupation, and retains associations with a recent history of rural oppression. Not one black African tourist was encountered by us on our many visits to nature-based tourism locations in KwaZulu-Natal. Indeed, entering the protected areas had the semblance of leaving Africa. Just outside the gates of the Royal Natal Park in the beautiful Drakensberg Mountains, there was a huge Zulu settlement living in crude huts on a hillside of bare mud. Once inside the boundary of the Park, there were sprinkled lawns, flower beds and a tastefully built reception and gift shop, where white visitors bought mugs and safari gear as souvenirs. This was held to be the norm by a senior manager in Satour, himself a Zulu and responsible for the improvement of relationships between African communities and the eco-tourism industry (Luvumbo, 15/11/95). At a People and Parks conference held in Durban, 23/5/95, the Minister for Economic Affairs and Tourism for KwaZulu-Natal, Jacob Zuma, commenting on the dominance of whites within the tourism industry (as tourists and as employees) argued that black communities in the past had regarded themselves as playing no part in tourism, and had been mere objects for tourists to view and photograph (Carruthers and Zaloumis, 1995).

It is also the case that many of the local projects of social amelioration have been slight in impact, and often wholly inappropriate. In conversations with NPB officers, the creation of a vegetable garden outside the perimeter fence at Hluhluwe Reserve was cited as a success story for the Zulu women who had been taught how to grow vegetables for sale. During a visit to Hluhluwe, it was noted that the garden was, in fact, in a rather sorry state. Members of Interface Africa had also been to look at the garden, and had discovered from some of the women who had been working there that they did not have the means to transport the produce to market, and that the vegetables were not popular with the local people. The result was that the vegetables were rotting in the ground, and the women themselves were disappointed and disillusioned (Mahlangu, 14/11/95). Numerous as the community improvement schemes were, they were insignificant in comparison with the needs of the people. They were not integrated into the wider economy of KwaZulu-Natal, nor were the important linkages between development and conservation made explicit.

The NPB was having to deal with illegal land invasions and the obvious threat of further encroachments in several of those very areas where it had been most active in providing villages with educational and other facilities (NPB, 1995a). As Wells and Brandon (1992) point out, within those projects, ostensibly based on a putatively symbiotic relationship between conservation and development, the paramount concern for state agencies is the preservation of biodiversity. The distribution of resources among villages is as much a part of the strategy to build a buffer zone as it is a contribution to the upliftment of impoverished communities. The NPB, like so many other statutory conservation agencies, was militaristic (its staff wore uniforms not unlike those worn by service people everywhere), and conservative. It had built for itself a sound reputation for efficiency in the protection of biodiversity. The demands upon it now were profound. Ethical and philosophical transformations were needed in addition to logistical expertise. A new agenda had been set, which required movement away from confrontational relationships with neighbours to concil-iatory arrangements involving transparency of purpose and co-operation.

In the past, white environmental groups have regarded conservation as a non-political issue. However, because environmental protection entails ownership and authority over land and other scarce resources, it is in fact a highly charged political matter, which requires attention at all levels of the new administrative system. Capacity building among African groups is necessary for them to take advantage of new political and developmental opportunities. This in turn entails the transfer of power to communities so that their participation in conservation-linked development programmes gives them the will and authority to make best use of their natural resources in the sustainable development of their agrarian economies. It is also envisaged that within this new discourse of 'eco' development, indigenous ecological knowledge will be attributed the credibility that it has been denied in the past.

Communities require more factual information on the income potential from conservation and tourism, and should resist attempts to bully them into what is regarded by many as a fickle and risky way to make a living. There is also concern that, within communities themselves, there are marked differentials in resources, and some individuals have acted as brokers between the various actors, and have been able to direct benefits towards themselves. There seems to be little understanding of community group dynamics on the part of the NPB and similar organisations, but this is not unexpected – government and quasi-government organisations the world over have found this a hard lesson to learn (Baumol, 1991).

Among many people living close to the perimeter fences of NPB protected areas there is the beginnings of an awareness of the potentially central role that eco-tourism could play in their respective futures. But there persists an old resentment over land, and rural communities are becoming increasingly impatient over land restitution. There is also a growing suspicion that the Neighbour Relations Policy was in effect a subtle means of extending the Service's authority beyond the fences. Within the communities there is concern over who should represent their interests vis-à-vis KZN-Wildlife and outside commercial agencies. While chiefs retain much of their old authority, the desire for democratisation has touched rural society, and a considerable proportion of the agrarian population is tired of old systems of patron-clientism. At the same time, there is no clear vision of exactly how local concerns are to articulate with the new political structures created since the elections of 1994.

In sum, there is anxiety that models of eco-tourism development are being adopted uncritically, and with insufficient consultation with neighbouring communities. The fundamental assumptions upon which such plans are based remain untested, and African communities, dangerously poor already, have the most to lose if eco-tourism fails to deliver. There remains deep mistrust of conservation authorities, who are suspected of promoting tourism as a pretext for pursuing their obsession with conservation at all costs. The existence of the protected areas reduces the land available for diversification to mitigate risks in times of hardship, placing additional pressure on those who are less educated, and least likely to gain employment in the eco-tourism trade, to poach game animals for food or for sale.

Although there is now some evidence that elected community representatives are being included in some committees concerned with the management of conservation areas, African people, in their dealings with the former NPB and currently with KZN-Wildlife, have not and are not participating in the decision-making process to the extent that they would like and to the extent deemed necessary for significant political and economic transformation for poor peoples. Nor does their role in eco-tourism initiatives match the concept of 'empowerment' that serves as a major focus for the Reconstruction and Development Programme (RDP) and the Rural Development Strategy (RDS). It is also becoming clear that tidy notions of eco-tourism as mutually beneficial arrangements between partners on an equal footing, which empower the historically disadvantaged while protecting the environment, are too simple when compared with the asymmetric relationships of power, and with the various perceptions of the environment, and what it is for, that prevail in rural KwaZulu-Natal.

In 1994, the first year of multi-racial elections, in recognition of the requirements of the RDP, the Natal Parks Board developed its Integrated Conservation and Development Model, in which it acknowledged that the necessary integration of conservation and development would require the Board to take on a new role as development agency, and would therefore lead to the organisation implementing fundamental changes to its institutional structure (NPB, 1998). This new model encompassed the marriage of environmental protection with eco-tourism, and would enable significant contributions to the social and economic development of communities living close to the protected areas.

Having considered the principles of the RDP, the Board concluded that the environment had a crucial role to play in improving the lives of poor South Africans. This role would be facilitated by improving access to natural resources by local communities. This in turn would include the enabling processes of including communities in the decision-making procedures involved in conservation and eco-tourism, and through education in environmental protection. The Board felt that substantial economic growth could be achieved by targeting both the domestic and international tourists in the expected tourism boom now that the age of apartheid was over. The Board urged caution and patience, arguing that early action might have long-term and deleterious repercussions for the natural resources.

The Integrated Conservation and Development Model was based on the interdependence of local communities and protected areas. The conservation agency was to act as a catalyst for rural development that would focus on both the use of natural resources themselves and on economic improvements within the surrounding villages. The model argues that resources will be used efficiently and, most important, sustainably within and outside the protected areas.

Within the parks and reserves under the authority of the Board, opportunities for development would emerge from the controlled use of wildlife resources, and from eco-tourism. In the areas adjacent to the reserves, efforts would be made to encourage eco-tourism and agricultural development. It was hoped that in this way, cross-sectoral linkages would arise, and facilities such as eco-tourism accommodation, and the improvement of retail and service industries established.

Stated activities identified by the Board, included the provision of infrastructure such as fencing, staff accommodation, roads, power and water supplies to rural areas; the development of eco-tourism facilities; human capacity development through training, and environmental education; craft industries based on local natural products, and other small industry opportunities linked to eco-tourism (NPB, 1994).

The fundamentals of the programme comprised the following elements:

- The development of the rural areas of the province depended upon their natural resources.
- The primary responsibility of the NPB was to protect biodiversity, which entailed the control of its exploitation.
- The sustainable use of natural resources would provide economic opportunities within protected areas, such as the controlled harvesting of resources, and immediately outside them for neighbouring impoverished African neighbours, in non-consumptive activities such as eco-tourism.
- The direct benefits would include the conservation of soil, water and biotic resources, and the safeguarding of life-support systems.
- Indirect benefits would take the form of the development of retail and service industries, craft production and accommodation, and human resources.

By 1995, during our first year of research, the NPB had established its Neighbour Relations Policy that required the Board to participate in Neighbour Liaison Forums, its support of economic development projects in neighbouring villages, and the enhancement of environmental awareness among communities living in the vicinity of the protected areas. The Neighbour Liaison Forums were set up to help create trust between local people and the Board, to identify and establish boundaries, create wildlife resource harvesting programmes and provide controlled free access to the reserves. The economic development included addressing the basic needs of the neighbouring communities, the involvement of local entrepreneurs, developing wildlife areas on the periphery of the protected areas, and the training of field staff (Ecoserv, 1995).

Environmental education programmes included creating an appropriate problem animal policy, undertaking staff training and creating a Neighbourhood Trust to fund these actions. However, these were early days and the efficiency of these activities was already under question. At that time, regional activities of the Neighbours Programme included community markets, school buildings, water schemes, market gardens, research projects, block-making, health projects, sanitation projects, chicken farming and community conservation areas. The benefits enjoyed by communities included income from salaries, collection of natural resources and the improvement of business opportunities. Several private sector ventures had been initiated in the province as a whole, and these entailed the development of private sector investment in the funding of accommodation within the protected areas, with the NPB providing guidelines and management of the reserves. Examples of such co-operation between the Board and the private sector included a general store and beach take-away, a dive shop selling equipment, air and boat tours, curio and basket sellers, and the harvesting of natural resources such as medicinal herbs within parks.

By 1997, the Neighbour Relation Programme had been reassessed and, as a result, was given a new title of the Community Conservation Programme to reflect both of its central concerns, conservation and community objectives. The change in title had implications for field staff working among communities in areas adjacent to the reserves. Prior to the change in focus, staff had concentrated on assisting communities in their efforts to attract funds for their developmental projects. But with time, it became apparent that such an approach did not lead to sustainability because the communities concerned often lacked the skills to pursue their goals into the future. Consequently, attention moved towards the building of capacity and away from straightforward infrastructural improvements (Morrison, 1997). This renamed programme incorporated local management teams, with the public responding in partnership to environmental issues within the province. Part and parcel of this programme were the Community-based Tourism Partnership Projects which aimed to support eco-tourism and conservation developments in rural communities. The NPB was clear in that the key concern was biodiversity conservation, and that the understanding of the need for conservation was the basis of all other activities.

At a workshop held jointly by the Board and the KwaZulu-Natal Tourism Agency, Paula Morrison, a Community Conservation Officer, cited three examples of interaction between communities and the Board near the huge and impressively well-run Hluhluwe-Umfolozi Park in northern KwaZulu-Natal. The first example is of a community-based bed and breakfast business sited close to the Umfolozi gate. This initiative was established in 1997, was owned by one family, and consisted of traditional Zulu huts that could sleep 30 people. Guests eat Zulu food, and can watch dancing and singing performances. Their stays here are usually of one or two nights, and are combined with visits to the Park itself. This project required little investment, and is the main source of livelihood for the Zulu family. However, Morrison (1997) indicates that there were serious constraints on the economic progress of the project. English was not spoken by the adults, book-keeping skills were poor, and the business has not been well marketed. Also there were signs that other members of the community were envious of the family concerned.

The second example is the Mpembeni community conservation area. This community occupies land adjacent to the western boundary of the Park near Mkhuze, and has surplus land that was made available for eco-tourism. Private sector funding and management were needed to develop this initiative with the help of the Board in providing access and guidance on conservation management. The Board also offered to contribute by allowing utilisation of its marketing networks. This community has also considered the potential of offering opportunities for cultural tourism: Zulu dancing and singing; visits to traditional healers and the tribal court (Morrison, 1997). The sale of crafts could provide a further source of income. In its favour, the community has strong supportive leadership from the Kwajobe Tribal Authority, a tourism association, a development association, and an Izinyanga (healer) association. Further, Morrison, contends that the community enjoys an open and trusting relationship with the Board. This claim was repeated by a senior NPB officer during an interview with us at Hluhluwe-Umfolozi. However, difficulties had arisen over attracting private sector investment, and the project remained in embryo until April 2001, when R68,000 was made available from the Community Levy Trust Fund to the community of the Kwajobe Tribal Authority (Hans, 6/4/01).

Since 1 February 1998, the Community Levy has been paid by visitors entering some of the protected areas under the authority of the Board. Each tourist is charged R1 extra on entering the selected reserves, and R10 extra on the cost of accommodation there. All of this money is channelled into the Community Levy Fund (NPB, 1998). The additional charges are justified in terms of the benefits they provide local people, and a substantial amount had been collected and was languishing in the Trust account, but the Board experienced legal and political difficulties in the allocation of the monies to community projects, and none had been invested in community projects by early 1999 (Münster, 31/3/99). By April 2001, the Levy Trust had collected about R12 million, and of that amount about R1 million had been transferred to two rural communities in KwaZulu-Natal.

A KZN-Wildlife spokesperson, Maureen Mndaweni, described how the Mpembeni Conservation Game Reserve, which had just been opened, was funded by the Trust, and the Kwajobe community now had plans to build a hall at the local school to be used as a classroom during the day and as a community hall during the evenings. At the handing over ceremony, the outgoing Chief Executive Officer of KZN-Wildlife, George Hughes, acknowledging the tragic history of conservation in which poor people had been abused, emphasised that although the Community Levy Trust had been originally established to facilitate rural development, priority was to be given to those communities living immediately outside the protected areas of KZN-Wildlife (Hans, 6/4/01).

The final example given by Morrison (1997) which we also visited, are the craft outlets near the Mambeni and Memorial Gates of the Hluhluwe-Umfolozi Park. These stalls provide a modest income to a group of women who, because of a lack of education would otherwise have few chances of supporting their families. Comparisons with tourist expenditure elsewhere suggest that there is room here to increase the income from the stalls. But the group is not supported by local tribal leaders, the women are not highly skilled, and there exists a lack of funding.

KZN-Wildlife has inherited an immensely challenging cluster of developmental responsibilities at a time when government subsidies are declining. Indeed, in 2001 large-scale job cuts were announced by George Hughes, as a cost-cutting exercise. Hughes was troubled by reports of declining standards in the conservation work of the agency and hoped that by trimming the workforce of 660 staff, more funds would be available for biodiversity protection. At the same time, eco-tourism development which was demanding so much of the organisation was not providing the expected income.

The other conservation authority in the province still in existence in 1995, the KwaZulu Department of Nature Conservation (KDNC), was first set up in 1982, as the KwaZulu Bureau of Natural Resources. By the elections of 1994, it had grown in responsibility over land area from 0.5 per cent to 2.5 per cent of the KwaZulu-Natal Province as a whole. Under its authority were 12 small parks and reserves, some of them newly created and others transferred from the NPB. These reserves are found in the more remote and less accessible northern regions of the province, and had experienced little or no tourism development. Like protected areas elsewhere in KwaZulu-Natal, they had their origins in the removals of local people, and consequently the KDNC was very unpopular in KwaZulu. But immediately prior to the 1994 elections, the KDNC made known its plans to end forced and uncompensated removals (Honey, 1999).

The KDNC also had a poor reputation for other reasons. Within its upper ranks it had employed many former Rhodesian military officers, including Nick Steele who was serving as the head of the organisation. Under his leadership, the KDNC had been accused of operating a covert division that spied on local politicians and had participated in complex schemes of ivory and rhino horn smuggling. The South African Military Intelligence Directorate had admitted training paramilitary units for the Inkatha Freedom Party on a KwaZulu game reserve (Ellis, 1994). Port Durnford Forest Reserve, on the north coast was being used for 48-hour training programmes. For some time, the counter-insurgency leaders of the South African security forces had regarded Inkatha as an important ally in the struggle against the ANC. KwaZulu game wardens for the KDNC were trained by the 121 Battalion of the South African Defence Force. In 1991 it became known that the KDNC had created a secret intelligence unit, which had kept the anthropologist David Webster under observation prior to his eventual murder in 1989. Webster had come across evidence of the illegal ivory trade between Mozambique and South Africa, and of the smuggling of weapons and drugs by South African security men.

During many of our interviews with stakeholders in tourism within the province, the KDNC was strongly criticised for the unprofessional behaviour of its staff. The NPB had also been troubled by reports that military training was taking place at the KDNC Mlamba Reserve close to the Umfolozi Game Reserve that was under the authority of the Board (Stober, 1995). By 1996, it was known that a senior member of the former homeland office of Chief Buthelezi had played a major role in the illegal funding of the Inkatha paramilitary self-protection units, with R8 million of public money (Eveleth, 1996). Further, it had become clear that the covert activities of Buthelezi had continued long after the KwaZulu homeland government and the Natal Provincial Administration had merged following the multi-racial elections, and that direct communications over the issue of clandestine military operations between the office of Chief Buthelezi and the KDNC had been maintained throughout this period (Eveleth, 1996).

These criticisms and suspicions notwithstanding, and in contrast with the Natal Parks Board, the KDNC had, from its very beginnings, developed a policy of sharing the profits from eco-tourism initiatives with local communities; a policy which was announced publicly and reinforced by Chief Buthelezi in 1989 (Koch, 1994). From its inception, the KDNC had admitted its impoverished neighbours to its protected areas to collect traditional resources such as reeds and grasses, to purchase low-priced meat, and to visit ancestral graves. The organisation had also helped local communities to establish game farms on unwanted land. In its literature, the authority repeatedly argued that conservation was dependent upon rural communities taking responsibility for the environment, and that there existed a direct link between poverty and environmental degradation (Roberts, 1997). A well-planned strategy of eco-tourism development had offered itself as the optimum use of resources while maintaining the integrity of the environment. The KDNC had realised that it did not have the resources or expertise to run and market a commercial eco-tourism enterprise and, because of this, under the directorship of Nick Steele, it had created a developmental model of innovative eco-tourism promotion. The basis of the model was a tripartite relationship between the Department, the private sector and the affected local communities. The model entailed the construction of small-scale, middle-income tourist camps and lodges. This arrangement, the KDNC contended, went beyond merely providing employment for its neighbours. It was an opportunity to enjoy meaningful participation, ownership and decision-making powers.

The benefits of the model included a reduced dependency on the environmental budget of the Department, investment in otherwise neglected rural areas, improved access to loans, the harnessing of commercial business skills, the stimulation of secondary, spin-off, entrepreneurial activities, and capacity building through the new decision-making responsibilities and activities. However, the KDNC conceded that there were major risks in such a model, namely, the rigours of commercial competitiveness, a relatively smaller role for the Department with the fear that commercial imperatives may take precedence over conservation, and the likelihood of misunderstanding each other's dynamics. The projects might also falter over the extended timescale of the negotiations (arising from the need to convince communities of the open intentions of the KDNC), and the lack of experienced institutions and other bodies to act on behalf of neighbouring communities.

In 1986, elected representatives of local communities were accepted onto the committees established by the Department, and a plan was created to give tribal authorities 25 per cent of the profits from culling and from tourism to use for local social upliftment programmes. However, these schemes had been criticised by local people in the belief that the KDNC had not been completely honest and open about the amount of profits secured, and that the funds that had been made available had been passed into the hands of tribal leaders who had, in turn, used the money for their own private purposes (Koch, 1994). But ill-feeling over past mistreatment by the organisation still characterised attitudes towards the KDNC, and small separatist movements campaigning to take Maputaland out of the homeland of KwaZulu were still active during the early 1990s.

The KDNC did not possess the level of tourism infrastucture enjoyed by the NPB, and in 1994 it was facing the widely publicised cuts in subsidies from the government. To overcome this disadvantage the organisation moved to form new relationships with the private sector and local communities, to construct lodges and hotels. A trust company, Isivuno, 'to harvest', was established through which funds would be channelled towards projects that would directly benefit local people. The Department had identified over 30 sites within its protected areas for eco-tourism development. The KDNC saw itself as a pioneer in such collaborations.

As strong examples of such ventures, Roberts (1997) refers to Rocktail Bay Lodge, and Ndumo Wilderness Camp in the far north of the province, where Isivuno, the local communities, Wilderness Safaris, and the KwaZulu Finance and Investment Corporation have collaborated in successful eco-tourism initiatives. At Rocktail Bay, ten wood and thatch A-frame chalets on stilts under the forest canopy have been built in the Maputaland Coastal Forest Reserve. A wooden walkway runs from the solar-powered lodge and over the tree-covered dunes to a beautifully secluded beach, where guests can pursue all kinds of watersports, and where loggerhead and leatherback turtles lay their eggs during the summer (Honey, 1999).

Initially established in 1924, and acquired by the NPB in 1954, the site of the Ndumo Wilderness Camp, the Ndumo Game Reserve, was hated by the surrounding Thonga people who were moved out when it was fenced. During the bitter and protracted civil war in Mozambique, the Ndumo reserve and the neighbouring Tembe Game Reserve were at times overrun by poachers, refugees, rebels from the Resistência Nacional Moçambicana (RENAMO), and smugglers (Ellis, 1994). In 1989, Ndumo and other reserves in the area were taken over by the KDNC. The Department immediately wanted to consolidate the Ndumo reserve with the Tembe reserve so that the elephant population of the latter would have access to river water in Ndumo. But there were families living in the corridor between the reserves, and they were already antagonised by their earlier removal from Ndumo, and by the denial of access to the water supply there. Eventually, in the mid-1990s, a compromise was reached whereby the communities agreed to move further south in return for guaranteed access to water supply at Ndumo.

When the civil war in Mozambique ended in 1990, Ndumo and the other reserves on the border looked more attractive to eco-tourists keen to see the abundant bird populations, the plentiful supply of black and white rhinos, blue wildebeest and other wildlife. Because of this interest, in March 1995, Wilderness Safaris opened Ndumo Wilderness Camp as a collaborative venture with the KDNC and the local Thonga communities (Honey, 1999). Eight upmarket and solar-powered tents on raised wooden decks were built in a secluded and beautiful spot surrounded by water and game.

Ndumo Wilderness Camp is owned by both Isivuno and Wilderness Safaris, but Rocktail is owned entirely by Isivuno. In both examples Wilderness pays Isivuno a modest rent, and Isivuno and Wilderness are co-managers. The local tribal community receives 25 per cent of Isivuno's receipts. Because the tribal leaders do not actually live in the area, Wilderness feared that there was an increased likelihood of funds not reaching the community members themselves, and therefore, to avoid complaints and dissent, decided to create trusts, into which all revenues are paid and which are administered by elected representatives of the communities.

In spite of the well-intentioned structuring of the projects at Ndumo and Rocktail, the participatory opportunities experienced by the communities and the economic benefits received by them, have been slight. Some local people have found work at Rocktail Bay Lodge. But while the lease payments have provided the communities with modest payments, by 1999 no management profit payments had been received by the trust fund in place there (Honey, 1999). Wilderness Safaris, for its part remains upbeat about the initiatives and is arguing that, in time, accumulated profits can be used by the communities to buy out Isivuno, thereby increasing their ownership of the projects to 50 per cent. The conservation authority (now KZN-Wildlife) also continues to believe in its tripartite model because it is not prohibitive to community participation, it takes advantage of the business acumen of the private sector, reduces leakage of income, creates employment and a sense of ownership for the local Thonga people, and may turn out to be the solution to the conflict between the local need for economic opportunities and the essential goal of conservation (Roberts, 1999).

For a deeper understanding of the conservation/community encounter, we turn now to a small selection of examples in which local communities relate in different ways to official agencies, to the commercial sector, to NGOs and to each other in eco-tourism planning and implementation. The peculiarities of actual case studies may also be useful in identifying some of the factors that assist or impede the rural poor in their efforts to promote their own upliftment. We have visited all three examples of eco-tourism development several times, and we have monitored their progress closely since 1995. Of paramount interest is the extent of community participation in decision-making, and the degree to which that participation is based on patterns of land ownership. With further research, it might be possible to develop typologies of eco-tourism projects that throw light on the dynamics of sustainable rural development and on the mechanisms necessary for a more equitable distribution of benefits to the most marginalised sectors of society.

Summary

Although tourism in northern KwaZulu-Natal has immense potential, it remains poorly developed. The profoundly excluded African communities of the region share a history of violence, political oppression and landlessness. Against the background of the fundamental principles of the RDP, the provincial con-servation authority has found itself under pressure to take an active role in the economic development of the communities surrounding the protected areas. While the NPB had a fine reputation for conservation, it had little commercial experience or expertise. The Board has been criticised for its lack of dynamism in tourism development. Many of its efforts to improve living conditions within African villages have been tokenistic and slight. Further, local people continue to doubt the motives of the Board, which at best they interpret as an exercise in public relations. There are also widely held doubts over the levels of transparency demonstrated by the conservation authority. Meanwhile, the authority is having to deal with reductions in public subsidies which threaten its primary concern, the conservation of biodiversity.

Chapter 3

Community-based eco-tourism in northern KwaZulu-Natal: ownership, management and participation

All three case studies discussed here are located in Maputaland, in northern KwaZulu-Natal, where there are several large and internationally important protected areas. The population of Maputaland is almost entirely rural, and while landlessness is not the problem it is in other parts of the province, the Zulu communities are living in a state of crisis (Centre for Community Organisation, Research and Development [CORD]a [no date]). Indicators of extreme poverty such as child abandonment, illegitimacy, high levels of dependency, illiteracy and early removal from school are commonplace, as is the sense that the region has been left out of South Africa's development during the twentieth century. Fewer than 28 per cent of the adult population are even functionally literate, and in the 20–64 age group, 35 per cent of males and 85 per cent of females are unemployed. Throughout Maputaland, 50 per cent of households earn less than $250 per annum. In addition to these symptoms of destitution, there is a high degree of dependency on male migrant earnings, which in turn leads to a disproportionate distribution of social goods in favour of the male population (CORDa). More than 30 per cent of the people have been removed from their land at least once in their lifetime, and communities feel themselves to be powerless in the face of external pressures, and in finding solutions to their chronic problems. This latter feature of rural society in Maputaland constitutes a major obstacle to the successful pursuit of community development programmes. Overcoming this profound social anomie, is a critical challenge to development agencies.

Eco-tourism and the struggle for land in the Greater St Lucia Wetland Park

> They will try to convince us of the value of tourism, but once they win they will chase us away [settler in Dukuduku forest; Mathenjwa et al., 1995, p.4].

The Greater St Lucia Wetland Park consists of a large and beautiful estuarine and lake system on the sub-tropical coastline of Maputaland, some 250km north of Durban. Within the boundaries of the Park lie St Lucia Game and Marine Reserves, Mkuzi Game Reserve, False Bay Park, Sodwana Bay, Cape Vidal, Maputaland Marine Reserve, and several smaller interconnecting protected

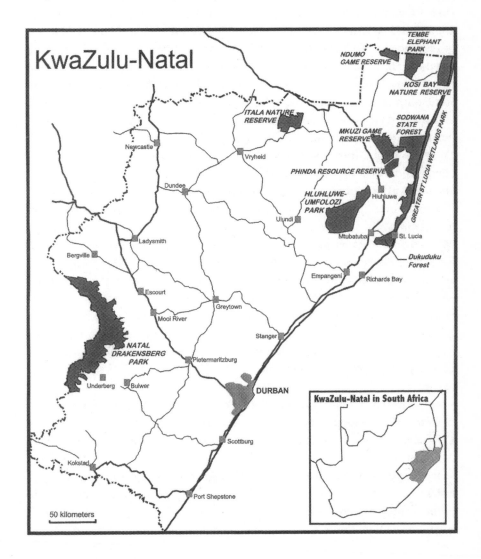

areas. St Lucia contains a remarkable variety of habitats and eco-niches including mountains, grasslands, forests, wetlands, mangroves, dunes, beaches and coral reef. The region was extensively hunted during the latter years of the nineteenth century but, more recently, native species of large mammals have been successfully reintroduced to the Park (R. Taylor, 1995). Hippos, crocodiles, flamingos and pelicans abound in the wetland area, along with rare species of antelope and migratory birds. The holdings of rhino, giraffe and buffalo are growing in number, and elephants, previously hunted to extinction, have been reintroduced to the Park for the first time in more than a century. Two areas of the wetland habitat are registered as regions of international stature by the Ramsar Convention. Some parts of the Park have been formally protected for almost a century and constitute one of the oldest areas set aside for conservation in Africa (South African Wetlands Conservation Programme, 1999).

In December 1999, the Greater St Lucia Wetland Park was accredited World Heritage Status, and was recognised as being of outstanding environmental value to mankind as a whole. As a result, the KwaZulu-Natal Minister of Agriculture and Environmental Affairs was confident that the province could look forward to substantial eco-tourism development in the St Lucia region, and that local communities and businessmen would benefit alike (KNCS, 1999). The Provincial Minister of Economic Development and Tourism immediately announced plans to turn the Park into a world-class tourist attraction, and announced the commitment of the government to upgrade its infrastructure.

The Park has been environmentally abused in the past by activities at military installations, by adverse agricultural practices in neighbouring regions, and by the planting of non-indigenous pine forests within the protected area itself. KZN-Wildlife, is currently working to eradicate evidence of ecological damage as part of its plan to attract private investment in eco-tourism development. All of the land within the Park is state owned, and its management has been delegated by the KwaZulu-Natal Provincial Administration to KZN-Wildlife.

Land rights and plans for eco-tourism development in St Lucia have been contested publicly in a long-running debate between rival interest groups, which can be broadly categorised as:

- conservationists, including the Natal Parks Board (NPB), over 150 environmental lobby groups, and white ranch owners;
- African settlers, many of whom were illegally occupying land controlled by the NPB;
- Richards Bay Minerals (RBM) a local subsidiary of Rio Tinto Zinc;
- large numbers of return tourists, mainly from the white communities in the Transvaal and Johannesburg, who enjoyed fishing from the beach at St Lucia.

In 1989, RBM made known its plans to dredge mine a 12km stretch of the Eastern Dunes in the south-eastern corner of the Park. These vegetated beach dunes, which line the eastern shores of the lake, contain rich sources of titanium and other similar heavy minerals. Between 1950 and 1970 two large Zulu communities had been evicted from the dunes. During the late 1970s a further 3000 people were removed so that a missile testing site could be built for the South African army (Honey, 1999).

The company stated that the mining would not cause any lasting damage to the ecology of the dunes, and that any disruption would be minimal. RBM pointed to its record of environmental reparation work (for which it had won an award), and further argued that much of the tree cover on the dunes was of exotic pines, or other alien species, which would be replaced (along with the topsoil) by indigenous trees and plants, returning the dunes to their original state. In addition, the mining would provide jobs for local people, and would earn foreign exchange for the country (Preston-Whyte, 1995). The NPB (and its allies) disagreed strongly with the assessment by RBM of the ecological harm that would be caused by the proposed mining activity on the dunes, and argued forcefully that the plans of the company constituted a serious threat to the internationally important wetland and wildlife area. The dredge mining would, they claimed, cause the dunes to slump on the seaward side. Moreover, the re-vegetation that RBM had claimed would occur once the mining activities were completed was unlikely, and changes in the soil structure would alter the hydrology of the local ecosystem. It was the view of the environmentalists that the loss of income from potential eco-tourism receipts alone, would exceed the anticipated local benefits from the proposed mining.

The consortium of environmental pressure groups made particularly good use of the media in their well-organised and high-profile campaign against RBM, and in favour of an integrated eco-tourism development strategy that the NPB had drawn up. The Campaign to Save St Lucia collected over 300,000 signatures, including that of Nelson Mandela, on petitions arguing against the proposed mining of the Eastern Shores (Honey, 1999). The advocates of the NPB plan claimed that community-centred eco-tourism projects would be more sustainable, and would provide more jobs than would be generated by mining. Loosely aligned with these agencies was the sector of prosperous, white farmers and ranch-owners in the region, who had plans of their own for upmarket tourism development, and who feared that the likely environmental degradation caused by mining activities would diminish the special sense of place, and would deter tourists from visiting St Lucia (Preston-Whyte, 1995).

The central government found itself in a troublesome dilemma over the application to mine the Eastern Shore. The foreign exchange earning capacity of the mining operation was highly attractive, and the development would fit well with the national policy of extending the range of minerals extracted (Baskin and Stavrou, 1995). But the government had committed itself to protecting the Park when it had signed the Ramsar Convention, and the environmental campaign against the mining was gaining strength at home and internationally. Unable to come to a decision, the state leadership requested that an environmental impact assessment (EIA) be carried out by the Council for Scientific and Industrial Research. When, in 1993, the comprehensive, and extremely lengthy report was finally completed and published, its conclusions caused great concern among the environmental campaigners, The EIA in fact concluded that under strict conditions to be stipulated by the state, either option (mining or tourism) could go ahead without causing irreparable damage to St Lucia.

The public outrage, and the government's waning confidence in its own authority, led to a sense of worrying indecisiveness over the issue. However, the Review Panel, appointed to make recommendations on the basis of the EIA, was convinced that the mining of the dunes should be prohibited. The decision of the Review Panel was not based on the wealth of scientific evidence made available by the EIA, but on the grounds that the mining would destroy the 'unique and special sense of place'; a feature of the wetland regarded as an essential component in the development of 'higher order' eco-tourism (Baskin and Stavrou, 1995). During the period of transition leading up to the first national democratic elections in 1994, political violence was rampant in KwaZulu-Natal. Africans were anticipating, and pressing for, radical changes in their circumstances, particularly on the issue of land rights. The National Party was reluctant to take decisions on such important, but sensitive matters as the application for a lease to mine the dunes in St Lucia. As a consequence, the problem was shelved, to be dealt with by the new government.

The politically strong mining company continued to argue that eco-tourism and mining could co-exist in St Lucia, and that the environmental lobby had exaggerated the potential impact of the latter on the former. RBM was also claiming the mining would only last for 15 years, and that at the end of that period, all evidence of its activities would be covered. The NPB on the other hand, responded by pointing out that the true time lag would, in effect, be much greater. At that time, the mining was not even planned to commence until 2001, and would require a minimum of six more years to complete the rehabilitation of the dunes. The total time span of the operations would therefore be much greater than RBM was arguing (Baskin and Stavrou, 1995). The Land and Agriculture Policy Centre (LAPC) in an attempt to expedite the decision-making process, commissioned six independent specialist reports on suggested alternative strategies for the development of the dunes. The reports consisted of an assessment of:

- alternative land uses;
- the hydrological impact of different land uses;
- the development potential of eco-tourism as described in the EIA report;
- the development potential of eco-tourism; a post-EIA report analysis;
- the development potential of mining;
- community perceptions with regard to the development of St Lucia
(Baskin and Stavrou, 1995).

In its evaluation of the original EIA, the LAPC conceded that those involved in the research had at least begun the process of engaging the South African public in important decision-making procedures, and had produced enormous amounts of helpful technical material. But the LAPC was concerned that the adjacent African communities had not been given the opportunity to contribute to the study, which had been largely academic in tenor. The technical bias of the EIA obscured the issues, and precluded the emergence of any form of consensus. What was needed, as we discuss more fully in chapter 10, was some plain speaking through which effective stakeholder involvement could be identified and assisted, and communications between the interested parties facilitated (Baskin and Stavrou, 1995). The LAPC was also worried about the geographically narrow focus of the EIA, which ignores the important socio-economic dynamics with the larger region. Moreover, the focus of the EIA was predetermined by the 'either/or' terms of reference, rather than by the needs of the local people to make optimum use of their natural resources.

The questions to be addressed were:

- How would local people survive once the mining operations were completed?
- How effective would eco-tourism be in providing benefits to the population of the district?
- Given the fickleness of tourism, and dependence of mining on fluctuating commodity prices, was either option genuinely sustainable?

Government at all levels in South Africa remains desperately short of resources, but the most effective way of utilising those resources entails the analysis of the problem in relation to the local economy and to the structurally determined poverty of local rural societies. The dunes are situated in the magisterial district of Hlabisa which, in 1995, was the fourth poorest in terms of economic production in South Africa; the sixth poorest in levels of service provision, and has the third highest rating of economic dependency (Baskin and Stavrou, 1995). Hlabisa, in turn, forms part of the sub-region of Zululand, and is one of the most deprived areas in the province. High levels of unemployment and male absenteeism, low levels of literacy, low per capita income and restricted access to basic needs ensure that the sub-region compares unfavourably with all other sub-regions. According to the 1991 census, 73 per cent of the population live in poverty. The priority for decision-makers must be the alleviation of the terrible deprivation that characterises this isolated part of the province. Taking into account the environmental and socio-economic factors that prevail in the sub-region, and having considered the research findings of all of the independent reports, the LAPC concluded that any land-use option other than tourism or mining on the dunes would be a wasted opportunity. However, the synthesis report acknowledged that it remained difficult to establish which of the two options would have the most secure, sustainable and beneficial impact upon the lives of the local population.

As far as the government was concerned, mining had the appeal of not requiring funding or other support of any kind. Moreover, RBM had shown itself to be a reliable and efficient organisation and had recent experience of mining on dunes at Richards Bay. Mining would bring job opportunities, tax revenue, infrastructure and services to the area. The planned duration of the mining operation implied that the adverse impact on the environment would be minimised and the dunes could be rehabilitated soon after.

On the other hand, the planned brevity of the work was worrying in that the area would soon be abandoned to poverty. Also, taking into account the near absence of relevant skills among the local population, it was likely that the inhabitants of the district would fill only poorly paid jobs. Such a scenario would not lead to any form of proactive role for the community in its own development. Moreover, the merit of the mining option would have to be judged in the light of the fact that it would almost certainly have a deterrent effect upon eco-tourists.

The development of eco-tourism offered the same benefits as mining, with the advantage that this particular form of tourism would not have as serious an impact upon the environment. The NPB had compiled an attractive package of tourism development and community participation that accorded well with the Reconstruction and Development Programme (RDP) and popular notions of sustainable development. In line with its conservation and development model for rural development, the NPB had produced a plan for the Wetland Park which would encompass its founding aims of conservation which were to be integrated with eco-tourism and contributions to the social development of local communities (Ecoserv, 1995). Based on the assumption that the mining application would be rejected and the eco-tourism option selected by the government, the Outdoor Recreation and Tourism Facilities Development Plan (NPB, 1991) made plain the aspirations of the Board for the Eastern Shores and for the neighbouring communities, who were to be offered substantial opportunities for community participation (Ecoserv, 1995).

The Plan was to incorporate the construction of a 200-bed hutted camp on the Eastern Shores, a similar hutted camp in the Dukuduku Forest, two lodges in the Futululu Forest and a 500-bed camp close to the Dukuduku Forest. All of these developments were seen by the NPB to be contingent upon the settlement of land tenure agreements, the ratification of boundaries, the support and approval of the local communities, and access to funding from such organisations as the World Bank, and the French Development Bank (Ecoserv, 1995).

As a statutory body, the NPB did not have a substantial capital base, and very little progress was made in raising the necessary funding. There were also doubts over attracting the number of tourists needed to provide the income and employment levels predicted by the Board. Given that conservation was the undisputed priority of the Board, there would have to be limits on the numbers of visitors allowed to stay in the Park, and establishing carrying capacities is always problematic. There was acute concern that the dunes might lose their special quality. Also if, as seemed likely, the local economy was unable to provide the goods and services essential to the tourism trade, there would be debilitating leakages of income and government revenue. The difficult task of integrating the eco-tourism initiatives into the tourism economy of the region as a whole would have to be faced.

In spite of the recommendations made by the LAPC, that integrated development planning was necessary to limit the costs and spread the benefits of a more participatory approach, a final decision on the fate of the dunes was slow in coming. More surprising, perhaps, was that, for all the rhetoric of community-led development, very little research into the needs and hopes of the various groups in the locality had been undertaken. One remarkable exception was a fieldwork report by the Community Resources Optimisation Programme (CROP), an NGO active in the province, which investigated opinions among residents on the choice of mining or tourism on the dunes in St Lucia. Defining 'community' as 'affected parties', the report by CROP took into account the perceptions of the environment and of its future use held by tribal authorities, local community-based development committees, white farmers, private sector enterprises as well as conservation agencies (Mathenjwa et al., 1995). CROP had high ambitions for the communities in St Lucia. Based on the interviews carried out among the various affected parties, CROP recommended that an integrated programme of resource use which took into account all helpful forms of sustainable development – not solely eco-tourism – was the only means of ensuring that all participatory interests were served (Mathenjwa et al., 1995).

In March 1996, the new South African government finally rejected the application to mine the dunes, preferring an integrated development and land-use programme, based on eco-tourism (Derwent, 1996). However, more than a year later, Jacob Zuma, the ANC leader in the province, hinted that the mining option might be revived if the eco-tourism plans did not deliver the promised social and economic benefits in the near future (Barker, 1997).

The threat to the Eastern Shores was not the only land-use problem faced by the NPB in the Greater St Lucia Wetland Park. From 1988, several thousand displaced African subsistence farmers, many of whom had been removed from the contested area of dunes when it was initially declared as a nature reserve, had settled illegally in the protected, and highly valued coastal state forest of Dukuduku, to the west of St Lucia, and south of the Matubatuba road. Dukuduku comprises 5960 hectares of coastal lowland forest, grassland and swamp, and contains many Red Data plants and animals. Formally incorporated into the Greater St Lucia Western Park in 1994, the forest plays a crucial role in the functioning and survival of the wetland system and is considered by the NPB and environmentalists an integral component of the Park as a whole (Menne, 2/10/98). An educational and eco-tourism resource, Dukuduku is viewed by many environmentalists as a national treasure.

A substantial number of these settlers were attempting to direct official attention to their claim of past ownership of the Eastern Shores, and were objecting to the fact that their concerns had been largely neglected in the white, middle-class dispute between environmental groups and the mining company. Their lives were blighted by unemployment, by insecurity, and by the violence along the same African National Congress (ANC) and Inkatha Freedom Party (IFP) lines experienced throughout KwaZulu-Natal. Ever since the Land Acts of 1913 and 1936, Africans in the region had been removed so that game reserves and white farms could be established. Land restitution was paramount to the settlers, who were themselves divided over their claims. Two strong applications had been made, and the settlement of these claims promised to have enormous implications for development plans in the future (May, 1995).

The illegal occupation was causing widespread damage to the fragile environment of the forest, and large areas were cleared by slash-and-burn farming. Some settlers laid claim to Eastern Shore dunes that were targeted by RBM, and were unhappy about being excluded from the largely white, middle-class debate over the dunes. They refused to move from the forest until land claims had been settled (Mathenjwa et al., 1995). Others occupied Dukuduku to obtain jobs in the case that mining applications were granted, and yet others claimed the forest itself as their ancestral land, strongly rejecting any claimed authority of the NPB over Dukuduku. The authorities did not have a good record in Dukuduku. During the 1960s the government had used large areas of the forest for timber and sisal plantations (Barker, 2/12/98). Living conditions in the forest generally were characterised by environmental health problems (there was no sanitation system in a near-swamp environment), high levels of crime and violence, intimidation, poaching, and all the symptoms of extreme poverty and insecurity (Münster, 1996). Furthermore, the proximity of Dukuduku to the central regions of the Park led to poaching of game animals, and rival chiefs encouraged occupation of the forest to enlarge their own support base (Carnie, 1997).

At first, the NPB refused to negotiate with the settlers until they moved out of the forest, and the Natal Provincial Administration attempted to resolve the problem by sometimes heavy-handed intimidation. Later, settlers were promised secure tenure and services at an alternative 3000 hectare site on the north side of Matubatuba-St Lucia road (Carnie, 1993a). By May 1993, many of the 1040 half-hectare family sites had been allocated, and a school and community centre completed. The superior living conditions and promise of legal rights to land, persuaded some 6500 people to relocate to the new site (now called Khula) and to seek opportunities for economic advancement in the new community. To this end, the Dukuduku Development and Tourism Association (DDTA) was formed, and a committee elected. As a consequence, the NPB argued that it was making positive and supportive moves towards settlers who had relocated, and was introducing members of the DDTA to the complexities of integrated conservation and developmental planning (Münster, 1996). Because of this more conciliatory and open approach, officers of the NPB felt that advances had been made in building trust between the community in Khula and the conservation agency (Creemers, 23/3/1998). Subsequently, an ambitious plan for eco-tourism development in the GSLWP, the Gateway Project, was optimistically considered by both parties.

Despite the improved conditions in the new site at Khula, many settlers in the original site, now called Dukuduku South, refused to move to the new settlement. Those who stayed accused the others of 'selling-out', and relationships between the two communities soured. To compound the problem, many new settlers in Dukuduku South occupied the space vacated by the residents of Khula, taking the estimated number of illegal occupants to around 20,000 (Münster, 1996). Widespread violence among the settlers, between settlers and police, and between settlers and the NPB, became major problems for the provincial authorities (Carnie, 1993b) to the extent that NPB officials, mandated to protect the forest, were ordered not to enter it.

CROP interviewed representatives of the Monzi sugar farmer settlement, living fairly close to Dukuduku South, but in conditions of high security. These prosperous families were deeply worried by the proximity of the illegal settlement. They were troubled by the prospect of the impending 'empowerment' of their African neighbours and by future negotiations with the settlers over the cost of providing public services in the settlements. Their own economic plans were for the development of a golf course and upmarket tourism accommodation close to the lake. To this end, the farmers would have been happier if the uncertainty over the land claims were ended. CROP felt that there were solid opportunities for positive and mutually beneficial interaction between these wealthy landowners and the inhabitants of Dukuduku, both in agricultural development, and in the staffing of the planned eco-tourism ventures.

In St Lucia town itself, there was a well-established tourism infrastructure already in place. The town was popular with Afrikaans-speaking holidaymakers, and caricatured as 'a stomping ground for beer-swilling cowboys with more horsepower than brainpower'. During the summer season the local population of about 400 white people swells to 6000, staying in tatty accommodation (Barker, 1997). The town had a reputation for its racial exclusiveness and during the local elections of 1996, the white residents and employers were accused of preventing their black employees from voting (Eveleth, 1996).

However, the contrasts in material well-being with the Dukuduku area were striking, and there was obvious potential for further tourism development in the town and in the adjacent land currently under the authority of the NPB. Local entrepreneurs were critical of the lack of commercial dynamism shown by the NPB, and were unequivocal in their dread of mining in the area, which would, they felt, almost certainly destroy their businesses. The consensus among the business people was that private sector, upmarket tourism would provide far more in terms of employment and general betterment of the area than either mining or eco-tourism. CROP agreed with this consistent position held by the local business community, but would like to have seen the tourism sector take the form of partnerships between the entrepreneurs and the local African communities in line with the RDP, and in a way which would provide local inhabitants with the opportunity to improve their skill base (Mathenjwa et al., 1995).

The restitution of land was of paramount importance to all the groups we talked with. The form that restitution takes would be critical. On the one hand, if the settlement were made on a tribal basis, then it appeared likely that both mining and tourism would be developed. On the other, if the restitution were on an individual household footing, returning it to those who had been removed from the dunes, or to their descendants, the reoccupation of the dunes in an unplanned and unstructured way could lead to irreparable damage to the ecology of the area by the much larger numbers of subsistence farmers involved. The hopeful occupants of Dukuduku appeared to be divided in their aspirations for the future of the dunes. Younger people, with less personal attachment to the place wanted to explore alternative developmental opportunities, while older survivors of the removals were more interested in living out their lives in 'their place'.

In spite of the apparent conflicts of interests between and within the communities interviewed, CROP was confident that an integrated and sustainable development plan could be constructed which would benefit all parties concerned, and accord with the RDP. However, the authors of the report were not convinced that satisfactory arrangements could be made between the settler groups and the NPB. The latter had a poor public image in the area, and was associated with all the injustices of removals in the past. The private tourism sector did seem to offer the best opportunities for alleviating the dire poverty of the settler communities, and for protecting the environment while doing so. Ultimately, it is significant that CROP felt that partnerships between the white business communities and the African groups would be far more efficient and financially rewarding than the long-term plans for eco-tourism in the region.

The Park has been identified as the South African anchor project for the Lubombo Spatial Development Initiative (SDI), a programme initiated by the three governments of Swaziland, Mozambique and South Africa, and covering the area from Maputo in the north, to the Lubombo mountains of Swaziland in the east, and to Richards Bay in KwaZulu-Natal in the south. This ambitious tripartite initiative, which was signed in October 1996, aims to make optimum use of the natural and cultural resources of this severely impoverished and erstwhile neglected region, and of its underemployed labour force, while creating attractive conditions for private investment. Among the main aspirations of the participating governments is the exploitation of the enormous tourism potential of the Lubombo region, and it is envisaged that community-based eco-tourism projects will feature in developments as well as more capital-intensive private sector enterprises. With the opening up of the borders between the three countries, with the hoped-for reduction in crime levels and environmental health problems, and with massive improvements to tourism infrastructure, it is hoped that the region will attract large numbers of overseas tourists.

In January 2000, 15 sites selected for private sector development in the Park were put out to tender as part of the Lubombo SDI. Public funding had been secured to upgrade infrastructure in the Park, in this effort to increase the number of local tourist beds from 11,200 to 18,200 within ten years. However, the proportion of community-owned beds remained very small, and potential benefits for local people were seen to lie more in improved employment opportunities rather than in ownership of businesses.

As a result of this more conciliatory and open approach, it was felt by officers of the NPB that advances had been made in building trust between the community in Dukuduku North and the conservation agency. Subsequently, an ambitious plan for eco-tourism development in the GSLWP was optimistically considered by both parties. However, a lack of resources, and the continuing sense of uncertainty arising from several land claims, including those made in respect of the eastern dunes, have forestalled the implementation of that plan (Venter, 2000).

Relationships between the settlers and business people in the area were worsening, and there were concerns among the local white population over the cost of providing services for both communities in Dukuduku. There were also well-founded fears that the continuing occupation of the forest would encourage some of those who had moved to Khula, to reoccupy the sites they had originally farmed there (Menne, 2/10/98). Indeed there was plenty of evidence to show that many of the residents in Khula were feeling resentful over the loss of their land in the forest, and this resentment was aggravating the already hostile relationships between the two communities. There were fears too that if the settlers in Dukuduku South were able to resist the official pressures to remove them from the forest, the occupation might act as a precedent for other illegal encroachments (Menne, 2/10/98). Social and environmental conditions had deteriorated so markedly that enormous efforts were being made to find a solution acceptable to all sides. In 1994, the NPB produced a plan to resettle the occupants of Dukuduku South on an area of farmland near to the town of Monzi, with a forest strip (a buffer zone for the GSLWP) to be made available to the settlers for their own eco-tourism projects. Access to part of the forest would be retained by the settlers, and a camp of 200 beds would be established alongside the St Lucia-Matubatuba road for further eco-tourism development.

By December 1998, it appeared that agreement had been reached whereby settlers in Dukuduku South would be relocated on the proposed site and the Dukuduku Declaration was signed in Durban by the National Minister for Water Affairs and Forestry and the Provincial Minister for the Environment. At the same time, the government made it clear that it would not negotiate on the issue of land invasion, and that settlers would have to leave the forest (Barker, 2/12/1998). A process of registering the forest dwellers would begin, and the South African Police Service and the South African Defence Force were to be deployed to prevent further encroachments in the forest, the protection of which was a national duty. But the mood of the settlers had been misinterpreted, their response to the Declaration was openly hostile, and they rejected it in its entirety. At a meeting convened to assess community reactions, it was apparent that they strongly objected to being labelled 'squatters' by the press and in official documentation, and still regarded the forest as their rightful home. Many of the settlers had become so well established in the forest that they had built cluster-housing units, and were renting out accommodation to newcomers (Barker, 2/12/98). They especially resented the intervention in the dispute by the government, continued to reject the authority of the conservation agency (now the KNCS) over the forest, and felt that acceptance of the alternative site at Monzi would be shameful (Barker, 14/12/98). Press reports later suggested that activist protesters were intimidating settlers considering the move and preventing them from registering for plots in the new site at Monzi. By April 1999, only 270 families had submitted their names to the register. In May 1999, a heavy gunfight broke out between settlers and the police after the settlers claimed that the conservation authority had unilaterally given permission to outsiders to cut incema grass on the boundaries of the forest. Rubber bullets, stun grenades and teargas were employed to quell this angry protest over the grass, which is an important resource for weaving.

The eventual settlement of land claims over the Eastern Shores did little to improve relationships between the occupants of Dukuduku and the authorities. In September 1999, the Commission for Restitution of Land Rights decided that the dunes would stay as part and parcel of the Park as a whole, and that every family that had been removed between 1956 and 1974 would receive R30,000 in compensation. However, although the environmentalist campaigners and the Chief Executive Officer of KNCS were delighted, there was little rejoicing at this outcome among the local Zulu communities. Even those 550 families who benefited financially from the judgement, were sad at the loss of their ancestral territory (Gowans, 1999).

In spite of the immense natural beauty of the Park, and its potential as a major tourist attraction, progress in the development of community-based eco-tourism initiatives has been minimal. There are strong doubts over the ability of the conservation authority to operate effectively in the commercial world of tourism. Barker (2/12/98) points to the long chains of command in the organisation, which often leave central decision-makers out of touch with locality-specific circumstances. In the field, officers tend to be committed conservationists rather than profit-motivated managers, and are often unavailable during hours when tourists need assistance. The booking service is slow, its office hours do not fit the characteristic unpredictability of tourist needs, and its accommodation prices tend to be uncompetitive. There have occurred numerous examples where tourists in St Lucia have been disappointed by the quality of tours and services provided by the NPB, and where relationships between guides and tourists have been less than friendly and informative. Cuts in funding have even prevented the conservation authority from meeting its environmental responsibilities in the Greater St Lucia Wetland Park. The all-important tasks of dredging the St Lucia estuary and monitoring the effect of its permit system (devised to minimise the environmental impact of tour operators and visitors) have been neglected. The authority relies upon state subsidies, and members of the commercial sector in St Lucia feel that this dependency has possibly robbed it of entrepreneurial dynamism. Given these commercial shortcomings, business people and environmental groups are not convinced of the wisdom of looking to the conservation agency to lead the way in eco-tourism development in St Lucia. The NPB has been criticised for its failure to tackle the occupation of Dukuduku with sufficient haste and clarity of purpose (Menne, 2/10/98). There are also strong doubts that positive and productive relationships can be established between the newly named KZN-Wildlife and the settlers in Dukuduku who associate the authority with so many past and present injustices.

As Wells and Brandon (1992) point out, within those projects, ostensibly based on a putatively symbiotic relationship between conservation and development, the paramount concern for state agencies is the preservation of biodiversity. The distribution of resources among villages is as much a part of the strategy to build a buffer zone as it is a contribution to the upliftment of impoverished communities. The NPB (and now KZN-Wildlife) has built for itself a sound reputation for efficiency in the protection of biodiversity. The demands upon it now are profound. Ethical and philosophical transformations are needed in addition to logistical expertise. A new agenda has been set, which requires movement away from confrontational relationships with neighbours to conciliatory arrangements involving transparency of purpose and co-operation.

In the past, white environmental groups have regarded conservation as a non-political issue. However, because environmental protection entails ownership and authority over land, it is in fact a highly charged political matter, which requires attention at all levels of the new administrative system. Capacity building among African groups is necessary for them to take advantage of new political and developmental opportunities. This in turn entails the transfer of power to communities so that their participation in conservation-linked development programmes gives them the will and authority to make best use of their natural resources in the sustainable development of their agrarian economies. It is also envisaged that within this new discourse of 'eco' development, indigenous ecological knowledge will be attributed the credibility that it has been denied in the past.

The private sector and socially responsible tourism in Maputaland

Phinda is acclaimed as South Africa's most responsible wildlife tourism project, with its goals of wilderness, restoration and community participation. Visit Phinda and play your part in the affirmation of a dream [Conservation Corporation, 1997, p.17].

The Phinda Resource Reserve is situated in the former KwaZulu region of southern Maputaland, approximately 25 miles west of Sodwana Bay. Although there is some commercial farming activity in the area – mainly livestock, pineapples, sugar and cotton on smallholdings – much of the land is of poor quality and is uncultivable. Because of this, and because of the rich wildlife and other natural resources in this part of Maputaland, nature-based tourism offers itself as an obvious alternative to the more traditional means of liveli-hood. Tourism is the largest economic sector in the area. Phinda is owned by the Conservation Corporation, now renamed as Conservation Corporation Africa, or CC Africa, a highly successful private company that is the largest private investor in eco-tourism in South Africa (Carlisle, 9/11/95). The Corporation offers luxurious accommodation and services at all five of its reserves and lodges in South Africa. The company has managed to attract enormous investment from overseas, even during the transition period when there remained an effective international investment boycott (Grossman and Koch, 1995). This success is explained by the company as stemming from its emphasis on aspects of sustainability and social responsibility in its develop-mental planning. The company has gained a reputation for providing luxurious eco-tourism while caring for the lives of its employees and local communities. According to its Mission Statement:

> The Conservation Corporation is committed to wildlife conservation in Africa by applying a balanced approach to tourism, conservation and local community involvement which promotes ecological sustainability, whilst providing guests with a quality wildlife experience and investors with viable returns [Conservation Corporation].

The company owns five reserves in South Africa, including Londolozi, situated on the boundary of Kruger National Park, and also offering luxurious accom-modation in a wildlife-rich environment. Within this reserve is a small village where 150 of the 230 people who live there are employed at Londolozi. The village has a community centre with television and other forms of entertainment, a library, clinic and two schools. There are workshops where villagers work as weavers, potters, brickmakers and drum makers. The schools are multi-racial and literacy classes are held for adults. In general, the conditions in the village are greatly superior to those in the region as a whole. The Conservation Corporation encourages enterprise and training among its staff, and makes low-interest credit available to those in the village hoping to set up their own businesses. However, the company does not make these services available free of charge. Small fees are charged for the healthcare and educational facilities (Honey, 1999). The profits made by the company on the loans made to the villagers is, in turn, invested in making further improvements to communal amenities. The general philosophy at Londolozi and at Phinda, is to assist communities to become as independent as possible, rather than remain reliant upon handouts (Carlisle, 28/3/98). The staff elect a mixed race committee to oversee the village, and efforts are made to break down racial boundaries by mixing white and black housing. This has not been a comfortable process, and the manager of the company admits that serious mistakes have been made in the past (Honey, 1999).

At Londolozi the focus has been on improving the lives of staff and their families. But at Phinda, social development programmes have been directed more at the surrounding communities, and has become the prime model of eco-tourism for the Corporation (Carlisle, 28/3/98). The high cost of building the luxury lodges at Phinda, and the remoteness of the region from the main tourist areas, has limited profits here, and the staff housing and other facilities provided to local people are not of the same standard as those at Londolozi.

The enterprise has its origins in the late 1980s, when the company bought approximately 7500 hectares of land previously used as a private game lodge. Since then, further purchases and the arrangement of long leases have enlarged the holding to around 17,000 hectares. In 1991 and 1993, two luxurious lodges were completed at the same time as a programme was carried out to rehabilitate eroded land and enlarge the stock of game animals. Phinda is situated in an area of acute poverty, among three economically and geographically isolated neighbouring Zulu tribes. There exists only a meagre provision of healthcare, education, water supply or good roads. Industrial development, if it were possible, would be ecologically disastrous, and most local inhabitants survive on subsistence farming on poor soils. Communities are dependent upon migrant labour, with an average of 47 per cent male absenteeism throughout the year (Carlisle, 1997)

The marketing strategy of Conservation Corporation Africa (CC Africa) appeals to a wealthy clientele, with all the facilities and services that characterise the more exclusive game reserves, and with reference to the social and ecological principles that guide the activities of the company during this environmentally and politically sensitive time in South Africa. In its own literature, the Corporation talks of its developmental interactions with local people, identifying projects such as joint business partnerships, small charcoal-producing initiatives, the setting up of produce markets, and the construction of clinics and classrooms. The Corporation acts as a conduit for donations made to the Rural Investment Fund – established by the company – which channels capital from sources outside South Africa into community development initiatives in southern Maputaland (Carlisle, 19/11/95). The fund constitutes a link between the conservation and tourism activities of the Corporation and the neighbouring communities. In 1992, following a generous donation to the Rural Investment Fund, the Phinda Community Development Trust Fund was established and, by 1995, at the beginning of our research, $625,000 had been accumulated for community development projects.

In its applications for low-interest RDP loans, the company makes explicit the relationship between its own commercial aspirations and the socio-economic improvements – such as the provision of water facilities to remote villages – it hopes to achieve in the future (Grossman and Koch, 1995). In the same applications, access to the communication facilities at Phinda is offered to local people establishing businesses, along with the services of two full-time members of staff whose work is to be dedicated entirely to community welfare.

In contrast to the landholding pattern in St Lucia, Phinda is based entirely on privately owned land, a factor which effectively excludes the reserve's Zulu neighbours from direct involvement in decision-making that would come with ownership. The security of that land, and the appreciation in its value are attractive to investors. It is possible, however, that the economic and political power of the Zulu neighbours will be transformed if current, and large land claims are settled in their favour. Should this be the case, conservationists may be all the more enthusiastic to assist in the programmes of social upliftment in the extensive, and possibly community-owned buffer zones around their protected areas. It might also be the case that these new land rights will stimulate imaginative partnerships, in which formerly muted African groups can take creative steps in their own choice of sustainable land use. Claims made by the Conservation Corporation in its literature, published and unpublished, that substantial improvements in the livelihoods of local people have already been achieved, were questioned by Interface Africa (Mahlangu, 16/11/95). Some members of this NGO regard the impact of the community programmes as minimal and unsustainable. Attention is drawn to the marketing value of these programmes, and to ways in which the discourse of eco-development and community empowerment can be utilised in applications for precious RDP loans. Moreover, Grossman and Koch (1995) feel that among the local people, those most likely to benefit are among the more educated of the Zulu population, and that the more marginalised groups, particularly the aged, will enjoy few improvements in their standard of living. They also note, that the charcoal produced at Phinda is costly, and that local villagers are unable to afford it.

Les Carlisle, the highly driven regional developer at Phinda, sees his role as similar to that of an NGO or local government body, in that one of his major activities is the bringing together of various agencies and local communities with the aim of providing or improving essential services (Carlisle, 28/3/98). Conservation Corporation, with the consent of the chiefs and *ndunas* (headmen) helps establish development committees in the neighbouring villages. These bodies then identify their developmental priorities, and the company looks for the funding. At the same time, it is hoped that with experience, local people themselves will become more adept at raising their own funds. Among the successful projects of which Carlisle is very proud are the construction of several schools, a health centre, water pumps, and the development of small businesses such as brick making, and the production of charcoal. This latter enterprise has been based on the use of wood made available by the carefully managed thinning of the trees on the reserve itself. The local communities provide the labour force and, in line with Conservation Policy, are charged a very small fee for the use of the new facilities.

Of particular interest has been a long-term project of developing a community reserve, close to Phinda, on land donated by the Natal Parks Board, and stocked by the company. The World Wildlife Fund has been attracted by this initiative, and has assisted with the provision of a water supply and solar panels. The reserve is run by the community, employing local guides, with mainly white hunters bringing their clients to shoot game (Honey, 1999). For Carlisle, conservationists make excellent development extension officers. In these efforts, the company co-operated with the NPB, local tribal chiefs, NGOs and civic leaders under the auspices of the Southern Maputaland Development Forum (SMDF), a developmental association of which it is a founding member. The SMDF is primarily concerned with stimulating indigenous people to further their own development strategies, whether they rely on tourism or on other land-use options, rather than converting communities into joint shareholders (Carlisle, 19/11/95). Grossman and Koch (1995) believe that, given the wealth and range of wildlife resources in southern Maputaland, the best approach for many of the neighbouring African communities would be for them to initiate low-capital tourism ventures such as guided bird-watching trips, or other similarly specialised forms of eco-tourism. As things stand, local people have no voice in the actual administration of the tourism and conservation activities of the Phinda Resource Reserve, their role being one of partners in peripheral initiatives or as providing labour for the reserve.

Carlisle emphasises that community development, which is contingent upon local commitment and support, takes a great deal of time. He also argues that rapid 'kick-start' approaches can cause more harm than good, particularly to the most vulnerable in the community. With sustainability in mind, Conservation Corporation has learned to move away from short-term goal-thinking towards the more demanding but eventually rewarding aim of training and capacity building (Carlisle, 1997). As the managing director of Londolozi advocates 'don't give a man a fish; teach him to fish. We don't believe in aid, it's a black hole, and patronising' (McKilvey, cited in Honey, 1999, p.372). Carlisle also focuses on the need to reverse the images often held of the helplessness of African communities, and of the need for handouts. The company has taken on board the necessity of consultation with local communities in order to generate trust and understanding; both of which are seen to be critical to sustainability. Respect for local custom, political systems, and knowledge is also essential, as is reliability and the meeting of commitments made by the company.

Having argued for sensitive management, Carlisle also points out the weaknesses and flaws in the community development model. Within the organisation, it is held that impoverished local communities rarely have the resources and technical knowledge to develop their own projects, and that development initiatives must be managed to attain optimum economic and environmental benefits (Carlisle, 1997). His experience at Phinda leads him to argue that actual communal ownership and leadership of initiatives is rarely achieved. Development needs to driven by commercially minded professionals, while aiming for the least possible dependency of the neighbouring tribes. Community politics have caused problems and have informed outcomes of well-intentioned initiatives.

Kosi Bay: community participation and the role of NGOs

The complexity of the issues surrounding democratic participation can be usefully examined through another, contrasting case study carried out during the current research in KwaZulu-Natal. Kosi Bay consists of a series of lakes, marshes and pans that flow into the Indian Ocean in the north-eastern corner of Maputaland, 2 kilometres south of the border with Mozambique. The Kosi waterway is one of the few pristine estuarial systems in South Africa. The system that is about 18 kilometres long, consists of four interconnected lakes, each with its own ecological characteristics. The mixture of fresh and salt water provides the environment for a wide spectrum of river and marine life. The beaches are nesting grounds for ocean-travelling turtles, and the edges of the lake hold the last swamp forest in South Africa. There are large numbers of hippos and crocodiles in the lakes. The system is a Wetland of International Importance under the Ramsar Convention. Kosi Bay was declared as a nature reserve by the KwaZulu Department of Nature Conservation (KDNC) in 1988. It comprises 11,000 hectares and includes the Malangeni Forest, the only swamp forest in the country. The entire area was fenced off, in places with electric fences to restrict the movements of the resident hippopotamus population. Many of the indigenous people resented the fence, particularly when it impinged upon their homesteads and fields.

Local people in Kosi Bay rely on traditional fishing techniques to feed themselves. At the mouth of the system a complex set of fish traps has been constructed from local wood, and is designed to catch the fish as they swim out of the estuary with the receding tide. Net fishing in the reserve is allowed on a permit basis, but such regulations are commonly flouted. The reserve provides grasses for weaving, herbs for traditional medicines and wood for fuel. The lala palm is tapped to make the lala palm wine that is highly popular in the region.

When the nature reserve was inaugurated, the KwaZulu government, the KDNC, the NPB, Satour, and representatives from the commercial sector proceeded to set up a luxury tourism resort, and to evict the Thonga inhabitants, whose ancestral presence in the area goes back for more than 1600 years, and whose livelihood was earned mainly through fishing using traditional stick kraals, or through male migrant labour (Munnik, 1995). Many of the indigenous people moved out under the harassment of the KDNC, but about 150 families resisted and refused to leave, and were consequently fenced-in. Living under the constant vigilance of armed guards, and in response to the harsh treatment, drastic measures were taken by some of the local people, ranging from tearing down parts of the fencing to attacking outsiders (Pleumaron, 1994).

The plight of the inhabitants of Kosi Bay attracted the attention of members of the newly formed non-governmental organisation CROP. In 1993, CROP, funded by the South Africa Human Sciences Research Council, began working with communities in the former homeland of KwaZulu, many parts of which are extremely impoverished, with all the problems of unsustainable, slash-and-burn agriculture on too little and poor-quality land. Nowhere in the sub-region of Maputaland do African tribes people grow enough food to support their families all the year round. Households throughout Maputaland supplement their food supply by the gathering of veld foods. The NGO recognised that the environmental resources of Kosi Bay made it a prime site for nature-based tourism, and CROP, while working to improve relationships between the local people and the various stakeholder authorities, began research into the feasibility of such an experimental initiative (Zaloumis, 16/11/95). At the same time, a great deal of adverse publicity over the militaristic activities of the KDNC had led the conservation agency to take (albeit reluctantly) a more lenient attitude towards the remaining inhabitants of Kosi Bay. Eventually, Derek Hanekom, Minister Land Affairs, personally intervened and assured the communities that their status within the reserve was secure.

Once an atmosphere more conducive to developmental planning was achieved, CROP initiated successful fund-raising, and a four-wheel drive vehicle and a motorised inflatable dinghy for ferrying personnel and tourists across the lakes to a tented camp were purchased (Zaloumis, 16/11/95). The camp itself was built around the old research base of David Webster, the former anthropologist and anti-apartheid activist who was murdered in 1992, allegedly by state security agents (Carnie, 1996). Dr Webster had spent 15 years researching the local communities of the region, and had taken a professional interest in the relocation of the indigenous tribes by the KDNC to create the Kosi Bay Reserve.

There was considerable enthusiasm among the local people for the tourism experiment, and a small-tented camp was established. Here, groups of tourists who were prepared to rough it a little could enjoy the physical beauty of the surroundings, while becoming more familiar with the culture and livelihoods of their hosts (we discuss one tourist experience of Kosi Bay in detail in chapter 6). Development committees representing the three tribal communities (KwaDapha, eMalangeni and Nkovukeni) provided the local institutional support for the project (now known as KEN, from the initial letters of the three tribal names). From the outset, the initiative was based on the fundamental principles of empowerment through proactive participation as advocated in the RDP, and emphasis was placed on the importance of incorporating the most disadvantaged, including women (Russell, 10/3/99). The first tourists arrived in December 1994, and bookings from various interested groups, including wildlife societies, schools and fly fishermen, soon followed (Munnik, 1995). The Wildlife Society of South Africa was a major supporter of the project, which it saw as a low-impact, non-consumptive alternative to the environmentally threatening activities of tourists elsewhere in the region (Carnie, 1996). Among early visitors to the site were Jacob Zuma, Provincial Minister of Economic Development and Tourism, and Derek Hanekom. The experiment was seen to have become a modest success.

Confidence in the project grew, and negotiations with the conservation authorities became less tense. The KDNC gave informal approval to further expansions of the enterprise, and catering and hospitality skills developed among the members of the tribes active in the experiment. The local communities were keen to push ahead with the development, and some interest was shown by potential outside investors (Zaloumis, 16/11/95).

The highly dedicated members of the NGO saw themselves only as facilitators in the process of training the community in hospitality and business skills. However, crucial decisions had to be made about the future operation of KEN. It was accepted that further funding was needed, and that contractual arrangements with external investors would have to be made, but CROP was anxious to ensure that tribal groups retained their decision-making role, that they would not be displaced by more powerful agencies, and that sustainability and the meeting of basic needs should remain paramount (Grossman and Koch, 1995). In addition, members of CROP were also keen to remind the communities that eco-tourism was only one of several sustainable development options, including agriforestry and fishing. Unfortunately, the project did not attract sufficient resources to pursue these alternative strategies simultaneously.

The people of Kosi Bay have been socially and geographically marginalised for a long time. Northern Maputaland is badly served by the state. Few inhabitants have enjoyed secondary education, and the general infrastructure is terribly inadequate. This political neglect has led to an unskilled adult population, with too few choices in terms of livelihood. The location of Kosi

Bay is another negative factor in the planning of tourism initiatives; it is distant and difficult to reach from the main tourist-sending regions. The absence of the big attractions, such as elephants and lions, also deflects demand from tour operators.

At Kosi Bay, crucial decisions had to be made about the future form and *modus operandi* of the eco-tourism enterprise. Contractual arrangements needed to be made with external investors, but CROP was keen to ensure that the communities stayed at the heart of the operation, and were not side-tracked by more powerful agencies. The interest of external investors in Kosi Bay was to be welcomed, because of the skills, experience and access to capital they could bring with them, but sustainability and the meeting of local needs must remain paramount in the long-term planning of the initiative. The optimum situation, and the one for which CROP was striving, would be a partnership between the communities and a number of small investors, at least one of whom should have had experience of eco-tourism in South Africa. In this scenario, CROP foresaw the communities (through their respective committees) holding 40–50 per cent of the equity in the business, investors having 40 per cent, and a local NGO, there to monitor the progress of the initiative, would hold 20 per cent. CROP reasoned that by owning the project, and by accepting risk, all parties would see themselves as agents for change, and would experience sufficient incentive to make it work. Grossman and Koch (1995) share the opinion that this high degree of participation is essential to overcome both the geographical isolation, and socio-economic marginalisation.

It would not be logistically possible, nor even desirable, for every individual in the communities to participate directly in the management of the eco-tourism business. The central role of efficiently run committees in rural development figures prominently in the core principles of the RDP. It was hoped that the planned capacity building would generate jobs and other benefits which would be fairly distributed for developmental purposes.

It is also a principle of the RDP that small enterprises be given every support by integrating them into the wider local economy. Experience has shown that such ventures founder quickly when they are not linked to larger, more established businesses. In Kosi Bay, it was the plan to encourage individuals within the communities to set up their own peripheral initiatives, and to form direct linkages with the core eco-tourism project as it expanded (Zaloumis, 16/11/95). In the initial stages of the project, it became the goal to develop four further small sites, which would cater for different types of tourists, offering different levels of luxury and comfort. The expansion would in time lead to economies of scale, and would make the enterprise as a whole eligible for more substantial loans. Problems over land tenure promised to be the largest single obstacle to economic success for the communities in Kosi Bay.

The business did not own the natural resources upon which it was based, and would not enjoy the normal financial benefits of appreciation in the value of land and buildings. The small scale of the project meant that tourism receipts were slight, and discontent increased among tribes people impatient for an improved standard of living.

The possibility of eventually negotiating a lengthy lease with the conservation authorities was regarded with some apprehension by the members of CROP. Such a step could tie the communities to goals that have lost their purpose, or restrict the communities to such goals, or restrict them in their efforts to diversify at a later date. It might also preclude new partnerships. However, investors were sure to be hesitant in the absence of security. CROP had proposed that a lending institution be approached to provide all the capital needed for the initial development phases, and that the private investors, and the NGO, underwrite their loans through individual guarantees. Subsidised loans from organisations with a commitment to the RDP would, it was hoped, encourage further investments from the private sector (Munnik, 1995). The poor availability of low-interest loans for sustainable rural projects, such as KEN, was a major inhibiting factor, and CROP felt that it was incumbent upon the state to help those Africans who had suffered so much at the hands of conservation authorities in the past.

Sadly, even early in the operation, the KEN project encountered difficulties of another sort. Rivalries between committee members began to emerge and crystallise. Some individuals made demands on facilities that conflicted with the wider needs of the eco-tourism project, and tourists were concerned at the presence of strangers in and around the camp (CROP, 1995). Relationships between members of KEN and the conservation authorities had soured over the demand by the former for a new access road within the nature reserve, and large sections of the perimeter fence were substantially damaged (Shepherd-Smith, 1995). The communities were angry that although they had been granted funds to build the road by the Maputaland Development Organisation, the KDNC had refused to permit the work. During a heated confrontation, officers of the KDNC pointed guns at angry members of the communities, who saw the fences as barricades preventing their development. In fact, the project was faltering because of poor management and worsening relationships among its members, leading to a general inability to adopt effective decision-making procedures. There was a need for professional advice on a long-term basis. Problems of this kind require sensitive handling. Members of CROP, for their part, became profoundly disillusioned with KEN. They recognised that personal obligations of participants in such initiatives should be clarified, and advocated a more professional and commercially oriented approach for future initiatives. One leading member of CROP told us that there had been a distinct lack of sincerity among the community members active in the initiative, and that questionable local politics had drained the project of energy and direction (Russell, 10/3/99).

However, another community-based eco-tourism development in the Kosi system has enjoyed longer lasting, if modest, progress with the leadership and financial backing of an external investor (Gowans, 1999). In contrast, these Thonga people who lived on the side of Lake Shengeza just outside the boundary of the protected area, were coming to understand the potential value of eco-tourism to the area, and asked the KDNC to include their land within the reserve. After a protracted but unsuccessful effort to find a financial backer, support was eventually offered by an investor with a strong history in eco-tourism within the province. Complex negotiations with the KDNC, an environmental impact assessment, and consultations with environmentalist groups, resulted in the community giving their developer a 30-year lease for a five hectare site in the sand forest. In return, the investor pays a fixed rental, and a share of the profits are donated to a community trust. With the consent of the KDNC, the community has also agreed to develop a further 400 hectares of their land as a small game reserve, and has negotiated tourist access to other parts of the reserve. Local labour and materials have been used to build a tasteful, low-impact 16-bed lodge, and community members act as guides for bird-watching, fishing, canoeing and other nature-based activities. Vegetable gardens have been established to supply the core eco-tourism business. The aim of the initiative is to provide an authentic Thonga experience. But it remains to be seen, in post-apartheid South Africa, just how attractive domestic and international tourists find such a concept. As Les Carlisle of Phinda told us, in his experience, most tourists do not want to be 'rubbing shoulders' with local people when they are on holiday (Carlisle, 28/3/98).

By 1995, the KDNC had formulated and announced a more clearly stated policy on eco-tourism development in Kosi Bay, and in the other protected areas under its authority. Stressing its determination to place the environment before all other concerns, but acknowledging the necessity of providing local people with opportunities to secure a sustainable livelihood, Nick Steele, the director of KDNC stated that eco-tourism initiatives within reserves would in future be considered by the authority, in partnership with indigenous communities and developers, but under specific conditions. The three most important of these were, firstly, the authority would identify the sites; secondly, it would specify the nature of the development; and thirdly, developers would be expected to include representatives of the relevant communities as share-holders in the ventures. This approach has in turn been criticised for being too restrictive on entrepreneurial activities but, in reply, Mr Steele defended the guidelines as essential for the protection of the beautiful but vulnerable natural resources of Maputaland. Notwithstanding these restrictions, the KDNC has more recently taken part in a number of negotiations with private developers and communities, and, in 1997, as part of the preparatory phases of the Lubombo Spatial Development Initiative, was considering the construction of a much larger and more luxurious hotel/resort complex at the mouth of the Kosi system.

Summary

While the language of justice and empowerment is seductive, experience in KwaZulu-Natal shows that participation is a slow and costly exercise. The case studies indicate a range of participation by community stakeholders in eco-tourism development. At Dukuduku, the conservation authority took positive steps to bring communities into the decision-making arena, but to an extent determined by itself and other official agencies. In disputes over land-use in Dukuduku and over the eastern dunes, planning and negotiations were steered by environmental lobby groups, by the conservation authority, by the provincial administration, and by the national government. Although genuine participation by African communities has grown, it remains modest and is regarded as contingent upon behaviour that accords with the aspirations and strategies of official agencies.

By contrast, local people at Phinda are expected to enjoy many benefits of conservation and eco-tourism, but largely as passive beneficiaries in terms of services and jobs provided. Jobs that do become available tend to go to the most educated rather than the most needy (Grossman and Koch, 1995). Local residents do not participate in managerial operations or become shareholders in the company. At best, the Corporation appeared to be playing a supportive role that in other locations would be occupied by local government.

In the KEN project at Kosi Bay, the level of participation enjoyed by the stakeholder communities was high and most closely reflected the principles of the RDP. However, internal rivalries impeded economic progress, and tourists were dissatisfied with the quality of hospitality and security. In such circumstances, the highly principled stand of CROP on participation, democracy and sustainability, and strict adherence to the tenets of the RDP, were possibly a disadvantage. Access to decision-making had led to some abuse, and CROP was possibly asking too much of eco-tourism. Taking the spirit of community-based development to its logical conclusion may well have restricted choice and limited opportunities to expand. If high principles themselves prove to be unsustainable, the best could be the enemy of the good.

At the heart of the problem of participation is the assumption that community members share interests, and are likely to pursue shared aspirations as a group. However, the evidence in this chapter strongly demonstrates the need for developmental models based on notions of self-interest and diversity within communities, rather than initiatives based on notions of community spirit and stability. Olson (1971), doubts that individuals will always work for the common economic good if they are unlikely to benefit themselves. Such co-operation occurs only in special circumstances, where there are strong negative or positive sanctions, or where the group itself is small. Assuming that there are always opportunity costs to participation, Olson's basic argument is that where the benefits of collective action cannot be ring-fenced by those who have actually invested in the cause, then those who will benefit in any case have no rational incentives to bear the cost of active involvement (Olson, 1971).

Public authorities and private companies continue to set the agenda for negotiations, and the existence of forums and civil organisations is no guarantee of a fair representation of the most disadvantaged in KwaZulu-Natal. In particular, the rights of women in Zulu society have changed little since the 1994 elections. Their empowerment – a central tenet of the RDP – would entail a radical transformation of the patriarchal structure of rural society in South Africa, including new restraints on the powers of tribal chiefs. Notwith-standing the Communal Properties Association Act (1996), which insists upon their fair representation, women have been effectively muted in committees established to expedite the land reform programme, an exclusion considered by Ritchken (1995) to be inevitable.

In the following chapter, we shall look in more detail at the socio-economic factors that hinder the development of eco-tourism in KwaZulu-Natal. The discussion there will use these case studies as exemplars, but will also question the fundamentals of the RDP and notions of the primacy of democracy, empowerment, and participation in developmental initiatives in South Africa.

Chapter 4

Eco-tourism in the real world

In St Lucia there is evident, chronic and dangerous conflict over scarce resources. As Preston-Whyte (1995) points out, the intensity of the conflict is directly related to the degree of scarcity. If titanium could be found everywhere, if there were no shortage of cultivable land, and if wetland sites were common, then the national government would not have been faced with such a seemingly irresolvable dilemma. The allocation of resources, and policies designed to guide those allocations, are of huge political significance, particularly so in the context of a country in which the majority of the electorate is looking for unequivocal indications that proper restitution is being made for the injustices of the past. In addition, the former rights of the mining industry to operate more or less wherever precious minerals are found, and the sophistication of the environmental campaign have also contributed to the intensity of the debate over mining, eco-tourism and land rights in St Lucia. The government's declared intention to promote economic development along community lines, encouraging the empowerment and proactive participation of local people in democratically organised sustainable initiatives, has added yet another dimension to the dispute. The ensuing politicisation of the previously disenfranchised black population has helped to draw attention to the desperate nature of their needs, and to the awful circumstances of the rural poor. It has also reinforced the moral and political arguments for a more equitable distribution of land.

Land and land reform in KwaZulu-Natal

Land rights continue to dominate the discussion of eco-tourism development in the Greater St Lucia Wetlands area. The harsh treatment sometimes inflicted on settlers in Dukuduku reflects a lack of understanding of traditional ties to land and attachment to ancestral graves (Carnie, 1991). Eco-tourism development will not attract sufficient public resources or private investment until rival land claims are settled. Meanwhile, many settlers in Dukuduku are convinced that KZN-Wildlife's plans for eco-tourism and community amelioration are little more than pretexts for retaining control over contested land areas. And environmentalists fear that, if eco-tourism fails to deliver on its promises, the mining application might be revived (Barker, 1997). In Kosi Bay, the KEN initiative has suffered from the outset because it has no legal claim to the natural resources upon which it was established. By contrast at the Phinda Resource Reserve the land is held entirely in private hands, and there is no claim pending for any of it. The lack of ambiguity over land ownership has contributed to the Conservation Corporation's successful appeals to investors and to the RDP for low-interest credit. If land rights are in doubt, community-based projects are at a disadvantage.

The social and symbolic significance of land to agrarian people is not always understood by urban planners. For peasant populations, land can comprise more than a means of livelihood. Ownership of, or secure access to land carries with it status, political power, honour and dignity. It may also have a deeply religious value, and require traditional stewardship to appease the ancestors. Enforced removals such as those in KwaZulu-Natal, then, are all the more tragic and humiliating in that a whole system of social values is ignored or trivialised. In St Lucia, many of the settlers are convinced that the socially responsible elements of KZN-Wildlife's eco-tourism proposals have been hurriedly cobbled together to counter the threat of mining, and to retain control over the land the inhabitants claim for themselves. In other words, local African people feel that, at best, they are being used to establish a buffer zone protecting the Greater St Lucia Wetland Park.

The ANC has set itself the task of generating productive rural development for the sustainable reduction of poverty, and for overcoming the legacy of economic distortions inherited from apartheid that have collectively held the country's black rural communities in destitution. To this end, and within the principles of the RDP, programmes of targeted transfers (land reform, housing grants and pensions) have been implemented (Deininger and May, 2000). At the same time and to replace the protected, highly mechanised but inefficient agricultural sector supported by the apartheid regime, markets have been liberalised, and price incentives have shifted towards high-value labour-intensive crops to improve employment opportunities in the countryside. Market conditions for land have improved, and land prices have fallen. The government has seen these changes as creating favourable conditions for a programme of land reform based on market transactions supported with a grant, rather than on a more radical approach of expropriation. The formidable challenge facing the ANC is to produce a programme of land reform that empowers the poor, improves productivity and creates sustainable livelihoods.

The Native Lands Act of 1912 prohibited the development of farming operations by blacks outside the native reserves, which at the time amounted to only 7.7 per cent of the country's land area. Inside the reserves, a newly invented form of 'traditional' tenure was imposed giving enormous power to chiefs in the allocation of land. Between 1960 and 1983, the policy of 'black spot removal' transferred the majority of black farmers who had legitimately owned land outside the reserves into the homelands, where overpopulation and tenure restrictions made commercial agriculture almost impossible (Deininger and May, 2000). Further, labour laws that discriminated against black farm workers and in favour of white employees also led to evictions of many black labour tenants. In attempting to reverse the impact of these measures, the ANC government has to deal with an extremely unequal distribution of land where the average area held by black farmers is 1.3 hectares compared with the average of 1,570 hectares in the hands of white commercial farmers (Deininger and May, 2000). Obstacles to change in 1994 when the ANC came to power, included the lack of an effective local government structure, established subsidies to capital, and a legislative legacy that undermined factor markets such as land. Subsidies to fertiliser prices had, under the National Party, also led to the widespread and excessive use of agricultural chemicals and to the consequential damage to the topsoil and the rural environment.

In KwaZulu-Natal, land reform has become an icon, compelling in itself. But the government is fully aware that, even if there were enough cultivable land to provide all rural households with a livelihood (and there is not enough), its redistribution on anything like an equitable basis would encounter all the problems already discussed, as well as the intractable obstacle of traditional power bases in rural society. The ANC has made known its dislike for atavistic structures and institutions that hinder the progress of modern democratic development. But the political reality of agrarian life is that chiefs retain much of their former authority, and that they resent the possibility of direct access to land among their tribesmen (DLA, 1995).

The national government, in its determination to settle the land issues in a non-adversarial way, has approached the problem of establishing a sense of equity in economic opportunities in the rural sector by means of a three pronged approach: restitution to compensate people who lost land through forced removals and other apartheid policies; redistribution to provide people with access to land through subsidies; and tenure reform to improve security of tenure and provide for a wider range of ways of holding land.

The legal and political obstacles to a smooth process of land reform have been compounded by the inadequate funds made available. In 1997, in a reprioritisation of funds, there were major cutbacks in the grants made to cultivators setting up on their newly secured land. Moreover, the Land Claims Commission had its budget for staff and legal work slashed by half in the same year. These cutbacks had serious implications for KwaZulu-Natal where the highest number of claims of any province had been lodged, and fears were growing that frustrated claimants and other landless cultivators were about to launch an illegal campaign of forcefully taking land from those white farmers who were resisting government pressure to sell some of their farmland. By 2000, in spite of repeated assurances by the new Minister of Land Affairs, Thoka Didiza, that steady progress was being made, there were growing signs that many black South Africans, angry at the slow pace of land reform, were considering land invasions similar to those occurring in Zimbabwe (Dickson and Streek, 2000).

The National African Farmers Union was also arguing that the government should take a much stronger line and expropriate white owned land at the lowest possible price. During the same year, Thoka Didiza conceded that market-based land reform was too costly and had failed to deliver large areas of land at a suitable price, and that only 0.81 per cent of South Africa's farmland had been redistributed under the land reform programme. In contrast, and in opposition to more radical redistribution measures, representatives of the mainly white commercial farming sector responded by pointing to the possible financial catastrophe that would result from a destruction of this important earner of foreign exchange. Arguing against the Minister, leaders of white farmers insisted that there was already plenty of land available at low prices, as a result of the slump in the market for some of South Africa's agricultural products (Dickson and Streek, 2000).

The DLA has endured a more troublesome than anticipated learning process in the implementation of its land reform programmes. Efforts to address too many problems using excessively centralised strategies of land reform alone have led to disappointing results and to terribly slow progress. Within the broad aims of the RDP (1994) three elements, pensions; housing subsidies; and land reform, had been identified as crucial in their impact upon poverty through targeted resource transfers. By 1999 it was clear that progress in all of these concerns had been unsatisfactory (Deininger et al., 1999). Moreover, out of these three elements, land reform had been the least successful. In addition, it is now recognised that even in those cases where land reform has been implemented, the levels of rural poverty have prevented the essential investment necessary to make the transferred land productive. The commitment by the government to implement a market-based approach respecting existing property rights, has not included an understanding that for a demand-led strategy to function well there is a need for a sufficiently robust capital base.

The other fundamental of the land reform programme is a strong focus on equity, and this has led to the small size of land grants made available. A trade-off between equity and efficiency may have achieved less in productive terms than a programme that targets those claimants most likely to succeed. The programme is poverty-oriented rather than productivity-focused. Moreover, the use of grants does not always generate a sense of ownership and participation among beneficiaries. Also, the centralised administration of the programme has led to a lack of integration with other economic planning within rural localities. By monopolising powers of decision-making, elite professionals have further created a sense of continuing disempowerment among applicants to the programme. The programme has also been criticised for the way in which locally powerful people have been able to direct the benefits of land reform towards themselves and their families (Deininger et al., 1999). Nevertheless, there are many examples in which the land reform programme has successfully reached out to the very poor, and to that extent, has helped to rectify, albeit on a small and local scale, one of the harsh and persistent injustices of apartheid. In many areas of South Africa, land prices have fallen in recent years making more land available to a reform programme based on market transactions rather than expropriation.

In spite of the flaws in the structure and delivery of the programme, land reform in South Africa does still show economic potential. Individual projects have been identified where participants have been able to generate profits by working the land they have gained through the grant system. Keeping projects small in scale, speeding up the process of approval, and selecting claimants most able to invest in their own future, are all conducive to successful transfers of land. Private sector participation also appears to facilitate a productive conclusion (Deininger et al., 1999). However, it should be remembered that the overall goals of the land reform do not focus solely on economic success. Poverty relief, and the provision of opportunities to farm at a subsistence level are fundamental to the programme. Minimising procedures and adapting these to suit target groups, such as dropping the requirement of a business plan from potential subsistence farmers, and decentralising the management of the programme, would improve opportunities for participation, and enhance its efficiency. Increasing the flexibility of the grant system would mean that the claims of those applicants who are primarily looking for a house rather than land need not add to the administrative burden of the programme. Perhaps most importantly, data on the poverty-reducing impact of land reform should be examined in detail, and compared with the other programmes with similar aims (the provision of housing and pensions), thereby assessing its real value to the rural poor of South Africa.

Land Reform in South Africa since 1994 has been based simultaneously on the need for growth and distributional equity. But there is a strong debate within development literature over the compatibility of these two aims. On the one hand, it is argued that development is actually helped by growing inequality, on the other, growth is seen to be contingent upon redistribution. The question to be answered is does land reform in South Africa successfully combine equity and efficiency? Deininger and May (2000) have used the limited available data to argue that land reform in South Africa has not only targeted the poor, it has also achieved this while combining the twin objectives of equity and efficiency. Many of those projects involving the transfer of land to the very poor have subsequently shown themselves to be economically successful, even in a context of a chronically distorted rural economy. However, they go on to suggest that their data leads them to think that, in future, economic viability should be the primary goal in attempts to reduce rural poverty.

At the same time, it has to be accepted that the actual number of successful initiatives has been limited, and that major changes are needed in the administration of land reform in the future to make further progress in poverty reduction. It now seems that a focus on community-wide integrated programmes, and a move away from the heavily centralised decision-making procedures are necessary. Also, land reform should be linked more closely with other government programmes so that local level synergies can be exploited, and a broader transformation of rural society achieved. Importantly, Deininger and May (2000) contend that administrative adjustments are necessary to speed up the painfully slow process of reform. The integration of land reform into a wider rural policy framework that allays fears by guaranteeing existing property rights and secures tenancy rights for farmers in former homelands is critical. Transparency in decision-making at the local level will help convince rural people that land reform is not another form of political favouritism. In our experience in KwaZulu-Natal, many rural Africans are extremely suspicious of and disappointed by the lack of rigour in the land reform programme. In many cases their negative perceptions of the intentions of political leaders have been confirmed. However ill-founded these perceptions may be, they are undoubtedly contributing to the government's political problems in the country-side, and to the lack of enthusiasm for eco-tourism development in areas where there are contested rights to protected areas.

Women in rural KwaZulu-Natal

Despite explicit government commitment to gender equity there is little sign of improvements in rights to land for women in KwaZulu-Natal (Billy, 1996). Even the development of the Land Reform Gender Policy (1997) has failed to improve the living conditions of women to any noticeable extent (Daniels, 2001).

African women in South Africa have not been drawn into land reform pro-grammes in any significant way. Most women we have visited in the regions of KwaZulu-Natal struggle to survive by growing subsistence crops on land they do not own. Large numbers of them have had to take the full burden of farming when their husbands and sons are forced to leave the province in search of work in mines and factories. As heads of household, many African women have brought up their children alone, and have the daily and ever more difficult chore of finding fuel and fetching water. Environmental conservation and restrictions on the use of natural resources affect the daily lives of women more directly than those of men.

In the rural areas of the province, African women do not have access to electricity or social services. Issues of race, class and gender ensure that rural African women remain poor and severely excluded. During the decades of apartheid, other than short-term insecure permits to occupy and farm in certain areas of the province, African women were denied ownership of land outside the homeland of KwaZulu. Further, customary law prevents African women in KwaZulu-Natal from owning land (Billy, 1996). Under the traditional communal system, grazing rights, and rights to occupy land, are allocated by the chief to male heads of household. Customary law continues to treat women as minors, and prevents them from holding rights in land and from inheriting land rights from their husbands. Women often become homeless when their husbands die or their marriages come to an end. Unmarried women may be forced to become squatters.

The difficulties for women over land rights are compounded by the fact that families working under communal tenure may lose their rights if their chief decides to sell common lands. There have been many examples in KwaZulu-Natal where chiefs, claiming proprietary rights over common lands have sold them to speculators, in deals which are illegal, and which ignore the needs of the landless. The prevailing ambiguity over communal land rights in the homelands is hindering efforts by the government to establish a more just land system. The rural violence and communal conflicts in KwaZulu-Natal often stem from rivalries over land, and warlords have been seen to take over land areas, granting access only to their supporters. Many of the trusts and other committees established to deal with land claims are dominated by men. Traditional values and the general lack of education among rural women together reinforce their exclusion from the land reform processes. Time constraints arising from excessive domestic responsibilities, geographical isolation, low self-esteem and the fear of violent retribution from husbands and fathers also work against the proactive participation of women in land issues. The Communal Properties Association Act (1996) allows communities to formalise the communal tenure system by establishing a trust and registering a constitution under the

Act. This piece of legislation stipulates that such associations must permit a fair representation of women. But equity in land rights for women will not emerge so long as the social and economic restraints on their activities persist. One important change that is needed is the reform of customary marriage and inheritance laws, which were codified by missionaries and the colonial authority (Baden, Hassim and Meintjes, 1999) and which prevent women from receiving secure rights to land.

Under apartheid, women from different racial groups and classes suffered discrimination differently. Most black women felt themselves to be closer to their black men than to white women (Baden, Hassim and Meintjes, 1999). During the decades of oppression at the hands of the National Party, women became increasingly active in the resistance struggle, not only against laws and taxes that affected all black people, but also against repercussions of apartheid for women alone. They formed their own campaigning groups, such as the Natal Organisation of Women, which worked alongside male-dominated trade unions and community organisations. In the late 1980s, there was a marked growth in the establishment of NGOs and CBOs caring for the rights of women, and the Rural Women's Movement became particularly active in the struggle to improve the lives of women in the remote areas of the countryside. In 1992, women from across the racial divide formed the Women's National Coalition, which drew up the Women's Charter of Effective Equality, in an effort to ensure that issues of gender were addressed in the constitution of post-apartheid South Africa (Baden, Hassim and Meintjes, 1999).

For the 1994 elections the ANC agreed that at least 30 per cent of candidates would be women. Subsequently, the South African parliament since 1994 has had more women members than any South African parliament before that date. In 1999, 80 of the ANC's total of 242 Members of Parliament, and four ministers out of a Cabinet of 25 were women. However, among women politicians, there is a strong feeling that parliament remains a man's world, and that procedures and timetables are not arranged to suit the family responsibilities they are still expected to meet. For parliament, social problems arising from differences in race are far more significant than those caused by gendered inequities. Moreover, the advancement of a small number of women to elite positions does not reflect the existential conditions of poor South African women, the majority of whom live in the historically deprived rural areas. Many of those women who do fill central political roles began their political careers in civil society, in NGOs or CBOs, during the 1980s when the battle against oppression was at its height. It was these organisations that made the most effort to ensure the inclusion of women in any future land reform policies, and successfully campaigned to have equitable access to natural resources included in the Constitution (Baden, Hassim and Meintjes, 1999). But while the government has made strides in developing policies to guide practice in issues of gender equality, changing historically established and institutionally entrenched values is more complex. Affirmative action with respect to race may have developed into a mechanism for favouring black men and for neglecting black women.

The pass laws brought in by the National Party prevented many women from finding work in the cities. In rural areas they were left behind to work unproductive land. Women were dependent upon the goodwill of chiefs in times of hardship. Poverty in South Africa is worst among the rural women living in the former homelands in KwaZulu-Natal, Eastern Cape and Northern Province. The strain of poverty in these areas often leads to problems within families resulting in violence against women by their husbands (Baden, Hassim and Meintjes, 1999). Moreover, those households headed by women are far more likely to be living in abject poverty than households headed by men. But even within male-headed households, women do not always experience an equal sharing of earnings. If they try to make claims on male resources, they may encounter a violent response. In spite of this, women remain in households where they suffer at the hands of men because they have few or no alternatives.

Financial poverty is not the only form of deprivation suffered by women in South Africa. In 1995, 23 per cent of African women aged 25 years or over had had no formal education, and 28 per cent were regarded as illiterate. In contrast, almost all white women had enjoyed primary and secondary education, and were literate. Historically there has been a tendency to send African boys to school rather than girls. Today, the overall numbers of African children in primary and secondary education has risen, and there are now slightly more girls than boys in school. However, the school experience is very different for girls. Many of them suffer serious sexual harassment, and are reluctant to visit libraries and classrooms in the evening for fear of violence. In employment the majority of African women are concentrated in casual agricultural labour, domestic work and the informal sector where they are poorly paid, liable to job loss, and to abuse. African women constitute the bulk of poverty victims in the country, with 71 per cent living below the poverty line. In the rural areas unemployment among African men fluctuates around an average of 45 per cent. Rural African women experience an unemployment rate of 62 per cent (Daniels, 2001). Poverty is gendered in South Africa.

Because of a general lack of safe clean water, sanitation, a varied diet, good housing and health services, black rural people in general have worse health than city dwellers in South Africa. Poverty-related diseases like TB are common. Poor women, in addition to having ill health themselves, are needed to care for their family members when they are unwell. Maternal mortality is estimated at 58 deaths per 100,000 live births for Africans, compared to 3 per

100,000 for white women. In most racial groups in the world, women live longer than men. In South Africa men have a greater life expectancy. Sixteen in every hundred African women visiting antenatal clinics in 1997 were HIV-positive, and more recent research suggests that the current rate of HIV-positive identifications has risen 30 per cent in KwaZulu-Natal. Poverty increases the likelihood of African women becoming infected with HIV, because it may force them into prostitution. Only a minority of rural women feel they can ask their partners to use a condom (Baden, Hassim and Meintjes, 1999).

Women and men often want land for different purposes. Men tend to be profit-oriented, while women often want land for subsistence and for a secure place to live and care for children. Women generally require smaller areas of land than men (Baden, Hassim and Meintjes, 1999). Men tend to benefit more from land reform subsidies because only one grant is made per household. Restitution also favours men because land rights in the past would have been in their names.

In KwaZulu-Natal, rural African women are commonly restricted to the domestic, 'natural' domain, while men deal with the 'cultural' and political issues, an arrangement often maintained by reference to custom or the sacred. Not all Zulu women have suffered subjugation without protest, but in the rural areas of the province that we have visited, many of those women who do attempt to make known their political or economic ideas are often censured severely by the men in their families. Wives whose husbands are away working in the mines or the cities may be particularly vulnerable and dependent upon the magnanimity of the chief in times of hardship, and may feel obliged to support his decisions in spite of their patriarchal foundations.

The empowerment of women, a central principle of the Reconstruction and Development Programme (ANC, 1994), would entail radical and fundamental transformations of the patriarchal structures of rural society, including new restraints on the traditional powers of tribal chiefs. However, many of the latter have found positions for themselves or their supporters in the newly established administration of local governance (Ritchken, 1995). Zulu chiefs, the majority of whom actively support Inkatha, have managed to retain a stronger hold on their authority than their counterparts in other former homelands. They recognise the challenge to democratically elected local government, and have linked their own campaign with Chief Buthelezi's political ambitions, based ostensibly on the struggle to save the Zulu kingdom and culture. The exclusion within an exclusion acts to counter women's opportunities to participate in eco-tourism initiatives, in anything like the proactive way specified by the RDP.

Domestic violence against black women in South Africa is often socially condoned within African communities, and is a recurrent theme in the press

(Billy, 1996). Women's groups see violence as a means of keeping women in a position of subordination to men. Rape is also a major focus in the media with estimates that a rape occurs in South Africa every 30 seconds, including attacks against young girls. Only one in 35 rapes is reported to the police. With an enormous AIDS epidemic in the country, rape can mean a heightened risk of early death for the victim. It is argued that men regard women as property, and that the continuing practice of *lobola* (bride price) is seen by many campaigners for gender equality as resembling a market transaction.

Social violence and eco-tourism development

The regular use of violence within households is not the only violent behaviour in KwaZulu-Natal that has a direct bearing on participation in eco-tourism development. During the 1990s, political violence came to dominate public debate, and to form something of a conundrum in South Africa (du Toit, 1993). In the past, violence had been more easily discussed and explained as a consequence of, and resistance to, the imposition of apartheid. But during the early 1990s, when state-led oppression of the black population was abating, other new forms of group violence were in the ascendant.

A great deal of research is needed into the origins of the present-day violence which continues to express itself in widespread and brutal murders, and which exacerbates economic stagnation. Apartheid is commonly argued to have been the most salient cause of the violence. However, as plausible as this theory appears, it does not explain why levels of violence were at their lowest during the period when apartheid was strongest. Nor does it explain why conflicts became far more common during the late 1970s, when the most severe restrictions of apartheid were slowly becoming eroded. Further, it fails to explain why relatively few whites have been the target for violent attacks (Olivier, 1992). One theory has placed the blame on resurgent ethnicity. But those authors who suggest that ethnic divisions are the prime cause of violence fail to recognise that a large proportion of attacks takes place between members of the same ethnic group, the Zulus. In other areas of the country where many ethnic groups live in proximity to each other, ethnicity is not reckoned to be a major factor in violent outbreaks. Socio-economic deprivation is also commonly posited as a cause of violence. That is, people who see themselves as unfairly deprived will organise themselves to commit violent crime. However, the extent of violence in South Africa has increased markedly at a time when there are signs that economic conditions for blacks have marginally improved in many areas.

Another obvious and important possible cause of group violence is political competition. In KwaZulu-Natal, rivalries between supporters of the IFP and the ANC have undoubtedly led to awful massacres and revenge killings, and to the province being described as the site of a civil war (Gwala, 1992). This argument does not help us understand why there is so little political violence in the Asian and white communities, where there is support for the whole range of parties active in South Africa. Linked to the argument that much of the violence is politically motivated, are the charges that the South African Police Service (SAPS) and the South African Defence Force (SADF) are not impartial in their efforts to deal with the violence, and that they have been arming and training members of the IFP to fight against the strongest reforming party, the ANC. Evidence that has been made public since 1994 supports these allegations, and also supports accusations that the SAPS were guilty of many criminal attacks on black political prisoners in police cells during the apartheid era. This explanation has been offered to us by concerned observers during our research in KwaZulu-Natal. The Goldstone Commission also revealed in 1992, that a group of powerful individuals in the police and security establishment were active in acts of terror, hoping to destabilise the country and derail the political progress of the ANC (Olivier, 1992).

In South Africa, a key problem in the explanation of the sometimes rampant violence is the understanding of how changes in the relative power of central organisations and in the repressive strength of the state itself, inform and prompt collective violence and social upheaval. The dynamics that underpin political conflict in the country have changed dramatically since the release of Nelson Mandela and the unbanning of the ANC in February 1990. Before that date, violence was largely committed by the state against the disenfranchised black majority. Now it could be argued that competition over the scarcest of resources, political power, is the strongest dynamic in group violent behaviour. Political structures and opportunities have become manifold and localised, and this competition operates at different levels.

There has been an enormous rise in crime-related violence during the past decade. This has included a rapid growth in burglaries, vehicle theft and hijacking, robberies, rape and murder. Many of the respondents we interviewed had personal stories to tell of violent crime committed against themselves or against family members. Some of these accounts were truly horrifying in their brutality. Members of the white population now surround themselves with security systems, and live in fear of armed burglars or hijackers. Indeed, much of the fury of the right-wing resistance to political change has been prompted by issues of personal security.

In truth, the widespread violence that continues to occupy the press has many interlinked causes. The social problems caused by apartheid, inadequate education, a chronic sense of cruel economic exploitation, high unemployment, debilitating poverty and exclusion and a sense of hopelessness, the availability of arms, poor police–community relationships, political rhetoric in which opponents are publicly blamed for instigating violent attacks, and a massive release of prisoners in 1991 have all certainly contributed to the emergence of a culture of violence in many regions of the country, especially in KwaZulu-Natal. Many violent acts committed in the province have been masked as politically motivated activities in order to decriminalise them in the eyes of fellow community members. Certainly, we found that some of those violent acts committed by blacks against whites are often rationalised as a transfer of wealth from the corrupt and historically powerful to the deprived and needy in the African townships and villages.

For Gwala (1992), there are three theoretical explanations for the rise in group violence in Natal and KwaZulu. The first is the struggle for political control between the state – and its extension the IFP – on one side, and the major liberation movement, the ANC, on the other. According to this explanation, the oppressive conditions imposed by the state caused a public response from the disenfranchised campaigning for their democratic rights. The second explanation suggests that the poor access to economic resources in the region became linked to political affiliations, and that this politicisation of economic issues raised tensions between the opposing parties. Finally, the third argument is that the violence is orchestrated by a third force, a secretive network of right-wing individuals and security forces which, by killing leading members of the opposition, would destabilise society in Natal and KwaZulu. Underlying all of these explanations, is the politicised conflict over material inequalities between the white and black communities, and within the black population itself. Changes in conflict levels in KwaZulu-Natal differ from those in other parts of the country in that they do not correlate as closely with events of national importance as they do elsewhere (Louw, 1994). The assassination of Chris Hani, in April 1993 was followed by surges of violence in Johannesburg and the industrialised zones, but in KwaZulu-Natal violence levels were not affected so markedly.

The prevalence of group violence in KwaZulu-Natal is not a wholly recent phenomenon, and the repeated calls for its cessation will remain largely unheeded until its dynamics are fully understood. In fact, as far back as 1896 legislation was enacted to deal with those involved, and large numbers of combatants have been prosecuted during the subsequent decades (du Toit, 1993). In spite of this long history of factionalism, little anthropological work has been undertaken on the subject, and remarkably, the major ethnographic monographs on Zulu social organisation hardly mention it at all (see Gluckman, 1940, 1973). Notwithstanding the scant literature on this major feature of Zulu life, the anthropologist, John Argyle (1968) of the University of Natal, suggests that factional fights be categorised as 'feuds' in line with anthropological studies of other societies where feuds are important factors in group politics. Argyle (1968, p.2) defines a feud as

> a series (at least three instances) of acts of violence, usually involving killings, committed by members of two groups related to each other by superimposed political-structural features (often involving the existence of an overall political authority) and active on the basis of group solidarity (a common duty to avenge and a common liability).

Criminal court documents certainly imply that many of the murders of Zulu tribespeople occur in retaliation for other killings, and that these latter were also responses to yet earlier murders (Argyle, 20/11/95). These records also show that a large proportion of the initiatory acts do occur between groups of one tribe, or less frequently, between closely neighbouring tribes, and are undoubtedly subjected to superimposed political-structural features. The absence among Zulus of a socially recognised mechanism to terminate the feuds with offers of compensation (a common feature of feuding societies elsewhere) can, in KwaZulu-Natal, lead to feuds having no end (we discuss the intractable nature of conflicts of interest and their implications for democracy in chapter 9). But the persistently retaliatory character of the faction fights does justify the comparison with similar violent group acts generally classed as feuds.

The fact that individuals are openly acting on a declared basis of group solidarity confirms for Argyle (1968) the usefulness of the concept of 'feud' to explain, at least in part, the frequency, scale and ferocity of violent encounters among Zulus in more recent times (Argyle, 20/11/95). There is a marked degree of solidarity within territorially defined and named groups. Some individuals can be seen to be in a position of authority, and there exist internal judicial structures, and systems of ranking, even among the lower orders of lineages. These groups can be thought of as corporations, having identity, presumed perpetuity, closure and membership, autonomy within a given sphere, and organisation.

The existence of such corporate groups does not in itself explain the hostility that can characterise their relationships with each other. Another defining feature of corporations that does help in the interpretation of the volatile relationships between them is the holding of estates (Argyle, 1968). In Zulu society, such estates can comprise land, cattle, water and other resources. Interaction between Zulu corporations frequently takes the form of long-running disputes over these estates and their boundaries. The claimed significance of these often territorial rivalries would seem to be questioned or contradicted by the frequency of clashes between Zulu groups in the urban centres, often far away from their homesteads. But Stephen Taylor (1995) argues that observers commonly under-estimate the very strength of corporate identities, which are recognised by many migrant labourers who continue to display corporate loyalty even in the less ethnically defined cities of South Africa. In the townships, group attacks may occur in retaliation for violent encroachments in the rural homes of the assailants, or may be responses to clashes between the same corporations over the monopoly of certain types of employment in the urban localities.

We are not implying that every member of a corporation is always ready to commit retaliatory violence, nor that corporate leaders expect such a unanimous response. In the cities there are innumerable Zulus whose ties with the politics of their villages have weakened. Nor is it the intention to suggest that corporate identities are immutable. New circumstances, such as natural disasters and crop failures, or changes in economic opportunities, can generate equally new group identities, or may lead to the symbolic enhancement of old ones. But it is argued that group identities and rivalries do inform economic and political activity in Zulu society to a greater extent than is often recognised (Mair, 1983).

The discussion so far, though, has failed to explain why such hostilities are so common among Zulus when they are far less so among other tribal societies also holding estates. Argyle (20/11/95) feels that four important factors contribute in important ways to the continuing perpetration of so many inter-corporate killings: the existence of a huge number of small territorial units; a similar number of chiefs; communal land tenure; and the historical forms of collective responsibility imposed upon the members of those small corporations. All of these have their origins in the colonial history of Natal and Zululand.

The sometimes diminutive Zulu territorial units came about partly because of the disruption caused to tribes during the tumultuous time of the Zulu leader, Shaka. More significantly, though, they arose out of the deliberate 'divide and rule' colonial policy, designed to pre-empt any mass uprising of the entire Zulu population (S. Taylor, 1995; Worden, 1994). By 1882 there were 102 Zulu tribes in Natal, and by 1904 there were 312, some of them with fewer than 400 huts (Argyle, 1968). This situation in tandem with the overcrowding in the reserves resulted in violent factionalism. Communal land-tenure prevented the settlement in court of boundary disputes between individuals. Whole tribes were involved. Customary law was nurtured by the colonial powers because, in the absence of individual ownership, a politically motivated middle-class of prosperous Africans was less likely to emerge. Moreover, such arrangements also suited the authorities because they placed collective responsibility on groups for the supply of forced labour and for the capture of criminals (S. Taylor, 1995).

Statistics of the continuing factionalism among Zulus seem to support this argument in that they show that fighting between Zulu corporate groups is often (but not always) particularly intense in those regions of KwaZulu-Natal where land shortage is most acute, and where farming conditions are the poorest (Argyle, 20/11/95). These factors cannot be regarded as anything approaching a full explanation of today's violence in KwaZulu-Natal, nor is it being implied that there exists a one-to-one relationship between the availability of land and the frequency of factional clashes. However, the above discussion does indicate the historical depth and the social complexity of the group attacks, and it also reveals the influential and pivotal role Zulu chiefs continue to play in rural politics in KwaZulu-Natal.

The resurgence in Zulu chieftainship

In the drafting of the Local Government Transition Act (1995), it is openly acknowledged that in South Africa, factional rivalries and traditional chiefs jealous of their powers, can cause acute difficulties in the transfer of democratic authority to rural and urban communities. A commitment to conflict resolution and negotiation is essential if old power bases are to be diminished in the construction of democracy in South Africa. RDP forums are to be established in the more acutely marginalised communities, forging links between CBOs, NGOs, political parties and other local bodies concerned with development leading to self-reliance. The central responsibility of these forums is to identify and prioritise local needs, and to allocate resources accordingly.

However, many chiefs have found positions for themselves or their supporters in the newly established administration of local governance (Ritchken, 1995). Zulu chiefs, with their active support of the IFP, have managed to retain a stronger hold on their authority than their counterparts in the other former homelands. They recognise the challenge from democratically elected local government, and have linked their own campaigns with Chief Buthelezi's political ambitions, based ostensibly on the struggle to save the Zulu kingdom and culture.

During the early twentieth century, chiefs and the Zulu royal family were becoming increasingly anxious over the trend away from traditional political systems and, in one sense, the segregation policies of Jan Smuts suited this section of Zulu society who were trying to rejuvenate old ways, at a time when urbanisation was accelerating. Later, under the Bantu Authorities Act 1951, chiefs were again rewarded for carrying out government policies, and in doing so were compromised even further in the eyes of the more modernising and often missionary-educated Zulus (S. Taylor, 1995). The IFP's strongest support has always come from the rural areas and, by 1980, the 'cultural' movement of Inkatha was the largest political organisation in South Africa. The founding tenets of Inkatha were the maintenance of tribal hierarchical values, which were argued to be the quintessence of African political life. Buthelezi converted Inkatha into a political party in 1991.

For many Zulus, the right to govern is determined by blood not by the vote. Councillors elected because they are nominated as candidates by chiefs are seen as members of the chief's court rather than as party representatives. One repercussion of this scenario is that chiefs can straddle civil society and state political structures, gaining access to developmental resources in a way that does not conform to the RDP's model of democratic development (Ritchken, 1995). When succession disputes occur, local government is sometimes compromised by a partial allocation of resources in attempts to secure communal support. Prior to the elections of 1994 in KwaZulu-Natal, there were many examples of factional politics and succession disputes overlapping and informing electoral campaigns. Candidates, unable to disentangle state politics from parochial rivalries, were often obliged to forge alliances with powerful civil and factional groups. For many observers, the IFP's political success in the province clearly demonstrates that, contrary to the ANC's modernising hopes for local and regional politics, chieftainship, the Zulu monarchy and ethnic identity retain much of their social significance (Johnston, 1993).

More than five times as many Zulus live in the areas formerly known as KwaZulu than in the remainder of the province, and during the years of apartheid, the homeland was a one party state in all but official designation. Free political activity did not exist there. The IFP has also striven to establish the fundamental differences between its own plans for the Zulu nation and those of the ANC, and has gained political mileage by repeatedly reminding the Zulu electorate that most of the important positions in the ANC are held by Xhosa speakers.

The ANC's refusal to develop a more federalist model of political organisation in South Africa, and its determination not to consider the Zulu nation as a special case and allow it a degree of regional autonomy, eventually led Buthelezi to threaten to boycott the elections in 1994, until he was given the pledge that international mediators would be invited to investigate the particular needs of the Zulus and their royal family. In the event, amid accusations of ballot-rigging by both sides, the IFP did win control of KwaZulu-Natal. However, even among those traditional chiefs who had shown some degree of support for the ANC's modernising goals, there has been a sharp transformation of opinion because of the latter's reluctance to recognise tribal authorities in any more than a symbolic role (Mbhele, 1997). In 2000, rural Zulu chiefs put up strong resistance to ANC plans to make their lands part of new municipalities which would include rural towns where ANC support was strongest (Makele, 2000). The proposed boundaries would in effect reduce the tribal authorities' representation to less than 10 per cent. At the last minute before the elections in that year, the ANC, in a conciliatory move, made minor concessions to the chiefs so that some tribal areas remained under their control.

In spite of evidence that a new pride in Zulu identity is beginning to attract younger community members and lessen the risk of violent conflict between them and conservative leaders (Koch, 1997), the images of mass violence, the resurgence of Zulu chieftainship, and the venality which characterises much of the developmental activity in the rural areas of KwaZulu-Natal, together effectively dissuade tourists from visiting the province. Similarly, when criminal violence is perpetrated against tourists and reported in the press, there is an immediate downturn in tourist demand. In St Lucia village, muggings of foreign tourists have led to cancellations of bookings for accommodation on a substantial scale (Barker, 2/12/98). It is our experience that this, in turn, has caused many local tourism operators to become increasingly sceptical about the possibilities of developing a model of eco-tourism that involves close contact between white domestic and foreign tourists and Zulu communities. Perhaps most importantly, the continuing authority of traditional chiefs, and the propensity to utilise violence in political disagreements, together inhibit the emergence of those democratic institutions deemed necessary for the sustainable upliftment of rural populations in eco-tourism initiatives, and for their empowered participation in democratically elected decision-making forums.

Eco-tourism and participatory development

As the previous chapter shows, the tribes – people active in the eco-tourism case studies we have monitored – have participated at different levels. The proposal that local people should take a more proactive and empowered role in nature-based, eco-tourism initiatives is not an original one. Integrated Conservation Development Projects (ICDPs) have been set up in a large number of countries in the developing world, and have attracted attention in the literature (Andriampianam, 1985; Barratt and Arcese, 1995; Hales, 1989; Poole, 1989; Wells and Brandon, 1992). Although not all of these projects are based on the promotion of eco-tourism, the lessons to be learned from their analysis are transferable to the discussion of eco-tourism development in KwaZulu-Natal.

Community participation is the factor Wells and Brandon (1992) regard as most crucial to the developmental goals of ICDPs, but they also point out that it is the most elusive component of projects designed to reconcile conservation with the needs of local people. In an important and pain-staking contribution, Wells and Brandon (1992) examine 23 case studies of ICDPs from Asia, South America and Africa. The socio-economic, cultural, political, and environmental circumstances vary widely between the projects, but the case studies do highlight many of the achievements and disappointments in these initiatives, that attempt to reconcile what are often regarded as the conflicting goals of biodiversity conservation and development. The strategies generally employed in these ICDPs are threefold: first, the management of protected areas; second, the creation of buffer zones around those areas; and third, local development operations, involving the active participation of communities themselves, and sometimes taking the form of employment, or the provision of basic needs such as education and healthcare, or payments in compensation for the loss of access to land previously occupied by local people. This last type of operation is thought by Wells and Brandon (1992) to be vital, but is also the most difficult to implement.

The dangers to many of the world's conservation and protected areas arise, in the main, from the desperate poverty of the surrounding populations; poverty which may have been caused at least in part by the setting up of the conservation areas themselves. In the past, protected area managers have concentrated on security; on keeping (local, indigenous) people out at all costs. This militaristic approach has, in some countries, led to the use of severe sanctions: fines, prison sentences and even death. As such, these approaches have met with fierce hostility from local people, who have seen themselves excluded from economic opportunities in the development of tourism and other enterprises. The sense of unjust exclusion from regions where, prior to the establishing of the protected areas, full access was once enjoyed, along with increasing pressures on land use outside the perimeter fence, has frequently led to illegal and sometimes destructive encroachments (Mendus, 1988; Wells and Brandon, 1992).

Recently, there has been a growing acceptance that conservation projects can only survive if local people are actively involved in their management, and have access (albeit, monitored) to the natural resources of the protected areas. An awareness of the urgency of environmental protection has accelerated efforts to incorporate the meeting of basic needs of neighbouring communities, and to provide alternatives to land invasions. A pillar of these programmes is the creation of buffer zones, where incomes are improved, education on environmental issues made available, and sustainable agriculture and agro-forestry encouraged. Programmes of resource management with ownership rights to the natural resources will conserve the soil, forestry, fresh water and wildlife, while increasing the incomes of resident populations. In these zones, the evaluation studies of ICDPs indicate that more intensive farming practices will be substituted for the extensive, and land-hungry, farming methods commonly utilised in the developing countries. Community social services will be improved, roads to markets constructed, and appropriate income-generating ventures, such as eco-tourism, assisted (Wells and Brandon, 1992). Local groups can participate in a number of ways, and to varying degrees, in the progress of the ICDPs through information-gathering, consultation, decision-making, initiating action, and finally, evaluation. Participation can be promoted and supported by employing agents of change, and by building and supporting appropriate institutions. The former will depend on the growth of trusting relationships, and the latter will serve as a focus of mobilisation and as links with external agencies (Fukuyama, 1995). The significance of trust in tourism development is the theme of chapter 10.

The longitudinal study of the 23 ICDPs discussed by Wells and Brandon (1992) has allowed the authors to identify many of the flaws in planning and implementation in these projects. One lesson that has been noted is that even if there are marked improvements in the material circumstances of groups living in the vicinity of the national parks and other protected areas, the non-violation of the parks is not guaranteed. In fact, it may be necessary for government to draw up new legislation containing even harsher penalties than those implemented under the earlier 'fences and fines' regimes. This problem has arisen recurrently because communities do not perceive the connections between the conservation programmes and the socio-economic benefits they are experiencing. It is a common fault in many ICDPs that the linkages between environmental protection and development are not made plain to all concerned and individuals and groups may feel that others are benefiting more than themselves. Under these circumstances, it is unrealistic to assume that relatively (and absolutely) poor communities living adjacent to seemingly limitless sources of game and other natural resources, will wholeheartedly accept the principles and practices of conservation programmes (Wells and Brandon, 1992).

Part and parcel of the ethos of these initiatives is the empowerment of rural communities. In those cases where local participation has been achieved, it has proved to be a more effective means of attaining sustainability than approaches that rely on the delivery of economic benefits without an active commitment on the part of the beneficiaries themselves (Olson, 1971). But, as Wells and Brandon point out, eliciting that participation can be time-consuming. While it may have been the earnest intention to include communities at all levels of decision-making, the process of implementation of short-term measures taken to gain credibility in the early stages of a project, have tended to encourage those communities to take a more passive role. Wells and Brandon are in no doubt that only long-term planning expressing the precise aim of incorporating communities in all stages of decision-making and evaluation will have a chance of developing sustainability. The provision of jobs and other benefits is not equivalent to local participation (Pateman, 1970; Wells and Brandon, 1992).

ICDPs should be integrated into larger development frameworks and strategies. The pressures and biodiversity that lead to ecological degradation have their origins in wider political and economic relationships of power and marginalisation. Sudden rises in unemployment as a consequence of a drop in global commodity prices, for example, can place rural communities in dire situations, forcing them to make illegal land invasions, or to hunt game, in protected areas. The ICDP model has value only to the extent that neighbouring communities accept the existence of the parks and recognise that game animals are worth more alive than dead. In their present form, ICDPs can only have limited impacts upon the welfare of rural people and in the protection of biodiversity. It is the role and responsibility of government to provide more generous funding, and to facilitate the formation of new partnerships between all agencies involved.

Most ICDPs operate on a scale considerably smaller than the problems of environmental degradation and rural poverty they are designed to alleviate, and can only be seen as worthwhile if their experiences are translated into the funding of much larger projects in the future. Moreover, it is government's task to address the tangle of multi-layered land claims, which has been seen to generate discontent and mistrust of conservation programmes of any kind. It would be a mistake, though, to expect unlimited support from government departments with responsibilities of natural resource conservation. These ministries are typically under-resourced and politically weak. In fact, governments may be incapable of managing large areas of land, and may not be able to resist pressures from commercial corporations keen to exploit forestry or mineral resources within the boundaries of protected areas (Baumol, 1991).

The understandable temptation to expand individual ICDPs as quickly as possible has placed onerous demands on local communities and on the smaller participatory institutions and agencies. In some cases leadership and control can be taken out of the locality and away from those very people who were expecting to have central roles to play and contributions to make. In other cases, where the initiatives are driven by the enthusiasm and expertise of small NGOs and individuals working for them, benefits can be visible, substantial and fairly distributed. However, when these dynamic representatives leave for other projects, or when disputes over funding are impeding progress, the initiatives can become bedevilled by internal strife, corruption or widespread disillusionment. This is a common scenario in rural development pilot projects in many developing countries.

The evidence provided by Wells and Brandon (1992) and others, so far, does not permit the construction of models applicable in a general sense. The study of ICDPs is the history of attempts to deliver, in one strategy, the means of conserving biodiversity by eliminating threats to protected areas, while promoting sustainable rural development through the empowerment of local people. Enormous problems remain, especially in the identification of suitable agencies to facilitate and monitor the progress of these initiatives. In a sense, neither conservation nor sustainability is the issue. Cruel poverty and the lack of life-choices are the factors that drive people's actions in agrarian societies all over the world (Doyal and Gough, 1991). Rural people are marginalised in political and economic structures that favour the urban, the white, the prosperous and the male; these institutionalised biases must be taken into account if development strategies are to have any meaning for their intended beneficiaries.

In the cases of relationships between local communities and the Phinda Resource Reserve, the KEN project in Kosi Bay, and KZN-Wildlife, there exist three very distinct trading arrangements, and degrees of participation. First, at Phinda, neighbouring inhabitants are encouraged to contribute to the development forum, and to negotiate over the utilisation of the available funds in a series of diverse projects. However, they are not invited to take part in managerial decision-making in either the conservation work or in the core tourism venture, nor are they expected to become shareholders in the Conservation Corporation. The local community fills a dependent and peripheral role in the reserve. Second, unemployment levels in the locality are particularly high, and, therefore, the impact of the reserve in terms of the generation of jobs and the creation of small businesses, is all the more conspicuous, and impressive. In the context of a weak and unstable local government, the Southern Maputaland Development Forum has taken on some of its enabling functions. But there is insufficient evidence to claim that the benefits enjoyed as a result of the setting up of Phinda are reaching the most needy.

In contrast with arrangements at Phinda, the levels of community partici-pation were high in all aspects of the KEN project in Kosi Bay. The residents have also shown a readiness to diversify into other forms of sustainable land-use that are compatible with eco-tourism, but insufficient funding has precluded any substantial extension work. Participants were optimistic, and the initial modest success of the initiative encouraged the conservation authority to consider promoting similar enterprises nearby within the boundaries of the nature reserve. The most disadvantaged members of the communities were urged to take part and, for a while, the stability of the project contributed to a strengthened self-confidence among the participants; a self-esteem that contrasted with that of neighbouring tribes, including those people who moved out under pressure from the former KDNC.

CROP's commitment to KEN was exemplary and inspiring. The admirable dedication to the project that has included individual representatives of the NGO putting themselves in personal danger, was at the cornerstone of the whole initiative. CROP took heed of local aspirations at all stages of the venture, and showed constant respect for customary values and procedures. Traditional fishing and farming techniques were made features of the tourism experience. However, the highly principled stand of CROP on such issues as participation, democracy and sustainability, and strict adherence to the tenets of the RDP, have shown themselves to be stumbling blocks, and it is possible that CROP was asking too much of eco-tourism. Taking the spirit of socially responsible development to its logical conclusion may well restrict choice and limit opportunities to expand.

Not all observers of economic development in KwaZulu-Natal are content to accept an analysis that blames internal, cultural factors alone, for the lack of progress in improving the welfare of rural communities. The Centre for Community Organisation, Research and Development (CORD), based at the University of Natal, argues that much of the government-sponsored research into rural development in the province has centred on the need to modernise Zulu society, and on the importance of dispensing with anachronistic organi-sations and irrational ways of doing things, such as witchcraft and political systems dominated by traditional chiefs and headmen (CORDa). The authors believe that such an analysis constitutes little more than a smokescreen and is instrumental in concealing the racially based, disadvantageous and structurally determined relationships Zulu society has endured with the white capitalist economy. In contrast to Argyle (1968), whose emphasis is on the internal political and economic segmentary form of Zulu organisation, CORDa rejects traditional anthropological models that, in the main, are besotted with notions of the primacy and determinacy of kinship, lineage and tribal allegiances. These generally structural/functionalist analyses, based on *a priori* notions of 'social equilibrium' and 'checks and balances', fail to consider or explain change, and ignore the impacts of external agencies.

CORD has carried out extensive research among Zulus in Maputaland, and in an informative if irascible paper, is condemnatory of the majority of earlier ethnography which portrays Zulus as living out their lives within communi-tarian structures and support systems, and according to age-old custom. Poverty, not lineage obligations, determines the actions of Zulu people. Innate rural conservatism is not the major factor inhibiting development (CORDa). The authors are, perhaps, unfair in their wholly dismissive, and somewhat acerbic assessment of the attempts by anthropologists to explain social behaviour among the African peoples they study. Even Gluckman (1940, 1973), who insists most strongly that the 'function' of social forces is the maintenance of equilibrium, concedes that, among Zulu tribes, there exist ambiguities in social rules that provide 'loopholes' for individual ambition and, eventually, for major political and economic change. These 'inconsistent actions', such as aligning oneself with white colonial authority when such an allegiance is beneficial, and, at the same time, condemning that authority at home, actually contribute to the balanced functioning of social systems (Mair, 1983).

CORD's research among the rural people of Maputaland is concerned primarily with the difficulties in making a living, and with the shifting allegiances that arise out of the struggle for survival. Because their work covers a considerable period, the authors of the various papers are able to take account of social formations resulting from temporary problems as well as adjustments made by the Zulu inhabitants of Maputaland in response to their long-term and legislated poverty (Derman, 10/11/95). Social movement, CORD insists, is determined by the structural relationship between black agrarian society and the wider capitalist economy. In a sense, black rural people constitute an internal colony. Rather than looking at Zulu society as if it were self-contained, we should be concerned with such issues as rivalries between generations, widespread illiteracy in an increasingly literate world, poverty and vulnerability in the context of asymmetrical relationships of power with the mainly urban, industrial and post-industrial economy (CORDb). In this scenario, ethnicity itself is manipulated to take advantage of economic possibilities, and clan names and corporate loyalties can be swapped when it makes political sense. The extreme pressures brought about by apartheid have resulted in a cultural resourcefulness and opportunism essential for survival.

This focus on individual behaviour does not imply that tribal boundaries are meaningless. Instead, what is being claimed is that, in times of hardship, the struggle for survival is paramount, and that rational economic decisions are taken within a very limited range of options. Joining the huge number of migrant labourers is one of those options, and in Maputaland this is a common strategy in spite of all the family and personal hardships that may ensue. Another preferred option involves approaching an educated relative who has employment, and who might feel obliged to help. Young uneducated Zulus often see no future for themselves other than dependency on their literate kin (CORDb).

If poverty produces pathologies, then urgent efforts should be made to improve material circumstances, particularly in the overcrowded former home-land of KwaZulu, where living conditions are manifestly appalling. The fact is that rural communities in KwaZulu-Natal are wholly dependent upon the white national economy, and the latter has contributed to the institutionalisation of the political and economic impotence of Zulu society. This structural dependency within one national economy has resulted in enormous leakages from the African sector to the white sector. Clearly, the best use of available resources is essential in diversified and sustainable development projects. Given the dearth of good farmland, CORD feels that this diversification could well include eco-tourism initiatives in those regions where environmental conditions and wildlife have a strong appeal to the growing number of visitors looking for a nature-based holiday experience.

In agreement with CORD it is easy to see that Zulu tribes do not participate in community-based eco-tourism ventures on anything like an equal basis with their partners. The conservation authority (now KZN-Wildlife) in spite of its intentions stated clearly in its literature, has tended to keep local people at arm's length, and to allow a more tokenistic and limited degree of involvement in the affairs of the protected areas under its authority. Although the authority has channelled funds from outside donors into village improvement projects, and claims that locals can now negotiate over access to natural resources, this does not accord with the RDP's notion of participation, nor would it be regarded as such by Barrett and Arcese (1995) or Wells and Brandon (1992).

The environment, eco-tourism and the state institutions in KwaZulu-Natal

The conservation authority in the province sees itself, not the villagers, as taking a proactive role in rural development, and the linkages with conservation are tenuous. Local people are suspicious of KZN-Wildlife's efforts to establish buffer zones, and are disconcerted by the lack of candour in its plans for the future when land claims are settled. Experience has shown that soil and farming conditions are already poor in buffer zones; a situation arising, at least in part, from the setting up of the protected areas in earlier decades. In the main, it can be seen that the role allocated to the authority's African neighbours is a more passive beneficiary one, with locals having almost no voice in the actual administration of the parks, or in forming links with sustainable development. A major fault with ICDPs, as with so many other models of rural development, is the common failure to recognise and take account of the social, political, cultural and economic differences between local communities. The initiatives are often based on assumptions of shared experience and ambitions, ignoring vital contrasts in population densities, length of residence in particular areas, indigenous knowledge and technology, and in land-use. The policies and practices of ICDPs may have very different meanings for semi-nomadic pastoralists and fully settled cultivators or fishermen.

Conservation authorities are often puzzled and disappointed by the persistence of illegal harvesting of game in those areas where there have been noticeable improvements in social welfare, where compensation has been paid for the loss of access to the reserves, and where the animals can attract more income in the form of tourism receipts than the cash value of the meat. But as Barrett and Arcese (1995) argue, the poaching may not be strictly pecuniary in motive. The foraging for wild foodstuffs, and the hunting of large mammals retain considerable status in many parts of South Africa, particularly so at times of important ceremonies, such as rites of passage and marriage. Africans are prepared to take enormous risks to capture animals in protected areas, and will also travel great distances to do so. This lack of cultural understanding characterises and sours the relationships between many statutory bodies and their neighbours.

In the case of St Lucia, the NPB did not consult the inhabitants in the formulation of its plans for eco-tourism, and stated that it would not negotiate with the settlers until after they have left the Dukuduku forest. This stance is typical of government agencies when dealing with the residents of illegal settlements. In spite of this, Baskin (16/11/95) feels strongly that the conservation authorities must accept the responsibility of incorporating African people in the active management of ICDPs. The official authorities, he states, are the only organisations in KwaZulu-Natal with the resources and ability to provide villagers with the opportunity to take their own development in hand. In interviews with a number of NPB officers, there was an air of anxiety about the changes being foisted upon them by a government with commendable principles, but without full knowledge of the realities of conservation surrounded by a land-hungry and impoverished rural population. The understandable ambivalence felt by the NPB as a whole was manifest in the organisation's relationships with local communities in development initiatives, which were tentative and small in scale.

The whole principle of democratic participation through civil forums in South Africa has come under severe criticism (Boshoff, 1996). In a review of the progress of developmental forums, Boshoff argues that because of the range of interests existing within communities, and because of the lack of education and professional experience among members of these agencies, CBOs and NGOs have been inefficient in prioritising needs, allocating resources, and in keeping their constituencies to agreements already reached.

Evidence from programmes of community development undertaken in many other parts of the developing world indicates that consensus is particularly difficult to sustain in regions with a history of conflict such as that of KwaZulu-Natal, and that in these situations traditional power holders typically feel threatened by the notion of democratic decision-making (Gaventa, 1998). According to Boshoff (1996), grassroots organisations tend to be dominated by powerful local interest groups, and impoverished communities might be best (and ultimately more equitably) served if local government takes full control and operates in an accountable way while heeding the advice of CBOs and NGOs.

The role of the state in the development of eco-tourism has attracted considerable attention (Jenkins, 1994; de Kadt, 1990; Leslie, 1994; Preston-Whyte, 1995; Smith, 1994). Jenkins disapproves of state intervention in tourism planning and management, suggesting that the commercial ineptitude of state departments, and their ignorance of the special dynamics of tourism, make the incorporation of local interests all the more difficult and unlikely. By contrast, Leslie emphasises the need for government control. For Lea (1993), the tourism industry cannot be relied upon to regulate itself, nor to arrive at an appropriate code of practice. Drawing lessons for tourism from development studies as a whole, de Kadt suggests that only the state has sufficient authority to offer necessary incentives, impose negative sanctions, and ensure that companies fulfil their environmental and social responsibilities. Baumol (1991), as outlined, warns that governments may be the least bad (compared to firms, for example) of institutional hegemonies. Similarly, Wells and Brandon (1992), in their wide-ranging study of integrated conservation and development projects, insist that initiatives operating without full government support have the least chance of being integrated into the wider economy, and therefore the least chance of success. However, much support for eco-tourism in South Africa ignores the bald fact that none of the conservation areas under state protection are profitable. All depend on state subsidies (Grossman and Koch, 1995). By contrast, only those game reserves in private hands are financially successful and thus (financially) sustainable.

What is certain is that the successful implementation of the RDP requires a new organisational culture in both the public and private sector (Cook, 1995). However, the institutional framework reflects and is informed by wider political and cultural values. In KwaZulu-Natal, the cluster of organisations directly or indirectly involved in tourism development is a structural legacy of the apartheid era. The racial and class partiality of the institutional framework of tourism in the province has contributed enormously to its lack of legitimacy in the eyes of the black population. Although the need for a 'people-friendly' system is self-evident, changes so far have been minor and curricular rather than fundamental and ethical (Schutte, 1995). The prioritisation of apartheid over developmental goals contributed to the proliferation and survival of a considerable number of ineffective agencies in the province (Barnes, 11/11/98). Professionally trained and qualified officials are competent in procedures but ill-equipped to deal with the legacy of separate development.

Compounding these problems and, like public services elsewhere in Africa, state organisations in South Africa, including the South African Tourism Board (Cokayne, 1997) and the provincial administration of KwaZulu-Natal, have been prone to corrupt practices (Lodge, 1998). While much of this was inherited from the apartheid era, particularly in departments responsible for the homelands, reports of financial graft at every level of government feature regularly in the national and provincial press. Such publicity gives little incentive to African communities to trust official policies and procedures.

The tendency of grassroots organisations to be dominated by locally powerful interest groups has resulted in self-defeating participation traps. The only efficient and equitable way of promoting development may be for local authorities to take full control and operate in an accountable way within the guidelines of the RDP, while heeding the advice of community organisations and NGOs (Boshoff, 1996). The history of complete exclusion from developmental decision-making has provoked a full ideological swing to its polar opposite, the central participation of all interests through civil organisations. Any challenge to this new way of doing things in South Africa is interpreted as authoritarian or anti-democratic (Rubenstein, 1995). CBOs and other civil organisations were initially established during the 1980s, when they earned the respect of many Africans through their efforts to rectify the economic and social imbalances of apartheid. However, more recently, the apparent inability of these agencies to represent the poorest members of South African communities, who are also the least experienced in promoting their own development, has led some observers to doubt the fundamentals of development through participation (Rubenstein, 1995). We continue this discussion when we talk about democracy and disagreement in chapter 9.

The discussion earlier in this section of the political chaos and venality in KwaZulu-Natal's rural communities, questions the assumption that the state system is the best means of promoting socially responsible tourism. In the near absence of efficient and representative local government, alternatives must be found. At Phinda, the Southern Maputaland Development Forum fills that role. In Kosi Bay, CROP has guided the process of developing KEN, and of assessing the optimum choice of sustainable land-use. Several authors have emphasised the need for an appropriate institutional framework to facilitate the engagement of African people in their own development (Baskin, 1995; Cook, 1995; Picard and Garrity, 1995). They are convinced that only the planned evolution of new organisations, or the major reorientation of old ones, will enable rural African communities to take a proactive role, and experience the incentive to commit their time and energy to sustainable initiatives.

The relevant institutions and agencies that already exist in KwaZulu-Natal have their origins in white minority rule and the furtherance of apartheid. Important transformations in policy and practice are essential, if new, small-scale African enterprises are to receive the support they need. But public resources are clearly limited, and there is a gulf between what is needed and what can be afforded. The movement for community-led development is not new, but it picked up momentum during the 1980s, when professionals active in diverse sectors of the development enterprise were undergoing personal crises as a result of the early obsolescence of mainstream development theories. Old paradigms of development were seen to be failing the poor populations of the developing countries. Development theory was often preoccupied with the politics of blame, rather than with the production of more helpful models for the future. However, at that time Chambers (1983, 1986) detected an important shift in attitudes among active participants in most areas of development, and within associated institutions. Chambers argued that a 'new professionalism' is emerging, replacing the old biases and ways of doing things in development. 'Normal professionalism', the thinking, values, and methods within institutions, is stable and conservative, and faces the challenge of change only with the greatest reluctance. Although development theories come and go, normal professionalism survives (Chambers, 1986).

What is at stake is power (see chapter 7) which is defended by procedures, specialisation, and most importantly, by knowledge. Normal professionalism displays 'first' biases, which are urban, industrial, high technology, the quantifiable, and the interests of the rich. It is also sustained by education, hierarchy and career patterns. Individual careers are built on inward and upward movement within organisations, away from the periphery and the radical. Normal professionalism does not believe that poor people can know anything of consequence. In contrast, 'new professionalism' which is, Chambers concedes, dependent upon massive reversals, 'puts people first' (Chambers, 1986, p.1). The institutional reverses needed to gain a closer knowledge of the needs of the poorest are of several orders; the political, economic, ethical and strategic. However, new professionalism recognises that societies and their environments are complex, and that they interrelate in even more complex ways. Recognition of that complexity necessitates the development of innovative frameworks that can contain and address these seemingly incommensurate orders.

Clearly, the whole enterprise of developing sustainably, with the empowerment of local people uppermost in mind, is dependent upon effective management that will concentrate on the improvement of human capacities, and on the provision of appropriate opportunities to perform. The successful implementation of the RDP would require a new organisational culture, within which there should be a rapid and widespread growth in the number of African managers and other decision-makers who have been active in the liberation movement or in the NGO sector. The old-style system of top-down managerial directives is not conducive to the proactive participation of impoverished rural communities. Schutte (1995) advocates a 'paradigm shift' in the administration of South African development. He argues that although the need for a 'people-friendly' system is obvious to many observers, changes so far have been minor and curricular, rather than fundamental and ethical. Moreover, research carried out in 1991 revealed that 40 per cent of the administrative elite in South Africa continued to support the principles of apartheid (Schutte, 1995).

Professional training and qualifications have provided strata of officials who are competent in procedures, but are ill-equipped to deal with the legacy of separate development. The problems that have emerged within the new political context have been dealt with by responsive crisis management rather than by pre-emptive and integrated strategies.

Summary

The selection of 'situations' discussed in this book demonstrates that even within the relatively localised context of Maputaland, there exist variants of eco-tourism which share certain important features, but which contrast in equally significant ways in their outcomes. Factors that are common to all the case studies presented in chapter 3 include climate, environment, levels of education and skills, the historic and continuing subordination of women, unemployment levels, the disproportionate distribution of land, mistrust of the conservation authorities, and unrelenting poverty. The projects cited differ, though, in the degrees of participation experienced by local people, the scale of the initiatives, the levels of luxury offered to tourists, the nature of the host–tourist encounter, the types of benefits generated by tourism, and in the nature of the project partnerships with the indigenous communities.

At the heart of the problem of participation is the assumption that community members share interests, and are likely to pursue shared aspirations as a group. However, the evidence in chapter 3 strongly demonstrates the need for developmental models based on notions of self-interest and diversity within communities, rather than initiatives based on principles of community spirit and stability. Olson (1971) doubts that individuals will always work for the common economic good if they are likely to benefit without bearing the costs of community participation. Such co-operation occurs only in special circumstances, where there are strong negative or positive sanctions, or where the group itself is small. Assuming that there are always opportunity costs to participation, Olson's basic argument is that where the benefits of collective action cannot be ring-fenced by those who have actually invested in the cause, then those who will benefit in any case have no rational incentives to bear the cost of active involvement (Olson, 1971).

Public authorities and private companies continue to set the agenda for negotiations, and the existence of forums and civil organisations is no guarantee of a fair representation of the most disadvantaged in KwaZulu-Natal. In particular, the rights of women in Zulu society have changed little since the 1994 elections.

Much of the economic argument supporting the case for socially responsible tourism is speculative and based on extrapolations from meagre evidence. It actually is not yet known whether or not community-led initiatives will result in development that is sustainable in terms of jobs created, income and other benefits. The extent of economic leakage from these initiatives is yet to be determined, but, given the scale and type of projects discussed in this book, eco-tourism in general and the impact of Good Tourists (see chapter 8) in particular, will not solve the enormous problems of the impoverished population of Maputaland or the inequalities of the Durban beachfront populations. In Maputaland, difficulties in funding, and the near absence of low-interest credit available to rural communities, will continue to hinder their involvement in attempts to reconcile developmental imperatives with the widely recognised need to protect biodiversity.

The South African government has to promote new developmental policies while dealing with crises in the fields of health, crime, access to land, employment and other major problems inherited from the apartheid system. However, existing and reluctant institutions, irredentism, political volatility and the continuing power of important vested interests are all obstacles to administrative transformations. The RDP is strong on ideas, but weak on mechanisms. New legislation alone cannot overcome the chronic and deeply institutionalised exclusion of vulnerable and poor members of rural society in northern KwaZulu-Natal, and the smell of poverty dominates our memories of research visits to rural African settlements.

The feasibility of attempting to link conservation with development in the context of dire needs, a history of violence, political venality and an expanding population is laudable but questionable. Many of the infrastructural improvements in African villages have been funded by outside charitable sources, not from eco-tourism itself, and because of this we have found that there is little perception of a direct link between the protection of biodiversity and improvements in welfare. For community-based eco-tourism to become sustainable, it must be able to support itself, and despite the arguments of environmentalists in KwaZulu-Natal, implementing conservation policies requires power over the distribution of resources. It is a political issue. In the province, parks and other protected areas are painful reminders of apartheid's extreme injustices, and of the privilege of whites who enjoy looking at wildlife while Africans suffer from land starvation. Community-based eco-tourism has in reality achieved little in securing protected areas for the future, and divided communities have few grounds for optimism over plans of the conservation sector. Community participation has been elusive, costly and minimal, and may even prove to be a wasteful goal in itself. In the face of enthusiasm for eco-tourism in the province, we have found significant disparities between rhetoric and actual opportunities, and between the desirable and the affordable. Eco-tourism is essentially an ideal promoted by well-fed whites, who ignore the brutal facts of the political economy we have covered in this chapter.

What emerged in 1994 in South Africa was an othodoxy stipulating that poverty cannot be eradicated without the direct and democratic involvements of civil organisations working at grassroots level. It is incumbent upon accountable and representative CBOs and NGOs to elicit community participation in their own development. But, as we have already discussed, it is not entirely clear just how representative such agencies really are. While it is true that civil organisations have been at the forefront of the drive to democracy in the country, a substantial proportion of them have come to be led by local elites, have conflicting aims, employ corrupt individuals, and are unaware of the special needs of the weakest members of African communities. There is almost always a disjuncture between the rational, tidy, conceptual frameworks for development practice, and the multiplicity of changing realities and strategies for survival at the local level. The morally powerful models for change that were so eagerly supported by the ANC during its early years of power, may prove wholly irrelevant to the comprehensively excluded populations of KwaZulu-Natal. Eco-tourism is a prime example of a model for development which does not fit the severity of exclusion, commonplace in the province today, and urgently needs to be re-examined.

Acting as the central dynamic of developmental planning in South Africa during the early 1990s was the belief that democratisation and good governance would lead automatically to improved material conditions among the poor. The ANC in 1994 was confident that efficient public sector management, enabling legislation, accountability and transparency of state institutions, in tandem with the co-operation of civil society organisations, would successfully address the chronic problems caused by the disproportionate distribution of resources along lines of race. The ANC was also convinced that eco-tourism provided a strong redistributionary mechanism for developing sustainably and protecting the country's immense natural heritage. But eco-tourism has proved to be a disappointment on both accounts, and serves to question the principle that equity and distribution constitute the optimum means to poverty relief. The land reform programme, which is critical to eco-tourism development, has not satisfied the hunger for land in KwaZulu-Natal, and the trade-offs that have been made between equity and productivity have failed to stimulate the rural economy. The drive to rectify historical injustices has spread national resources too thinly, and it now appears that a 'betting on the strong' approach might, in the long term, hold more economic promise for impoverished Zulu communities. To those with more radical aspirations for growth from redistribution and the spread of democracy, the lessons of the recent past in South Africa might well appear unpalatable. But the history of development during the late twentieth century provides a convincing number of examples, where authoritarian governments have achieved levels of growth far in excess of many countries proud of their democratic foundations.

These issues are discussed in more depth in the coming chapters, but it can be said here that in KwaZulu-Natal, the intensity of the political strife and conflicts over resources has created an infertile ground for genuinely participatory eco-tourism. The proponents of eco-tourism initiatives have not convinced local people that they can deliver benefits on anything like the scale needed, and the shared history of racial exploitation restrains the development of trust. In the context of awful poverty, small-scale eco-tourism projects, with corresponding levels of still potential income, based in part on virtuous notions of sustainability and democracy, lack legitimacy in the eyes of those most in need. Without taking full account of the prevailing political economy, eco-tourism cannot be regarded as a convincing paradigm for future developmental practice.

Chapter 5

Toleration, truth, reconciliation and the 'tourist–host' relationship

Truth claims

Whenever we talked to South Africa's people about this inquiry into aspects of tourism development in South Africa, we always did so with some trepidation. We were and still are very aware that South Africans consider their country to be such a complex place that any attempt by people, even South Africans, to write something that gets close to the reality of South Africa, what is going on and what might be working or could work to bring about a desired future for South Africa, lays us and them open to the obvious charges of arrogance at worst and presumption at best. But we were equally aware that one of the motivations for our study was that we were unhappy with much of the academic tourism studies literature. Studies of tourism development had tended to shy away from understanding tourism inside an analysis of the political economy of everyday life for hosts and tourists. We could justify our work on the well-used basis that it takes outsiders, sometimes, to flirt with the meaning and significance of everyday life as they observe it, since their mistakes and simplifications are no more distorting, so the argument goes, than the barriers to truth that can be put up by being too close to the action.

However, in the South African case, it is difficult to sustain the notion of 'outsider' and 'insider'. South Africa has kept 'open house' since 1994 and has been inundated with friends and well-wishers. Many nation states and individuals, such as ourselves, have established or felt a deep identification with South Africa's development and future and feel real pleasure and pain at its successes and setbacks, often without knowing much at all about the country's past and present and having no vision of possible futures. South Africans we met and worked with on this project were critically sympathetic to our aims and objectives, encouraging us to stick with the task, yet pointing out, at times, that we seemed to be getting it all wrong.

The questions arise as to what images dominate the perception that people have of South Africa, how influential these images are in affecting South Africa's development through their determination of aspects of South Africa's external relationships, where the images come from and how true they might be. In particular, we are interested in how significant these bench-mark perceptions might be in affecting the contribution that the development of the international tourism industry can make to a good future for South Africans. Perhaps the strongest recent and current image of South Africa, apart from the interest in former President Mandela himself, is in the way in which South Africa is trying to repair the damage of the past, in order to create an agreement about a desired future. The South African government, since 1994, has set itself the task of deconstructing the old politics of apartheid, of outlawing the traditional non-politics of ethnic or tribal violence, and establishing a new politics of South African and, indeed, through ambitious diplomacy, a new Sub-Saharan African democracy. And these processes are vital to our understanding of the actual and potential role of tourism development to national progress in South Africa.

Our starting point to developing an understanding of this national project is to focus on the meaning and significance of the Truth and Reconciliation Commission, directed by Archbishop Tutu, and discuss the idea and practices of conciliation, reconciliation, politics itself, and toleration. This will lead us into a more detailed discussion of violence, in the next chapter, especially political violence in South Africa and into a consideration of the role of international tourism as a potential peace-keeper or as an agent of social development in post-conflict societies. We shall address the theme here of the 'ownership' of South Africa's past and future through an extended discussion of the politics of toleration and obligation, and the ways in which the tourist or visitor 'learns' about a host society. The 'host society', in our case, a particular concern for KwaZulu-Natal, is a vague enough construct, but people who would say that they are in the presence of 'guests' know that one category of guest is the tourist. More interesting than the host–guest relationship, in any case, is the nature of the host society and its political, economic, social and cultural forms and dynamics and how this shapes the international tourist experience. We clearly cannot contextualise our work on tourism through a detailed account of the political economy of KwaZulu-Natal (the sketch in the previous chapter illustrates the scale of the task rather than solving it) but reference will be made to the need to recognise that we should be analysing the personal and social position of the tourist within the intellectual construct of a complex system, inside of which international tourism activity is one of the complex process elements, defining and being redefined.

Samuel Huntington's influential book, *The Clash of Civilisations and the Remaking of the World Order* sums up South Africa in a single paragraph that is notable for its facility to get things just about wrong on every count:

South Africa's peaceful and negotiated transition from apartheid, its industrial strength, its higher level of economic development compared to other African countries, its military capability, its natural resources, and its sophisticated black and white political leadership all mark South Africa as clearly the leader of Southern Africa, probably the leader of English Africa, and possibly the leader of all sub-Saharan Africa [Huntington, 1996, p.136].

Visitors to South Africa can be verbally accosted by South Africans who want to tell them all the latest stories (that, incidentally, may be stories about events that happened many years ago or stories that form the main narrative of an imagined past) about violence and its victims, especially political violence and violence associated with theft. They will also point out how poor people are, some people living in absolute poverty and others suffering from relative poverty brought about by the volatile nature and general weakness of the rand. They will cruelly caricature the army as populated by unreconstructed thugs of low intelligence, and give copious examples of the wasting of South Africa's natural resources. Levels of corruption in politics and the latest scandals are part and parcel of gossip in the University common rooms, shebeens and on the beachfronts of Durban and Cape Town. This country that Huntington claims to be a 'leader' of nations is being deserted by a white economic elite who fear for their personal safety and for their wealth and future earning power, and by middle-class people, white and black, who claim to see no future in South Africa for themselves, and, in particular, for their children. And poor people who live in the townships, or on the edges of the cities and towns, and on the fringes of the roads leading to the tourist attractions, such as the game parks, will say that they are already impatient for the political reforms that actively address, and where necessary, redress inequities of land and property ownership. This is their reasonable expectation, and the government's promise, for the 'new democracy'.

These are elements in the story that the visitor or tourist might be told, as we have been told during our visits since 1994. And the overall 'message' we received from discussion, often in conversation following interviewing or observing, was that things are getting worse rather than better (strong version), or things were not getting any better, or not getting better fast enough (weak version). The South African image of their nation, as we experienced it, is dominated by a special cocktail of fears and hopes, the latter always laced with pessimism.

Internal affairs

These impressions do not, of course, amount to a paradigm, to a way of mapping our understanding that may prove to be indispensable. Indeed, we may deny the need for any such macro-intellectual guide and simply go by what we take to be the facts of the situation and only consider the detail of life as we observe it without generalisation or extrapolation. However, there are always images, or assumptions, together with the usual mixed bag of bias and prejudices, that qualify our acceptance of and the significance we attach to the 'facts' and to the merits of each 'case'; including the examples of tourism development we outlined in chapter 1. For us, the politics of South Africa today is bound up with two interrelated and mutually dependent dynamics, one chosen, the other not. The latter is the impact and the significance of world economic forces and organisations on the South African economy and the economic welfare of its people. This exogenous dynamic will be discussed in chapter 10. The former is the ambition and struggle to establish a politically reconstructed nation state, and aspects of this endogenous dynamic and its implications for tourism are discussed below.

The relationships between the internal and external dynamic is, of course, extremely difficult to specify and the conceptualisation itself into 'internal' and 'external', masks an array of theoretical and policy-orientated issues. This dynamic can be thought of as a complex system (Dicken, 1998) or a set of complex processes for which there is no single theory. Complex processes, such as the dynamic between attempts at community power-building in tourism destinations, and movements in the relative purchasing power of the local currency because of the anticipatory actions of international currency speculators, suggest an interrelationship, interaction and an interconnectivity of the elements within a system, and between a system and its environment, over time. A decision or action by one element will affect all other related elements. This effect will not have equal or uniform impact but will vary with the status or degree of potential influence of each related element at that time. And the status of an element will be determined by its own history, organisation and processes. Moreover, the complex system is 'complex' partly because it is in constant transformation brought about by the dynamic of each element, through adaptation or learning, and its impact on the adoption and learning of other elements, who may, too, have their own internal dynamic.

The nature of complex systems and processes are in themselves a growing field of study by natural and physical scientists as well as social scientists (Hirshleifer, 1987). But the main point here is that if we are concerned with the possibilities of political, social, economic and cultural shifts, both brought about by current tourism activity and by the planning activities of individuals, communities, organisations and government seeking to continually re-create the tourism industry, and brought about by the unintended consequences of current or planned activity outside the tourism industry but affecting it, then we should recognise that our descriptions and analyses will be less than ideal (Sher, 1997).

We can begin, though, to recognise the need for analytical sophistication through getting beyond simplistic conceptualisations of the main agents or elements in a system. This would begin to address properly the issue of complexity. For example, when we examine individual elements, we could get beyond the assumption that people exist as persons with assumed competence, to considering people in terms of what they actually do. The officers of the KwaZulu-Natal Nature Conservation Service (KZNNCS) who we talked to about the relationship between a nature reserve and the needs of people living on the edge of the reserve, focused on the 'capacity' of local peoples to change their way of life, of what locals might be able to do to change their own behaviour or to be educated about their long-term interests (in plant and animal conservation) by the Service's officers. The conceptualisation of the individual should be rooted in what they do rather than in what they might do. Similarly, organisations, such as firms or regional planning authorities tend still to be studied in relation to a single, predictable outcome, such as contribution to increasing tourism revenues, and then evaluated against a single contested criterion such as 'best practice'.

A more explicit recognition of theories or models of complex processes would emphasise that organisational behaviour can lead to multiple outcomes, intended and unintended, with no single outcome being 'the' outcome in terms of undisputed prime significance. How, for example, the KwaZulu-Natal Tourism Authority develops as an organisation, could reflect this real world of influence and action through the evolution of the Authority and the ways in which it is eventually structured: its levels of hierarchy and the nature of the relations between those levels; relationships between 'core' activities and its main stakeholders; and the very way in which work is done within the Authority – its organisational culture. The Authority's work already includes some impressive studies of the tourism market and how that might be modelled in terms of how it is (Seymour, 1999) rather than presuming that the tourism market operates according to textbook models of allocative efficiency, via equilibrium between suppliers and purchasers. Modelling the actual tourism market conditions and feeding this data into its policy advising and co-ordinating functions, will prove to be a vital service to tourism development in KwaZulu-Natal. We shall discuss later (chapter 9) the problems of aggregation from the individual to the community in terms of the logic of political or community action, but the point that needs to made here is that when people talked with us about the social and political system we label 'KwaZulu-Natal' and when we recount our work in the region to our friends and colleagues in the UK, there is a tendency to describe this regional social system in terms of aggregate behaviour, the latter based on assumptions about individual behaviour that may not hold up empirically.

Theories of complex systems, including social systems, imply models based on observable behaviours with the higher or community-level phenomena allowed to emerge, rather than being specified *a priori*. In a nutshell, we need to achieve explicit models of the relationships between individuals and groups, in order to begin to understand the dynamics of social change. Influential tourism bodies also need to ensure that their planning for change is constrained by a theoretical realism of individual-community aggregation difficulties. How the new tourism bodies, such as the KwaZulu-Natal Tourism Authority, and the old organisations with new agendas, such as the former Natal Parks Board, now KZNNCS, acquire appropriate knowledge, and apply this knowledge within a social system where intrapersonal and interpersonal processes and structures co-evolve and feed-back into the planning and decision-making processes, is a major challenge to these organisations and to the study of such organisational learning (Allen, 2003).

More generally, one of the excitements of studying tourism development within a tacit recognition of theoretical as well as practical difficulties is that familiar social scientific puzzles can be aired in relatively new and undeniably important contexts, where, in this case, the actions of the tourism bodies are major determinants of present and future welfare for poor communities of people in KwaZulu-Natal. This latter claim raises the question of access to knowledge – to really useful knowledge.

We live in a historical context that presents a knowledge paradox: there is so much knowledge around – and the stock of potentially useful knowledge continues to grow in accessibility and volume – yet the ability of any single agent or agenda to prevail in applying this knowledge to meet their own needs is decreasing or static (Preston-Whyte, 1995). The educational and public relations work of the tourism companies and bodies in South Africa will inevitably lead to new asymmetries of power embedded in the elements of tourism's complex system. In economics, the concepts of information asymmetries, information externalities and informational inequalities are well known (Williamson and Masten, 1999). There is also a growing body of thinking that connects knowledge with concepts of uncertainty (Allen, 1997). The choices that we make are taken within bounded certainty, or with often unknown degrees of uncertainty (when we know the level of uncertainty, we are in the risk business). Uncertainty and information asymmetry are part of the equation of power relationships and we shall focus on power and the dimensions of power and tourism and crime, as a special case of power relations, in chapters 7 and 8. They define, for example, who or what are assumed to be experts or what is expert opinion in a given context. The KwaZulu-Natal Nature Conservation Service and its employees are world-renowned for their expertise in plant and animal conservation but not, as yet, for their community development work in attempting to secure and promote the interests of local people, tourists as well as animals and plants. Emerging networks of knowledge production and learning are creating new patterns of political and economic power in KwaZulu-Natal.

Who or what controls information about the real and potential direction and degree of change embedded in the tourism industry in KwaZulu-Natal proved very difficult to assess. Asymmetries in knowledge may arise from intentional acts by those who benefit from possessing more knowledge than others and it would be unwise to look to altruism as a prime principle, as yet, for the holding and withholding of knowledge among the various tourism stakeholders. A long and distinguished history of conservation activity and associated organis-ational learning is unlikely to be gifted to other organisations or communities. Others will have to duplicate this knowledge or find substitutes for it or attempt to get rid of the activity on which the knowledge is based if they are to turn the asymmetry around. Governments, for example, cannot assume that the collective interest of a region, or the common good, will be best served by the 'free' flow of information and it remains a main function of the KwaZulu-Natal Tourism Authority to give a gentle nudge to stimulate this flow of know-ledge around companies, organisations and communities with a stake in the tourism industry. Informal property rights controlling the stock and flow of information will have to be dealt with first and the attempts (in April 1998) to constitute an Advisory Board for the Authority were bedevilled in part by this issue. Really useful tourism industry research and development knowledge is not a public good.

In any case, the ability to absorb and make use of new information is limited by many different elements. When talking with people in the province, they often said, discussing those they perceived to be influential over them, that such people or organisations simply 'didn't want to know', nor did they listen to or empathise with their views. Political, economic and social advantages are conferred inside complex systems because of variation in the capacity and willingness of the elements to generate, distribute or use knowledge. The earlier distinction between 'internal' and 'external' sets of elements acting through complex processes creating complex systems suggests that one of the meanings and significance of globalisation theories (Mishra, 1999) is the impact of tech-nological capacity and the nature and growth of technological change in affecting stocks and flows and inequities in knowledge. Satour has little control over the managerial decisions of those large travel and tourism companies whose business it is, if they choose it to be, to supply South Africa with the bulk of its international tourists. Nor can Satour know – and thereby potentially influence if need be – the basis on which company decisions are taken about where to sustain, introduce or shut down business.

Reconciling the past

Where, in any case, are the roots of the international tourist demand for a South African experience to be found and what do we, as outsiders, (tourist-researchers) witness when we visit South Africa, or what do South Africans tend to commonly say when they talk about their country? Ignatieff (1998, p.168) asks:

> What does it mean for a nation to come to terms with its past? Do nations have psyches the way individuals do? Can a nation's past make a people ill as we know repressed memories sometimes make individuals ill? Conversely, can a nation or contending parts of it be reconciled to its past as individuals can, by replacing myths with fact and lies with truth? Can nations 'come awake' from the nightmare of their past, as Joyce believed an individual could?

The answers are not at all clear but we often talk about whether a community, such as a nation state, has the 'political will' to address such questions, which means that we must begin with a brief sketch of the nature of politics, as opposed to violence, as a means to achieving and sustaining social order. We know, from Bernard Crick (1969), a follower of Aristotle on such fundamentals, that politics exists because organised states, which define themselves as the aggregate of different tribes, religions, interest groups and traditions, accept the complexity of the social structure and the diversity of interests, and seek a political resolution to the problem of governing or maintaining order. Politics in South Africa, as seen through the microcosm of the establishment and workings of the Truth and Reconciliation Commission, is, in a major way, defined by the attempt to find specific, effective, pragmatic and dynamic solutions to what will no doubt prove to be long-standing problems of conciliation and toleration and reasonable expectations of the possibilities of political reform and reconstruction. Crick (1969, p.160) neatly and powerfully sums up the challenge:

> Conciliation is better than violence – but it is not always possible; diversity is better than unity – but it does not always exist. But both are always desirable. Perhaps it all comes down to the fact that there are two great enemies of politics: indifference to human suffering and the passionate quest for certainty in matters that are essentially political.

In South Africa, the existence and ways of working of the Truth and Reconciliation Commission demonstrate the active rejection of indifference to human suffering, so in Crick's terms, politics is possible. But a deep and widespread condemnation of the quality of political life, seen through the daily media accounts of political corruption, for example, and the current economic disenfranchisement of the population (for businesses, seen through the lack of economic confidence in the government's ability to control the influence of world economic forces and organisations on the pace, direction and distributional effects of economic development; and experienced, directly, by all, through failure to establish, quickly, land reforms and acceptable quality public systems of housing, education and health), underwrites the use of violence rather than politics to comment on and create changes in the social structure and in social organisations. This does not mean that violence as a means to establish order is ruled out – for some peoples, it may be a form of ideal conduct, an absolute ideal or something simply worth doing to express feeling or create changed circumstances. But the morality of political life today in South Africa, usually referred to as the 'new' politics, is that a context is in the process of being established within which legitimate non-violent means for settling disputes can be defined and implemented. And in this fundamental development process, which will take some time, violence, including state violence, should be ruled out. Hence, one of the major meanings and a main significance of the creation and implementation of a Truth and Reconciliation Commission is the signifying of a return to the first principles of democratic politics, to establishing the common interest in sustaining the political means to make public decisions and in defining the boundaries of toleration (Mendus, 1988).

The Truth Commission toured the country attempting to create a new political agenda and process through publicly offering the opportunity for the country to 'work through' its past. The chance exists and has been taken by both victims and perpetrators to 'work out' their experiences of apartheid. Choosing truth, for the guilty, through disclosure of what crimes against humanity were known to them and what they actually did themselves that they now regret and apologise for, means choosing amnesty and pardon and the avoidance of judgement. It is not at all clear, as the Commission itself knew full well (Shapiro and Jung, 1996) that the individual public virtues of truth, justice and reconciliation are linked holistically such that achieving one leads to the achievement of the others, and failure to achieve one leads to failure to achieve the others. Ignatieff (1998, p.170) reminds us of the old African proverb which cautions that the truth is good but is not always good to say, and he goes on to quote Archbishop Desmond Tutu's aims for the Truth Commission: 'The promotion of national unity and reconciliation ... and the healing of a traumatised, divided, wounded, polarised people.'

Ignatieff gently attacks Tutu's words on the basis of the assumptions that appear to be made, such as a nation only having one psyche, not many; that there is one certain truth, not an array of possible truths, each needing to be contested; and that the emergence and acceptance of a certain truth has therapeutic or healing powers, leading to reconciliation of deep difference. But there is a more fundamental assumption behind the establishment of the Commission, as we have hinted, that overrides Ignatieff's critique, which is that the Commission exerts the moral supremacy of politics. Within politics, as Crick (1969) argues, coercion as an instrument of political power needs justification but conciliation justifies itself if it works. 'For it is, after all, too hard (indeed perverse) to respect the morality and wisdom of any who, when politics is possible, refuse to act politically' (Crick, 1969, p.31).

Tourist tales

This is the challenge to South Africa, or the South African project, which the international tourist visiting South Africa is party to and that the internal tourist must learn, cannot forget or leave behind them. There are two main ways in which this project is mediated between international tourists and hosts, or between strangers: the first is through the tourist experience itself and the second is through television. We shall focus on the first of these here and comment on the influence of the latter in the next chapter, in setting and framing the tourist perception of South Africa. We begin a short series of selective descriptive accounts of travelling to KwaZulu-Natal, South Africa, from the South West of England, and later tell and develop another tourist's tale, from Kosi Bay.

> Some twenty kilometres west of Durban, just off the main Pietermaritzburg road, and en route to a major tourist attraction, the Valley of a Thousand Hills, the twisty but well maintained road has a number of lay-bys for people to pull off the road and enjoy the view across the hills and back towards Durban and the Indian Ocean. The lay-bys have trees planted or preserved, to provide shade, and have concrete tables and seats for picnics or for simply sitting and absorbing the magnificent scenery. Hidden from view and living in or near to the lay-by, are families who, as soon as a car stops and international tourists get out, appear with artefacts to sell, or simply sell themselves as willing subjects for the tourist's cameras. The artefacts sell for only a few rand and there is no set fee, or necessary fee, for appearing in snapshots. For such families, alternative ways of getting money are limited so prices for the beads and wooden animals are low, photographic services are cheap.

Speeding onwards north from Durban up the coast to Shakaland, a well-known Zulu theme park, the car is flagged down by two black policemen using a radar gun. They thank us for stopping, show us the metered reading that is well in excess of the speed limit, and ask for personal details. Seeing that one of us has three points logged on his British driving licence, the conversation turns into a consideration of the relative merits of points, fines, community service, compulsory education programmes and so on, for dealing with road traffic offenders. We are thanked for our help, told to behave ourselves in the future, and asked politely to be on our way.

A black American family, man, woman and teenage daughter, are also visiting this popular theme park some 200 kilometres north of Durban. They are staying at a hotel in Durban and have hired a middle-aged white male guide, via the hotel, to 'interpret' their day out for them. This interpretation includes carrying their copious and heavy camera equipment and talking in Zulu to the Zulus (who speak perfect English) who work at the theme park in order to get the camera shots the Americans desire.

On our return to Durban, heading eventually back west to the Drakensberg mountains, the unofficial beach-guard at one of the beaches at North Beach, Durban, makes a point of looking out for us when we call in for a brief swim and guarantees to protect our car from theft. There is no necessary fee. She is part of a co-operative who dress to look like City officials but have no official authority at all. People could simply park and ignore the car parking and protection service.

At our hotel in the Drakensberg mountains, a newly trained male Zulu waiter decides that it would save time for him and us and the kitchen dish-washing staff if he brings our breakfast of porridge, bacon and toast and marmalade all together on the same plate. We point out that this is not the way we would prefer our breakfast and the white middle-aged Afrikaans couple we share a table with say we should make an angry complaint about him to the manager. We don't like to do this so we don't complain, but we tell the waiter how we would have preferred to have had our breakfast served.

Each of these situations made demands on our conscience and the feeling of unequal power relations (a theme we will return to in chapter 7) rarely left us. Television, for many visitors and tourists, introduces and may prepare people for visits to destinations where the tourist is undeniably more powerful, politically, economically and socially, than they are in their usual environment. These new-found riches for, in particular, the first-time tourist to Sub-Saharan Africa, and the way in which this novel power base gets worked out in terms of actual behaviour, can be understood within the framework of the political and moral relations between the tourist and local people. There is an interactive and complex relationship here between the ways in which, prior to a visit, television serves to set the moral agenda between strangers that then is reassessed (and confirmed, denied or adapted) when the tourist and stranger come face to face. A moral relationship only exists, as it did for us, when either being directly involved with or witness to interactions between hosts and guests, when those involved understand themselves to be potentially (at least) under obligation to those less powerful than themselves.

This possibility may make tourism a very unusual form of consumption behaviour. We may not be able to afford to be empathetic to all those people we meet on a normal round of consumption in the low-paid retail industries at home and certainly there is not a usual expectation that on returning from a shopping expedition in our neighbourhood, town or city, we have to emotionally debrief. Western capitalism may not engender the same level of historic guilt as European imperialism in Africa. The Good Tourist, as we shall develop further in chapter 9, may be trapped by history and television inside what Ignatieff calls, 'a descending order of moral impingement' (1998, p.14). This order puts the indeterminate stranger last, the claims of kith and kin first, and neighbours, friends, co-workers and so on somewhere in the middle. We know, from the abusive letters that appear in the British press following any suggestion of an increase in the real value of the British government's overseas aid budget, that the propensity to 'aid' the stranger closer to home can be part and parcel of a strong nationalistic ideology. But it may be that South Africa now has a special place within Ignatieff's insightful characterisation of the moral confusion that arises from what he calls the 'supposed natural outflow of charitable empathy overseas' (1998, p.15).

Ignatieff is discussing the response in the North to the terrible tragedies of famine and other disasters in the South but the argument can be extrapolated to add meaning to our understanding of the Good Tourist in South Africa. The tentative argument here is that the special place of South Africa within the 'long-standing conflict between the conscience of ethical universalism and the demands of a private property system' (Ignatieff, 1998, p.15), arises from the South Africa project. This project is to create a new politics using the symbolic and substantive importance of the Truth and Reconciliation Commission as the main reform instrument directly under the control of the country. This may alter the obligation and compassion stakes, ensuring that, at least within the British moral universe, South Africa sits squarely, for the time being at least, within the ranks of the deserving rather than undeserving nations. This is why it may come as a surprise to the British first-time tourist to South Africa, in particular, to be faced with rather more despair and pessimism than expected.

Mediating human relations

How, then, is the tourist to make sense of the rationality and emotion of obligation, toleration, guilt and empathy and privilege? What tourism does, as does television, is to present political and economic relations as human relations. The internalisation of the experience and icons of the tourist in South Africa, the 'charge', thrill or glow South Africa may create for the tourist, need not necessarily displace the capacity for reflection and analysis. The impact of thousands of hours of television viewing for the average adult international tourist will include possibly hundreds of hours of what could either directly or indirectly be called development issues, and the influence of this exposure on political and moral consciousness may be considerable for many people. And we know that people's economic conscience is far more complex than classic economic theory would have had us believe (Titmus, 1970; Taylor-Gooby, 1998). People in England who would never buy a copy of the 'Big Issue' from a street vendor, or under no circumstances ever give to someone they see begging on the streets, will contract to support a worker's co-operative in Rwanda if Oxfam ask them to and will sponsor a street child in Delhi if Save the Children Fund set the deal up for them. We have earlier used the traditional academic tourism studies language and constructs of 'hosts' and 'guests' but this serves to create an oversimplification of 'them' and 'us'. It is quite clear, from what some people do, that they feel closer bonds to people they have never met or have no possibility of getting to know, than they do to people in their own neighbourhood, or from their own social class.

What might be particular about the South African tourist experience, at least for the British, is an empathy towards a country that has witnessed and been internationally vilified for crimes against humanity. The British tourist need not know that the British invented and built the world's first concentration camp at Aliwal North, in order to contain Boer women and children; nor may they have seen Stanley Baker earn the cinematic Victoria Cross at Rorke's Drift; nor have travelled with the British dockyard workers and their families who went overland to Durban from Plymouth some 60 years ago to help repair the British ships that were damaged by German U-boats. We are not qualified to examine these experiences and to comment on what they tell us about the particularities of the heritage-tourism industry in South Africa. But the distinguished South African historian, Jeff Guy, in a paper titled 'Battling with Banality: Tourism, Historians, and the killing fields of Zululand' (Guy, 1998, p.6), writes:

> Thus in the case of the Zulu war, explanations why thousands of armed men
> from Britain and the South African colonies marched into foreign territory,
> looted cattle, burnt homesteads and killed their occupants, are unnecessary.

The fact that an independent African kingdom was destroyed with consequences that can be discerned to this day can be ignored. That this was
done with deceit and racist brutality can be brushed aside. British soldiers
killed and were killed for no other reason than because they were there. As
a result, a century later, the glamour and the tragedy, adventures in Africa,
approach can be revived without qualms. And associated with this is the
perception that these scenes of past slaughter have the potential to make
money: to sell books, to attract visitors, overseas tourists in particular, and
create financial opportunities for those well placed in the tourist industry
and its adjuncts.

A full page profile of the South African novelist, Nobel Prize and Booker Prize
winner, Nadine Gordimer, on 1 February, 1998 in the *Observer* 'Review', one
of Britain's most respected newspapers, is headed 'The new South Africa. It
was worth fighting for – but does it make great novels?' We could ask, rather,
does it make for great holidays and does international tourism in particular,
do anything at all to meet the main political challenges facing South Africa?
One response would be to say that international tourism will not of itself solve
the resource scarcity currently paralysing the reform of schools and the drive
towards education for all and universal literacy, nor will tourist expenditures
increase the supply of effective housing and meet the universal need for decent
shelter. But it is quite clear to us that abject poverty should not be conceptualised and marketed as a product by the tourism industry. The rise of so-called
political tourism (it is nothing of the sort) where, for example, one South
African-owned tourist company organises tours to Soweto, should have no
significant role in the drive towards reco-tourism – trade that directly promotes
reconstruction.

Action for Southern Africa (ACTSA), the successor to the Anti-Apartheid
Movement, has urged Britain's tour operators to play a more constructive role
in South Africa. ACTSA's demonstrations at the World Travel Market at London's
Earls Court on 13 January 1998 sought to encourage travel companies that
operate in the country to ensure that more of the cash spent by the 250,000
tourists who visited South Africa in 1995 (ACTSA's figure) remains in South
Africa. ACTSA commissioned a survey of holidaymakers to South Africa which
showed that more than 75 per cent of tourists wanted more information from
the tour operators on how their holidays affect residents of the new South
Africa. More than 30 per cent of those questioned said they would be
prepared to pay up to 10 per cent more for their holidays if they knew this
would help resident South Africans. Ben Jackson, a director of ACTSA, is
reported as saying (*Guardian*, 13 January 1998) that 'More and more people
today are using their powers as consumers to press big business to give poor
people a chance. This is a clear message from the British consumers to the

travel industry that they should support this new vision of tourism and support the new South Africa.'

One reason why ACTSA was able to report such enthusiasm from British tourists to understand and influence the level and direction of their holiday expenditure may well be to do with the respect that accrues to a country that embarks on a public project to learn the terrible truth of its past. Any such respect, of course, has to be an emotional response rather than a cognitive response to the project since, yet again, there are important informational difficulties in analysing the 'truth' (even in typing the word, according to Antjie Krog, one of South Africa's leading poets – *Guardian*, 18 January 1998). People are now being encouraged to visit a country because of its moral attraction. We, therefore, can usefully begin to extend our analysis of the reality of tourism development as a complex system through calling on some fundamental moral questions and principles, and it is to two of these that we now turn (Krog, 1999).

The attraction of Kosi Bay

When we visited one of the visitor lodges in the Kosi Bay area, we were struck by the boyish and infectious enthusiasm of the owner and his family, staff and friends for the experience that the Lodge offered: access to a beautiful natural environment composed of a unique configuration of land, sea, lakes, people, forest, plants and wildlife. The Lodge was run on what seemed to be a vibrant mixture of entrepreneurship and stewardship, making money through opening and thereby preserving and popularising the locality through the owner's cele- bration of the facility. One possible excursion from the main lodge is to visit the mouth of the Kosi River by four-wheel drive truck. This involves a journey of some 15km, taking one and a half hours, through tribal lands where there are scatterings of people living and a few villages, each with a small school and shop. En route, local people wave to us on the truck and, because of the terrain, which restricts the speed of the vehicle, can talk to us and, potentially, climb on board the truck as we travel through to the sea. Young children, in parti- cular, chase after the truck and would climb on if the driver allowed them to. He repels any who try with multi-lingual expletives and a stick he always carries.

The driver is a relative of the owner of the Lodge and another good friend of the owner is also on board, together with six international tourists, including ourselves. Two of the other tourists are from England, a father and son travelling together, 'doing' Southern Africa, and the other two are Belgian medics, taking a vacation from their work with a German NGO supporting a hospital in Nelspruit. Much of the conversation is led by the friend of the owner and is focussed on his views, illustrated by jokes, about the local people, in particular, their sexual and criminal habits. When we return to the Lodge, we talk to the other tourists and find that they were equally as offended by the derogatory comments about local peoples made by the owner's friend, but, like us, they said nothing to him nor did anything to show their displeasure. Given the context, slowly bouncing through wonderful countryside en route to a snorkelling expedition in the mouth of the Kosi River, known locally as the 'aquarium' because of the clarity of the water and ease with which one can see and approach the fish, and feeling privileged to be the paying guests of our host, the owner and his family and friends, it seemed inappropriate to change the tone of the day. We all operated a tacit policy of non-interference and we left the situation alone – we did not reach nor breach the limits of toleration.

Toleration has to exist on two fronts, a legal front and a social front, in order to guarantee a tolerant community (Scarman, 1981). The law can and should define actions that we should repress because they do not deserve our toleration, and irrespective of the law, we should have values and attitudes that preclude toleration to certain behaviours. The main pragmatic (historical and linguistic) forms of toleration (and intolerance) have been sexual, racial, religious and political and certainly three of these were potentially present on the Kosi Bay river-mouth journey. Historically, toleration has meant to permit by law but not to endorse or encourage. Nonetheless, it is clearly the case that as well as 'live and let live', a toleration of diversity, there is a position that actively welcomes and celebrates difference. Within this theme of diversity sits uncomfortably, as we shall see, a form of dogmatism. For the justification of intolerance is through an appeal to the truth, the right way to behave. Toleration fuels the assertion that there is a correct way to live and nothing is to be gained by allowing people to live in a manner that is deeply misguided or morally wrong. Toleration, too, can be more than just about non-interference or leaving alone and can involve the acceptance or active support of the repression of wrong behaviour. This leads us, later, to discussing the paradox of toleration.

Linguistically, we usually distinguish dislike from disapproval. Dislikes do not need toleration and indeed one can like someone and still disapprove of their beliefs or actions. There can, of course, be a fine line between the two but, like rights, it is easy to trivialise the concept of toleration if we attach it to matters of minor importance. The circumstances for toleration require first, diversity and second, that the nature of the diversity leads to disapproval or, more strongly, to disgust. The undesirable or the undesired are the prime candidates for both toleration and intolerance. Toleration is more than simply allowing something to exist (freedom to) or to allow legally (licence by law) or to ignore (through indifference). If we speak of liberty or freedom, there is no criticism implied. However, toleration means criticism since it has the property of disapproval or disgust. Otherwise, toleration is not needed.

Moreover, to distinguish toleration from indifference, we need to add that the tolerant person must be in a position to influence behaviour, and it may or may not have been the case that we could have changed our fellow traveller's thoughts of the sexual habits of the Tsonga people of Kosi Bay. For example, we can't be tolerant of someone getting too fat if this is linked to an incurable medical condition but we can be tolerant, if we choose, of someone who eats too much and gets fat (where we disapprove of fatness). We are tolerant when we could successfully interfere with, influence or stop a behaviour but choose not to, but the point we are making here alongside this formal analysis of the concept of toleration is that, acting on the construct is, in part, situationally determined, as it was for us on the truck journey.

The ideological or intellectual roots of toleration, as Susan Mendus (1988) shows, are embedded in liberalism. When we begin to compose questions to do with the nature of liberalism, what is its justification and what are its proper limits, the word 'liberalism' can be replaced by the word toleration. It is part of the liberal tradition since liberals often explain, describe and defend their position as the arch promoters of liberty and toleration. This is why the perception and experience of toleration is so important in the South African political project. Securing agreement about the limits of toleration is one of the litmus tests for a mature democracy. Toleration may be a necessary condition for the promotion of freedom as well as being more than simply part of the circumstances of freedom. A pluralistic community requires toleration because it recognises that not all values have their citizen's approval and that this disapproval cannot necessarily be reconciled harmoniously.

The source of much unhappiness in liberal states is caused by the need to be tolerant, for those of us who find it distinctly uncomfortable allowing activities we disapprove of to continue. If all conflict could be eliminated with nothing of value lost then we would be in a single, utopian state where equality did not conflict with liberty, nor justice with mercy. From the point of view of the individual, pluralism claims that no person monopolises all virtues; hence, perhaps, our reluctance to complain to our fellow passenger on the Kosi Bay truck ride, about his comments and gestures. Indeed, some virtues may displace others (as does equality and liberty in the liberal state) because they are incompatible. It may be that creativity is incompatible with patience, yet both are virtues and value is lost if either is displaced or reduced. We tolerate the behaviour of others because we recognise that it is only, perhaps, because of the behaviours of which we disapprove that we have the virtues or good qualities. In the Kosi Bay situation, we knew that our friend from the Transvaal had been a tireless worker and propagandist for the need to maintain the environmental stability of the local environment. If the personal limitations did not exist, neither might these virtues.

Within bureaucracies the need for toleration is often towards people or structures that govern our behaviour and, as we have said, we felt we were the guests of a benevolent host when staying at the Lodge (his home was on site). Most frequently, proper thoughtfulness or sensitivity in some circumstances can seem like (and be) infuriating indecision, prevarication or plain fence sitting or deviousness. The decision-making process needs to be transparent. The workings and principles of the institution need to be well known and available for scrutiny and, in our visit to the Lodge, they were. The Lodge culture was masculine, geared up to have fun, do good works and make money. This culture should not and was not to be misunderstood through mystification, mythology or the 'noble lie'. This, again, is a basic principle of liberalism, since we need accurate information in order to come to a position of intolerance and, certainly, we need the truth to justify action against the potentially offending behaviour.

Toleration, as it is emerging in this analysis, is to do with leaving others alone at its weakest, and certainly with refraining from persecuting them (unlike in totalitarian states). In a country desperately seeking democracy, and within the micro-liberalism of the Nissan truck, toleration is limited by consideration of the truth (Williams, 2002). We need to decide whether people or their beliefs, practices or behaviours are morally wrong. If they are morally wrong, we can be reasonably intolerant. Where they are morally right and alterable and we disapprove, we need to be tolerant. For the tourist or stranger, where does the confidence come from to judge a situation in such terms? Racial discrimination need not be tolerated. It is morally wrong to disapprove of qualities that are not freely chosen and unalterable. People are not responsible, as individuals, for the colour of their skin and can't alter it. Racial discrimination is wrong and nothing (virtuous) is lost if it disappears.

Why then should we ever tolerate that which we disapprove of, where we claim that someone or some action or belief is morally wrong? The claim of moral correctness can only be made if all rational people could agree with the claim – it has universal validity being the claim of a rational agent. One problem, as we have seen in this case, is that if we get rid of some 'bads' we simultaneously get rid of the 'goods' (racism goes but so does conservationism). The strongest form of disapproval, where things become intolerable, leads to things being unbearable. Something that is unbearable is to be stopped. But we know that within liberalism, diversity must, at least, be accepted and normally celebrated. We need some mechanism for deciding whether intolerance is justified or not – should the unbearable be so labelled? If we can never be sure about what is a moral truth or good, if we remain sceptical, then in the liberal state, we err on the side of toleration, as, in this sense, we tourists on the truck rightly did. If there is nothing to choose between lifestyles, then there are no moral truths and, therefore, no-one can presume to impose or rule. We then must allow different and possibly competing lifestyles. Within liberalism, of course, freedom and then equality set the boundaries for this moral relativism so that lifestyles that deny or reduce either of these principles are deemed to be intolerable. These principles are a weak form of perfectionism, contrasted with a strong form such as fundamentalism.

If we are then to let diversity flourish, are we to allow a belief that scepticism or neutrality is mistaken? It is a view, if left to flourish, that competes with all other views and may lead to their downfall. Someone may believe, fundamentally, that there is a way of life so morally superior that they feel morally obliged to impose it on others and this is what we tourists were subject to during the physically and morally bumpy ride to the Kosi Bay river mouth and back. This is a well-known paradox of toleration; the need for neutrality is created by the facts of diversity and scepticism, but can we be neutral about a view that denies the truth of the latter proposition? The liberal state would not allow or sponsor the dominance of one concept of the good over another, and the work of the Truth and Reconciliation Commission can be partly understood inside this claim. The state and all members of it will remain sceptical and, therefore, neutral about competing moral truths and will be tolerant of all of them. Each person within such a state is autonomous in the sense that each person is then able to live their life in their own way (Mill, 1978). Autonomy is logically derived from the toleration of diversity within a framework of moral truth, and certainly the macho world of the lodge included a culture of 'do your own thing' and 'go for it'.

Fundamental behaviours

There is a problem here, of course, which postmodernism addresses. If we ask 'Am I free?' then we need to distinguish whether freedom is defined as satisfying the needs or desires I have or whether it is about satisfying the desires I would have if I were more rational, better informed, self-willed, self-disciplined and less confined and/or manipulated? Autonomy is about rational self-determination, the precondition for human flourishing within the liberal state. The paradox of toleration, as earlier defined, is resolved here through only remaining neutral towards people's beliefs, practices or actions which arise from rational self-determination. For example, a subculture of non-autonomous-seeking individuals (based on religious fundamentalism) who withdraw from society to avoid contamination from it, will not warrant neutrality from the state.

The unity of diverse, plural, liberal societies and that which gives them their collective identity, is derived from the fact that they all subscribe, within their separate solidarities, to the application of rational self-determination. Solidarities or collectives that refute this are not members, as groups or as individuals, of the state. They are not sceptical and their lack of scepticism denies the scepticism of others and precludes neutrality. This is a limit of toleration and is currently being worked out and defined in the everyday political and moral worlds of people, including international tourists, in the new liberal South Africa and, of course, as Mendus (1988) argues, liberal societies are less tolerant than their advocates would have them believe.

The question remains, should we have tried to interrupt our South African companion's stories, jokes and observations in some way or other? We now know that the limits of toleration were not breached because of judgements we tourists independently made about the nature of the situation, and, moreover, that we felt that it would be socially irresponsible to contaminate the beauty and exhilaration of the occasion with politics and morality. However, we will not shy away here from this important discussion. The concept of social responsibility is usually treated in political philosophy as part of a discussion of obligation and political obligation in particular. Obligation has a number of interesting features. To begin with, there is a tension between the claim that obligation is a primary moral concept and the claim, from linguistic philosophy, that obligation suggests an unwilling acquiescence. So, if we are obliged to do something, we do it because it is the right thing to do. Not to do it would be wrong. On the other hand, it is normally used in connection with some burdensome interpersonal behaviour of some social benefit.

It is usual to identify three different types of obligation (with the accepted caveats of non-exclusivity): social obligation, where an action is recognised by the consensus of public opinion or some relevant group of society; legal obligation, something done that is valid in the courts of law; and political obligation, an outcome of some established political process. We are specifically interested here in the first of these, social obligation. Generally, our obligations are the sum of what is required of us as members of a society, a polity or a jurisdiction. They reflect our public lives. Obligations and interests need to be distinguished since, although they sometimes coincide, they are logically distinct. Obligations are not always in a person's interest, that may explain our inaction on the truck. For example, we may be obliged to be honest but there are occasions when we want to lie. Obligations, however, are unconditional imperatives, but the obligation we felt concerning the abusive discourse from our instant friend from the Transvaal was to feel guilty about not directly and openly resisting the tone and substance of his manner and words.

Social responsibility describes a situation where self-interest is overridden by community interest whenever the two conflict (strong version), and whenever people act so as always to do what can be done in promoting the community's interest (weak version). Social responsibility is part of public life and is not found in anarchy. It sustains communities not through the abandonment of self-interest but through the pursuit of self-interest in ways at least compatible with the community's interest, which is, in our case, to preserve a certain tight-lipped integrity about our trip to Kosi Bay river mouth, in order to keep the moral and political peace, and there to sustain our tourist experience.

Terms such as the public interest, community and mutual benefit indicate that our actions usually impact on others. Obligations, we have seen, are often grudgingly acknowledged, but rights, which, at the level of the individual, are usually expressions of human needs, are stronger evocations of a demand for mutuality. Any genuine right must involve some normative direction of the behaviour of others (the relationships between obligation and duty is often blurred and may not be worth clearly distinguishing). Socially responsible behaviour is often argued for, given a high profile, by claiming rights to such behaviour. In our sense of obligation as a primary moral concept, people have rights, they might claim, to be able to see out their obligations as any virtuous person would do. Interesting questions arise that include whether such rights and their duty correlate or whether associated normative behaviour should transcend community boundaries? The international tourist (and, perhaps, the traveller) might claim rights to travel (liberty of conduct), with the correlate behaviour of others not to interfere; to avoid injury (secure protection), with the correlate behaviour of others to interfere if they think we are in danger; consume services, with the correlate behaviour of others not to interfere with the exchange. However, imagine people from two dissimilar political and moral communities brought into direct proximity through tourism. For example, if the tourists were Islamic, visiting a non-Islamic community. Where people do the will of God, as Muslims must try to do, there is no specific system of rights that locks together self-interest and public interest. This problem of particularity can be overcome, as we have seen, by recourse to claims made about practical matters of surviving or sustaining a situation and/or psychological allegiances to (common) humanity, or, more specifically, to a technical concept of global village or the community of one world (as we discuss in chapter 9). In any case, if visitors, including tourists, are allowed in, they must be tolerated; if visitors chose to come, they are obliged to be tolerant, as we were.

Chapter 6

Crime, conflict and the precautionary principle: the rise of the fearful tourist

Fear of travel

In a society where a particular industry is seen as an essential part of a planned process of economic and associated social and political reconstruction, the position tourism occupies in South Africa, any threats to the actual or potential beneficial impact that tourism is supposed to have will inevitably receive significant attention from all parts of the industry and the society in general. Moreover, crime in significant international tourism destinations can get extensive coverage by the news industries worldwide. An examination of the main daily and weekly newspapers in KwaZulu-Natal, in Cape Town and in Johannesburg and a content analysis of news and features items on South African television during the period March 1997–February 2002, reveals a regular, expansive and intensive reportage of the impact of crime on the tourism industry and versions of these reports are carried, sometimes following further investigation, by the world's press and television.

The basic starting point for the public debate about the causes and consequences of South African crime rates and the incidence and significance of particular types of crime, is that crime is a business that is bad for most other businesses and that the level and patterning of the tourist market, both national and international, is skewed by the public perception of safety. This scenario is not, of course, unique to South Africa. Tourism in Florida, Egypt, Fiji, China, the Lebanon, the Turkish Republic of Northern Cyprus, Northern Ireland, the Yemen, and, most recently, Mombasa, in Kenya, for example, has or may be affected by reports of violence, including violent crime, in such locations. In South Africa, the most widely reported incidents of violence that are thought to have reduced the international tourist flow and redistributed the demand from domestic tourists has been the Planet Hollywood pipe bombing in Cape Town in August 1998 and the killing of two young female Scandinavian tourists in Umhlanga Rocks.

The Cape Town incident and its effects on the tourism industry is the subject of current research work being carried out by George (1998) and the following comments are based on his first research report, 'Measuring the effects of the Planet Hollywood incident on international tourist numbers to Cape Town'. The basic argument George presents is that Cape Town, following the death of two people and serious injury to many others, including tourists, as a result of the pipe bomb at Planet Hollywood right in the centre of the main tourism area of the city, is now in danger of winning an unwanted prize, beating off the competition from Johannesburg and Durban, as South Africa's most dangerous city to visit. Over 1.4 million international tourists visited South Africa in 1997 and the vast majority of these, 1.2 million, visited Cape Town, and Satour expects the rate of growth of international tourism to be in the order of 10 per cent per year in the foreseeable future (George, 1998). George also quotes Richter's claim 'Tourism as a discretionary activity is incredibly vulnerable to crime, violence and political instability. Even natural disasters such as earthquakes and hurricanes do not have the lasting impact of crime and violence' (Richter, 1984, p.308, quoted in George, 1998, p.5).

The response to the Planet Hollywood and Umhlanga Rocks incidents by the local and national tourism industry and tourism authorities and agencies has been to focus on what can and should be done to lower the possibility of tourists being subject to actual criminal acts, especially violent robbery including car hijacking, through programmes of tourist education via tourism companies, hotels, and tourist attractions and through improving crime prevention and detection procedures and rates. For example, the KwaZulu-Natal Tourism Authority has public relations resources and strategies ready to swing into action to ameliorate and contain the potential impact of reported criminal activity thought to affect the tourist decision to visit KwaZulu-Natal. A vital issue here, among many, for the future development of the South African tourism industry, is the relationship between the perception of crime, the perception of risk, the personal need for safety and the influence of these three interrelated elements on the tourism industry. The way in which we shall approach this issue is to begin with a discussion of the influence of the media and other sources of knowledge on the tourist perception of a place as a potential tourist destination. We then consider the significance of the late twentieth-century majority obsession, in the Northern Hemisphere, to avoid or to minimise uncertainty in life and a contingent need to take precautions. This will allow us to begin to understand where the perception of crime in South Africa by the international tourist from the North emanates from, and how this perception both defines and resonates with a person's belief system and decision-taking processes, in particular, the choice of where to visit as a tourist and what to do or not do when they get there.

Moral order on the beach

Tourists who visit South Africa may, as we did, read the local newspapers and watch local television in their hotel rooms, and if they do, they will see that the debate about the future for the tourism industry, as covered in feature articles and editorials and news stories and letters in the newspapers and news, news-magazines and documentaries on the TV, is dominated by fears about the impact of local violent crime and its reportage on the local tourism industry. And, of course, violent crime in any society is of interest to the worldwide media and it is possible that the British tourist contemplating visiting South Africa will also have been exposed to extensive media coverage, through news and features and so on, but also through specialist tourism programmes (for example, the BBC's *Holiday Programme*). In any case, people have a perception of countries and places that they may never have visited and these perceptions are an important dimension of our personal belief systems or ideological frameworks. We 'know', for example, that life in the UK is tolerable partly because we believe that social life in most other countries, none of which we may have visited, would be much worse for us (Harré, in Warren, 1999). We 'visit' other places through a complex process that can include personal, direct experience, as a traveller or tourist, through other people's accounts of places they may or may not have visited, through the media, including travel books, novels and films (for example, through the latter, all of us know what a tropical island should be like).

What is of interest here is how we use this information to make judgements about whether places are as they should be; more particularly, of how secure they are. In considering the impact of travelling to a place as a tourist, or in analysing the personal decision to choose a specific tourist destination rather than feasible vacation alternatives, we might dwell on Ignatieff's claim that 'television has become the privileged medium through which moral relations between strangers are mediated in the modern world' (1998, p.10).

ACTSA, in the UK, as we have seen, have concentrated their campaign for 'People First Tourism' on the activities of British tour operators running tourists to South Africa (the choice of 'running' here is deliberate – tour operators, worldwide, may be subjected to the same moral outrage as gun-running arms traders). Ignatieff is particularly concerned with images of the casualties of civil war or structural violence, of poor, thin, oddly shaped children, for example, and the response of the relatively affluent to such images. He says,

> At first sight, the moral relations created by these images could be inter-
> preted in radically different ways, either as an instance of the promiscuous
> voyeurism a visual culture makes possible, or as a hopeful example of the
> internationalisation of conscience. The difficulty, of course, is that both of
> these opposing interpretations may be true [1998, p.10].

A British tourist sits on a metal seat on the Durban beachfront promenade, at South Beach, in the early evening. He has rand in his bum-bag and he is sleepily deciding how to spend the evening. The beachfront is still ringing with activity – there are surfers coming out of the water, rollerbladers traversing the boundaries between grass and concrete, joggers, glistening with body oil, glued to the inside of their Kevlon shoes, strollers, arm in arm, vendors selling ice cream and samosas, watchers sitting on the grassy banks, sunbathers catching the last rays of the sun, and fishermen unloading heavy gear from their trucks and heading out on to the piers. And the beachfront police horses stand to attention while their uniformed riders decide which area of the beach-front to head for, where they will pose, impress and intimidate during their last sortie of the day. The sex industry workers are already in their usual spots, waiting for regular clients or to pull the actively inquisitive tourist, and the car parking and protection industry is in full swing.

All of this activity, and more, is currently the subject of ongoing research work by Professor Robert Preston-Whyte at the University of Natal (Preston-Whyte, 1997) where he is studying the regulation of space between the various beach activities. What is of interest to us is to look at this scene, as crudely sketched above, and consider the significance of the perception of risk and urge for precaution as important elements in the tourist experience. And the framework for this analysis, briefly outlined, is that the tourist experience of a place or situation arises from a complex interaction of a belief system at a point in time with a place or situation. Within this interactive process, as we saw in the last chapter, our tourists will, as part and parcel of their moral selves, be working out their obligation to act in certain ways or not (pay for sex?) and to leave others free to behave as they wish or not, testing the limits of toleration (to swear at the rollerbladers who see how close they can get to tourists while performing their party tricks for each other as part of the on-going competition between the bladers to increase difficulty and danger?). Our tourist, sitting on the bench in the early evening sun, vaguely watching the changing patterns of the beachside activity around him as day shifts to evening, is brought, potentially, face to face with the suffering of others, with the need to make a living for the beachfront workers, legal and low-paid, or illegal with wide variations in income, such as the prostitutes and their pimps. If necessary, the economics of survival may require exploiting the international tourist who, worldwide, has the aura of an 'easy touch'.

Watching a television programme in England about crime in South Africa and the risk of tourists becoming a victim of crime gets translated by travel, into a decision set, facing our bench-mark tourist on the Durban sea-front, involving choosing whether or not to respond to the approaches of others (people offering him goods or services) and/or to initiate contact with others, through visiting a particular place. Through choosing to sit on the beachfront in the early evening, we could exclaim, what did he expect to experience if not the night trade of a large seaport and tourist centre? Of course, the very presence of attractions that exist in the illegal economy do not themselves create a moral claim or dilemma. The tourist has to believe that he is potentially under an obligation to those other people acting out their lives on the beachfront. In the case of South Africa, and for a British tourist, it may be that what Ignatieff calls 'the mechanics of empathy' (1998, p.12) that is at work in the decision to consume something (a parking space from a poor person who could easily be ignored, informally but authoritatively waving the hire-car driver into a parking bay) that could be free and need not be purchased. And informing this personal moral dynamic may be a history of political, economic and social relationships that help form conscience, and maybe guilt, that dominate the individual decision to act at a moment in time and space and that can only subsequently be understood through reference to an ethical universalism. In early evening terms, this can lead to a view that 'these people shouldn't have to do these things, but if they do, maybe it's best for me to do what I can to help'. So the sex worker is paid but not otherwise experienced. Now, the interesting feature of such an outcome is that this situation may not ever be replicated, for the tourist, in his home setting. The tourist as a stranger, at least for some part of the tourist experience, also means that the tourist may be a stranger to himself. There are features of the Durban beachfront that are similar to the waterfront of the city of Plymouth in the UK, but our British tourist, travelling from Plymouth to Durban, and occupying his seat in the sun beneath the Equator, is both the same person and a different person – a cultural and moral dualist.

The pleasures of compensation

In order to really understand the moral and political position of the South African international tourist, when faced with the sorts of choice outlined above, is to engage in some difficult and under-explored philosophical work on the nature of remorse and reparation (Thomas, in Cox, 1999). In particular, we need to understand the differences and the relationships between such feelings as guilt, shame and remorse. If our tourist were to claim feelings of guilt, for, say, being rich where all around is poverty, then we are conceptualising his position in terms of identifying with a set of standards – to do with preferred distributions of wealth and well-being – that he is conscious of violating. The tourist comes to the situation with an orientation to a framework of moral standards and an internalisation of these standards such that they authoritatively determine behaviour in a situation. Our tourist, as we have hinted, may have violated his own moral being, simply through the choice to leave the hotel room and head out on to the beachfront. He is his own victim and international tourists to South Africa may knowingly put themselves into this position. In any case, such a philosophical and psychological conceptual framework may be useful in understanding the position of the tourist in such settings.

The analysis of eco-tourism (WTO, 1999a) seems to have largely ignored the basic philosophical and practical importance of remorse. This is unfortunate since the distinguishing feature of remorse is that something of value has been destroyed that can never be replaced and, moreover, that a moral agent would not have engaged in such destruction even though no rules or codes of conduct may have been broken. It has no natural outlet since the act of destruction has happened in the past and cannot be put right. We contemplate and reflect but we cannot otherwise act to repair the harm. For example, the relatively rich white tourist from the Northern Hemisphere did not choose when and where to be born, nor to be in a particular economic relationship to the poorer black person from the South. All that people might do is 'get through it' or 'live through it' in the hope that it will be lost in the inadequacies of memory. In the South Africa situation, this sort of analysis might be a way of making contemporary sense of the so-called 'white man's burden'.

The tourist relationship to crime and to the valuation of others as people and to a location as an attractive place to be or not, is clouded by a unique set of moral, political and economic frameworks, forces and situations that will never be satisfactorily revealed but we must acknowledge are there to be explained. Giving money to the informal parking attendants for providing a service that the tourist may not want and doesn't have to make use of, may be part of the process by which an incurred debt for being more privileged is expressed, a debt from that we seek to be released. In this sense, rather than remorse, we are experiencing and responding to guilt. The tourist then becomes a compensatory mechanism to pay off his nation state's moral debt through economic actions.

We do this, too, when perhaps we are too tolerant of behaviour, or tolerant about words or actions that would otherwise have breached the limits of toleration. The situation described with the Zulu waiter in the previous chapter could be revisited and analysed from this perspective. Indeed, it may be possible to sustain the macro-philosophical argument that North to South tourism is a compensatory mechanism, akin to a tax willingly paid to alleviate guilt. But there is no way of offsetting remorse through compensation.

What we seem to expect is reparation. The reflective tourist from the North, on the Durban beachfront, particularly if he is British, may imagine a collective identity, a shared remorse with all the other tourists in his moral position. In this case, he may demand reparation:

What role, then, is played by the demand for reparation? Its role seems purely expressive and symbolic, reflecting one aspect of our concept of legitimate punishment – as expressing and symbolizing our collective emotion as to the wrongful act and as demanding a similar acknowledgement on the part of the agent [Thomas, in Cox, 1999].

Now, of course it would be possible for our tourist to have taken the advice of his hotel or his tour operator and not gone near the beachfront after 6pm. In this way, the tourist is excluded from aspects of the domestic economy and culture and is an implicit agent in the suppression or realignment of the local economy and morality. Green tourism (WTO, 1999b) of course, wants to conceptualise the political and economic relationships between visitor and host as human relations. This leads to an assertion that there is a connection between the Northern (Western, British) conscience and the needs of strangers from the North on the Durban beachfront and that this connection has its roots in a respect for commonality in human nature that transcends and excludes the inclination to exploit (say, for one-sided pleasure). And more than this, there are the assertions from Green reconstructivism, that we should look at strangers through an idea of a universalism that rests on hope rather than fear and an optimism about the human capacity for good rather than pessimism about the inherent or learnt capacity to be bad. This is the upside of Green Fascism. What the international and tourist operators and agencies in Britain and South Africa are telling the British tourist is that, in a nutshell, you will be OK as long as you stay alert, careful, are streetwise, treat others as moral agents or as human beings, and, above all, take precautions, and it is to the latter that we now turn.

Once again, there is a number of related themes that we need to bear in mind here and these include the notion that the North and the West have experienced an erosion of social relations based on trust (Fukuyama, 1995); a fear of strangers, induced, perhaps, by a feeling of lacking control in a situation, or akrasia (Gosling, 1990); a heightened awareness of the presence of uncertainty and risk in everyday life (Giddens, 1999); and a reaction against a culture of personal abuse (Furedi, 2002). Such themes are highly significant for understanding the social and moral condition of the international tourist from the North visiting South Africa. One of the interesting features of tourism is that it can reflect the personal need to take risks. We have already made the familiar claim that the tourist can be 'a stranger to themselves' and part of this strangeness can be a different outlook on risk and uncertainty. The classic conceptual-isation of the urge to travel (McCannell, 1976) as stemming from an urge to escape from the certainty, and, hence, boredom, of life in the usual place, coupled with the close association between tourism and hedonism (Inglis, 2000) has led to a tourism paradigm of enhanced risk and uncertainty. Other places are places where indulging oneself is acceptable and expected (more drink and food, less sleep and exercise, quick friendships and faster sex).

Paradise lost, paralysis found

This traditional perception of the uniqueness of the tourist experience is now knocking against a culture that exudes safety and precaution in social life, that sees risk-taking or a lack of worrying about how to be, as disorders needing therapy. Americans who claim not to have concerns about their own persona, have been said to suffer from a perfectionist syndrome (Furedi, 2002). Young people who beat each other up during drunken brawls on Spanish beach-fronts, then have their wallets stolen while dazed and inebriated and end up in jail, may find themselves in a similar physical and economic position as a middle-aged tourist who gets mugged through recklessly getting too close to South Beach, Durban at the wrong time of day. Both situations can be seen as exemplifying an unreasonable disregard for personal safety at the same time as being understood as part and parcel of the tourist experience. Frank Furedi's thesis, in his appropriately titled *Culture of Fear*, may be of major significance for understanding aspects of the contemporary tourist experience, and what follows is underwritten by an admiration for Furedi's creative work on the Western and Northern culture of safety first:

> The evaluation of everything from the perspective of safety is a defining char-acteristic of contemporary society. When safety is worshipped and risks are seen as intrinsically bad, society is making a clear statement about the values that ought to guide life ... Risk has become big business. Thousands of consultants provide advice on 'risk analysis' and 'risk management' and 'risk communications'. The media too have become increasingly interested in the subject, and terms like the 'risk society' and 'risk perception' now regularly appear in newspaper columns ... There is a definite, anxious con-sensus that we must all be at risk in one way or another. Being at risk is treated as if it has become a permanent condition that exists separately from any particular problem. Risks hover over human beings [Furedi, 2002, p.4].

Our man in Durban is not expected to enjoy let alone put up with the 'risk' of the beachfront. Risk, according to Furedi, has been turned into an exogenous force, that acts on us but is outside our control, and is always with us, the Millennium 'Big Brother'. If we accept the force of this thesis, then we must also say that every human experience, or every place in which human beings find themselves and their subsequent actions, can best be understood in part as action and reflection inside a constant search for safety. Let us say, for example, that our tourist decides to catch the last tourist bus taking sight-seekers up and down the Durban beachfront. What are the risks here? Well, he should know that, according to anxious Diana Lamplugh, a leading British 'safety expert' quoted by Furedi: 'The wise passenger never loses sight of the fact that public transport is still a public place. There is open access to stations (and bus stops). No-one is vetted, everyone is acceptable as a passenger. Moreover, when we travel we are often unable to move easily and avoid trouble' (Furedi, 2002, p.5).

To translate into action the logic of Lamplugh's argument is to create a fear of any action at all and would lead to a personal and social politics of paralysis (akin to the impact of remorse on action, to create inaction, as we have argued above). That is not to deny the significance of the sense of risk as a social construct and this social construction of risk may itself be built on another social construct, a perception that because society is becoming progressively more complex, decisions about what to do are increasingly taken in a context of uncertainty. Such matters have been explored in great detail (Beck, 1992) and it is not the intention here to begin to integrate this work into mainstream tourism studies literature concerning visitor–host relationships, though this is a task worth doing. The point we wish to stress is that the relationship between the fear of crime and the choice of tourism destination, and behaviour in a perceived risky tourism environment, is only one manifestation of a general cultural phenomenon that places the assessment of risk at the forefront of our thinking about decisions and situations. We are told that we are unlikely to be able to predict the outcomes of decisions we take or the dynamic of social situations we find ourselves in.

According to Furedi (2002), we have seen the translation of risk assessment and management in the natural world, in environmental management, into many other spheres. These include crime and personal safety more generally, for example, sexual activity, eating and drinking and fitness or personal health and well-being. Clearly it is possible to see this precautionary tendency as a radical attack on unnecessary dangers, risks we should not have to live with and need not live with if we stay alert and adjust our lifestyles accordingly and work for changes in the social and material worlds that bring a new, safer world into being. It is also possible to see the sanctity of safety and the precautionary imperative as fundamentally reactionary, trying to return social life to a simpler golden age of minimal uncertainty, where the risks are known, alternatives and their consequences are clear, and people could be trusted, even strangers. As Giddens more generally argues, 'the current world economy has no parallels in earlier times' (1999, p.9).

We have hinted already that the precautionary fundamentalists, in unknowing concert with the international travel and tourism corporations, would insist that our early evening Durban beachfront tourist should be locked up in the cocoon of turned down sheets, the mini bar, room service and the BBC World Service on the hour, every hour, by the time 6pm comes around. He brings a cultural cloud to the decision to leave the hotel room and to sit on the bench (alongside and merging with the moral cumulus) limiting what is thought to be possible and appropriate to do. For the tourist, this culture of risk aversion converts into an intense and wide-ranging fear of strangers and strangeness. The main aim for our Durban tourist, if he internalises all these cultural imperatives, is not enjoyment or pleasure, but survival. He is seen not as a guilty party but as an innocent victim of circumstance, for some reason choosing to visit a society where high crime rates and the associated lack of respect for people and property are endemic. His decision to brave the beachfront may be thought to be foolish, and socially reprehensible (there will be social costs as well as private costs following any loss or damage to his property or self). What he has begun to overcome by sitting on the bench is a collective failure of nerve; he is in the business of resistance. 'The secret of the problem of trust is the belief that we are so pathetic that we cannot trust ourselves. In recent years this belief has helped to shape a new morality based on the themes of mistrusting people, exercising caution and avoiding risk' (Furedi, 2002, p.145). This postmodern etiquette derived from the guidebooks of moral fascism diminishes the tourist experience of South Africa.

The tourist is faced with situational informational asymmetry – he has to rely on imperfect information in coming to decisions about what to do, where to do it and who to do it with, guessing that others, such as his local relatives or friends, if he has them, or tour guide or local people if he is allowed out to meet them, are streetwise where he is street-foolish. When this is coupled with the Furedi thesis of the unfortunate influence of the general fear of taking risks and the elevation of safety into a deity, it is no surprise to see a continual exaggeration or mystification of the problems facing society; whereby, in tourist contexts, the host needs to be anxious and cautious about the visitor as well as *vice versa*. Here, we are encouraged not to trust our own judgement about others and situations, and to do nothing to expose ourselves to uncertainty. The outcome is less autonomy and community, and 'a world view that equates the good life with self-limitation and risk aversion' (Furedi, 2002, p.147). No wonder the holiday market for cruise ships has expanded so much in recent years; regulatory bingo at 6pm in the lower after-deck lounge with Darren is a safer bet than early evening on the Durban beachfront with Natalie.

It might be argued that this rational timidity is underpinned by the lack of a moral framework that informs the lonely Durban beachfronter's ability to choose a course of action, or rather, that the dominant moral framework in the Northern Hemisphere is risk-consciousness. And, moreover, this personal morality is deeply reinforced by an obligation to others as well as to oneself, not to take risks. Leaving the delights of applauding the terrible weather back home, courtesy of the satellite's gift of CNN's World Weather Review and heading out and into the early balmy, salty evening, contravenes our moral responsibilities to others: to tour representatives, who might have to pick up the pieces; and to friends and families at home, who have to bear the ill-temper of the anxieties that are part of the unreasonable costs to others of risky encounters. On the other hand, this stress can be matched by the restrictions on personal feeling that come from this risk-related moral authoritarianism, from a personal resentment about the cultural imposition of a Good Life that precludes and excludes certain social experiences for the tourist and host communities.

We have seen that ACTSA's responsible tourism campaign slogan, 'People First Tourism', from the point of view of the foregoing analysis, is better conceptualised as fundamentally reactionary, in its outcomes. Tourism companies are urged to protect their tourists from being put into a position where they tacitly support the exploitation of low-paid workers through their consumption of hotel services. What this leads to is a trip down the slippery slope to the moral straitjacket of caring capitalism, where First Choice means no choice at all if any risks are involved for the industry, client or host. The industry's public relations or marketing machinery, of course, would describe such policies as promoting and supporting sustainable tourism.

We came into this discussion considering the meaning and significance of the perception of crime and its relation to tourism demand and the tourist experience. We have argued, following Furedi (2002), that risk-consciousness creates a moral position that shifts the burden of responsibility and obligation from the social to the personal plane. This leads inevitably to the individualisation of crime, to a view that it is individuals who should know better. From the point of view of the tourist in a strange place, the onus is on him not to allow these out-of-control individuals ('locals') to exploit him. Interestingly, he must not put the young potential thief at risk of being able to rob him. He owes this to his host community, and his lifestyle as a tourist is conditioned by this fear. If he is robbed, otherwise taken 'for a ride' or given a 'raw-deal' or catches a sexually transmitted disease, he should feel guilty, even remorseful, and suffer accordingly. He has 'asked for it'.

Chapter 7

Power and the relations of tourism

A rough guide to power

It is easy to slip into claims that 'it's all to do with power' when discussing potential resolutions of undesirable states of affairs, whether for nations, groups or individuals. The discussion often then quickly proceeds to an elaboration of the relationship between the powerful and powerless and possible strategies for changing power inequalities. Often, power becomes a residual factor for inquiries into the causes of and solutions to social problems, such as the relationship between the nature and rates of crime in South Africa and its impact on the tourism industry and tourists. All other factors are identified and prioritised although, perhaps, with little agreement about the relative importance of each factor, but with agreement that, in the end, nothing can be done unless power relationships change and become less unequal. The power of the tourist and host needs discussion through an analysis of the concept of power and here we need to draw on the work of political philosophy (as well as moral philosophy) and, specifically, on theories of power and of democracy to do this.

If South Africa is a democracy, it will have power relationships congruent with democratic political principles, procedures and practices. At the micro-political level, our protagonists on the Durban beachfront, our man from the North, other tourists and the host communities working and recreating at the front, all learn about how to 'be' on this political battleground through a rational analysis of the power relations they hold and the possibilities for redistributing resources, legally or otherwise, that follow from the nature and positions of relative power. This is the political overlay, or the foundation, for the moral and cultural territory. Dennis Wrong's (1979) work is useful in offering a witty and stimulating counter to the intellectual slippage indicated in a general tendency in tourism studies literature (Boo, 1990) to highly weight the importance of power yet be unable to discuss effectively the forms, bases and uses of power, and we have drawn on aspects of Wrong's approach in what follows.

Wrong (1979, p.2) suggests that 'Power is the capacity of some persons to produce intended and foreseen effects on others'. He quotes Hobbes ('Man's present means to any future apparent good') and Russell ('the production of intended effects') as guides. Empirically, people have asked: 'Who runs this town?' (Who runs Durban?) Such questions have created a division between reputational and decisional analyses of power in practice. People can be asked to identify power holders (over them, over a recognised geographical territory) and, phenomenologically, their answers are true. That is, if they say that X has power (over them), then X does have power. The source and boundary of power is attributed by personal truth claims. If X is reputed to wield power, they do wield power through, at least, their reputation. Historical analysis or direct sociological observation of some sort, might confirm or seek to deny the truth claims of people. Indeed, people may be poor at accurately defining their own power situation because, as we shall see, they may be manipulated by their power holders. The beachfront parking attendants use various strategies to make us think that it is our choice to pay them; the trick may be to leave the tourist with the illusion of choice in order to meet the British tourist's moral need to choose to pay a collective, historical debt.

Conceptually, power is slippery because it can be argued that we all have it. Or, we can prefer to reserve a restricted view of power as an instrument for determining the outcomes of struggles between competing groups for scarce resources. The potential to wield power is associated by Wrong with Gilbert Ryle, the epistemologist. Power is defined as capacity (inclination + ability) to produce a particular level of performance that can influence others. Intentionality raises the issue of whether power is being exercised when its effects are not intended. Can someone be said to be in a power relationship with someone else when neither party would recognise that any power relation exists (for example, grain farmers in the American mid-West and the urban poor in Durban)? This is not a problem for decisional methods that recognise that people can be blind to both the intended and unintended outcomes of power holders' actions. It is also not a problem to those reputationalists who accept the widespread prevalence of manipulation (see later).

Capacity, latency or potential has two major lines of development: capacity that leads to inaction since, as long as the power receiver acknowledges the capacity of the power holder to effect change or sustain the status quo, the power holder may need to do nothing; and capacity that leads to failure to effect intended change because, for example, the power holder chooses the wrong forms of power or over-exploits the basis of power. This is not discussed by Wrong, but, empirically and conceptually, it seems there will be times when power holders only create unintended change (maybe counter-productive outcomes) or achieve no change at all. In these cases, their power of potential influence is presumably diluted and may need reaffirming through direct remedial action.

In South Africa, as we have seen, the tourist will be severely warned about the dangers of car-hijacking, and a favourite local story for international tourists, first told to us in 1998 and still doing the airport international lounge rounds, is about a deterrent device that some unnamed firm is producing that is fitted to cars and allows drivers, in the tradition of James Bond, to zap attempted hijackers with flame-throwers built into the skirting of the car. Here we have an interesting example of a potential or mythical (and still potential) crime deterrent meeting the probability (greater than zero but not much) of hijacking. What sort of power game is being played out here? At the least, we would expect to see a car hire company installing and capitalising on the invention and responding to the fear of hijacking through its car hire rates (already very high in South Africa compared to rates in major tourism destinations in the Northern Hemisphere).

Power relations vary, of course, and individuals normally have many different relationships as both power holders and power casualties, where power is misused. Tourist and host power relationships may oscillate according to the evolution of a situation that brings them together where the power relations seem initially clear – for example, a particular type and degree of inequality of influence. Wrong distinguishes integral power (centralised, monopolised, asymmetrical) with intercursive power (countervailing, pluralistic) and the scope of influence is clearly different in each of these general positions. With integral power, as in South Africa under apartheid, resistance is difficult. Integral power shades into intercursive power the more civil liberties, legal processes, rights of appeal, and guarantees to the possibility of alternative successions to power exist. In South Africa, we could argue that the politics of everyday life should push or be pushed by the politics of the state. It is a moot point how far the claim to a macro-political world of democracy, or a New Democracy, is offset by contradictions at the micro-level of people's power relationships with each other and within the nature of civil society. These arenas of political thought and action, the politics of the state, of civil society and of the everyday life of the Good Tourist (see chapter 8) is the political world that the international tourist enters, bringing their own political culture with them and their media-induced political expectations for the new South Africa.

Observing the effects of power holders, as we have seen, is fraught with difficulties. Some effects are subjective (only claimed by the power holder or receiver) or internal (altered mind states with no behavioural changes). There is a considerable level of uncertainty over the effects of a power holder's capacity for action, both in the mind of the potential power holder and the person possibly under the influence. Doubts over whether asymmetrical power does exist, in what form, for how long and to what effect, lead some power holders to employ multiple methods of influence, a grapeshot approach. We also discern, in some people, a disposition to hold power, to acquire the potential or recognise their potential as a power holder. Richard Bierstedt (1981) locates disposition within the capacity-potential-ability set, but Machiavelli (1998) among others, suggested that there is a lust for power. The sexual metaphor implies that a disposition to hold and exercise power is a fundamental part of being human and, if so, will be part of the 'urge' to be a tourist. This 'natural' trait is more prevalent in some than others, Machiavelli claimed, and leads to dominant ruling minorities that have most successfully realised the fruits of this innate capacity. This is an accurate description of the temporary position that any international tourist holds travelling from North to South and the long-term position the international tourism industry encompasses. Machiavelli was led then to claim that since the lust for power was inevitable, it was virtuous, and that those who extended their potential to exercise power should be applauded. Hobbes (1962) saw integral power as a way of safeguarding value in a world of scarce resources. Everyone needs power (or an agency of power) to feel secure.

Freudian analyses of aggression suggest we should distinguish people who desire the power to do things, from people who overtly desire power over others. Wrong (1979) argues that organisations rather than classes are the real focus of the demand for power, being arbitrary creations to which we are forced to accommodate. In Bachrach and Baratz (1963) terms, organisations are powerful since they compel obedience. In this sense, leaving the hotel room, the safe base camp, to go to the (beach) front is an act of resistance or a signal that the power of the tourist industry and its organisations is ineffectual. Empirically, these are difficult matters to decide truthfully and we tend to rest on *a priori* reasoning. Wrong, characteristically, forcefully expresses his own frustration:

> Yet the formal definitions and distinctions made by different writers scarcely succeed in dispelling this confusion, for they reveal at least as much diversity as uniformity. Power is regarded as a form of influence, or influence as a form of power, or they are treated as entirely distinct phenomena. Power is held to rest always on consent, or it must always confront and overcome resistance. Authority is a subtype of power, or power and authority are distinct and opposite. Persuasion is a form of power; it is not a form of power at all. Force is a form of power; it is not power but a sign of the breakdown or failure of power. Manipulation is or is not a form of power. Personal leadership is or is not a form of authority. Competence is a basis for persuasion and has nothing to do with power or authority, or it is the fundamental implicit ground of all

legitimate authority. All power is reducible to the unequal exchange of goods and services, or the offering of benefits in return for compliance is simply one form of power [Wrong, 1979, p.65].

Nonetheless, if we reduce the discussion of the genesis, cause and solution to social problems as being fundamentally about power relationships, then we need to sustain the work of intellectual clarification.

For some, power is a burden. They seek to avoid exercising it. This escape can take a number of forms. For example, it can be described as apathy (towards political processes); it can be seen as withdrawal from personal relationships (psychologically, depression); and as physical or economic isolationism (refusal to contribute to collective interests). Politics, briefly, can be defined as, positively, a struggle for power or, negatively, as a struggle to limit, resist or escape from the influence of power holders. Escaping from the potential to exercise either positive or negative power is anti-politics. If we accept this interpretation and couple it with Freud, escaping from being a power holder is both anti-social and unnatural, and, phenomenologically, may be a *non sequitur*. The process of acquiring the anti-power-holding position will be a political process but the outcome (as with a recluse or hermit) may indeed be 'odd'. Resisting or combating power holders can take several forms: power subjects can attempt to exercise countervailing power (turn integral power into intercursive power); limits can be set to the span and nature of control through avoidance strategies or through increasing the costs of influence; claiming integral power through supplanting power holders; and destroying the bases of power.

Each of these strategies (they are complementary rather than exclusive) is potentially within the grasp of both tourist and host. Wrong suggests that these positions complement a distinct type of political organisation. The first is concerned with the search for democratic government; the second is often combined with a search for constitutional government; the third is more about political processes, for example, a putsch, rebellion or electoral contest; and, lastly, the fourth leads to anarchy, or the elimination of government.

A politics of influence and difference

A politics of everyday life in significant tourism locations would stress the setting of agendas as the key political process. Empirically, answering the question 'Who set the agenda?' would reveal the asymmetry or balance of power relations. In terms of tourism and criminal behaviour by hosts, criminal behaviour can have the effect, if not the intention, of reversing the asymmetry of power relations through the failure or the unwillingness of the tourist to 'read' local situations. We were not able to find any studies of the reaction of tourists to South Africa who, for example, had been robbed. Speculatively, for some tourists, the experience could be cathartic, allowing them to experience the emotions associated with the cleansing of cultural imperialism. More prosaically, they may say, 'We asked for it'.

Wrong uses the work of Bertrand de Jouvenal (1958) to outline a model of the variable attributes of power relations. These may be better thought of as boundaries of influence that limit the effects of a power holder and, we shouldn't forget, the great twentieth-century treatment of boundaries of political influence is George Orwell's *Nineteen Eighty-Four* (1949). De Jouvenal identifies three dimensions of influence: extensiveness, comprehensiveness and intensiveness, each of which underwrites the narrative of Orwell's great novel, and has the universal force and appeal to illuminate tourist–host relationships. Extensiveness limits the number of power subjects within the boundary of influence of a power holder. This is sometimes referred to as the 'span of control' (a military term) and, numerically, can be described as the ratio of power holders to power subjects. Another approach is simply to determine the ease of avoiding surveillance from the power holder. An autocratic political regime, such as South Africa under apartheid, using modern media and military and psychological technologies, may potentially influence millions of subjects and effectively limit, through the mass media and agents of the state (such as a youth wing of the party) people's ability to avoid receiving commands. A Zulu chief, in rural KwaZulu-Natal, in contrast, had major surveillance problems (and costs). This is often referred to as a visibility constraint; Orwell, through the omnipresent TV screen, satirised the latter as a partial solution.

The political correctness of contemporary South African broadcasting in the immediate post-democratic election period, using, for example, black and white newsreaders within strict protocols of rotation of 'lead' presenter, and growing criticism of the practice, reflected a new controversial take on the surveillance function of public broadcasting. If we consider the perceived extensiveness of influence of the international tourist in South Africa, this belief may be more rooted in the widespread perception that tourism is a panacea for economic problems, a new economic correctness, rather than being a function of the growth in the numbers and visibility of the international tourist. Individuals are the sum of a number of parts, emotional and cognitive, some of which can be kept separated (Harré, in Warren, 1999).

Comprehensiveness refers to the range of potential effects on a power subject that a power holder can successfully produce. Certain types of behaviours, such as consumption decisions, might be under the influence of, say, the state, but not others, such as friendship patterns. Some thought processes (belief in God) may be outside the boundary of influence but not others (belief in Mandela's competence). Power holders, other things being equal, would wish to control total conduct but this is rare (except in total institutions).

We have seen that one of the traditional ways of conceptualising the tourist is as someone who travels to a social situation that they temporarily inhabit where they are 'the other' in their lives. This 'other' has a different emotional and cognitive mix, at least potentially. When British travel and tourism companies are encouraged by ACTSA, as we have seen, to market their products as a form of ethical consumption for the 'new' breed of tourists, we can anticipate the limited success of this sort of campaign through remembering that companies, as well as individuals, may be adept at appearing to accept a moral line but flaunting it in practice. How much of our emotional and cognitive selves are susceptible to short-term, selective campaigns to be different than we would otherwise be, perversely for example not to be different when we are on holiday? These short bursts of potential influence become part and parcel of the lifelong learning that goes on which, together with our genetic makeup, lays down the deep values that make us what we are.

This elementary discussion of the nature of human nature is simply meant to make the point that some situations are indeed such as to transform our thinking and our behaviour. Being in South Africa may lead to a different view, via, perhaps a personal discovery of a new spin on an old issue such as income inequalities. The power of a situation to teach us about ourselves may well be the strongest (strongest in that we are deeply affected and the affect is sustained) power relationship we experience, even if only to affirm a belief or value position. This is why people may talk about the anticipatory thrill or buzz they get about travel and why our Durban beachfront tourist may overcome his risk-aversion self and venture out into a situation that may lead to significant impacts for him and others.

Intensity of power relationship, according to Herbert Simon (1969) is a function of where the boundaries lie that define the 'zone of acceptance'. This concept refers to the willingness of the power subject to obey a power holder without resistance, with compliance. The less resistance, the less has to be invested in processes of influence. It is also legitimate, here, to include the notion of depth of influence. This has an historical dimension (How long does it last? How often was reinforcement necessary?) and a thought–action dimension. People may think differently but behave the same and *vice versa*. Some power holders will want to change thought or action or both. Is a minimal acceptance of influence acceptable to a power holder and does the subject have to totally take on the intended change, unquestioned, indefinitely?

The boundary is usually set by a number of well-known considerations, in particular, whether one person or agent has more money than the other and whether one is in an authoritative position over the other, through charisma or vested authority in a job or role. We have mentioned, in chapter 5 the moral dilemma that can arise from being in a position where a small financial gesture to one person, the tourist tipping or not tipping, or of buying from roadside traders or not, as at the Valley of a Thousand Hills viewing point, is of major significance to the other (poor) person from the host community. This is clearly an intense power relationship since it really matters to at least one party what the other does. And, indeed, as we have seen in our discussion of guilt in chapter 6, the altruistic act may be understood as something that needs to be done as a form of cleansing, benefiting the giver as well as the receiver. Technically, where these are the features of a transaction, this is not altruism since the latter should be best left to describe transactions where one person suffers real loss (of income, wealth, time) in order for the other to be better off. Chapter 10 will have more to say about the links between altruism and tourist behaviour when we argue for the application of a more truthful economic psychology and rationality in tourist–host economic relationships than is usually the case in the academic tourism studies literature.

These three power boundaries, comprehensiveness, intensity and extensiveness, obviously cross one another at several points, rather than running in parallel. Intuitively, it seems that the greater the extensiveness (the number of subjects) the less the comprehensiveness and intensity. Clearly, there will be great variations within a population of the effect of power holders. Some people are more prone to compliance (thereby raising the intensity level) than others. The boundaries can be used to describe and rationalise power strategies. Power holders are faced with a choice of methods. Rational power holders want the most (extensive, comprehensive, intensive) they can get for the least cost. Their choice of methods of influence should be determined by this calculation. We now are in at least the position where we have a way of talking about power relations in the tourism industry that hopefully transcends the characteristic generalised commentary that fails to describe, and, therefore, to analyse significant power dimensions, especially between international tourist and local peoples.

The outer reaches of politics

Wrong's analysis of the forms of power is clearly (acknowledged) influenced by his own value position. The literature he uses (never uncritically) and his own arguments assert the moral superiority of non-violent forms of power and of persuasion over manipulation, that is, he is implicitly recommending the power relations that should be defining features of democratic states. South Africa's claim to be constructing a 'New Democracy' can be tested against the nature of the power relations that are called on to examine and either agree to accept or to resolve the differences of views characteristic of democratic states. The discussion of toleration in chapter 5 highlighted the importance of continually keeping under review the limits of toleration within democratic states and, in so far as the meeting of the international tourist with host communities involves a bringing together of associated political cultures, we need to examine the limits of toleration between these cultures. Analysing the nature of prevailing power relations is one way into this issue.

We have seen the importance of violence and violent crime as being part of the reality and perception of South Africa today. The key identifying feature of violence is the treatment of humans as physical objects, and violence is a particular form of force. Force can also involve non-violent methods, such as sit-ins, strikes and curfews. For Edmund Burke, the possession and use of legitimate force defined the nature of governments. *Parens patria*, the legal basis for conscription into armed forces and custodial arrangements for children, defines the state as knowing best, as being in the position of a wise parent, specifically, a wise father, an illuminating description of South Africa under Mandela. As we have seen earlier, power exists where it is used and where there is potential for its exercise. Similarly, force can be threatened or (then) applied. The threat of force we call coercion. One of the meanings of liberal states may be that the use of force is seen as a last resort. For Bernard Crick (1969), the use of force signals the failure of politics; for Machiavelli, (1998) as we have seen, the use of force is the beginning of politics, a legitimate outcome of the possession of power. At any particular historical movement, societies are politically characterised in a major way by the range of political actions deemed legitimate and illegitimate and the degree to which the latter definition is contested and ignored.

Where a power subject is unaware of being in an unequal relationship with a power holder, the possibility of manipulation exists. Where the international tourist is not aware of the intentions of a local person and the street trader, say, succeeds because of this ignorance, manipulation has taken place. Fraud is the crime that signals the illegitimate use of manipulation. Manipulation, through fraud, may simulate free choice, and evoke initiative and enthusiasm in the power subject, especially where fraud is the real basis for a commercial transaction between tourist and host. David Easton (1953) has referred to 'pseudo Gemeinschaft', the faking of personal concern, and we intend to explore the descriptive and analytical force of this construct in future work on tourism; intuitively, some tourist–host relationships lean this way.

Manipulation can't be properly resisted because, by definition, there is no awareness of the need to resist. In this sense, manipulation, like violent force, is dehumanising. The cliché 'you can fool some of the people some of the time, but you can't fool all of the people all of the time' suggests that manipulation has to be used sparingly and sensitively as part of a political strategy. Empirical studies of the extent of economic fraud suggest, however, widespread use, and, of course, we have the widespread description of the economic function of tourists, as far as some host communities are concerned, as being a 'soft touch'. The reverse is also sometimes true. In Portugal there is an old joke, reflecting the flow of British tourists who visit the Algarve and then seek to take up residence there through buying land and property, that goes something like: 'How do you make a small fortune in the Algarve? Arrive with a big one.' The joke seeks to ridicule affluent British (and, increasingly, Southern African) prospective residents who buy grossly overpriced, useless land and property from Algarvian land-owners (white-flight Southern Africans, since the early 1990s, have also been buying land in the Algarve).

Persuasion as the dominant form of power relations is the linchpin of claims for the existence of liberal democracies. Persuasion is where a power subject independently evaluates a power holder's intentions or actions and chooses to accept the influence. In this case, the Durban beachfront worker would present a series of arguments to our man on the bench and these points can be tested for their rationality and truthfulness. However, the qualities that lead to effective persuasion are not usually equally distributed. Reputation, charisma, oratory, money, sexuality and other resources arise in such ways as to restrict and protect the scarcity of their supply. The main benefits of persuasion as a form of political power is that it is likely to be successful and, when unsuccessful, has little risk of creating antagonism or oppositional strategies. Since it is visible, unlike manipulation, it can also be more readily learnt (the degree to which this learning is possible will offset distributional inequalities, and whether this political education is possible in schools is a major issue for South African education policy and practice). Inequalities of influence are at the heart of the politics of everyday life and, of course, are important determinants of the social and economic relationships thrown up by the tourist experience.

Authority in South African international tourism: a user's guide

Wrong (1979) provides a detailed taxonomy of the types of authority (competent, inducement, legitimate, personal, coercive). The basis of authority as a form of power is that unlike persuasion, there is no need to offer reasons. Commands, that either order a course of action or thinking or forbid some behaviour of belief, are the method of authority. Like persuasion, there is little risk of antagonism or opposition, since, *de facto*, authorities are acknowledged and obeyed without question. According to Easton (1953), anyone who is regularly obeyed is an authority (although neither in Easton nor Wrong is there a formal discussion of obedience). Now both tourist and host can present as an authority to each other, the one, perhaps, because of being seen as rich and white; the other as having local knowledge worth accessing. As we saw from Ignatieff (1998), both are in a position of moral authority vis-à-vis each other, the poor host a victim as a member of the deserving poor, and the rich British tourist a victim of a colonial tradition and the need to travel.

Images of carrot and stick are prevalent within inducement-based authority, otherwise known as economic power. Rewards, or the fear of deprivations, are passed from the authority to power subjects and are the basis of obedience. In competent authorities, shading into persuasion, an authority is recognised to be superior in judging a subject's interest because of what they are (e.g. as professional or expert authority). Expertise, unequally distributed, can be a mask for privilege. When competent authority is claimed by the state, Wrong offers the following metaphors as the characteristic language of this political position: the ruler as helmsman of the people and the statesman as physician or healer. We could add, the party as teacher and the ideology as God.

These metaphors are widely used in South African society as we experienced it in our visits. Legitimate authority is compulsory for the individual but voluntary for the collectivity. For example, parental power is exercised through commands as far as children are concerned but the legitimate authority of parents vis-à-vis children, or the state vis-à-vis children, can be changed. Each of these forms of authority can be analysed, as we have seen, in terms of de Jouvenal's (1958) divisions of extensiveness, comprehensiveness and intensiveness. Rationally, any power holder will want to have recourse to a repertoire of forms of power because of the uncertainty of outcomes and the possibility of (counter-productive) unintended outcomes. Power holders also, when creating a strategy for long-term control over targeted power subjects, need to understand the logical interrelationship of different methods and evaluate these (often a job for Ministries of Propaganda or Heritage or Culture). For example, if force is used, persuasion may be ruled out in the future; if persuasion is frequently successfully used, the persuader becomes a competent authority and reasons or arguments need no longer be offered. Jürgen Habermas's (1975) utopia of citizens emancipated from domination, through establishing the political discourse of ideal speech situations, suggests that the potential disappearance of persuasion, overcome by competent authority, is to be resisted. Command and obedience relationships are anathema to Habermas and are, in the extreme, a characteristic of totalitarian states, described by Raymond Aron (in Wrong, 1979) as 'ortho-doxies without doctrines'. Orwell, of course, in *Nineteen Eighty-Four*, satirised the continual invention and destruction of doctrines (e.g. through rewriting history) as the maintenance of command – obedience power relations. Red

Guards in China in 1968 were trained in the daily designing, printing and posting of political slogans, often contradictory to the previous day's slogan.

The forms, bases and uses of power at different political levels are mentioned but not treated in detail by Wrong. It is clear from political socialisation research of the 1960s (Schwartz and Schwartz, 1975) and subsequently, that many people identify only with a restricted concept of politics: a politics of the state. They are disinclined to follow the move of political scientists, sociologists and philosophers in general, to identify also a politics of (mediating) organisations and a politics of everyday life, as described by Belgian and French situationalists (Allen, 1997). These three levels call for different strategies of influence if power is to be exercised at any level and/or across the levels. Anarchism would eliminate the first and second levels, the state and organisations; authoritarian populism (in the UK, 1980s and 1990s Conservatism) would eliminate level two; and totalitarianism would establish the party as the dominant power at all three levels (for example, within Fascism) and as compressing all three levels into one (as in Maoist Marxism).

Tourists are not, of course, a collective political force because that they don't have their own political party. There is no single pressure group that represents the 'voice' of tourists and 'tourism' is not a social movement in the same sense that feminism or anti-racism is. The 'ism' in tourism is not patently ideological. However, tourists do collectively exert power under three main conditions: when they switch demand at short notice; for example, American tourists staying at home for the duration of the Gulf War; when they assert consumer sovereignty through complaining about a facility or the lack of it; and when they choose to engage in certain personal and social relations rather than others.

Schattschneider (1960) has defined organisations as collectivities concerned with the 'mobilisation of bias'. Mobilisation refers to processes that attempt to change inequalities in power holding, and may aim to equalise power distributions or create different forms of inequality. These processes, as mobilisation, involve some form of collective behaviour. Harold Lasswell (1936), famously, described politics as to do with, paraphrasing, who gets what, when and how? Wrong (1979), discussing mobilisation, transforms Lasswell's line to who gets mobilised, for what collective goals and when and how? Empirically, at a moment in time in a liberal democratic state (by definition) it should be possible to find numerous examples of organised groups fully mobilised to seek power, some organised but not politically organised and some (quasi-groups?) disorganised or not politically, but potentially a political influence.

Differently named polarities can be imagined and have been used to describe (and evaluate, maybe) degrees of organisation, collectivity or solidarity. One polarity, for example, is ephemeral (single, transient issue-based) to permanent (general, long-term issue-based). The stability of mobilised political organisations seems to evolve around their ability to produce structural changes as solutions to social problems (if successful they can then fade away?). Mobilisation is detectable, according to Wrong, when there is common commitment to goals and/or values that are markedly different from any other existing (or past?) organisation; when there is conflict with other groups (this seems tauto-logical); there is a shared perception of the need for action; and, lastly, an organisation exists to promote the cause. Political parties, pressure groups and social movements all can be identified through the four criteria. The degree of solidarity, of course, within an organisation will vary widely, maybe inversely to the degree of coercion required to sustain or initiate membership (e.g. health promotion as a social movement?). Successful social movements, as we have hinted, are doomed to create their own downfall through 'incorporation'. The iron law of decadence (Crick, 1969) is a powerful dynamic force determining any given array and the health of political organisations.

Why do people get mobilised? Aristotle, after studying slaves in order to maintain what might now be unacceptable inequalities in power, concluded that only an intense, collectively felt feeling of injustice would lead to the mobilisation of the powerless. In this sense, the powerless (for example, slaves) became powerful through exercising an anticipatory influence. Whether this then leads to their interests being taken into account, for example, through 'cooling them out' by growing welfare state institutions as part of the evolution of liberal democracies, depends, in part, on the ability of power holders to manipulate the so-called powerless. Hence, the Marxian concept of false consciousness (via elite manipulation). Whether the claimed apathy of the powerless reflects relative contentment or hopelessness (Mann, 1973) is an empirical question that has resisted historical analysis (although, see Fox Piven and Cloward's, 1977, monumental work).

Why, in any case, should people need collective action? Olson the Nobel prize-winning economist, as we mentioned earlier, in his influential work on the logic of collective action (1971) substantiates the human nature of the 'free rider'. No such rational, self-interested individual need invest in action, that usually has large opportunity costs, to achieve needs held by others since as long as others act together, the individual will benefit anyway, unless the collectivity is able to exclude non-members from benefit. In well-known cases such as feminism, few 'belong' yet many benefit. In wage-bargaining, non-members of trade unions are not normally excluded from the successful wage-improving activities of trade unionism. Some people may be driven by an influential personal value position that elevates collective goals above welfare. The potential personal refutation of Olson lies in empirical studies of voluntarism, charity, philanthropy and altruism as a means, in part, to denying a single view of the rational economic actor.

Certain collectivities, such as slaves, prisoners or peasants, or host populations in tourism destinations in poor societies, may have latent interests or power. The powerless may have an anticipatory influence, media created, that leads to their interests being taken into account by power holders and thereby watering down the claim to powerlessness. The so-called apathy of voters (when low turn-out rates at local and General Elections are being explained) may reflect relative contentment or hopelessness. Being able to stipulate the ideal size of collectivities mobilising (or having the capacity to mobilise) for political directed changes has attracted academic attention. Concepts such as 'critical mass' and 'laws', such as the superiority of small numbers, have been elucidated. Seymour Lipzet (1959) has analysed relationships between class inequality and political mobilisation. The failure of the working classes to effectively mobilise in the UK in the twentieth century, as described by Michael Mann (1973) would be explained by Lipzet as a complex mix of the following: the lower classes may share the elitist values; socialism, as a movement, has too many contradictions to warrant mass support; left-wing parties appeal to change and all voters prefer stability. Wrong suggests we need detailed work on the interactions between ethno-religious differences and class divisions before we can test either Mann's (in the UK) or Lipzet's (in the USA) claims.

This discussion of power and the logic of individual and collective political action, or the lack of it, is crucial to an understanding of the general power position of the tourist. More specifically, tourists are limited by the transitory nature of their involvement in the local political economy of their destination. While it is true that, say, regular tourists to an area can join a group of residents, often 'expats' who have formed a 'Friends of' organisation to work to stop or slow down processes of change, most tourists simply come and go. If British tourists to Durban wanted to support the local exhortations, on behalf of some beachfront residents, to move the sex workers back to the Point Road, how would they do this? What is actually happening is that the tour companies are increasingly putting tourists into hotels in Durban's Central Business District (CBD), to sustain them through containment. This tendency may act as a magnet to the sex industry, pulling workers away from working the promenade in front of the beachfront apartments. However, the only reason that the CBD is 'safe' at the moment is because at night, no-one goes there – and there is nowhere to go for tourists. Only locals know the territory well enough to define a reason for spending the evening in CBD, and they choose not to.

The tourists then really are confined to a night of CNN and hotel cocktail bars. It is the tour companies who wield the political and economic influence here since, certainly for first time 'packaged' international tourists to Durban, the latter may have little rational option but to defer to corporate authority. The holiday brochure captions of a modern CBD hotel in Durban offers no insights at all into what they actually offer in practice – safety through the manufacture of familiarity. In any case, the CBD in Durban is fast being depopulated by the flight of foot-loose companies, financial and property services, for example, to the safety and more convivial surrounds of the beach communities north of Durban. International tourists in the Durban CBD enclave may meet no-one other than other international tourists. They could just as well have stayed at the Heathrow Holiday Inn in the UK.

Chapter 8

The anatomy of the Good Tourist

Tourist goods and bads

We know that there is a widespread belief, held worldwide, that tourism development has not brought the promised nirvana to either visitors or host populations (Inglis, 2000). Countless examples are available that tell how tourism development has created more costs than benefits for known stakeholders and there is probably a silent majority who could scream about the bad impact that tourism has had on their lives (WTO, 1999b). New types of supposedly acceptable forms of tourism now proliferate – major tour companies, for example, claim to behave in ways that respect people and habitats (WTO, 1999a) and specialist tourism companies have grown up that aggressively market a socially responsible tourism product (Wheeller, 1990). Tourist destinations worldwide may seek to market eco- or sustainable or green tourism as a way of telling potential tourists and, indirectly, the host population, that they will enjoy and otherwise benefit from the tourist experience without suffering pangs of guilt and remorse through having a bad overall impact.

Individual tourists, by now, will have found it hard to ignore the exhortation to behave well, perhaps presented as an exhortation to behave in a way they would wish visitors to their own habitats to behave. Tourists have to respect – weak version – or celebrate – strong version – differences in culture while leaving things untouched by their presence in the other culture, leaving things more or less as they found them in all respects. Other than, of course, where they can act in a way that unequivocally is in the interests of the host community – such as expenditure that goes directly to the worse off members of the host culture with no costly externalities (Rawls, 1999). We cannot, of course, conclude an analysis of the desirability or otherwise of the impact of tourism on the distribution of power and resources without a clearly acknowledged vision of a socially just society. We shall return to this theme in the final chapter.

Governments know they need to control the potential downside of tourism development, either through owning key resources (land, companies, attractions) or through controlling development through laws or through a mixed economy of regulation and ownership. International tourist activity requires control, it can be argued, because it is at the forefront of a more general political correctness movement (Dower, 1998, MacIntyre, 1981) that makes demands on people and organisations to behave in ways that match the dominant contemporary morality. This behaviour may not be freely chosen, especially by hedonistic tourists. Tourists may want and expect to behave badly and host communities may tolerate this because they trade off their gains from high-priced, low-quality products. This is the classic media conceptualisation of the British tourist abroad (Inglis, 2000).

The literature on alternative or good tourism has grown rapidly alongside the growth of the industry and has underwritten the mass media's interest in telling the story of tourism development through both TV Tourism or Travel Programmes, through features on bad tourism (Butler, 1990) and through the occasional dramatic and tragic account on news programmes about people or habitat damage caused by tourism. It is difficult to avoid tourism as a social activity in a world where tourism is a very popular pastime, a major employer and is media sexy. Popular and academic, oral and written and visual accounts of tourism proliferate alongside the long-standing literary tradition of travel writing. The study of tourism has fed off and fed into the growth of tourism experience, of popular tourism and travel writing, including storytelling, and an increasing inter-disciplinary and multi-disciplinary interest in the analysis of tourism in higher education (WTO, 1996).

No self-respecting programme of tourism studies could avoid engaging with a critique of tourism development and international tourist behaviours and we suspect that the thousands of postgraduate theses that appear worldwide each year on tourism are dominated by themes that arise from assumptions or hypotheses about bad tourism and tourists and what the industry and people need to do if they wish to achieve the applause of the moral audience. Such issues are now thought to be of interest to the 'Guardian-reading' public. For example, in the UK, in 1999, an interesting partnership between the pressure group, Tourism Concern, the Guardian newspaper and the University of North London, was behind a series of public debates about the virtue of tourists, the social responsibilities of the tourism industry, and the application by states of good governance protocols and their significance for tourism development.

Good persons and good international tourists

The context is now appropriate to offer the beginnings of a formal specification of the virtues of Good Tourists. This task will call on political and moral
theory, two hitherto neglected disciplinary perspectives in tourism studies; and
much that has been implied about human nature and virtue in previous chapters
will be made more explicit here. A responsible tourist, as part of being a virtuous
human being, will know how to act properly in tourist settings, will want to act
in the right way in whatever contexts they find themselves in and will have
the ability to act successfully in their chosen ways (failed intentions or buried
motivations are not good enough). The Good Tourist will draw on deep-seated
values that muster universal acclaim when identified as informing choices or
other forms of decisions, and will have sufficient information and inclination to
make the right choice in often complex situations. Intentions must be realistic
and realised with limited, if any, unintended consequences, unless these add
to the general good. And the 'Good Tourist', like Doris Lessing's (1986) 'Good
Terrorist', will know that their own very existence suggests a moral paradox.

Tourists, as Good Tourists, will be human beings acting out their personal,
moral and political selves in contexts where they are not on home territory,
seeking pleasure from the decision to leave their home community and to take
the hedonistic and/or enlightenment road to other people's home territory. When
they travel as tourists, their personal, moral and political personas travel with
them, often with the need and motivation to make some significant adjustments.
We know from experience that some people transform themselves when becoming
tourists; they behave and think in ways that would make them strangers in
their own communities.

Tourists can call on a number of political identities or an alternative mixture,
as most obviously, citizens of the nation state as global or world citizens; or as
citizens of their local state; and, clearly, some mixture of two or three of these.
Different degrees of personal transformation take place when they travel, with
various levels and types of responses to the new situation they temporarily
find themselves in. These transformations, we are claiming, can be politically
or morally judged against our model of the Good Tourist.

People live out their lives in association with the major social relationships
they create and inherit. A standard and useful division is to assume that people
live in some relationship to the state (including global society, for some), to
civil society (or to major social institutions other than the state) and to their
families and friendship groups. Good Tourism will take place where there are
good governments, where civil society offers opportunity for virtuous people
to flourish, and where human beings consciously seek the good life in mutual
association with others. This utopian thinking is necessary since, in order to

get beyond the specifics of the concrete experience of people as tourists, we need a vision, derived from preferred moral and political life, of how they should behave in specific contexts. The traditional Western philosophical approach to this vision is to argue for a direct relationship, through rationality, between beliefs, values and action (Goulet, 1995, Hare, 1981).

This is no small task but it is straightforward enough. We need to specify what the Good Tourist will know and believe, what their deep values and attitudinal dispositions should be and what sorts of motivations and skills they will call on in order to feel the need to act well and to act as a Good Tourist should in practice. Since tourism involves travel, then, preferably, these belief, value and action specifications should also be transportable. That is, be more or less acceptable as leading to good outcomes from tourist activity wherever tourists are to be found. This raises the difficult but unavoidable issue of the relationship, as the individual experiences it, between universal propositions about human behaviour, such as equal chances for men and women to acquire income and wealth, and local and culturally diverse prevailing political, economic and cultural norms. The limits to the toleration of diversity, as we indicated in chapter 5, are key here. A particular British specification of the good life and of virtuous behaviour will not be sufficient to underwrite the specification of the British Good Tourist in Islamic or Zulu or religious and cultural settings (Mendus, 1988). But notice that because of the intermingling of host and tourist activities in long-standing tourist destinations, the so-called 'host culture' is itself an outcome of the progressive weathering of tourism's elements; of hosts and tourists interacting and moulding the social, economic and political landscape.

In KwaZulu-Natal, the KZNTA has created 'The Tourist Guide Code of Conduct and Ethics' (www.zulu.org.za), stipulating 17 prescriptive behaviours for professional (accredited) tourist guides. One of these is that they 'shall be impartial, unbiased and positive, and represent South Africa objectively' (in another code, a sub-text, meaning: don't ever dare to denigrate South Africa to international tourists!). So, as we have predicted in chapter 5, the limits of toleration of all interested and involved parties will be tested.

We can return, briefly, to a three-fold division of the main spheres of social life – the individual, the firm and the state. The virtuous individual, as a tourist, will think, judge and act in ways that are universally recognised as good conduct. Moral and political philosophy will help with this specification although we have no intention of trying to introduce and summarise the long-standing and contested philosophical debates about virtue, the good life, the general will and other meta concepts. In context, we can nearly always tell when people are behaving badly. For example, in a small Durban harbour-front restaurant, two young Australian women who were drunk, were refused entry (sensitively) to a Chinese restaurant, and proceeding to claim, loudly, that they were being victimised, received embarrassed attention, at first, from the onlookers, and then universal condemnation. These were young international tourists behaving badly and older international tourists behaving well. In KwaZulu-Natal, in a hotel lodge in the Drakensburg mountains, a white tourist from Johannesburg asserts loudly and vehemently, in conversation with fellow guests at dinner, that 'blacks lack the courage to play rugby'; while being served by a Zulu male waiter. This is a tourist behaving badly.

The good firm can be identified through the application of criteria derived from the growing theory and, hopefully, practice of business ethics, for example, through subscribing to practices that exude corporate responsibility (McIntosh et al., 1998; Allen, Acres and Tromans, 2001). The swiftest way into defining good state or good governance (a term used by the main international aid donor countries and agencies) is to start from a working definition of government. The monopolisation of legitimate force in a society is a strong distinguishing feature of government. Force is a form of power and good governments can be viewed as making the right decisions about the form, uses and bases of power, as we saw in chapter 7. Contrasts in powers of arrest, especially in the use of force, are clear and strong examples of major differences between governments that regularly put tourists into the public gaze. Englishness, alcohol and 'laddishness' are not treated as kindly by the police in Durban as they sometimes are in Newcastle.

What, then, underwrites responsible tourist behaviour? First, we need a model of the autonomous tourist, a travelling or travelled pleasure or enlightenment seeker, and second, a model of the tourist in social context.

Figure 1: The autonomous, responsible tourist

Knowledge	Values	Skills
will know what they do know and what they don't and need to know in order to act responsibly; will be able to make rational and moral decisions about behaviour in context	will acknowledge their obligations to other human beings and habitats through a respect for toleration and the exercise of power; will have a capacity for empathy and sensitivity to human needs, and a celebration of the need for pleasure/enlightenment in theirs and other people's lives	will include political skills and cultural skills, appropriate to control or mediate the activities of themselves, other individuals, firms and governments

Figure 2: The political contexts and arenas of tourist activity and good tourism

Context	Good tourism
The individual	has knowledge values and skills so they know what they need to know, feel what they need to feel and can do what they think they should do
	Key concepts: obligation, toleration, power, human needs, pleasure, enlightenment
The firm	exercises corporate responsibility through active recognition of the need to meet economic and social goals through minimising its bad impacts and maximising benefits for all potential beneficiaries
	Key concepts: corporate responsibility, social and economic objectives, impact
Government	exercises responsible power, has legitimate (non-coercive) practices
	Key concepts: prohibition, restriction, compensation

We have argued that we cannot separate the concept of the socially responsible tourist from a vision of human virtue. We have also argued that the Good Tourist will not only know what they need to know to behave well but will want and be able to behave well. At this stage in the development of the specification, the focus will be on the 'key concepts' identified in Figures 1 and 2, listed in the 'individual' segment. The justification for this initial and fundamental focus is that the attempts to get beyond exhortations for tourists to behave well and to work out the implications of how tourists and hosts should behave from the numerous case studies of bad tourism that now dominate the literature, are remarkably scarce on the ground (Seabrook, 1996).

Humility, identity and citizenship

Bad behaviour is easy to identify and label as such but, as in criminal behaviour, there is a major debate always waiting to surface about who or what actually defines what counts as crime, and behaviour that is morally intolerable. This debate has its roots in philosophical questions about the nature of human nature and about the form and shape of causality and determinism in social life. The literature about reformed tourism practice seems to have skipped a necessary stage in the argument, that is to search for some universally accepted values and a behaviour base that coherently and consistently informs thought and action, and, as has been stressed in our KwaZulu-Natal focus, arises from an accurate cultural awareness of the political, economic and social contexts. This sounds daunting and unrealistic, and if it proves to be so in practice, then the tourist response should be to behave with due humility in the face of uncertainties.

What follows is a focus on the concept of identity, and citizenship as a key identity concept, that allows us to theorise about the actions of tourists and, indeed, to be judgemental about tourist activities. Since individuals are the prime moral agents in both industry and government, a stress on the features of the Good Tourist will illuminate the concept and practice of Good Firms and Good Government. We need to separate out the pleasure and/or enlightenment principle as an end state, something that defines tourism and that is an intended outcome of tourism, from other features that are more procedural in that they are concerned with how the pleasure-through-travel aim is met. These features are few in number since the claim is being made that these are universal, although it is simultaneously argued that their application will need to be determined by accurate information about and sensitivity to the cultural specifics and dynamics of any social situation.

The strongest descriptor here, given our stress on the political and cultural and the international, national and local, is to use the concept of citizenship. We argue that tourist-as-citizen allows us to develop the persona of the Good Tourist. We need to analyse the nature of citizenship and the possibilities of local, national and global citizenship (Wringe, 1999; Dunkerley et al., 2002) in tandem with an analysis of the ethical dimension in relationships between localities; specifically, between nation states, given our particular interest in international tourism and international tourists visiting South Africa (Dower, 1998; Goulet, 1995). What we are seeking to understand is what Kidder (1995) refers to as situations in which 'Good People Make Tough Choices'.

A surgeon in one of the north coast hospitals in KwaZulu-Natal told us that hospital records suggested that about 80 per cent of all hospital cases he dealt with were either crime-related, especially crime with violence, or AIDS-related. In the same breath, he went on to celebrate the 'ideal' working conditions he experienced, where there was little red tape, he had freedom to experiment, where his black patients trusted him implicitly and where there was no fear of litigation if things went wrong, compared to the dreadful lawyer-dominated worlds of medicine in the USA and Britain. This social dualism, of repulsion and celebration, is, in general terms, unsurprising since all societies have elements that can be described in such dualistic terms, but the specific forms in which these social 'surprises' presented themselves in KwaZulu-Natal led to the salutary reminder that we knew very little about the province and its peoples. This state of comparative ignorance, and its logically correlated behaviour, driven by humility, should define and condition the experience of the international tourist, both domestic and international and, of course, will in part determine the behaviour of host populations. What we are doing in this chapter is showing the shape of a model that identifies some common features and issues that potentially 'tie together' people from different localities, regions or nation states.

Seymour (1999), a senior research officer with the KNTA, estimates that, in 1998, 40 per cent of all international tourists to South Africa visited

KwaZulu-Natal. His survey work indicates that they came for the wildlife, the scenery and beaches, and for the Zulu culture and some 3/4 of these visitors were independent travellers, usually combining a holiday with visiting friends or relatives. So, we can safely assume that a significant proportion of the British tourists who visited South Africa in 1998 had a tourist experience mediated by their friends or family. Indeed, the female partner of a male British academic working at a University in KwaZulu-Natal, on a three-year contract, set up a tourism business specifically designed to take the decisional and organisational pains away from local people who felt obliged to arrange tourist itineraries for friends or family visiting KwaZulu-Natal. We mention this because there is little commentary in the tourism literature about this aspect of the management of the tourist experience, especially for the so-called 'independent' traveller, whose independence may be significantly constrained, quite willingly, by becoming putty in the hands of local residents or temporary workers in South Africa, known to them as friends or family. This factor adds to the complexity of the process through which the tourist and local people experience tourism.

Local people in KwaZulu-Natal, such as the residents of Kwa Mashu in Durban, a predominantly black community famed for once housing Mahatma Gandhi and, more recently, for being the site of severe political violence, experience the tourist gaze when they visit the Durban beachfront for religious ceremony or to collect sea water to sell back in Kwa Mashu for its magical and medicinal properties. The town of Matubatuba, some 20km inland from St Lucia, is home to the waitresses who serve on tourists visiting the up-and-coming restaurants of St Lucia town. These young women sleep, illegally, in Dukuduku South forest, in insecure accommodation monopolised by landlords who charge only just little enough to make it cheaper for the waitresses and cleaners to sleep in the forest, after a day and night's work, than to try and get back to Matubatuba. Their wages, of course, do return to Matubatuba since, in Zulu society, as in some other African cultures, anyone who is earning income from work is obliged to share this with the immediate and extended family. The casual tourist tip for service at the restaurant can pay for a nephew's schoolbooks. The culture of communal ownership of earned income can lead to obvious moral dilemmas for people in work (to fail to declare income, to resist any higher wages for more difficult work, knowing that any additional income will, at best, have to be shared).

These economic, moral and political alignments are the DNA of citizenship. We cannot know their precise makeup in any full sense but we can always behave so as to recognise that human beings and human interactions and relationships build and build on the lived experience of individuals. This rather bald point is made in order to urge caution when we read, for example, that:

The emphasis of this book has been on the need to take account of the context in which tourism takes place, with the suggestion that it acts as a barometer of the global political economy rather than a driver of it. The idea that tourism is a response to the need to escape from the division of labour arising from the present political economy would clearly fit in with this... However, the desire to escape everyday life long predates industrialisation and is common to most cultures – even if it has been realised in different ways [Brown, 1998, p.103].

The June 1999 elections in South Africa led to a range of different press and media coverage in Britain. One type of treatment was to draw pen-portraits of the 'new' or the 'old' South Africans. One such article in the *Guardian* (28 May 1999), by Gary Younge, was headed: 'I know things have changed because I can eat with white people', quoting one of the featured characters, and under this, 'As they go to the polls, Gary Younge asks four very different South Africans how much has changed since the bad old days of apartheid' (that could conceivably, of course, have been, for some potential black respondents, the good old days of apartheid, but not these chosen few). Each character interviewed and whose portrait is drawn is subject to a summary, echoing the *dramatis personae* of Peter Greenaway's erotic and violent film, *The Cook, the Thief, his Wife and her Lover*.

We are introduced to four people:

- 'The cook, Maria Zulu. Having watched her older children suffer under the old school system, Maria Zulu now hopes her younger ones will get a better start in life.'
- 'The wife, Margie Morrell. When her husband was held up at gunpoint, and security costs on their cul-de-sac rocketed, Margie Morell began to contemplate a fresh start.'
- 'The thief, Colin Nkabinde. Sentenced to five years for theft, Colin Nkabinde had his term cut by Mandela – he now attends church and intends to marry and start a family.'
- 'The lover, Bheki Moutlong. Gay Christian and trained flower arranger Bheki Moutlong feels things have improved for homosexuals in his country; he hopes to get a job soon.'

These pen-portraits fit perfectly inside the political rhetoric of the ANC's Reconstruction and Development Programme, where the primary motivation (Mandela, 1999) is 'the desire to attain a nation at peace with itself and be able to build a better life for all'. In the same article, Mandela stresses the theme and need for reconciliation, which we discussed in chapter 5.

The path towards reconciliation touches upon every facet of our lives: it requires the dismantling of apartheid and the measures that reinforced it;

and that we overcome the consequences of that inhuman system that live on in our attitudes towards one another as well as in the poverty and inequality that affect the lives of millions. (Reconciliation) is inseparable from the achievement of a non-racial, democratic, and united nation that affords common citizenship, rights, and obligations to each and every person, while it respects the diversity of our people.

This political pen-portrait overlays and conditions the projected futures for our residents of Kwa Mashu, Matubatuba and the four Guardian Angels, and the other 40 million South Africans (Christopher, 1999), eight million of whom, according to the 1996 census, live in KwaZulu-Natal Province. Of these eight million, approximately 80 per cent are African, 1 per cent are Coloured, 9 per cent are Indian (mainly living in the Durban metropolitan area) and 6 per cent are white (Christopher, 1999). Racial and gender inequalities, as Mandela alludes to, are manifest in, for example, relative income levels, which are significantly determined by economic activity and unemployment rates.

Recollection and human rights and wrongs

We may now ask, how do notions of identity, citizenship and community enable us to relate the experience of tourism to the experience of being a human being? One obvious theme, which Mandela, among others, can't escape from in their aspirational speeches, is the concept of human rights. It is easy to forget that human rights, as part of world order, are younger than Mandela himself, being debated in the 1930s and given some political clout as part of the processes that led to the United Nations and its Declaration of Human Rights, to the Nuremberg trials and to the European Court of Human Rights. Human rights are a global fashion, leading some people to explore the possibility of an enforceable world Human Rights regime (Robertson, 1999). Such a movement rests on the moral proposition that every crime committed against humanity is a crime against all of us, and we all therefore suffer from a loss of rights as a result. This underwrites the special place that South Africa may hold in the hearts and minds of British citizens, for example, whereby the experience of apartheid infuses the relationships between the two nation states. British tourists to South Africa may indeed, as we have sketched in chapter 5, suffer from the 'Exploitation of Our Longings for Connectedness', the subtitle of Freie's stimulating book, *Counterfeit Community* (1998).

'Genuine community', for Freie, is:

an interlocking pattern of just human relationships in that people have at least a minimal sense of consensus within a definable territory. People within a community actively participate and co-operate with others to create their own self-worth, a sense of caring about others, and a feeling for the spirit of connectedness [1998, p.23].

In contrast:

Counterfeit community is composed of images, symbols, structures, and suggestions of association and connectedness that are false and ultimately exploitative. Unlike genuine community that demands that we actively participate, counterfeit community superficially and symbolically links us to others. It is more spectacle than substance. Counterfeit community projects images of community but keeps us at arm's length by never asking that we act responsibly to maintain the kinds of relationships necessary for genuine community [Freie, 1998, p.5].

Tourism, of course, has long held out the possibility that it will develop a sense of community between peoples from different nation states and will, in so doing, also promote world peace. In Var, Ap and Van Doren (in Theobald, 1994, p.27), we find a bald claim for tourism – 'I have watched the cultures of all kinds blow around my house and other winds have blown the seeds of peace, for travel is the language of peace' – quoting, appropriately for us, the former resident of Kwa Mashu, KwaZulu-Natal, Mahatma Gandhi.

In the same edited volume, we find a section headed 'Milking the macabre' inside a chapter entitled 'Tourism: the nostalgia industry of the future' (Dann, in Theobald, 1994). The force of Dann's thesis is that we may decide, as tourists (or our friends or family may decide for us) that we should visit Kwa Mashu not because we can see where Gandhi lived but because we visit the sites of political violence, as spectators not only of violence as an attractive way of dealing with political or culture differences to some communities, such as Kwa Mashu used to be, but to celebrate violence as an Attraction. To develop this argument, we would argue, as we have begun to do in chapters 6 and 7, that the academic tourism specialists need to engage with the work of people like Ignatieff (on nostalgia and voyeurism and civil war) and Cox (on remorse, reparation and guilt).

Part of our political identity, our citizenship, comes from what we learn, and the main political curriculum in South Africa, as we have seen, is the past. The role of recollection, especially from what Dostoevsky called 'preserved, sacred memory' (quoted in Dallmayr, 1998, p.145) underpins the particular influence that the complex mix in human lives of action and circumstance and purpose and contingency has in forming political identity. The force of the past in shaping the present in South Africa goes beyond the usual formulation of rationalist philosophy that sees the past only as a prelude to the present, which in turn is merely a milestone on the way to the future. In this way of thinking, remembered experience is of little significance, soon overtaken by or subsumed within a deeper form of reflection on the 'now'. The role of recollection, as the experience of the Truth and Reconciliation Commission (TRC) has shown (indeed, this point is part of the rationale for the Commission) recollection can be emancipatory in so far as it forestalls both forgetfulness and complacency (Dallmayr, 1998). But also, of course, in the South African context, it can be painful, keeping alive the memory of dislocations and the agonies of inequalities and associated unfairness.

The obvious connection to make here with mainstream tourism constructs is with the concepts of heritage and authenticity and their place in the task of understanding the international tourist's experience of KwaZulu-Natal. More particularly, the work of the TRC is a concrete example of the liberation of remembrance that, in so far as it may stress the retrieval of 'indigenous potentials' (Dallmayr, 1998, p.161), serves to keep the brakes on the move towards the realisation of Western-style democracy in South Africa. The latter, in any case, holds no natural monopoly over concepts such as truth and justice, despite the technological potential for a culture of 'universal' Western govern-ance to submerge non-Western cultures and political traditions. Nonetheless, the African peoples of KwaZulu-Natal live with and contribute to a complex duality of affirmation and defence of their cultural traditions and identities while at the same time holding out the possibility of radical transformation of the latter in the face of alternative futures. This difficult cultural and political project has to preserve a stress on distinctiveness without the reification of localness, parochialism or 'cultural difference'. This struggle has a major influence on the tourist experience of South Africa.

Into this arena of what Taylor has called the 'Politics of Recognition' (in Gutmann, 1996) strides the tourist who, we know, cannot be summed up in any convenient way – there is no such thing as the 'average tourist'. However, some generalisations do still seem to have currency, especially those of the 'mass tourist' and the 'alternative tourist' and we need to explore the identity of the latter and how this fits into the preceding political and cultural territory. According to Krippendorf (1987, p.37) the alternative tourists are those who 'try to establish more contact with the local population, try to do without the tourist infrastructure and use the same accommodation and transport facilities as the natives'.

We can immediately see the poverty of this now dated yet popular definition in the South African tourism context, and we have already discussed in previous chapters how the eco-tourists, a particular form of alternative tourist who focuses on being active contributors to the health and future development of the host ecology, has great difficulty, in practice, in deciding what is the best thing to do to meet the latter objectives – they suffer from major gaps in essential information to make rational choices (Sher, 1997). Being in harmony with nature and with local cultures is an onerous task for the international tourist-citizen.

Collective and political action

The possibility of an eco-trip is a considerable factor in the demand for KwaZulu-Natal tourism (Seymour, 1999), and we have discussed earlier the difficulties facing agencies such as the KwaZulu-Natal Nature Conservation Service in promoting opportunities for African employment, income and general improvements in well-being at the same time as ensuring that development decisions effectively and efficiently reflect the full value of natural and cultural resources for the tourist industry. What then are the possibilities of local political mobilisation in order to promote the interests of eco-tourism through the resolution of potentially opposing tendencies, of conflicting agendas? Under what conditions do citizens come together to offer a collective voice and put into place a force-field of solidarity against development thought to be in someone else's interest (Fox Piven and Cloward, 1977)? One theory or principle is the 'several among some' principle (Cioffi-Revilla, 1998, p.199). This is a subgroup solution to the classic collective action problem (Olson, 1971). The argument here is that collective action is not initiated by the group itself, say, the African waitresses who work in St Lucia and live in Dukuduku South forest, nor by a single individual, but that some core subgroup 'activates'. The classic shape for this core subgroup is well known; a charismatic and 'streetwise' leader and a few close followers, but we still cannot accurately predict the course nor outcome of events because of the position of uncertainty as a fundamental property of politics – we return, yet again, to the theme of risk: 'Uncertainty is ubiquitous, consequential and ineradicable in political life' (Cioffi-Revilla, 1998, p.3).

The strength of Cioffi-Revilla's work is that he tries to penetrate the properties of political uncertainty and put the resulting analysis up as a cornerstone of political theory. In this theory, what is of importance to our discussion of citizenship and identity is the presence of uncertainty in individual decisions where choices have to be made that seem less than ideal (Sher, 1997), and may also be interactive; and where uncertainty underwrites processes and outcomes of collective action. The late twentieth-century preoccupation with risk and uncertainty, a prevailing theme of this book, puts a new gloss on Olson's classic 1971 work, *The Logic of Collective Action*. We began this chapter by drawing a sketch map of the Good Tourist and we have now moved on to consider the possibilities of Good Tourists acting in unison through collective political action. What are the conditions under which the Good Tourist, as a leader, close follower, or supporter, becomes part of a recognisable group established to resist or to bring about change? Does the concept of 'global citizenship', for example, suggest that tourists, as world citizens, are notionally there to call or be called on to engage in political action for tourism development?

The starting place for Olson is a rehearsal of the claim that economically motivated groups of individuals, such as the residents of the newly gentrified apartment blocks of South Beach, Durban, who want to 'clean-up' the beachfront in order to raise the value of their properties, usually come together (to form a Residents Association in this case) to further those common interests. As Olson (1971, Introduction) writes,

> If the members of some group have a common interest or objective, and if they would all be better off if that objective were achieved, it has been thought to follow logically that the individuals in that group would, if they were rational and self-interested, act to achieve that objective (and) the assumption that organisations typically exist to further the common interests of groups of people is implicit in most of the literature about organisations.

Olson's argument, however, is that unless there are special circumstances, a very small group say, or the presence of incentive or inducement arrangements, or coercion of some sort, 'rational, self-interested individuals will not act to achieve their common or group interests' (1971, Introduction).

Thinking through the logic of Olson's argument and searching for empirical verification of the logic of collective action, are both absent from the academic tourism literature about community-led tourism development in general and, in particular, from the limited literature about tourism development in KwaZulu-Natal. Why should African people, for example, support the group with potentially the strongest identity, the national state? Will the rallying calls of 'Rainbow Nation' and 'African Renaissance' create the sort of modern nationalist community that the new South African government seems to want? Olson's basic argument is that where the benefits from collective action cannot be ring-fenced by those who actively invested in the 'cause', then those who know they will benefit in any case have no rational incentive to bear the costs of active involvement (assuming that there are always opportunity costs to such involvement). Free riders simply judge that they have better things to do and better places to be.

The power of this analysis for us is that it begins to explain why putting the emphasis on 'community-led' tourism development may be doomed to failure since we know that the largest 'groups' in a society are the unorganised groups that have no visible lobby, take no action and appear to have only the power of latent action. Poor African communities in KwaZulu-Natal may fit this description. Latent groups have no incentive to act voluntarily to further their common interests, and it is this feature that determines their unorganised and latent characteristics, and which also will act to effectively disempower them in a democratic social system managed to reflect the activities of organised groups. Olson's work also suggests that claims that some sort of new local and national forms of citizenship are beginning to appear, a movement perhaps thought to be part of the residue of the June 1999 elections, will need to be treated with caution.

Citizenship properly prescribes a person's relationship to a polity, primarily the nation state but increasingly the local and world politics (Wringe, 1999). This possible multi-layering of citizenship, and the particular forms it takes for individuals, could usefully inform a political analysis of the social interactions and their economic and political dimensions that define the international tourism experience. What Olson tells us is that we should not necessarily expect these political identities to lead to new forms of relationships for individuals inside groups or collectivities, or that individuals will gain a new or enhanced sense of community from such a label as 'world citizen'.

Moral universes

Does the claim to be a citizen of the world (a claim that could be seen to unite tourists and indigenous populations) lead to a claim that there is a world ethic (Dower, 1998)? For Dower, a world ethic would be an ethical theory that acted as a guide to how we should behave in our relations to all peoples through its defining sets of norms and values and obligations and responsibilities. A dilemma here, of course, is that what people take to be universal values, such as some of the procedural values that underwrite democratic societies (valuing honesty, trust, and tolerance, for example), may not be the moral framework that informs action in the real world. The search for universalism in the types and standards of personal relationships may not be worth the effort. We have already seen that the promotion of human rights as a form of universalism, as a way, for example, of arguing for an entitlement to minimum standards of well-being for all peoples (Doyal and Gough, 1991), which itself needs to square a cosmopolitan solidarity with a celebration of a localised culture, may not be able to take the practical strain imposed on it. The simultaneous need to respect cultural diversity and a plurality of values and to promote a sense of world citizenship (and stewardship) may fail under the burden of reconciling incommensurate norms and values. If there is no such thing as a generally accepted universal value system, then, as Dower argues, we are left with 'many different systems of knowledge, worldviews, and ways of life that may simply be incommensurable' (1998, p.34).

This is not to argue, of course, that each and every way of life is of equal moral standing, and, again, this is where dilemmas exist that can trap both international tourists and indigenous populations into a state of anxious paralysis. People feel uncomfortable with each other's behaviour yet recognise a need for caution (wondering whether the limits of toleration have been breached) before publicly objecting. We saw, in chapter 5 with the parable of the Nissan drive to the Kosi Bay river mouth, the attractiveness of caution (or the cowardice of quietism).

Apart from human rights, the other major contender for a unifying strand informing the values and behaviours of multi-layered citizens, is a commitment to global social justice. This theory rests on the proposition that the economies of the world are so intertwined that their distribution effects can be judged and, in principle, regulated, against a social justice gold standard. Dower makes the point that such a theory remains only a theory because we should not have empirical confidence in the proposition that we have an intertwined world economy. However, if people believe that this is the case, and certainly it is possible to see concrete evidence of this in the economic development of the new South Africa, then we can also believe in and thereby work for the realisation of global social justice.

The multi-layered citizen, co-existing in their local, national and world politics, has a complex ordering of priorities, though all informed, as we have seen through Olson's (1971) work, by rational self-interest (another theme we will return to). We can stay loyal to our local community and to our nation state, but the moral pull of an association with a global view of what should be, say in terms of human rights or distributions of resources and well-being, may cause tensions. But this is only to say, as we have already argued, that people suffer from information lapses (and information inequalities) when coming to a view about what is in their self-interest. Eco-tourists could choose to rationalise their behaviour in terms of self-interest but find it more difficult to do so, it seems, than to argue on behalf of the unborn child who they assert deserves a particular future. This does not mean that the self-interest argument could not be made but that it seems more elusive or less attractive to the Good Tourist as a comment on human nature.

Developing political understanding

Citizens trying to work out their priorities are faced with a daunting task that will present itself as a series of situational dilemmas, and tourism increases the frequency and, perhaps, the intensity of those dilemmas. Tourists and local populations will need to call implicitly on their political understandings of social and economic relationships (Allen, 1997), and in the case of British tourists visiting South Africa, will need to be able to begin to unravel the development knots. Conceptually, we can distinguish a number of strands that need to be disentangled and then retied to make a belief system that informs action and is rationally and morally defensible (inside the difficult arena of universalism versus cultural diversity, as we have seen, just to compound the difficulty). Development is about improvements in people's lives, but what counts as improvement?

Can we agree on how to assess whether improvement has taken place and why, and what priority we should give to the needs of the metaphysical worlds of future generations and the global village? Development has a moral imperative in so far as we tend to argue that things should be better than they are and then to seek ways of making them better and producing models and measures for estimating that improvement has actually happened and why. The problem is lack of agreement about what 'things' are of most worth. Irrespective of what we should want, we know that international tourism is seen by inter-national, national and provincial governments and agencies, as a universal economic panacea for the problems bedevilling development. We also know that, for individuals, the dominant claim made about the significance of international tourism in their lives is that they want to leave behind the problems of this life and set out in search of paradise that can be found on this earth: 'Travel brochures sell us paradise islands in which we indulge many potent dreams...This is paradise as a theme park. Paradise has to some extent become a leisure pursuit, a holiday destination' (North, in Whelan, 1992, p.66).

In part then, 'Better Government' and 'Good Governance' will have to grapple with the tension created by the political and economic role of tourism as a panacea for failed development, and its social and personal icons as paradise, or as respite care for stressed-out and risk-averse souls. When we talk about citizenship, we have seen that we are asserting that people identify with some collective polity that we can define spatially. Good Tourists, as Good Citizens, want their thoughts and actions to be regulated by Good Government, but, as we have noted, would prefer the latter to be brought about at least cost to themselves – they should ask themselves whether they are likely to enjoy the fruits of Good Government because of the political actions of others. In any case, in South Africa, there is an intense and high-profile struggle going on to determine the degree and ways (including meeting cost-effectiveness criteria) in which the recently elected government should regulate the lives of its citizens. The international tourist, as a citizen of the world, will be interested in the political changes going on and, in any case, will, as a tourist, be visiting a country where the tourist experience is clearly mediated by the contemporary political agenda and by tourism itself being part of that agenda.

Governments are about regulation and being a citizen means identifying with (if only to fight against) a particular regulatory regime. There are three main types of government regulatory activity and each, together with the conflict over its nature, conditions the nature of citizenship and the identity, therefore, of tourists and African populations in KwaZulu-Natal. Economic regulation is where it is thought to be essential for societies to compensate for market failure. Where possible, governments will promote competition between firms and where it is not possible to do this, consumers and firms themselves will be protected against or compensated for unfair, anti-competitive practices. Second, environmental regulation is thought to be required when it is predicted that improvements in economic welfare may only be short term, rather than sustainable, where Good Government is about taking the long-term view, and where the costs of any gains in economic welfare may be too high to bear, rationally and morally. The costs from the misuse of natural resources are a case in point.

Third, social regulation arises from preferences about the distribution of power and resources and about affecting the distribution of these, usually on the basis of some sort of social justice argument, so that citizens and groups of citizens are protected against discrimination or exploitation and are protected from absolute poverty. When we tracked the efforts of the KwaZulu-Natal Nature Conservation Service to make sense of the tourist demand for the paradise of the St Lucia wetlands area, in the context of Dukuduku South people's long-standing asserted rights; and when we talked to local African people about the visit of Prince Charles to the area, and read ministerial statements about the Dukuduku South problem being 'solved', all alongside the continual creation and re-creation of the Richard's Bay Mining Companies' corporate strategy for mining in the area, we saw the three sets of intertwined regulatory functions at play. We can reasonably ask: are we witnessing Good Government at work here in concert with Good Citizenship?

As far as the citizens of KwaZulu-Natal are concerned, they could be expected to ask the following question of their provincial government: Are the regulatory processes as open and transparent as they can be and are the enforcement mechanisms accountable for their effectiveness and value for money? Does the province need what we can call a Comprehensive Regulatory Review (*should* the responses to our first question be negative)? Can the province be expected to regulate, given the influence of the National government and the influence of international bodies and agencies, including large firms (such as international tourist companies)? Indeed, what lessons can the province learn from the international experience of regulatory reform? It could learn, for example, the lesson that regulation is usually an untidy mixture of formal, informal and *ad hoc* interventions, driven by political agendas rather than by administrative principles and practices.

The major themes of government reform in South Africa, unsurprisingly, have been a view that state intervention is usually a source of the problem rather than part of the solution, and that markets are the key mediators in the development process and in the globalisation process. The tragedy of a sterile central bureaucracy, sanitised and drained by the effort to police admini-strative and cultural inefficiencies in government, in unseemly cahoots with a mindless and out-of-control globalisation underwritten by hegemonic market forces, is part of the political nightmare of contemporary KwaZulu-Natal. The importance of this vision is that it is pushing the constant search for resistance through alternative political futures, the consistent 'alternative' being to recast processes of political change in a popular-democratic direction towards democratic participation, community development and, ultimately, an individual and group identity for all citizens. This push for political change should be based on being able and wanting to work at change politically when citizens accurately perceive existing situations and plans to enshrine and enhance injustice and unfairness. This vision of democracy, based on a knowledgeable and efficacious citizenry (Crick, 1969) has been summarised by Kothari, writing about India, as:

> not just electoral politics but a politics based on critical interventions that will once again give a sense of hope and confidence to the poor and marginalized sections of society, generate a process of empowerment, a new realignment of forces and, out of it all, a new agenda for the state... If minority (or, for that matter, the majority) groups in this country are to be weaned away from the influence of fundamentalism, they must be made to feel socially and economically secure. Their culture and religion must he protected from external violence and from unnecessary moralising. It must be recognised that social transformation can only legitimately come from within a society or community... External threats to the identity of such communities only strengthen the traditionalists and fundamentalists within them, and margin-alize the progressive forces [in Dallmayr, 1998, pp.228–29].

Kothari's sentiments are quoted at length because they are fine words that totally fail to deal with Olson's (1971) analysis of where the incentive to engage in direct political action is to come from. Echoes of Kothari's words are to be found on our interview tapes with officers and employees of the KZNNCS, the KZNTA and the Conservation Corporation at Phinda, who have learnt this new discourse of empowerment and reproduce it in their corporate mission statements and have internalised it to such a degree that it is written and spoken without any sense of parody or scepticism. We are also back in the territory of tradition and heritage and its commodification by the tourism industry, since underlying this empowerment thesis is a view that indigenous cultural resources can act as the critical buffers against the homogenising effects of nationalism and globalisation, where nationalism is a by-product of globalisation. The image and myth of Rousseau's 'noble savage' (Whelan, 1992) comes to mind. We saw no 'noble savages' at Shakaland, despite the costumes, only streetwise young Africans glad to be in work where they could have fun simultaneously guiding and ridiculing the common tourists.

The quest for universal procedural values

For the task of trying to understand identity, citizenship and tourism in KwaZulu-Natal, the relationship between heritage, culture, and development and social justice is of major importance. We have framed this book in part through telling about everyday incidents that can lead to dilemmas about how to 'be' inside those situations and what their implications might be for future thinking and action. One way of conceptualising culture is that it conditions our reflected judgement in ways that are specific and can be contrasted to other culturally specific contexts. Culture is a tool, also, to remind us of the human presence in development and, therefore, of the possibility of a common universe of discourse in social encounters with 'strangers'. This is not the place to discuss the difficulties of assessing and prescribing the significance of similarities and differences among peoples, and the influence of any subsequent analysis, on adjudicating the primacy of 'justice' or 'solidarity', whenever the two conflict, in social theory and practice. But we can say that when citizens come together, their remembered experiences will be, at least in part, anchored in concrete moral sentiments or situations, such as feeling 'ripped-off' by a shopping encounter, or the anger that comes from a failure to recognise generosity, or the frustration and exasperation, for the British, when they cannot get a 'decent' cup of tea or 'pint'. There are well-known philosophical and psychological issues here too, of course, about how far we are able to become moral spectators or detached observers, of our own remembered performances. But we can apply or assign some universal rules to particular contexts, as Rawls (1999) would have us do. We could prefer, for example, equal liberty and social justice for all, or sameness of treatment of citizens, to a primary celebration of 'difference'; to be, in effect, blind to differences of status, gender, race and so on, whereby we universalise the particular through the recognition of the unique identity of each individual or group.

We have seen earlier that all peoples may lay claim to multiple citizenships, local, national and global, or that an argument can be made for the possibility of multiple citizenships. This does not stop us from applying to this framework the notion of equal citizenship, whereby all, because of the common features of being a human being, are worthy of equal respect and treatment. This is the position that Dworkin (1996), following Kant, so lucidly argues for. A useful dualism here is to remember that we are individuals who exist among other persons and that we are also part of a culture-bearing group among other peoples. What we have outlined throughout these later chapters is that these two semi-detached propositions about identity come into contact with each other at prime moments, as part of the international tourism experience, and lead to all sorts of pragmatic accommodations, as with our lone, relatively wealthy male tourist on the Durban beachfront. The onus on the beachfront early evening tourist is to reconcile implicit, or reflective universal procedures, such as rights to equal respect, with the potential claims by Africans he might meet, that their own rational needs and their 'differences' as individuals be recognised. Despite the pressure here of a postmodern or post-structuralism discourse, the reality of the international tourist experience in the heartlands of KwaZulu-Natal, is that a prospective or reactive moral position on action or non-action in a situation is unavoidable. Moral indifference never made it to paradise.

An equal playing field and size 42 sandals

The problem remains of whether we can find a defensible moral framework to inform the international tourist experience in KwaZulu-Natal? In order to examine this question, we need to return to the possibility of global or world citizenship as part of the triumvirate of political identities that the thoroughly postmodern citizen might lay claim to. There are, for example, two major conceits that we have alluded to that condition the tourist experience. The first of these is the view that people from the North and the West hold the key to universal procedural rules of social relationships and discourses. The second is that the 'noble savage' is due respect simply because he is, by definition, closer to the essence and truth of things (a facility long since eroded by the weathering of industrialisation and urbanisation on peoples from the nation states of the North and West).

What we need, according to Taylor (1992), following Hegel, is a global 'politics of recognition'. Technologically, this can come from the forked tongues of the mass media, especially television, and tourism, as we began to argue in chapter 6. For the obstacles to learning – to get beyond compulsory mis-education by Murdoch and Thomas Cook – are rooted and routed in the asymmetry between North and South, more particularly, between Swindon, England and St Lucia, KwaZulu-Natal. We have known this for some time, notably through the vivid writings of Frantz Fanon (1967) that Africans need to liberate themselves from the colonial impact of 'Negrophobia'.

We are moving towards what might seem to be unreasonable and unrealistic demands on the political consciousnesses and competencies of visitors and indigenous populations. Alternative conceptions of social justice exist, for example, and arise from a particular mix of recognition of individual and cultural differentiation. We cannot pull down a simple rule to decide on the intellectual or moral superiority of alternative conceptions and nor can we reasonably expect individuals to be able to defend their actions inside a situation by reference to their preferred formulation. The issue, as Dallmayr (1998, p.271) so succinctly puts it, is 'how to recognise difference without sanctioning discrimination and individual and group privilege, and how to promote universalism without becoming a pawn in hegemonic power plays'.

His solution, which has a seductive charm, is to say that we – in our case, as international tourists – have to exercise 'prudential judgement'. Prudential judgement: 'is meant to adjudicate between justice as procedural norm and justice as goodness or the "good life", between the principle of universally equal rights and the ethical demands of particular relationships and situated life contexts, in a sense negotiating the difference between Western and non-Western modes of ethical sensitivity' (p.271).

Before we go further into the moral maze of multi-layered citizenship, we can see how far this approach may have simply informed the actions taken by one of the authors en route to St Lucia, from arrival at the international airport at Durban. The weather in Durban in the Spring is unpredictable and the experienced tourist, having to travel on from Durban in a hire car after leaving the cold and damp of Heathrow at 10pm the previous night, will prepare for a possible immediate change of clothing if faced with a regular 'high' sitting on Durban, producing hot and humid weather. The first job though is to sort out the hire car, and get out of Durban, making progress up north towards St Lucia, Phinda, and Kosi Bay. It is easy to pull off the main road north of Durban, into a small coastal community, draw breath at the sight of the Indian Ocean, thank God for the privilege of being on this earth, and then to change out of shirt, trousers, shoes and socks into cooler uniform. This ritual once resulted in an expensive, new pair of sandals being mistakenly abandoned. They were placed on the ground at the rear of the car, ready to be stepped into as part of the clothing change, when a pick-up full of young African men appeared in the deliberately chosen secluded changing spot somewhat off the beaten track. The decision was quickly taken, given that the boot of the car had suitcases and all stuff necessary for a field-working visit of some four weeks, to abandon the clothes change, drive off and try again further up the coast. The sandals were a casualty of this anxious moment, left on the ground at the rear of the car.

The immediate reflective reaction to this event was annoyance. Quality hot weather walking sandals that fit and have been broken in cannot be replicated during the four-week stay. Reaction and possible over-reaction to the crime-rate for robbery with violence co-existed with a recognition that the target was too easy to resist and that there was a moral obligation not to tempt these young men with such an easy and lucrative opportunity to explore the contents of the trunk. In any case, after a long flight and a long journey to complete before nightfall, there was only room for possibly inadequate first thoughts and actions. Of course, the economic, but not the moral, impact of this involuntary donation to the KwaZulu-Natal domestic economy was just the same as if the sandals had been offered as a gift. And it was the latter thought that smoothed over the anger and humiliation of not coping with the situation. The young Africans may, after all, have offered a cold beer and kind words for a safe journey and enjoyable stay in their country. So, the thought remained that there was now no need to worry about a failure to be generous in any subsequent situations, since a once and for all act of involuntary generosity meant that dues had been paid to the KwaZulu-Natal economy. We have raised earlier the moral dilemma, created by among other factors, a rich-tourist–poor-local divide, associated with the differences in relative impact on economic well-being, of the tourist offering a painless (philanthropic) gift that becomes temporarily at least, a significant source of personal and family income for the recipient. And, of course, the subsequent carefully chosen purchase of a new pair of sandals from a Durban street market, selling for a worker's co-operative based in the town of Stanger, KwaZulu-Natal, also eases the pain. It is interesting to speculate, too, how the truck load of young men actually decided who was to have the sandals (size 42 being popular) a dilemma it is easy to empathise with, as a fellow world citizen. We guess that they drew lots, or the toughest or the neediest of the size 42s claimed them.

Good tourists as world citizens

Dower (1998) has distinguished three different senses in which the claim of world citizenship might be made. The first of these is that we have no choice as long as there is a world political community, or something approaching a world government. Narrowly speaking, citizenship means belonging to a polity and world citizenship must mean belonging to a world polity of some sort, and, of course, we have no such structure in place. A wider citizenship, based on alternative frameworks of identity and belonging, could be the basis for an argument that the notion of world citizenship is not necessarily fatally undermined by the lack of a world polity. People may claim, for example, that they feel 'at one' with all others, that the prospect of a global community is a genuine rather than counterfeit (Freie, 1998) prospect for them. The second claim, therefore, is that we experience global society as a real place where we know we are in harmony with the thoughts and actions and values of others, irrespective of cultural difference. We experience, perhaps, a sort of emotional solidarity that we want to lay claim to as part of having a 'world view'.

Dower (1998, p.72) has little of interest to say about this second proposition ('The second claim may be to some extent true but the degree of established global community is not very high'). It is empirically difficult to verify any notion of shared anything when the sharing is claimed to take place on a worldwide front and, in this sense Dower's benign neglect may be understandable. On the other hand, the current influence and potential impact of information and communications systems, where television and tourism reign, suggests that this strand of thinking should not be dismissed all together. The third strand we have already alluded to in our discussion of the possibility of solidarity through identification with some supra-powerful of set of principles, with human rights and a linked vision of human needs being one contender, and a socially fair or just allocation of resources, linked to a regulatory system that produces this preferred distributional outcome of power and economic resources, being the other. This would place on us all certain duties and obligations both to control our own political and economic activities and to have them controlled in the search for the common world good. The latter, of course, would imply the establishment not only of a political world community but a moral world community as well. And the basis of this moral community would require a major reconceptualisation of personal and national economic interests, replacing self or national interest with, perhaps, a mixture of egalitarianism and altruism. Otherwise, Olson's (1971) free-rider problem remains.

The fusion of a new political and moral global citizenship will require a fresh conceptualisation of what counts as rational economic and political behaviour which, in turn, will be significant in completing our pen-portrait of the Good Tourist as the Good Citizen. In order to properly discuss the position of the eco-tourist as a Good Tourist, and as a Good (and World) Citizen, we shall also have to consider whether, how and to what degree future generations and non-human living creatures have moral standing. We shall return to explore these possibilities further, to consider, for example, the possible role of Good Tourists as inevitable transnational activists.

We now need to turn to the theme of reconciliation, but this time to consider how it is possible to reconcile the three layers of citizenship – local, national and supra- or world-citizenship. In particular, we need to recognise that the meeting of tourists and local populations involves a meeting of different bundles of citizenship, consciously and/or unconsciously held, whereby in principle, the persons concerned have filled their own political space with choices about preferred ways of living and the qualities that go with these. Out of these choices come the politics that we have created and that we decide how to relate to. Both the United Kingdom and South Africa might be described, by Wringe's (1995) useful label, as 'multicultural democracies'. Inside these, however, are multi-layered citizens who may also be members of cultural groups who may cling to beliefs and practices that are profoundly undemocratic. The subordination of women, for example, in Zulu society, is a central belief that helps give Zulu society coherence and continuity. The subordination of asylum seekers and refugees occupies a similar square in the UK's political status and economic rights game. Wringe states the position with characteristic succinctness:

> Wherever the interests of the individual may lie, however, to be committed
> to democracy is to be committed to protecting those interests against that of
> the group, even when that group is a cultural entity which, as a democrat,
> one wishes to respect and, within the parameters of democracy, try to preserve
> [1995, p.287].

The challenge for the governments and citizens of the UK and South Africa is to ensure that individuals do not suffer injustice as a result of their member-ship of cultural groups and that the cultural norms of these groups, as long as they are tolerable within the limits of liberal democracies, are not under outside threat. It is this sort of general analysis that can inform our thinking about how the international eco-tourist visiting St Lucia, and passing by Dukuduku South forest – often described as one of the last major examples of indigenous forest in South Africa (Preston-Whyte, 1995) – currently home for some 60,000 people who are progressively stripping the forest for fuel and food and shelter, might respond to this situation. As a citizen from a democratic nation state with its own cultural differences, the eco-tourist may be committed to lending positive support to the chosen ways of life of the Dukuduku South settlers, that might otherwise be under threat from current Provincial or National government policies. As a world citizen, however, the eco-tourist may identify with an overarching obligation to preserve the indigenous forest area of Dukuduku South even at the cost of pain and anguish for local peoples. And, of course, the Provincial and National governments may enshrine political and economic policies and practices that do actively discriminate against peoples of particular ethnicities, or practise reverse discriminatory practices that lead to more perceived injustices than they resolve. At the least, there has to be a move from the rhetoric of individual rights, equality, justice and autonomy (classic democratic values) towards their effective enshrinement in social life:

> It is the very practice of seeing oneself, and more especially those outside
> one's community, not as individuals suffering pain, deprivation, uncertainty,
> humiliation, the frustration of aspirations and so on, but as the occupants
> of roles ascribed to them by the mythologies and belief systems of one's

community that is at the root of much intercultural strife [Wringe, 1995, p.289].

The ascription of myth, of course, is one of the prime impacts of the heritage industry, and it is a moot point how far the social interactions between tourists and local populations that the industry throws up, confirm or deny legitimate relations within multicultural democracies. 'Legitimacy' is here defined by the defining features of democracy itself, whereby agreements are reached about such rule-governed behaviour through negotiation between equals, on equal terms (Gutmann and Thompson, 1996). This is the philosophical and practical political world that the South Beach Residents Association of Durban, intent on 'cleaning up' the beachfront informal economy, part of the Durban tourism industry, may acknowledge. These citizens will also need to acknowledge that on different occasions our individual identities are bounded by commitments to various collectivities larger or smaller, local, national or global, cultural, interest-based, or professional. The important feature of the modern multi-cultural democracy is that none of these identities need be subordinate to a single centralising nation state. The 'Rainbow Nation' and the 'African Renaissance' in that sense, are spot on as rallying calls, since they avoid an unthinking allegiance to anything other than a full-blown vision of democracy whereby people are able to choose freely ways of life on equal terms and this choice is informed by a creative imagination identifying and prioritising choices and their implications. Good Tourists and Good Citizens come together at this point.

Chapter 9

Empowerment, government and globalisation: possibilities and problem areas for tourism development

Democratic tourism

In a new democracy force-fed on the democratic structures of polities in the North, it is with no surprise that we see the unimpeachable authority of aspects of direct democracy, or participatory democracy, as a natural remedy for the well-known diseases of representative democracies where people suffer from disaffection, distrust, dislike and disgust with politics and political process. In South Africa, the moral authority of empowerment is welded, culturally, to a social process of rectificatory social justice, so that voices previously dormant or silenced have or should have due influence in national, regional and local politics. This process of empowerment is context specific, defined within the local, historical, political, economic and social context but is also universal in this sense of reflecting a practical response to the technical, procedural inadequacies and to the inequalities in influence typical of representative democracies. It also implies that there exists marginalised groups, with no recent history of political influence, and that power is effectively redistributed towards these groups even if it means taking power away from previously dominant power holders. More recently, the meaning of empowerment has been conditioned by the congruent quest for self-reliance and for sustainability.

In KwaZulu-Natal, the role of the tourist industry and tourist development in promoting economic regeneration, political confidence and stability and a new social and moral order (where the use of force as a means to settle dispute would be rare) is wrapped up inside the warmth of a high-profile blanket commitment by all the main tourist organisations to empowerment as the main political procedure for realising significant social change. Hence, the macro-political agenda of empowerment is replicated and reinforced by its mutually supporting sectoral or micro-parallel inside a major industry – tourism. Empowerment, however, does not grow on trees and has to be learnt, where learning is the active construction of really useful knowledge. Of course, the local communities of Kosi Bay and St Lucia, for example, have a wealth of technical and social indigenous knowledge, built up through survival in difficult circumstances with limited resources. One of the results of a successful political process of empowerment would be a higher profile and status for such knowledge to be put into the development process. Knowledge of local environments and the validation of this knowledge may be of crucial importance in facilitating enhanced self-realisation through self-confidence. We shall return to the general significance of confidence in our discussion of trust in the next chapter.

There is a complex relationship between gains in individual empowerment and community participation, and the models and practices of empowerment we heard about, and saw in action, in KwaZulu-Natal often failed to recognise this. We have already drawn on the work of Olson (1971) here and a challenge for research-driven tourism policy and planning in the province will be to explore and to act on the outcomes of questions concerning how, why and to what degree any change in individual self-realisation produces concrete impacts of some sort or other on marginalised people's actual participation in community organisations, in community development and in community action. The relationship may be a negative one, as Olson (1971) suggests – growth in individual self-confidence may be inversely related to the willingness to join with group activity. The main outcome may be an enhanced willingness and ability to look after oneself and one's family, through, for example, managing local food resources better or being more likely to compete in local labour markets, where other people in the community are perceived to be in competition rather than co-operation.

This may be especially true of men who see newly confident women as the main barrier to their own empowerment and indeed men may seek to block any gains in women's empowerment. The need for rectificatory social justice through policies and practices of reverse discrimination are at their strongest in the South African context, given the high-profile political commitment by the government to making South Africa a place fit for women to live in. The security-women we met in the parking lots of Durban; the women with their young babies and children we met at the arts and crafts markets at the St Lucia river mouth and at the exit to numerous game reserves; the young waitresses in the increasingly upmarket restaurants of St Lucia, living in Dukuduku South by night during the week and then back to Matubatuba on the occasional day off, having their income siphoned off by their dependants; and the women and their daughters working the tourist lay-bys on the 'Valley of a Thousand Hills' tourist drive in the Durban tourist hinterland; and a young Zulu woman completing her research degree at the University of Natal, in the teeth of tradition, may know nothing and may need to know nothing of the Aristotelian concept of rectificatory social justice but it surely applies to them. Aristotle developed his ideas on social justice because of a pressing personal need to know as an intellectual, whether if freed slaves took revenge against their former masters, they were philosophically and morally legitimated so to do. We remain unsure about how precisely to describe the power position of these different females and collectives (Archer and Cottingham, 1996) but we are sure that regional and local public policies that do not address the reality of their position will be failing to meet the aims of the national political agenda.

The theme of political mobilisation is crucial to analysing the future for South African tourism. South Africa in the early twenty-first century is uniquely at the juncture of being able to attempt to use tourism as a main engine of economic regeneration and income and wealth redistribution inside a major political project of creating a democracy that offers the prize of equal influence for all citizens. This will mean major changes in the economic and political position of many people, alongside potential changes in the political consciousness and actions of majorities of people. In KwaZulu-Natal, a central question for assessing the success of tourism development is how far it leads to real growth in poor people's well-being, through either lubricating or demonstrating the reality that life can be very different from how it has been and how it is.

One way of conceptualising and experiencing empowerment is as a new means of consumption, as a new model of the structures and settings that enable us to consume all sorts of things (Ritzer, 1999). Ritzer does not discuss the political process of empowerment as a form of consumption but he could have, given the arresting title of his latest book *Enchanting a Disenchanted World. Revolutionising the Means of Consumption*. For a distinguishing feature of consumption, as opposed to investment, is that consumption uses things up more or less immediately and satisfaction, or not, is gained from a once and for all act of digestion. This could mimic the experience of direct democracy in the new South Africa, whereby the act of political engagement through direct participation must offer immediate and tangible pleasure or fulfilment, or the consumer will switch back to an alternative product (apathy, violence). Ritzer (1999, p.x) writes about 'cathedrals of consumption', pointing up the quasi-religious or 'enchanted' nature of the new settings of malls, mega-malls, casino-come-mall, cruise-ship-come-mall and theme-park-come-mall. It may be hard to think of the community centres, schools and rough ground that house political meetings in the neighbourhoods and villages of KwaZulu-Natal as 'cathedrals' to a new means of political process, akin to consumption, but their promise of a new experience, of entertainment through consumption (openly personal, moving and sometimes provocative political speeches and their ripostes), may enable people to get beyond what Baudrillard has called the 'age of simulation' (1983, p.4) into a more genuine and authentic political world, where the real and imaginary and the true and false are kept demonstrably separate.

Clues for how the commitment to empowerment writ large in the brochures of the KNTA and the KZNNCS, and in the advertising of Kosi Bay Lodge and Phinda Game Lodge, might lead to real changes for the better in the political position of poor people can be found in Fox Piven and Cloward's (1977) prize-winning study of political mobilisation in the USA.

The role of government in initiating, building and sustaining empowerment, or suppressing, undermining and destabalising empowerment processes raises more general concerns about the role of government in facilitating a shift from representative to direct or participatory democracy. There is a sense in which empowerment cannot be 'given'; it has to be taken, or, more strictly, be seen to be taken if we are in the business of tokenism rather than an authentic shift in power. We have seen, from the recent history of Dukuduku, that the residents on the south side of the road have never felt they have experienced empowerment since the terms for any shifts or transfers in power, say, from the conservation authorities, have been dictated by the latter as the current power holder or power-bearing organisation. However, even in a truly direct democracy, government has a role as the regulator of due process. The point here is that the form of regulation should be radically different than under representative democracy. What sort of shifts in control or regulation by government would be needed to fit processes and outcomes of political empowerment as building blocks of a new democracy?

Democratic governments are under worldwide pressure to exhibit 'Good Government' or 'Better Government'. The OECD, for example, has been described as 'evangelical in its fervour to promote the spread of regulatory best practice across its membership' (IPPR, 1999, p.1).

There are three types of potential regulatory control spheres, as we have seen in the previous chapter, where the Provincial Governments and National Government in South Africa are currently rethinking purpose and method and ways of evaluating outcome. First, economic regulation is essential where there is a view that in a particular sphere of economic activity, market failure would not be acceptable and government should ensure that any costs of market failure are compensated. For example, consumers and companies need to be protected from anti-competitive practices and, more positively, effective competition between companies needs to be promoted and sustained. Second, environmental regulation, simply conceived, is required to monitor the impact of economic processes and to ensure that such impacts are environmentally sustainable and are not dependent on the short-term misuse of significantly scarce natural resources. Third, social regulation includes all the measures designed to affect the distribution of rewards that arise from economic activity and in particular, are designed to prevent poverty and reduce and eliminate, where possible, unfair discriminatory or exploitative impacts and processes.

We can begin to understand the challenge facing such bodies as the KwaZulu-Natal Tourism Authority and the KwaZulu-Natal Nature Conservation Service when we recognise that such bodies are part of a general move to rethink the way in which governments regulate both organisations responding to central and provincial agendas and attempting to influence such agendas. In South Africa, tourism development and the wider development project is significantly conditioned by the pressure to be radical in thinking through the appropriate roles of government and quasi-government bodies. What appears to be emerging in KwaZulu-Natal is a mixed-economy of regulation, whereby the National Government's priority is the setting of general public objectives but the specific form in which these objectives emerge as targets, and the procedures and methods for achieving these targets, are locally determined. This is the point at which the force of the individual and group empowerment imperative connects with an international pressure to rethink and reform the ways in which government in democratic states goes about its business. Obvious questions here are whether the costs of aggregate and individual (for example, community or firm) regulatory costs are worth bearing?

The governance of tourism

The Chief Executive of the KwaZulu-Natal Tourism Authority, when we first interviewed him in 1998, was clear that one of his major tasks was to promote private sector investment in tourism development in the province. We know that, both globally and, where appropriate, nationally, firms will direct investment and resources towards localities that offer the best (least cost, most permissive or malleable) regulatory framework for them to operate within. Over-regulation is a real danger for tourism development in the province and could be avoided if public bodies and officials had an informed appreciation of the real costs of regulation on private firms. The aim should not be simply bits of economic, environmental and social regulation, but an informed awareness and rational acceptance of the costs and benefits associated with alternative degrees and methods of government regulation, the latter arising from an active and dynamic understanding of the pace and direction of change of any indigenous cultural politics otherwise remaining behind its own Chinese wall. This could be identified, as we have earlier outlined, by what has become known as a Comprehensive Regulatory Review, whereby a baseline re-evaluation of all existing regulation takes place. Certainly this might be done at the sectoral level, for tourism development, that might mitigate any tendency

towards opportunistic short-termism, potentially very inefficient in a low spending financial climate. The introduction of a regular Regulatory Impact Analysis, subjecting new and existing regulations to cost/benefit analyses, however crude, would at least undermine any tendency towards complacency. The costs of effective regulation, by definition, are outweighed by the benefits, and the private tourism industry needs to overcome any knee-jerk hostile reaction to government regulation and to recognise that good regulation should protect firms as much as consumers, employees and other citizens. For any of this to happen, as we shall argue, the degree and distribution of trust in political, economic and social relationships must be conducive or permissive, and we see little sign of that in the KwaZulu-Natal we know.

The South African tourist industry has been constantly under threat from criticism that it has failed to achieve the economic regeneration potential both possible and desirable, and that other countries, close market competitors, have done comparatively better. One government response to this belief in comparative failure is to sustain a lax regulatory regime in order to encourage international tourism companies looking out for some cherry-picking of weak regulatory jurisdictions, to look kindly at moving business to South Africa or expanding business there. Such companies, of that the Conservation Corporation (see chapter 1) could be an example, would be denied the benefits of effective regulation. In any case, the perception that reducing the costs of complying with regulatory procedures could be part of the competitive advantage that any single tourist company could achieve will increase the likelihood of accusations of corruption in the province's government and quasi-government agencies.

Sustainable disagreement

Another – controversial – view here is that the South African government should be permissive in its application of laws and usual financial procedures and to make this permissiveness known, as other countries have done, if it is to compete on equal terms in attracting international businesses to be active in South Africa. We don't intend to get into the details of such disagreements but we do want to discuss the nature of disagreement in democratic societies (and we will pick up our discussion again in the concluding comments of this book). In particular, we are interested in thinking about the nature of disagreement in a democracy (Gutmann and Thompson, 1996 will guide our thoughts). Our interviews, discussions and observations of tourism development in KwaZulu-Natal illustrated for us the widespread differences of view held about how a preferred vision of the future of the tourism industry might be brought about and sustained. We are particularly interested in the nature of moral disagreement in a democracy, such as South Africa is building, and we think that disagreements about the desired aims of tourism development, who and what is planned to benefit and to what degree and for how long, and disagreements about how these aims are to be met, for example, the role of state regulatory agencies, reside in disagreements about fundamental values.

The challenge facing the South Africa political project is that democracies offer no guarantees that conflicts of interests arising from clearly different, possibly entrenched values, will be contained and coped with. The main vehicle for doing this is normally through reasoning with other people in order to persuade them to one's point of view or to revise one's own point of view. This process of reasoning through argument, will only take place where people respect each other as moral agents; that is, they respect the fact that it is legitimate for other people to hold other views, derived from a different value system, and they also are prepared to enter into public activity, such as discussion, to explore the bases and forms of the disagreement and be persuaded, potentially, to change their views and revise their value system. Where other people are witnesses to such a discussion, they themselves may alter or confirm their own moral stance as a result of the public and publicity features of the way in which moral disagreements are aired in a democracy. Sometimes these conflicts of interest, based on competing value positions, exist between public officials and citizens and when these differences are made public, we have the basis for public officials being made accountable for their actions or proposed actions. Where these political discourses, arising from a plurality of value positions about issues that really matter, are seen to work well, being based in themselves on democratic principles such as basic liberty and equal opportunity, we have the basis for deliberative democracy. That is not to say that a process of deliberation will of itself guarantee that the possible fundamental difference in values, such as a belief in a particular conception of social justice in resource distribution, will be eliminated. What it will do is to allow people, at least provisionally, to experience a mutually justifiable way of coping with their ongoing moral disagreements.

We are particularly concerned here with the significance of the South African democracy project for tourism development in South Africa and the possibility of achieving genuinely community-led tourism development. The word 'community', in this context, implies some shared view about what should happen and how it should happen and what needs to be changed. Moreover, it explicitly means that questions concerning the private and social costs and benefits of development are known or predictable, at least roughly, and are agreed. Our experience of tourism development in KwaZulu-Natal suggests that this conceptualisation of community has not yet been achieved, and this is not surprising. Why is it that people do morally disagree about

matters of public policy? There is, of course, a long-standing political literature to call on here if we wish to review this question (Crick, 1969). We
know that conflicts of interests are possible and probable when resources are
scarce, or rather, are perceived to be scarce, and they have to be fought for
unless human nature is so generous that some people are willing to have less
so that others can have more (practical altruism). We also know that people
disagree because they fail to understand each other's position or, if they do
understand, they cannot see how agreement can possibly be reached. So they
may not so much disagree but find themselves unable to agree. Finally, there
is the possibility that our values are formed in such a way that some of them,
at least, become so entrenched that they are not subject to change through
reason; we simply have to accept that some values are incompatible because
they are fixed and irreducible. Above all, there is the Hobbesian claim that
people's values are simply a mask for what would be better called self-interest,
especially economic self-interest. However, we now know, from a recent research
expansion in the psychology of economic behaviour (Parker and Stacey, 1994),
that 'self-interest' can take many different forms. It may be in our interests to
be altruistic, for example, where selfishness and selflessness merge.

We should not expect to resolve all or even most of the moral conflicts that
inform and surround community life but the basis for a process of resolution,
where there is disagreement, is always present because of the reciprocal
nature of moral argument in politics.

> If moral disagreement is so pervasive, how can we ever hope to resolve it?
> Some basis for hope is to be found in the nature of moral claims themselves.
> Just as the problem of disagreement lies partly within morality itself, so does
> the basis for its resolution. If citizens publicly appeal to reasons that are
> shared, or could be shared, by their fellow citizens, and if they take into
> account these same kinds of reasons presented by similarly motivated citizens,
> then they are already engaged in a process that by its nature aims at a
> justifiable resolution of disagreement [Gutmann and Thompson, 1996, p.25].

In the South African context, extending the domain of deliberation through
the empowerment of formerly marginalised voices bears the risk that even
greater conflict may arise than was previously the case. This possibility is
confused by a consideration of the intensity of disagreement, as well as its
spread. Certainly in KwaZulu-Natal, tourism development may be held up
or skewed simply by the historic weight of disagreements. Once citizens and
officials become more aware of their own value position in the context of
a public process of deliberation, they may be less likely to compromise or
reconsider. We attended meetings concerning the shape and pace of tourism
development in the province that were dominated by the discourse of

high-minded statements, unyielding stands and no-holds-barred opposition. Students of tourism studies who we met in the province, for example a group from the Natal Technicon at Phinda Game Lodge, might well be asked by their tutors to contemplate the significance for tourism development in the province of the following statement: 'There are moral fanatics as well as moral sages, and in politics the former are likely to be more vocal than the latter' (Gutmann and Thompson, 1996, p.44).

Tourist accommodation

This is a risk that the empowerment process throws up – that raised moral consciousness makes compromise less likely. On the other hand, low levels of understanding of one's own position on controversial issues of development may lead to unsustainable 'fixes', the impact of that reinforces disaffection with the political process. The risk is worth taking on the moral grounds that a political regime that does all it can to open up discourse is morally preferable to one that encourages or is indifferent to the suppression of disagreement. Green fundamentalism and its influence on tourism development in St Lucia reflects a view that some people already know what is the best resolution of conflicts of interest both for the citizens of the area and for the institutions, such as the KZNNCS, with major stakes in the area's future. But there is no place for any sort of fundamentalism in a deliberative democracy since a meaning of fundamentalism is that some people, extremists, know what constitutes the best resolution of a moral conflict, without having to deliberate with those other fellow citizens who have a stake in the outcome and may be bound by it. This does not mean that uncompromising positions are outlawed, such as, say, a decision to ban all RBM company activity in the St Lucia area for the foreseeable future, but that such an uncompromising position has no legitimate basis. David Harvey (1973), the enlightened geographer, has argued, in a nutshell, that a socially just society is arrived at in a just way. That is to say, the conditions of social justice are as important as the content of social justice in a socially just society. Similarly, in a deliberative democracy, the political process most be as morally defensible as political decisions.

> Deliberative democracy aspires to a politics in which citizens and their accountable representatives, along with other public officials, are committed to making decisions that they can justify to everyone bound by them. This commitment entails the integration of substantive moral argument into democratic processes that manifest the equal political status of citizens [Gutmann and Thompson, 1996, p.50].

The stress on reciprocity in the previous discussion deserves further comment. In the pluralist communities of democratic South Africa, people are likely to continue to hold competing views about the direction and pace of tourism development and its preferred associated costs and benefits and their distribution. How can people live with basic moral disagreement where the latter is unlikely to be resolved (and maybe social life would be impoverished if it were)? The democratic state with aspirations towards deliberation and participation as major means to empowerment will have to provide some guidance for how people live with difference and disagreement. Gutmann and Thompson (1996) stress the importance of the principle of reciprocity in providing standards in the practice of mutual respect, or what they elsewhere call 'principles of accommodation'. Where can we find accommodation in tourism development? The usual technical planning procedures for encouraging participation by citizens in projected development is either some form of consultation process or an impact/cost-benefit analysis, or a combination of these, such as putting the findings of an impact analysis to citizens for consultation.

What we are suggesting here is that what people might prefer and what is needed to really promote empowerment is reciprocity. The moral basis of cost and benefit, or impact, is what may be significant in people's feelings of well-being or otherwise as a result of living in a democracy (the latter being built into a model of objective well-being by Doyal and Gough (1991). Reciprocity relies on people behaving in a co-operative way after citizens reciprocate. That is, they work out their justification for the actual or potential distribution of desired things or 'ways of being', deciding whether others deserve (as an example of an operative principle) what they have or will have and make an appropriate return whereby others will know that the current and future flow of things can be justified by reference to some accepted (mutually agreed) principle. In a deliberative democracy, people's claims to things can be morally justified through a public test of reason. Some people may never agree to what counts as the latter, and if they do not ever agree with the nature of reciprocity, the point will be reached, as we suggested in the previous chapter, where they forfeit their right to be a member of that community, or voluntarily leave. Reasons will need to be recognisably moral in form and plausible in practice.

We can take as an example those nature fundamentalists who want to preserve the animals and their historic ways of behaving in the game reserves against any reform. For simplicity we can say they put the interests of animals before the interests of people, especially, in some cases, the interests of certain people rather than others. The nature fundamentalist, as we experienced them at Kosi Bay, might claim, if pressed, that they are indeed accommodating in Gutmann and Thompson's terms, because their moral reasons for adopting the animalist stance are readily accessible to anyone who lives the sort of life they do. It is living the life ('in communion with nature') that allows access to the public, moral justification for such a life. Personal experience is, here, the mother of moral necessity. Yet the moral validation of this experience breaks the requirement for reciprocity because experience is put first and is, therefore, exclusive. Other people have to adopt this animalist way of life as a condition for understanding this way of life and thereby, its morality. Not all people can or would be prepared to experience the animalist life in order to test the strength of the moral defence of that life. If they found the test failed, for example, they would have lived in a way that was morally unacceptable to themselves and why should they willingly put themselves in such jeopardy? When we were on our truck drive to Kosi Bay river mouth, this is why we did not join in with the joke-telling, because the jokes illustrated the moral dimension of the story-teller's personal experience of local people, an experience we could not and did not want to share.

We can now see that the role of the state in a democracy that is simultan-eously striving for participation and deliberation, the two processes that we now claim to be essential logical conditions for empowerment to occur, should be a reserved role. Deliberative disagreement arises 'when there are mutually acceptable reasons, accessible *now* that not only call into question our best judgement but also permit other citizens to reject our judgement and defend opposing ones' (Gutmann and Thompson, 1996, p.78; original italics).

Where we have deliberative disagreement, a collective decision must still be taken. The difficulty of coming to a view may be set by the impossibility of complete moral knowledge and a resultant unacceptable degree of risk in decision-making. Government exists to take decisions that otherwise would not be taken because of the limitations of deliberation by citizens. The size and nature of the state apparatus, in particular, its forms of regulation (economic, environmental and social, as we have outlined) must be evaluated against this criterion, as a decision-taker of the last resort. This position of the state would be congruent with personal and group empowerment, and would recognise that the state itself should be morally accountable for its actions. The Truth and Reconciliation Commission was a strong example of the capacity of the South African state to encompass a public morality through trying to base its practical work on transparent moral principles. But it is important to note that people have disagreed with the idea of the Commission, or disputed its ways of working and findings (Krog, 1999). The Commission does not represent a moral consensus but does reflect the point that the political agenda is never likely to be free of moral conflict.

The empowerment fundamentalists of tourism development in South Africa, those who see community consultation and participation as the only way to plan tourism development, seem to be implicitly asserting that empowerment in itself is the common good, that political process is more important than political outcome, or that process is outcome. This comprehensive moral conception is doomed to failure and so it should be. Just because a process of deliberation is established about the shape, pace and likely impact of tourism development, which in turn will mean deliberating together about substantive moral values (for example, the respective and comparative rights of the environment, animals, local people and international tourists) does not mean that citizens should come to agree collectively on a coherent set of those values. Moral disagreement about tourism development will persist. It can and may be reduced through refinement and boundary definition as a result of deliberation, whereby people accommodate their own and others' views, through a personal political and moral education induced by the deliberation process, itself grounded in the reciprocity principle. They thereby learn the principles and practices of mutual respect and accommodation that the reciprocity principle is defined by.

The Aristotelian principle of rectificatory social justice will be returned to as part of our analysis of the importance of trust in tourism development, the theme of the next chapter. However, we do need to locate the South African political agenda of increasing the power of previously disadvantaged or marginalised groups inside the framework of deliberation. In a representative democracy, the political situation of disadvantaged groups would be potentially improved by extending and changing in other ways (for example, taking power away from previously advantaged groups) the nature of group representation in the political process. In a direct democracy, previously disadvantaged groups will be able to define actively and significantly define the political agenda and determine its outcomes without the use of a representational filter or censor unless this is freely chosen, that is, not imposed by due procedure. The long-standing issue of the future for the forest dwellers of Dukuduku I, and arguments in favour of 'giving a voice to the people themselves' can be justified as part of a project to establish a more deliberative polity. The latter may be thought to require, in the South African case, more extensive representation in the public forum, justified by principles of compensatory and rectificatory group representation. However, the problem remains, certainly in the St Lucia area, that the majority of local citizens could claim to be members of oppressed minorities. The local fishermen we spoke to certainly felt this way about their political position; the forest dwellers of Dukuduku would not, we suspect, immediately recognise the fishermen as in any sense oppressed but might be prepared to consider the argument. In any case, the forest dwellers need to deliberate since this will define them as deliberators and identify them as members of a discursive political community, seeking reciprocity and material well-being.

What is at stake here is not tourism development itself but the welfare dimension in tourism development. By this we mean whether and to what degree tourism development creates basic opportunities for income and work and creates fair access to non-basic opportunities such as well-paid jobs and relatively high levels of income and wealth. We cannot go into the detail, here, that would be required to provide a full account of the tourism development-welfare relationship in South Africa, but we can outline the way in which we might think about this relationship and its significance for a deliberative democracy project. We adopt the well-known distributive principle that people should not be denied basic opportunities through factors outside their control, such as the exogenous and thereby morally neutral distribution of natural talents and its impact on future welfare. Deliberation is needed to arrive at those distributive policies that offset the effects of the exogenous determinants of our original opportunity position.

Doyal and Gough (1991) offer what is still the most convincing account of standards or criteria in human needs theories and policies but we are not so much concerned here with that issue but rather whether there is ever a case for arguing that people should be denied basic opportunities in income and work? From the point of view of compensation for past injustice, the welfare or distribution affects of tourism development is a crucial issue for deliberation. And the latter itself is based, as Doyal and Gough imply, on a basic opportunity of citizenship. So, we argue that the social conditions of a deliberative democracy are significant for the establishment and functioning of the latter because of the necessity for a basic opportunity of citizenship to be complemented by a basic opportunity of welfare. Top-down models of welfare reform are the obvious antithesis of empowerment.

The Green fundamentalists claim to protect the rights of future generations and the potentially disadvantaged (through not being able to benefit from currently available natural goods, goods that are threatened with short-term extinction) who otherwise would have no 'voice' in public affairs. Conflicts of interests between the predicted needs of future and current citizens will be a significant dimension in deliberation about tourism development when future citizens take on sacred value. When the latter is welded to the sanctity of the earth, as in the Green fundamentalist case (Worpole, 1998), then the process of deliberation itself is threatened and undermined because of the contradiction between fundamentalism and the principle of reciprocity. That is not to say that the heavenly twins of sanctity of earth and of future generations should not be present in deliberations but that they should take part inside the principles of a deliberative democratic process, and this excludes fundamentalism in any shape or form.

Chapter 10

Trust in tourism?

A stranger to trust?

Basic economic and political transactions require a minimum level of trust. In the history of twentieth-century South Africa, the society can be described as one where trust between groups within South Africa and between South Africa and other countries has been lacking. A major role of government in the new democracy will be to promote trust between groups who have a historical tendency not to trust each other. Into this task, in a small but significant way, comes the stranger, the international tourist and the whole range of potential tourist–host relations that tourism studies literature is replete with. Each of the latter has its own unique trust dimension that we have not seen formally described and discussed, and we cannot do so here (though it would be a job well worth doing). What we shall outline are ways of thinking about the meaning and significance of trust in the context of the future for tourism development in South Africa, inside the national political and economic projects.

John Stuart Mill claimed that differences in the degree and nature of trust between regions and countries are a major cause of differences in the level of economic and social efficiency in the society: 'The advantage of mankind of being able to trust one another penetrates into every crevice and cranny of human life' (Mill, 1900, p.68, in Humphrey and Schmitz, 1996, p.1).

Kenneth Arrow is also quoted in Humphrey and Schmitz (1996, p.1): 'virtually every commercial transaction has within itself an element of trust, certainly any transaction conducted over a period of time. It can plausibly be argued that much of the economic backwardness in the world can be explained by a lack of mutual confidence.'

The issue, then, is not that there is any disagreement over the general importance of trust but rather why there are variations in the volume and type of trust relations both within countries and between countries, both politically and economically, and how trust grows and whether trust can be made to grow, for example, by green-fingered governments. Indeed, the shift from represent-ative to direct democracy, where it is advocated, is itself a sign of distrust in the representative procedures and processes of liberal democracies. In KwaZulu-Natal, we would argue that the level of minimal trust needed to ensure that the province maximises the potential of tourism development in promoting development more generally, may not yet be there, or rather, is too patchily distributed for the bits to join up.

Trusting someone or something happens when we believe that the other person or body will not exploit us for their own benefit when they could do so. Trust implies an unequal political or power relationship since equality in relationships means that each is equally able to exploit the other but does not or cannot because it would not be worth the costs of trying to exploit the other. It is usually useful to distinguish trust from confidence, where confidence may be best thought of as a measurement of the degree of trust one has that one will not be exploited. Also, it is philosophically conventional to discuss trust alongside risk and the problem of lack of information which undermines our ability to be sure that we are correct in our judgements, when we assess the degree of trust we have in people, in specific situations. Tourists, as strangers, are prone to having an explicit need for trust yet are the least likely to be able to gauge whether they can have confidence in the way others will act during an economic or social transaction. Put simply, we trust others before they act and where their action will have consequences for our well-being, when we expect good behaviour, and we mistrust people when we act on the probability of bad behaviour. 'Trust involves making informed choices in situations of uncertainty that make one vulnerable to the actions of others' (Humphrey and Schmitz, 1996, p.5).

In tourist–host transactions, there may be specific cultural conventions that are designed to reduce uncertainty for both agents. These conventions might be a dynamic function of the expectations we have, set, perhaps, by home-based television coverage of the country or region we are visiting. When people visit South Africa from the UK, they may begin their vacation with generally lower levels of trust in the benefice of the relationships they will experience, because they have been encouraged to believe that exploitation is the rule rather than the exception. Indeed, we may partly define the concept of being a 'stranger' in a community precisely because of the low level of trust that, initially at least, surrounds all the transactions a stranger engages in. Strangers have not had the chance to learn from experience, who or what to have confidence in. In so far as trust is inductive, and requires us to look back and extrapolate from the past, the experienced tourist, visiting a country for the first time, will calculate the degree of trust he or she can have based on his or her past experience of being a tourist and hope that this experience will transfer and be a useful basis for learning about the new context. In any case, he or she can and will, if rational, build safeguards into transactions, such as avoiding any expensive purchases until he or she has a 'feel' for local prices and quality. In the South African situation, as we have mentioned earlier, local friends or relatives may help the visitor through the minefield of trust calculations, or simply take on transactions on behalf of their visitors who deferentially allow them to do so – this is where we shall eat, this is what you should buy, and don't for goodness sake ever go there.

The risk business

ACTSA has actively encouraged UK tourists to South Africa, and prospective tourists, to ensure that the company or companies they use to arrange the vacation subscribe to corporate responsibility. This is where, for example, they only book tourists into local hotels, game parks, excursions and so on where South African minimum wage legislation for employees is actively endorsed. We have briefly discussed, in chapter 5, the experience of an American family visiting Zululand and the nature of that theme park and the tourist experience; and also how hotels in the Durban Central Business District and on the local beachfront advise international tourists to return to the hotel before dark to avoid the uncertainties of Durban's evening tourist industry. We can now more formally consider whether tourists should do as they are advised. Certainly tourist organisations want tourists to behave responsibly, which is a morally convenient rationale for making sure that the tourist stays locked into the hotel's bars and restaurants, video rental systems and organised excursions. Whether tourists enter into this somewhat paternalistic contractual arrangement (if you stay with us, you must let us look after you) may depend on the degree of generalised trust they have in the tourism industry or on the more specialised trust they have in the South African enterprises that they have bought into.

We know the South African tourism experience for the British visitor to be partly conditioned by the possibility of a heightened risk of being the victim of crime so that, while the tourist may have a high level of trust in tourism enterprises, they may have a low level of trust in those tourist enterprises trying to sell South Africa to them as a destination. What the international South African tourist industry needs is for the tourist's preference for accuracy and honesty in risk assessments to be shared by local enterprises, so that what Platteau (in Humphrey and Schmitz, 1996) calls an 'honesty equilibrium' will then emerge. When the British tourist meets the South African tourist enterprise, calculative self-interest and opportunism (to make gains from the other) collide and we can then only expect tourism transactions to take place if this risky business is ameliorated by a suitable generalised morality. An important component of the latter for the international tourist would be the provision of accurate and trustworthy information about local conditions, and the possibility of compensation if one's faith in the presence of generalised trust proves unfounded by experience.

It may also be the case that a particular feature of the South African tourist experience for the British tourist is that the latter has a more than usual need to trust the local tourist industry to the extent, as we have mentioned in chapter 6, that the tourist is 'paying back' or seeking to make recompense for the experiences of disempowerment and poverty. They may be more willing to ascribe trust to local people and enterprises because of a strong political or moral identity with the country. The presence of such emotions could be built on and fostered by the local tourist public agencies, not by promoting trust by tourists in the public agencies but by promoting trust relationships between the tourists and the local tourist enterprises. This is one sense in which the concern of the KNTA with crimes against tourists and their encouragement of crime-reducing practices is to be understood. And, of course, we are now back in the territory of considering the impact on the international tourism industry in South Africa of the ways in which the development of both generalised and specialised trust is bound up with the emergence of the new democracy. In this political situation, trust relationships between tourists and local enterprises and peoples co-exist alongside the conflicts of interests or identities that underwrite the politics of social issues and problems that are a matter of public interest and potential collective action.

Trust reduces complexity for the stranger by providing them with a (realistic) sense of security by allowing the stranger to take for granted many of those aspects of social life upon which their well-being depends. Naming South Africa as a new democracy in itself may be promoting the assumption of trust. Some international tourists may want to get beyond the position of generalised distrust that seems to characterise the tourist experience, since the latter offers a sense of managed security but also an impoverished experience. This situation suggests another layer of meaning for the term 'authenticity' in tourist relationships (McCannell, 1976), and recalls the discussion of risk in chapter 6, and, in particular, our discussion of the risk and uncertainty dimension in the early evening Durban tourist beachfront experience.

Transitional democracy

Inglehart (in Warren, 1999) offers a general theory of stability in new democracies. He argues that people do not need high levels of trust in political
institutions themselves but they do need high levels of interpersonal trust and
feelings of well-being. In the transition to democracy, low levels of subjective
well-being defined by, say, economic security and fairness in educational
opportunities, and low interpersonal trust, may exist. The lack of subjective
well-being and minimal interpersonal trust are two prime sources of social de-
capitalisation. Moreover, trust may be in limited supply in political contexts
characterised by social issues and problems that, for their democratic treatment,
require dialogue based itself on shared understandings, procedures and
practices. If democracy is necessarily defined by deliberation about conflicts
of interests and perspectives on public issues and problems, then deliberation
itself relies on a minimal level of trust (Harré, in Warren, 1999). Further, one
of the challenges to South African democracy is that it has jumped feet first
into the relatively unknown waters of direct democracy rather than a purely
representational democracy.

We know far more about the type of trust relations needed to sustain a
representative democracy than we do about the bases and forms of trust needed
to promote and sustain direct democracy, although, as we have seen, Fox
Piven and Cloward (1977) offer significant clues. Their analysis can now
usefully be extended by considering Claus Offe's extremely useful discussion
(in Warren, 1999, pp.42–87) of trust and democracy, and what follows is
stimulated by his chapter entitled 'How can we trust our fellow citizens?' Offe
does not use the tourist to illustrate his analysis but we think that his work on
trust suggests an enlightened way of thinking about the international tourist
experience in South Africa and maybe elsewhere.

The basic social order model Offe examines has the following constituent
parts: first, money co-ordinates the actions of people engaged in economic
transactions; second, political authority, vested in laws, for example, provides
insurance for such transactions; third, learning through experience allows
people to make rational decisions about transactions; and fourth, and of most
importance to us, trust exists as the residual factor washing up the inadequacies
of the 'intelligently regulated market economy' (Offe, in Warren, 1999, p.43,
sceptically outlined). The international tourist, experiencing the reality of this
model, could rationally expect benign or at least non-hostile intentions on
the part of the local tourism industry and local peoples, and trust in this
presumption would act as a major form of social integration for, and between,
local peoples and strangers.

Trust is the cognitive premise with which individual or collective/corporate actors enter into interactions with other actors. This cognitive premise relates to behavioural preferences and inclinations of others in terms of their preparedness to contribute, to co-operate, and to refrain from selfish, opportunistic and hostile courses of action [Offe, in Warren, 1999, p.45].

Again we need to return, as Offe does, to a central question: if trust is so important, as a cognitive and moral lubricant for the simultaneous achievement of useful economic transactions sustained within the necessary conditions of social order, what determines its level and distribution in any society? One feature of the tourist experience that will always stick in the mind is when a local person is very helpful to them and this makes an impression precisely because the expectation of such behaviour may be low and the experience is, therefore, surprising. It is always the case that we cannot know in advance what others will do but we always face this unknown with various degrees of confidence in our ability to predict how others will act and, indeed, we try and influence the actions of others through incentives, such as the offer of payment, or disincentives, such as the threat of legal action. In some tourist situations, where the spectre of the 'noble savage' raises its head, tourists may start with what has been called 'wishful trusting', where we trust too early and too easily. This may be because we may not mind too much losing out financially from misplaced trust, because we gain moral currency from the interaction. This feature of wishful trusting extends the analysis of the encounter with the women and children at the Valley of a Thousand Hills lay-by which we outlined in chapter 5.

The link between trust and risk-taking is crucial to an analysis of host–tourist interactions and the specific form in which this link works itself out in practice will, of course, be specific to the region and situation. The main general point is that, certainly in South Africa, the management of excessive risk avoidance and distrust can impoverish the tourist experience because of the elimination of options. We have here what Offe rightly calls an optimisation problem, whereby too limited trust is costly, and trust that is extended too readily and too far leaves the tourist vulnerable. There is an interesting discussion to be had at this point about whether it would be useful to say that people, tourists and hosts, for example, have to 'decide' to trust or not trust or whether trust is either an input or an outcome of a decision to engage in an interaction with someone else, or both. The key point for us, however, is that the usual conditions for arriving at trust or non-trust is through experience, and people as tourists and hosts bring particular, often restricted, experience of each other to the act or otherwise of transaction. This may be a defining feature of the tourist experience, namely that the 'normal' dynamic of trust-building, as described so lucidly by Offe, may not apply: 'Out of past experience

develops a present orientation concerning the anticipation of future behaviour'
(Offe, in Warren, 1999, p.51).

Morality in transit

For the British tourist to South Africa, there may exist an obligation to trust
simply because there is a belief that tourist expenditure can help to put right
past inequities and it would be unfair to use normal criteria or accepted
standards in the application of such criteria for conceptualising and acting on
a perceived trust relationship. This may explain the phenomenon where tourists
may wish to pay more than they are asked to pay, or buy things they don't
really want, or buy things that are of poorer quality than they would normally
tolerate. They may not only feel obliged to act this way but it is in their self-
interest to do so. As we have implied, trust is usually a time-consuming activity
– as is suggested by the term trust-building – and, normally, this relatively
lengthy process can be dismantled in an instant by an experience that destroys
our generalised or specialised trust. Trust relationships conditioned by peculiar
forms of obligation and self-interest may confound this 'normality' too. When,
as described in chapter 5, we did not complain about the waiter in the
Drakensberg hotel who served us a strange concoction for breakfast, we did
not do so because we felt obliged not to and we felt better for not doing so. We
guessed (trusted) that he was new to the job, that he was not singling us out
for poor service, and so on. In any case, being relatively rich and powerful in
that situation, we could afford the luxury of not taking his inefficiency to
heart; being what we took to be well-informed about his social condition, we
could survive the failings in any trust that we might have had in him as a
waiter, in a hotel catering mainly for tourists, a hotel clearly part of the
international South African tourism industry. He had what we might call
economic and cultural credit – for making mistakes – because of our assumptions
about what we were, what he was, and what the situation called for.

   We can also link our brief discussion on empowerment and direct democracy,
on regulation and government and on globalisation to this discussion of trust
and its importance to understanding the international tourist experience in
South Africa to the situation facing the people of Dukuduku South. The
historic position of the former Natal Parks Board regarding Dukuduku has
been one of having an unlimited capacity for control and enforcement. In such
cases, there is no need for a trust relationship, except for trust in oneself or in
the organisation's ability to sustain its power position. When the people of
Dukuduku South chose not to conform to the Board's policies and practices,
they were forced to comply. The use and threat of force rather than trust is, of

course, very expensive, given the allocation of resources needed to ensure that people know about and, if necessary, feel the pressure of the potential use of force, and it is also very inefficient. The Board was always faced with a surveillance problem and the presence of trust serves to displace the unwelcome social costs of anxiety and suspicion and monitoring of behaviour. From the point of view of the forest dwellers of Khula, on the north side of the Matubatuba–St Lucia road, they could not and cannot afford to have misplaced trust in those others they depend on for economic survival. People in or close to absolute poverty have a deep need to be trusted and to trust, since they have no rewards or punishments they can bring to underwrite economic and social transactions. Such trust relationships that have been built up in this way are both an example of and the basis for empowerment (although we must remember that they can be dismantled in an instant).

This experience of trust emerging from the lessons of personal interaction over time is limited by the restrictive nature of such experiential learning. For the tourist and host, the interactions may at least in principle be characterised as a meeting of strangers, where the learning that accrues from normal mechanisms of trust-creation, from personal familiarity with people or situations, may not transfer to first-time situations. If no alternative trust-creating procedure is found, then, as we have seen, the perception of risk leads to an impoverished set of choices, either in an absolute sense or in the sense that we let others directly manage our experience for us – so much for the independent tourist. The classic transactional problem then has to be faced, which the tourist experience exemplifies, of how we rationally extend trust relations beyond the familial and the familiar. Fukuyama (1995, p.11) is instructive on this point:

> Law, contact and economic rationality provide a necessary but not sufficient basis for both the stability and prosperity of post-industrial societies; they must also be leavened with reciprocity, moral obligation, duty towards community, and trust, *that are based in habit rather than rational calculation* [my italics]. The latter are not anachronisms in a modern society but rather the *sine qua non* of the latter's success.

The legitimacy of suspicion

The term 'stranger' can be partly defined as a person who has no reason to trust or be trusted. Tourist and host, conceptually, are mutually ignorant and must logically, therefore, encounter each other in an attitude of distrust, caution and low confidence. Of course, the perception of tourists held by the informal Durban beachfront parking attendant is partly set by the latter's learning from her interaction with other people and other tourists seeking somewhere to park.

She does not know if she is going to be paid or not for her service but she can call on a sort of universalised trust, not based on concrete persons but based on her experience of people who park cars on the beachfront in bays controlled by herself and others like her. As we have discussed in chapter 5, we always paid, even though it is easy to avoid paying, because we felt an obligation to do so. Free-riding (Olson, 1971) tourists become free-parking tourists on the back of tourists like us. We have frequently used the word 'may' in this discussion of trust and tourism because there is a disappointing lack of conceptual, theoretical and empirical studies of trust in the tourist experience (a search through *Annals of Tourism*, for example, a major academic tourism journal, did not reveal any significant attempts to discuss trust in tourism formally).

Offe's work on what he calls 'Problems of building trust beyond familiarity' (in Warren, 1999, p.55) is worthy of a more detailed examination of its usefulness in illuminating the tourist experience than we can give here. However, we will continue to use Offe to link our discussion of empowerment, government and globalisation to this sketch on the significance of trust as a background to understanding tourism development in South Africa. We mentioned the problem of achieving stability that societies face in any transition from one polity to another, and one means to the maintenance of a new democracy will be trust among elites. The exact form these elites take will vary according to the degree that the democracy is representational or participatory, where elites will be restricted or extended respectively. What is true of either system is that much significant decision-making takes place behind closed doors. Sorting out conflicts of interests in this way, according to Offe, is extremely 'trust-sensitive', and, of course, these closed doors are not usually as watertight as protagonists might wish, certainly not to the press. Examples of breaches of confidentiality, failures to remember and honour concessions through reciprocal concessions and failure to honour agreements and compromises after they have been agreed, are writ large in newspaper coverage of the tourism industry in KwaZulu-Natal. What we may have here is a problem of 'new faces' around the table, say on the Board of the KwaZulu-Natal Tourism Authority, and whether they abide by the rules of informal bargaining derived from established trust relationships (though the latter are not static, the way in which they shift will be well known and predicted by the old faces).

Belonging, personal power and trust in organisations: a three card trick

The force of the global rhetoric of partnership in development is obviously contingent on the degree, type and sustainability of trust relationships within and between the key institutions or groups. The foundations of trust may well arise from a perception of whether an institution or group actually 'belongs' inside the bargaining process. Offe (in Warren, 1999, p.63) calls belonging a 'non-experiential assessment rule for trustworthiness'.

The meaning and significance of claiming to be a 'stakeholder' in some process of social change is clearly important here too, since claims to being a stakeholder may be tested against perceptions of whether a potential stakeholder can be trusted to play the game. The latter has to give out the appropriate trust-inducing signals and it is this sort of political or social leaning, or rather the lack of it, which helps to define and sustain the marginalised position of poor peoples. Indeed, such communities, for example, the people of Dukuduku South, or the casual workers on the Durban beachfront, may be treated as outsiders, with aggressive distrust by those already inside the tourism development project. The work of St Lucia's Nicky Moore (formerly Barker) the political activist, journalist and hotelier, can be understood as facilitating processes that might lead to a different and fairer distribution of trust allocations among current and potential stakeholders in the development of St Lucia. The high-living new residents of the newly renovated apartments in the art-deco masterpieces on the Durban beachfront, trying to raise the property value of their 'bargain' accommodation, need to 'clean-up' the beach as part of their gentrification (investment) strategy for their property. Local sex industry workers may resist such financial cleansing.

We have already alluded to the stress on the empowerment of previously voiceless peoples in the South African democracy as reflecting a preference for direct, rather than representative, democracy. This in itself suggests that people should be trusted since there is little confidence in the ability of representational institutions and procedures to act as fair and effective mediators and generalisers of trust. Institutions are partly defined through the impersonal operation of self-sustaining mechanisms for self-correcting mistakes, for being durable and, more or less, for being part of the furniture of the political process. Lack of trust in the perception of future well-being, as we have seen, leads to a lack of confidence in these hoping-to-be-taken-for-granted institutions and this in turn leads the move towards mass elites, or empowerment and the de-institutionalisation of politics. Any government institutions left inside a direct democracy will have their very existence continually contested and their boundaries will always be unclear or subject to change such that they could not operate a 'closed-shop' of membership and influence. 'Institutions are worthy of our confidence exactly to the extent that we have reasons to trust those who are involved in the defense, interpretation, innovation, and loyal support of institutions' (Offe, in Warren, 1999, p.67).

There is a well-known dilemma here that underwrites the political context of tourism development in the new democracy of South Africa: the need to trust in persons cannot be fully substituted by trust in institutions, but we know that market failures in the distribution of familiarity and community diminish the capacity to trust other persons. Offe (in Warren, 1999) refers to this dilemma through a brief discussion of both Weber, whose political sociology focussed on this issue, and of what Offe calls the 'libertarian solution' and it is the latter that is of major interest in the South African context. Libertarians argue that societies that face this well-known trust dilemma should reform and aim for a social structure where the need for trust as the bedrock of political, economic and social transactions should be minimalised. In such a structure, contracts have to be unambiguously enforced, it must be possible to exit from member-ship of the local state, and people must have the personal means, including use of force as a last resort, to defend their present and future well-being under conditions of high risk and uncertainty, or of restricted confidence in trust relationships. Once these conditions are in place, they, in effect, replace the oil and glue of trust in the social order. From our direct experience of travels through KwaZulu-Natal, and our discussions, observations, and general immersion in the region, preferences for a libertarian solution to the trust dilemma seem to have created a unique cultural and political mixed economy of democracy and libertarianism.

The role of rational perception here is vital to consider, since it may deter-mine the personal opportunistic inclination towards non-compliance with the elements of a newly defined social order. Take, for example, the poachers who rely on their well-being through infiltrating the perimeter fencing and farming the outer limits of KwaZulu-Natal Wildlife's regulated game reserves in KwaZulu-Natal (and they would defend their killing game, too). Why do local people 'farm' the game reserves and why should they not do this? The fence is the steel reality of the institutionalised rules of the KNW designed to enforce generalised trust and compliance in the KNW's capacity to defend the public interest. But, of course, the public interest is contested and, moreover, the rules are 'positive'; they are made and can be changed and part of the meaning and significance of the 'new' in the new South Africa is just that. If local popu-lations judge the KNW as lacking the inclination or competence to make fair and effective use of their powers, and to be subject to the temptations of personal opportunism, then the incentive to trust the system is diminished.

We need also, as we have done before, to call in Olson's (1971) free-rider concept to pursue this issue of non-compliance, for the latter is contingent on the degree of confidence or trust that any single potential poacher has, that other potential poachers will actually resist farming the reserves. No single potential poacher wants to be the only one from a community who misses out on promoting personal and family well-being, but if all comply with the regulatory framework, all stay equally disadvantaged. Offe (in Warren, 1999, p.69) summarises the game position of the potential poacher succinctly: 'In order to be motivated to comply, I must trust that, by and large, (a) legislators do not neglect their legislative responsibilities, (b) administrators do not act opportunistically, and (c) fellow citizens do not effectively defect even in cases where they can escape formal sanctioning.'

There is a sense in which the framework of the stranger works equally well for analysing the KZNNCS Officer (say, one of the new Community Development Officers) and poacher trust relationships, as it does for tourist–host relationships. For the Officer is historically and culturally a stranger to the local Zulu empowered farmer or poacher. How can the Officer develop a kind of abstract and inclusive (for all local potential poachers) trust in the co-operative dispositions of all those to whom the anti-poaching laws are addressed? The obvious point here, and we now have the beginnings of a more formal argument for it, is that institutions such as the KZNNCS in the new South Africa, in respect to the communities of interest that exist with a demonstrable stake in what the KZNNCS does and how it does it, remain viable or sustainable only in so far as there exists supportive understandings and dispositions from both those inside the institution and outside it. And the difficulty for the KZNNCS and for the KZNTA is that neither is well entrenched and time-honoured and it may prove difficult to understand, to offer support and loyalty to, and to empathise with these infant institutions' aims and methods.

> It is the substantive quality of institutions, their capacity to make compelling sense, that determines the extent to which they are capable of promulgating the loyalties of those whose actions they are supposed to regulate, as well as the trust on the part of agents that this support will be widely shared by other agents [Offe, in Warren, 1999, p.69].

This is also the point at which we can formally support the view, that comes from intuition and experience, that just one KZNNCS Officer can destroy trust relationships for all other Officers. Institutions such as the KZNNCS allow local peoples, potentially, to trust people whom they have never met, have never had any contact with and share no cultural or historical allegiance with. Institutions, as we have hinted, are strictly speaking simply sets of rules that create a particular form of political and moral authority but they embody 'personality' because of the persons who are employed by them. People who have every reason to trust the KZNNCS can instantly lose their trust in the authority of the KZNNCS because of one bad experience, with just one of their employees, say, an inexperienced KZNNCS Officer.

The problem that the KZNNCS seems to face in its relationships with local peoples is that it makes no sense to these peoples – its very existence is contested, despite its long-standing history as the Natal Parks Board, and subsequently as a newly badged conservation authority. The disjuncture of function for land and animals that exists between the KNW and some local communities is a formidable barrier to the development of trust. If the Service succeeds in meeting its transformation mission, this will be because its commitment to working differently has generated new forms of solidarity, co-operation and civic identification with the Service. The new agenda of the KNW and the agenda of the new tourism authorities in South Africa must have moral plausibility and operational efficiency. Compliance may then be achieved because they are perceived to be congruent with the political agendas of partnership and empowerment in control and regulation in a resource-depleted financial environment. In this way, the tourism institutions can also promote generalised trust in state institutions and thereby wean the social order off libertarianism towards a democracy that accommodates in a sceptical and critically supportive way, globalisation and its celebration of capitalistic democracies.

In South Africa, the power position between the tourist and local people is a complex one, bounded by and defined by different asymmetrical power relationships. But generally speaking, the tourist is in the dominant position because they can do more harm to the local person through what we can call negative sanctions, i.e. a failure to spend money that might lead to benefits for the local person. This power outweighs, usually, the power that the possession of local knowledge gives the local person over the stranger or tourist. And, of course, truth and honesty, such as keeping promises, in any transaction is a major causal factor in the nature of the trust relationships engendered. Variations in the ability and propensity to lie and be dishonest in transactions is directly related to the extent and quality of trust relationships.

A free-riding culture

A major factor in putting the 'strangeness' into the tourist–host experience of being strangers to each other, is culture. Meanings, perceptions and expectations based on the significance and experience of interactions underwritten by claims to truth, honesty, fairness and so on are culturally determined. Our interviews with the waitresses in St Lucia suggested that they had no choice, as they saw it, in making as much money as they could because they, and their job, were looked on as a source of family, dependants' and friends' welfare. This led to excellent service for us because of the waitresses' need to enhance income through tips. The tip, in effect, was a tax, leading to transfer income. The tourist is potentially a major contributor to the local welfare state. And we know from many surveys of attitudes towards expenditure held by tourists, the latest of which (reported in the *Guardian* 15 January 2000), by Tearfund, a

Christian relief and development agency, confirms the position. Most British holidaymakers claim to be willing to pay more for their holiday if this means that more of their expenditure stays local and can be seen to directly benefit poorer communities. If the British visitors to St Lucia knew how the Zulu family economy worked, they may be more willing to tip and to tip more generously than they otherwise would. We shall return to the relationship between globalisation, tourism and welfare in our concluding comments.

The point to stress here is that public policy cannot enforce a collective economic morality on individuals. In KwaZulu-Natal, the legitimate tourism authorities seem only to be competent in designing programmes of tourism development but are not able to implement and control these policies so that people behave in line with the aims of the programme. People need to be able to trust their fellow citizens to behave in ways that are congruent with collectively derived, legitimated and regulated policies before they themselves will commit behavioural support to those programmes. We are back, yet again, to the significance of Olson's (1971) work, which we have now implicitly tied into our analysis of the significance of trust relationships in tourism development. For the local people of KwaZulu-Natal to play along with centrally planned tourism development inside general policies of economic, political and social reform, then voluntary compliance and co-operation is a necessary condition for the success of such policies and the likelihood of voluntary compliance is sabotaged when individuals believe that others will take them for a free ride.

An important case in point, which we have referred to before but now we can add this further element into the analysis, is that of local people taking game from the KNW-regulated game reserves. If only one family from a village stops poaching or farming game in order to comply, they will become poorer because of this and since others still benefit from the game, the likelihood of alternative forms of food supply arising will not increase.

In South Africa, the experience of apartheid as a special form of centralised state power, gradually and cumulatively took over and buried any vestiges of the characteristically incomplete yet functional trust relationships in civil society. In the transition to a direct democracy, or a democracy stressing personal and local real political power, centralised state regulation is too weak to succeed in the usual paradoxical policy of imposing empowerment. One way of conceptualising this problem, widespread in the public voice of the KZNNCS and KZNTA, is to see it as to be resolved through the emergence of an idealised view of civil society, replete with co-operation and efficacy. The likelihood of the vision being realised is in part a function of the extent to which South Africa can, in the twenty-first century, escape from the bonds of an extended and deep experience of state-centred interventionism, especially since the underlying or 'suppressed' culture of associationalism and civic identity and solidarity were at best unevenly distributed. It may not ever be in the short-term interests of individuals to sign up to the processes of attempted empowerment that dominate the rhetoric of politics in South Africa.

The market for trust

There is what we can call a supply-side deficiency in the level and distribution of trust and we return to where we began, with the question of how to change the market conditions for trust in the new South Africa? The problem is three-fold: first, lack of trust between people in the same political, economic and social condition; second, lack of trust between 'the people' and the regulatory institutions; and third, lack of trust between the regulatory institutions. Offe (in Warren, 1999, p.85) argues that one solution would refer to a

> radical historicist answer, leaving, by implication, communities with a low perceived level of social capital with the not very helpful diagnosis that they suffer from the 'wrong' kind of history and tradition ... Is it conceivable that the 'social capital' of trusting and co-operative civic relations can be encouraged, acquired and generated – and not just inherited?

Offe concludes his important chapter in Warren's very useful collection of articles, with this question and a failure to identify and address this question directly may be endemic to the political process of tourism development in KwaZulu-Natal as we experienced it.

We are not in a position to prescribe how the supply of trust, the necessary ingredient for the presence of productive social capital, could be changed so as to underwrite processes of empowerment. Social capital is a moral resource, and generalised trust and social capital are in joint-supply – increase one and you increase the other. Fukuyama (1995) has argued that in certain cultures, economic performance and economic relationships are determined by the lack of generalised trust and determined more so by forms of particularised trust, say, preferentially trading, as in the Chinese economy, only with 'family'. And we can here draw on earlier discussion of toleration, and say that the degree of trust or confidence we have in strangers is in direct relationship to the degree to which we tolerate risk and uncertainty in our lives. More strictly, we appear to be faced with a particularised decision set if we are poor, when we choose not to engage in the sort of transactions that promote personal economic well-being. Should we tolerate our voluntary poverty because we refuse to tolerate the risk that we associate with this different array or level of transactional relationships, arising from, for example, co-operative behaviour that may or may not lead us out of poverty? Put another way, we might say that the nature of trust in a society may be directly related to the bases, forms, levels and distribution of optimism among the members of that society. If this is the case, it would begin to explain the significance of Nelson Mandela to South Africa, even in retirement, because of his symbolic representation of hope in a better future for all South Africans. It also underwrites, from another perspective, the importance of the work of the Truth and Reconciliation Commission.

Trust and optimism are not the same thing but, psychologically, they are major components of our world view. Some of the small B&B owners we talked to in KwaZulu-Natal were what we might call optimistic distrusters. They thought that life might get better for themselves and their families because they were 'closing ranks', limiting the boundary defining the toleration of risk, and trusting none but themselves to determine their own future prosperity. There may be a threshold point of optimism. When we get beyond that threshold, the urge to control one's own future through limiting reliance on co-operative efforts so to do, is outweighed by such a belief in the benefits from one's own tightly controlled actions that we will take the odd gamble in co-operation. For example, the St Lucia hoteliers may read, rather than bin, the promotional material of the KNTA advocating just what the KNTA can do for them. The point of this speculation is to stress the argument that the achievement of empowerment, of good government and of a socially just distribution of goods and services in the new South Africa, and the role of tourism development inside this more general development project, hinges on these interrelated goals. The latter exist as both targets and processes or are simultaneously inputs to and outputs of (just to complicate matters still further) the imperative of rapid, planned social change. And the latter is in a complex dynamic with the personal political, economic and social psychology of stakeholders.

Moreover, the stakeholder concept itself is confounded by what we take to be the meaning and significance of globalisation and whether it is unprecedented or not. As Marx and Engels, (in Giddens, 1999) assert, we should treat any claims to the uniqueness of contemporary political and economic relations with caution:

> The bourgeoisie cannot exist without revolutionising the instruments of production, and with them the whole relations of society...Constant revolutionising of production, uninterrupted disturbance of all social conditions, everlasting uncertainty and agitation distinguish the bourgeois epoch from all earlier ones. All fixed, fast-frozen relations, with their train of ancient and venerable prejudices and opinions, are swept away, all new-formed ones become antiquated before they can ossify. All that is solid melts into air...

Democracy in itself is no guarantee that the nature of trust in a society will radically change.

Democracies that are badly divided by ethnic, religious or racial clashes may be only marginally more trusting than autocracies that are similarly split. Generalised trust can be the engine of a society only where most people are willing to express at least a modicum of faith in strangers. And people are most likely to trust others (and not just their own kind) when they are doing well and expect to do better [Ulslaner, in Warren, 1999, p.143].

The time frame within which people perceive the possibility of a better future is clearly of vital importance. If, for example, the local people of Kosi Bay believe that the benefits from economic co-operation with private Kosi Bay tourism development will pay off in the near future, rather than filter through and have its main impact on the welfare of future generations, this will clearly affect people's assessment of whether they want to support co-operative economic development. We spoke to the local Ngunu when we visited Kosi Bay and learnt that the share which the local community had taken out of the trading profits of the Company for a number of years had yet to be spent because the group set up by the Ngunu to decide how the money was to be spent could not agree. The conversation we had with the Ngunu took place on upturned boxes outside a partly built school and community centre. This building had been started in the first flurry of co-operation based on joint ownership of a new resource, returned tourism profits from the white owner of the Company, but building soon came to a standstill because of disillusionment with the time it was taking for the local regulatory authorities to staff the school, when built, with a teacher. This lack of faith in the efficiency of a new democracy may be fuelled by the residual pessimism present, in this case, as a result of a long tradition of violence and violent relationships in and between local communities in the Kosi Bay locality (CROP, 1995).

Rom Harré's work on the semantics of trust (in Warren, 1999, pp.249–72) complements Offe's deductive work and stresses the double-sidedness of the notion of trust. 'To trust someone and to be trusted by someone constitute both a pattern of psychological dispositions and beliefs of an essentially pragmatic character and a pattern of moral obligations, of that duty to those who trust is the paramount one (Harré, in Warren, 1999, p.271).

Harré focuses on 'reliability' in trust relationships as the key behavioural element and there is clearly close substitutability between his notion of reliability and our treatment of confidence. Both are measurements of trust. The main lesson for our analysis from Harré's work is that he convincingly argues that the nature of the interrelated mix of psychological and pragmatic dispositions and moral imperatives that create a trust relationship is conditional to the form of democracy.

Alternative democratic futures

We have stressed in this chapter that the leap into empowerment underpins both the inappropriateness of the previous authoritarianism, prior to 1994, and the wish to adopt a radical democratic model, closer to direct democracy than to the politically bankrupt representative models offered by the democracies in the Northern Hemisphere. Harré talks about 'parliamentary' and 'consensual' democracies, also described as examples of 'thin' and 'thick' democracies respectively. The political economy of tourism development in KwaZulu-Natal, stressing the empowerment of all citizens with a stake in the distributional and welfare effects of tourism activity, in theory and in practice has to incorporate a model of how people's reliability or confidence in the trust relationships appropriate to a 'thick' democracy, can be identified and sustained or enhanced.

This, in itself, will require perhaps a shift in direction for tourism research in the province in order to focus on the nature of trusting practices, and their pragmatic and moral bases, significant to the tourism development project. The policy level research that would be entailed inside this new research agenda would include an examination of the relationship between the thin democratic simplicities of global political and economic institutions, such as the World Bank and its development agenda for South Africa, and the thick National and Provincial empowerment projects that South Africa appears to want to set for itself. It would also entail close anthropological accounts of how public order in significant tourism locations, such as the Durban beachfront (work on the geography of social and economic informal regulation has already been started by Professor Robert Preston-Whyte of the University of Natal, 1997), is established and sustained by the aggregate of the informal and unpaid contributions that individuals, including international tourists, make to the building up of trustworthiness through practising mutuality, reciprocity and so on.

We want to return to a previous element in our discussion in order to focus on the tourist experience in South Africa. We argued earlier that the British tourist to South Africa may occupy a particular moral position in so far as they may wish in some way to 'pay-back' local people for what the tourist takes to be the unreasonable hardships created by apartheid and, maybe, though more rarely, the tourist perception of the debt owed by current generations of Britons to current South Africans, because of the longer history of British imperialism and exploitation in South Africa. In any case, these forms of particularised guilt may mix up with the generalised view that when rich tourist meets poor host, a moral obligation exists that informs the political economy of interpersonal transactions. From the point of view of the poor host, there may be a prediction, derived from a perception of the trust relationship between herself and the tourist, that the tourist will act more generously than he or she would otherwise do in less guilt-ridden or more equal transactional relationships.

The problem for the international tourist, of course, is imperfect information – how can they know that the women they meet at the Valley of a Thousand hills lay-by are poor enough to warrant a relationship built on such a premise? The tourist has to trust his judgement. But the role of trust here is not simply to allow a prediction to be made, how far one can trust, but to practise what Mainsbridge (1980) has usefully called 'altruistic trust'. This is where we, as tourists, give the other local person or persons the benefit of the doubt. The point here is that we feel obliged to do this, to be optimistic and to get beyond an otherwise rational point where we would normally limit the transaction, given the nature of informational imperfections and their predictive value. The tourist here would be practising a trust relationship that arises from some sort of historically derived empathy with the current social condition of the local person overlain, perhaps, with some general principle that always informs their behaviour as tourist – such as to be more generous with poor people than with people perceived to be not so poor.

Altruistic trust occurs when we trust more than is warranted by our assessment of the objective probability of being exploited. It may be a feature of the Good Tourist visiting South Africa and possibly elsewhere, that they are prepared for the possibility of engaging in altruistic trust relationships. If they are, this will increase the sum of trust in the country (we know nothing about the size of the multiplier effects on the social order of injections of trust into a polity). The practice of altruistic trust is closely related to the concept of what we earlier referred to as wishful-thinking trust. Practising altruistic trust illustrates the view that we have of the other person: we show that we respect them, treating them as we would wish to be treated were we in their position; more generally, it shows we actually care about the nature of the relationship created by a potential transaction or encounter; and we might also think that our actions may indeed have a multiplier effect, persuading any doubting observers to follow our example. Tourists, or local people, who practice altruistic trust never warrant the label 'suckers', the common epithet used to label people who trust too much when trying to ration their trust to objective prediction. When the other person in the transaction outwits them, by in effect successfully selling them messages about themselves that lead to an inaccurate objective risk assessment, people are said to 'have fallen for it', to have been duped, suckered and manipulated. This cannot happen with altruistic trust. We are more here in the kind of territory described by Titmus (1970) when he wrote about the market conditions for blood in the USA and the UK, contrasting the classical economic market of the USA with the unusual 'gift relationship' market operating in the UK. The risk of exploitation, with altruistic trust, is zero since, by definition, there is no possibility of exploitation. The relaxation of the normal predictive procedure is in the nature of a gift to the recipient. Here, tourist transactions can be described as bearing the hallmark of a gift relationship underpinned by a moral intention.

An example of this form of trust relationship occurred to us when we were parking our car in a Durban multi-storey car park near Tourist Junction, the home of the KNTA, heading for interviews with members of the Authority. We parked on the sixth floor (the first available space) and had to walk across the floor to the lift. There, we were greeted politely by a young black man, who we judged to be local by his accent, as we waited for the lift. We thought he was waiting for the lift too but he didn't travel in the lift with us. We had heard all the stories and had seen the data about car theft in Durban and we wondered whether he was simply checking out that we would not be back for a few hours (he asked us what we were doing in Durban and we told him). We were tempted to return to the car and to shift it to another floor, but we resisted the idea of acting as if this friendly man was a car thief just because he was black (the necessary moral dimension in altruistic trust emerges at this point) just because he was friendly and just because he didn't join us in the lift. It could be argued that our actions represented a gift to him and others like him – we wanted to trust him beyond our objective assessment of the situation. As it happens, he was still there when we returned and we asked him why he spent so much time at the multi-storey. We had missed the pretty obvious point that he was a plain-clothes security guard and we were relieved that we had given him the benefit of the doubt (though he never knew this), based on either belief beyond reason or a conscious, moral decision to discount the data linking young black men to car theft in Durban. When we told some of our friends in Durban what we had done, they advised us to err on the side of pessimism and self-interest on all future similar occasions, and not to be 'stupid'.

We have begun merely to hint at significant ways in which the stranger-to-stranger transactional relationship characterises the particularities of the British tourist experience in South Africa and we conclude this aspect of our discussion by returning to the general South African political, economic and social project, of which tourism development is a significant congruent element, of achieving empowerment, well-being and fairness in everyday life for current and future citizens. We have seen that trust relationships are dynamic and trust-building can be dismantled in an instant. Stranger-to-stranger trust relations may be among the most fragile of all interpersonal trust relations and will only be extended and sustained in a culture where there is widespread trustworthiness. The paradox here is that a culture of trustworthiness may attract cherry-picking individuals seeking to benefit from the transference of general trustworthiness to themselves, even as strangers. Both locals and international tourists may be described as 'gullible' or easy to 'take for a ride'. We know little other than through speculation about how such matters define the tourist experience in South Africa and elsewhere, but our extended discussion here indicates the need for new forms of empirical research into the tourist experience.

Trust and its meaning and significance in different societies is a major indicator of the nature of political life. We expect to see different trust relationships according to the type of polity. According to Warren (1999) we do not yet have a well-developed theoretical account of trust and democracy. Equally, we do not yet have an adequate theoretical account of the tourist experience. If we put together these two claims, we can see why theoretical explorations in the political economy of tourism in democratic societies are so thin on the ground.

The beginnings of an elaborated account of the latter have been the focus of this book and we want to conclude this chapter with some final thoughts on the South African project to transform the polity and simultaneously to seek economic prosperity through the development of key industries, such as tourism. The importance of trust here is that the big political project smacks of unfamiliarity, of being riddled with uncertainty rather than risk (which we have defined as uncertainty, amenable to objective measurement – a risk assessment). Trust involves people in breaking with the security of familiarity and its inherently conservative bias and allows us to cope with the fact that we may perceive ourselves to lack information about what is likely to happen and happen to us. Politics, in so far as it is about the potential resolution of conflicts of interest brought about by inequalities in life circumstances, both undermines trust and establishes the need for it. We can never be sure that we know the interests of others, because of informational inadequacies of all sorts, yet we need to be able to predict the interests of others or to predict the moral position of others, in order to trust them at all. The exact ways in which different political systems facilitate this and the degrees to which they simultaneously undermine and reinforce the need for trust, is the focus of a significant intellectual and research effort among political scientists at the moment.

The point we make here is that not only democracy but the specific form of democracy, such as democracy South African style, will be based on and lead to congruent forms of trust relations and trustworthiness. These trust processes, whether and how quickly they emerge, may determine the success of the South African project. Since, as we have argued, trust relationships are vital in theory and practice in the tourist experience, putting tourism development at the forefront of the grander political and economic project makes good sense. In this way, the direction and speed of change in the South African tourism industry is a mirror of progress in the wider strategy of promoting well-being for all, through creating a prosperous deliberative or direct democracy. It remains simply to say something about the nature of trust relations inside the latter.

Deliberative trust

The shift to participatory forms of democracy makes sense when there is little likelihood that historic and culturally determined conflicts of interests that really matter, say over land and animal ownership and reform, will be treated inside the ring of warranted trust. One of the conditions of trust that is warranted is that there exists some degree of commonality of interests that mitigate against the risk of exploitation. Where this is largely absent, people have to participate directly in deliberative processes (meeting and speaking directly to people, for example). Of course, a well-known potential inefficiency of direct democracy is that things take a long time to get sorted out. More formally, the technical aspects of regular mass participation can prove insurmountable, and the motivation for people to commit time resources to deliberative processes may be lacking, people preferring to engage in wishful thinking trust. Moreover, there may be perceived or ascribed cognitive barriers to direct engagement, where it appears to be too difficult to come to a view (other than the one already held). We attended political rallies during our visits to KwaZulu-Natal that were held under the umbrella of deliberative democracy. At these rallies, people were invited to come forward to offer personal testimony concerning some view or experience. Some people, especially women, talked on their feet for a long time, often about things that were not signalled by the agenda, and no-one dared tell them to sit down to give someone else a chance to speak.

What might be functional is for deliberative democratic processes to be called on when, as we have seen, trust is limited by history and culture, and conflicts of interest really matter. The significance of trust then will be that people have confidence that such matters will be treated in a deliberative way and that competent authorities can be trusted to be just that, and confidently left to get on with promoting the public good. As far as institutions such as the KZNTA and KZNNCS are concerned, this mixed economy of trust relations will define their organisational culture and practices for them: minimally, they will need to be transparent in their employment practices and operations and in their public accountability procedures, and they will need to provide, as a special case of this first condition, appropriate information in an appropriate form. There will also need to be institutions with similar qualities that exist to challenge institutions such as the KZNTA and KNW and individuals in 'trusted' positions. Those that monitor the trustworthiness of the trusted, such as Interface Africa, must be subject to the same ethical criteria. Such knowledge might remain hypothetical until tested by a real need, so that the possibility of public scrutiny will limit the temptation to provide misinformation or to simply offer the veneer of accountability. People will not know that institutions are playing the game but they could know and will lose trust in institutions that were revealed as dishonest and employees who are found to be corrupt. It may be that people have a differentiated trust in institutions: they trust one feature of the organisation but not the other. This could clearly be the case with local people's trust perception of the KNW, whereby they know that the KNW are experts in animal conservation but not in people conservation.

Empowerment is congruent with deliberative democratic processes since the latter encourages people to combat what Warren (1999, p.340) calls 'the subjective cognitive biases towards the past'. The perspectives of individuals, (if deliberation is inclusive which it must be if it is deemed to be in place) can be enriched and possibly challenged by new or alternative voices being heard for the first time, whereby new alignments are achieved and new trust relations, which in themselves increase the supply of warranted trust. Logically, these new dispositions can displace the older narratives based on demonisation, distrust, conspiracy, betrayal and fear, the standard bases of historical narratives of the recent past in South Africa. And, of course, the more public politics is, the less opportunity there is for a non-public or corrupting form of influence to dominate, such as the promise of power and money; and the more dialogue and com- munication there is in political life, the more the likelihood that persuasion, the main form of influence in democracies of any sort, will come to the fore, displacing manipulation, coercion and force. As we have emphasised before, it is a moot point how far societies can lay claim to a political label, such as democracy, when the major political, economic and social institutions of that society are not in themselves democratic. The role for tourism development in South Africa should be to replicate, reinforce and lead the move to a new polity of democracy through its own structure and behaviour. This might also be congruent with what the British international tourist would wish to see too, if only they knew it.

In everyday speech, one of the popular uses of the term 'brothers' is to infer some deep solidarity between people who are not literally brothers. 'Brothers' are clearly not strangers, and what we have argued about the nature of trust relationships between people who are strangers to each other should not apply when we are describing and analysing trust relationships between so-called 'brothers'. But in South Africa, and elsewhere, people who have called them- selves 'brothers' are at war with each other or have resorted to force to resolve conflicts of interest between them. Indeed, Ignatieff (in Mendus, 1999), a writer whose work we found useful in developing our commentary in chapter 5, draws our attention to what he calls the 'Cain and Able Syndrome', pointing up the condition of hatred between the two brothers in order to make the point that toleration can teeter over into intolerance when people are very close to each other. This is not revelatory but it does suggest that to conceptualise tourist– host relationships as being essentially to do with strangers meeting each other and then to build models of trust relationships on that premise, would be to miss a very important feature of interpersonal relationships. The general proposition here is that those who know the most about each other and differ least from each other may prove to be the most intolerant of each other. This possibility is crucial for it may undermine the prospects of achieving empowerment through the establishment of a deliberative democracy in South Africa, and may, at the micro-level, mitigate against tourism development through empowerment. When we met the Ngunu in Kosi Bay after doing our background reading on the history of the region, we should not have been surprised to find that the transferred profits from the Company had not yet been spent by the local community. Those who are closest may also be the most divided. This is the first irony we should consider.

There is a second irony that further confuses the picture. Solidarity between 'strangers' may be on the increase, certainly in so far as we might, whether we like it or not, claim to share the impacts of globalisation. Doom and gloom environmentalism, for example, can unite people because of an identification with a common enemy, human nature, and the impact of technological trans-formations in the media and travel, resulting in international television and tourism, might be said to make us all neighbours or brothers and to be our brother's 'keeper'. The latter, if it is true, suggests that we cannot ignore an obligation to act on behalf of people who are poor and otherwise deprived and in difficult circumstances because we sense that we are in some way responsible for their condition. So, we would seem to be in a position where we can simultaneously go to bloody war with our brothers and make great sacrifices (in time or money) for people we have never met and are never likely to meet. The point of this possibility in the context of discussing tourism is that the complex and seemingly paradoxical or ironic positions we take up with respect to other people, should cast doubt on any simplistic analysis of the tourist–host relationship. Though we have made use of the language, the latter configuration may not be a very useful way of modelling tourist encounters.

In a liberal democracy, the state symbolises the fact that we accept the presence and value of diversity. People can take up their own value position and hold to this, following appropriate deliberation, but this conviction sits alongside a recognition that other people will want to live their lives in other ways and should be allowed to do so. A belief in the legitimacy of the political system, in the neutrality or impartiality that the state represents (though, of course, it enshrines the values of conviction and diversity so, in this sense, is not neutral or impartial) allows this dualism of conviction and accommodation to co-exist.

This is why, at the micro-level of the tourism development in South Africa, trust in the benevolence of state or quasi-state national and provincial institutions is crucial to securing a sustainable tourism industry. Seeking political and moral sustainability in tourism development would also guarantee environmental sustainability since the latter would be an outcome of moral deliberation inside a politics of everyday life in the new South Africa. And this political life would have to be characterised by action, authority, efficacy, toleration and curiosity, rather than passiveness, deference, indifference, intolerance and self-satisfaction. This would be in stark contrast to the experience of apartheid, a political and moral regime based on the principle that is was necessary and right for each ethnic group to follow what the apartheid government called 'separate development'. Ignatieff, (in Mendus, 1999, p.85) makes a more general point about apartheid:

> It insists that group identities are so all-shaping that they create moral worlds unintelligible to each other, and that groups therefore are incapable of living together in peace within the same territorial and political space. This form of intolerance underpins ethnic cleansing in Bosnia, Christian–Muslim conflict in the South Caucasus, Afrikaner claims to separate homelands for whites in South Africa, and perhaps also tribal warfare in Rwanda. This intolerance often tacitly presumes the superiority of a particular group, but it is more often relativist and separatist; it may only insist on the impossibility of sharing civic space with other groups.

Tourism development in South Africa is today contingent on a reconceptualisation of society itself. The latter is not to be viewed as bound together by the chains of birth and ascribed nature (if you are a Zulu then you must be…), but, rather tied together through a deliberative process that constantly reviews claims made on the basis of self and group interests, on property or ownership and human rights. This will take time.

What may happen, and this is why the process may be slow, is that even as people become more tolerant towards each other or their differences begin to disappear, they might tend to stay focussed on the differences that still remain and increase their capacity for intolerance towards these residual conflicts of interest. As we write, this is the case in Northern Ireland, for example, and explains a comment made to us by a nurse, a Zulu, working in a medical centre in northern KwaZulu-Natal who also worked part-time at a KNW-run game reserve. She told us that she was glad the (new) medical centre had been built, that her village welcomed it and were keen to use and promote its work. But her superior at the centre, a senior nurse, treated her badly at work. Revenge for this maltreatment, she said, was to be found through inter-village life, since the senior nurse came from a nearby village and the two groups of villagers had always been in competition for food, firewood and land. Both villages had a vested interest in the success of the medical centre but this apparent solidarity based on mutual interest may not displace emotional and historic or subjective response to the situation. As the two sets of villagers come together through joint interests in meeting the basic opportunity principle, (in this case, supporting the running of a medical centre) in contrast, their respective tolerance of each other may diminish. This complexity of social relationships acts as a cognitive and practical barrier to attempts by the KZNTA and the KNW to promote 'community-led tourism development' in the province.

We have not dwelt on the importance of education in this book, though chapter 8, when discussing the notion of the Good Tourist, suggests the crucial role that political and moral learning, or the lack of it, has in shaping political behaviour. For the democratic twin peaks of conviction and accommodation to co-exist, it will mean that people have to be able to break the ties of the uncritical absorption of collective identities and predestination. The motivation and ability to distance oneself from these two barriers is what South Africans might look to their education system to cultivate. This in turn would be congruent with the everyday political learning that will take place from deliberation, itself a form of political lifelong learning. Where individuals live with poverty and inequality and wherever they seek to find personal identity and pride inside group membership, then we have the basis for intolerance. As Ignatieff rightly claims, 'Racism, on this account, is the pride of those trapped in collective identities' (in Mendus, 1999, p.100).

Trust in disagreement

Tourism development will be conditioned by the experience of intense ethnic conflicts of interests and their associated disagreements about preferable outcomes from planned social change, but hopefully not for too much longer conditioned by the inhuman consequences of racism. Where there are *prima facie* good reasons for different and incompatible courses of action, and these arise from fundamentally different value positions, then, as we have argued, we must feel able to trust the state to make sense of the dialogue between conviction, diversity and accommodation and to resist any tendency to revert to racism or fundamentalism, with their shared features of suppression and disruption of discourse. The discussions that we had with people in KwaZulu-Natal about their preferred tourism futures and their personal aspirations and hopes for their family, indicated deep divisions within and between people and groups. What is clear is that the politics of tourism development in South Africa means in part establishing processes that allow people to come to as large a measure of agreement as is necessary to lead to effective and efficient policy implementation. Such a process would accept that disagreement and conflict are endemic features of democratic social life and in a deliberative democracy will go hand in hand with conversations that continually (or as necessary) review these alternative preferences and their practical consequences. The protocols of such conversations would include seeking to avoid either the suppression or disruption (the two are tactically related) of opinion unless the content or method of presenting and opinion is agreed to be intolerable at the outset. We attended, as we have mentioned, an ANC political meeting near Empangeni in KwaZulu-Natal in 1996, where people were allowed to stay on their feet talking for as long as they wished, irrespective of whether they appeared to be contributing to the matters in hand or not. No-one was prepared to ask them to conclude their speech to allow others to respond or to deal with reaction from others in the hall to the points made. This was neither efficient nor effective, as far as we could see, but it may have reflected a sort of political and community cathartic process of speaking aloud about one's attitudes, concerns and opinions.

According to MacIntyre (in Mendus, 1999), when we are involved in debate with those who hold possibly conflicting views to our own, we can take four distinct attitudes to the voices of others. MacIntyre does not address the issue of cultural differences in conversational discourse, nor does he directly refer to the fit or otherwise between forms of conversation and political systems. However, the logic of MacIntyre's analysis is convincing and, moreover, does lead to an analysis that is congruent with what we are searching for, which is to begin to elaborate a practical method for addressing potential or actual disputes about matters of common interest, including preferred tourism development impacts. He argues, firstly, that we can welcome the views of others as either reinforcing our own conclusions or as assisting in the adjustment and improvement of our views. Second, we may welcome them because they are so persuasive as to make us change our minds and adopt a new and preferable way of thinking, that we had not considered or not thought through well enough. Third, we may also productively engage with an alternative point of view because we believe it important to expose its weaknesses or its fallacies and, moreover, to encourage the other person(s) to adopt a better way of arriving at opinion that will avoid coming to untenable views. For example, others may present views based on an analysis of the consequences of a particular course of action that we believe is completely unfounded.

There is a fourth type of response we can make to what we hear others say and how they say it. We can seek to exclude the person from making any further contribution to the discussion because we find either the manner or the content, or both, of their utterance intolerable, and, therefore, they are deemed no longer to have any legitimate conversational standing. And, as MacIntyre points out: 'This is not primarily a matter of suppressing the expression of some point of view within the debate. It is a matter of expelling someone from the debate' (in Mendus, 1999, p.135).

A crucial question for the discourse of tourism development in KwaZulu-Natal is where the line is to be drawn that isolates the fourth possibility from the other three, or, put in the language of toleration, who or what is to draw the line between justified intolerance and unjustified suppression and how is the standard to be enforced? We know that these sorts of questions have to be explicitly faced in a deliberative democracy because disagreements are always present or potentially present and the degree to which we tolerate disagreement, in manner or content, reveals the nature of our own convictions and the limits to accommodation and diversity. These are well-known dimensions to an age-old problem in democratic theory and practice; they will not go away and must be addressed if tourism development is to be politically and morally sustainable. One of the most general sources of conflict, where toleration is likely to be breached, is over issues that, for their resolution, need agreement about the respective powers, roles and boundaries of the state, the market and the local community. This is why Preston-Whyte (1995) is correct to focus on questions concerning the mix of public, private, voluntary and community responsibilities in examining the significance of the organisation of Phinda Game Reserve and the legitimacy of the distribution of benefits from the Phinda Game Reserve's trading activities. He is also right, in our view, to claim that the state should not have sole or even dominant claim to be the authority that answers the questions we have set nor to set the conditions under which such matters are discussed, but it will, as we argued, retain a position of decision-taker of the last resort.

MacIntyre (in Mendus, 1999) argues that there are five conditions constraining the promotion of 'practically rational dialogue' and we outline them here, however obvious they may seem, because we believe they offer an effective baseline framework for deliberation about tourism development in the province. Into and onto this framework, appropriate historic and cultural preferences can be infused, the nature of the latter being the first potential source of conflict, of course. This is why there has to be a threshold level of initial agreement about what it is that needs to be decided, about criteria for determining the supremacy of preference, based on the superior nature of the reasons for holding that preference, and about what might be at stake in a decision – who or what are the potential winners and losers and to what degree.

The first condition concerns agreement about who is to take part in the conversation and we can note that this question should not be politically constrained by the technical form of the conversation. To take an easy example, a video-conference concerning the future for tourism in the St Lucia Wetlands area would be exclusive to those who have the facility or access to this technology and this could knowingly or unwittingly exclude legitimate participants. The second condition concerns the moral or polite conventions of discourse, to do with activities such as interruption, rudeness and so on, whereby failure to observe conventions could lead (temporarily, we suspect) to expulsion. These conventions will have to be learnt, starting in school, so we can already infer the timescale for the model we have in mind, which is not to ignore the point that learning will begin once the process of deliberation begins. Third, people will have to judge and be satisfied that a point has been reached when further deliberation is unwarranted, that certain questions have been settled. The residents of Dukuduku I thought that deliberation concerning the future for the forest had been conclusive, only to find no action being taken and conversations being started again in the future. Some people, we say colloquially, 'don't know when to give up' but inside a process of rational deliberation, they would know or be excluded if they tried to continue. And, fourth, as we have argued, certain things have already been decided as part of defining the initial starting ground (this may be the main and slowest task) such as to prioritise any suggestions for tourism development that appear to benefit women at least as much as men, if not more so, and to exclude any suggestions that are based on a wish to turn to features of economic and social development congruent with the politics of apartheid. And last, people must be prepared to be held accountable for the reasons given to support a position. The force of this condition is that, at least at the time of ongoing discussion, there will be different levels of information and understanding among participants, potentially allowing the most knowledgeable people to hold sway. They could, of course, simply be trusted that their claims to the truth are legitimate, but the possibility of verification would be a further brake on exploitation by a knowledge elite. The KZNNCS, for example, has unrivalled information about the projected population growth of game in the public reserves in KwaZulu-Natal and the KZNNCS needs to be controlled by an expectation held by others that this information will be used by the Service to promote the aims of the matters being deliberated. Officers who fail to disclose appropriate information, for example, could be excluded from participation and could, by their individual actions, exclude the KZNNCS as well, at least in the short term.

This construction of what MacIntyre calls 'a rational politics of local community' (in Mendus, 1999, p.154) is at odds with much of the contemporary global, national and local rhetoric of political and commercial organisations. Indeed, the local and the global appear to be incompatible, which is why any attempt to shift away from the rhetoric of 'community-led tourism development' towards a process of agreed development arising from deliberation, is to be welcomed.

Invisible voices

We want to return here to the position of different groups inside the political economy of tourism development in the province, especially those groups who Olson (1971, p.165) refers to as the 'forgotten groups – those who suffer in silence'.

By definition, we know least about these groups and can say little about them with any confidence. In KwaZulu-Natal, there will be groups with a clear stake in tourism development, who have no effective lobby and currently take no collective action. Why is this? The reason is that they can see no incentives, as individuals, to voluntarily coming together to act jointly to further their own interests. This is a paradoxical position because it is the people who could claim membership of these marginalised groups who have some of the most vital common interests. We can think, for example, of the migrant workers in the province, of the hospitality industry workers, of all the people seeking restoration of land rights in the province and of the informal labourers working the Pacific Ocean beachfronts. Rational poor people will not be willing to make any sacrifices (measured, by the costs of joining the group and conforming to group behaviour) to achieve the objectives they share with others. This is why the forest dwellers in Dukuduku South may not, as individuals, refrain from burning the forest to get charcoal and energy, or why people may not stop poaching or farming the game reserves. 'Community-led' development is undermined by the illogic of collective action and may only be a practical way forward when the conditions of trust between individuals is such as to guarantee the benefits of collective action. Community-led development does nothing, either, to attack an age-old paradox in democratic theory and practice. Questions about boundaries of decision-making and membership of decision-making processes, which we have earlier called issues for initial agreement before a deliberative process can properly begin, themselves demand democratic resolution. 'The great majority of mankind are satisfied with appearances, as though they were realities, and are often even more influenced by the things that seem than those that are' (Machiavelli, quoted in Freie, 1998, p.1).

The promise of community as a planning construct and method still holds sway in KwaZulu-Natal in part because of the unimpeachable authority of its inseparable twin, empowerment. As we have seen earlier, Freie (1998) offers the term 'counterfeit community', to describe a process of social change that allows people to sustain their individualism and engage in collective activities; the latter is not allowed to subsume individual identity. Community remains symbolic and therapeutic, acting both as a political and personal marketing device and inside what we might call this personal 'front', another more private person co-exists. This model is helpful since it reinforces the challenge to find ways in which personal and family self-determination is compatible with democracy, and we applaud any attempts in South Africa to make the new democracy more deliberative, since this seems to be a promising way in which individuality and connectedness can interact. We cannot here provide a detailed account of how we see this dynamic working itself out but we simply want to say that it is, and will continue to be, at the root of disagreement.

We follow Shapiro (in Shapiro and Hacker-Gordon, 1999) in believing that the most fruitful way of understanding the origins of political identity is to see them as a complex, interactive mixture of what he calls 'primordalist' origins, leading to unalterable value positions, and 'socially constructed' origins, that are malleable and dynamic. Political identity, including the possibility of belonging to what Freie (1998) calls a 'genuine community', is shaped by basic constitution, context and circumstance and we do not yet have an explanatory model that helps us predict the limits to a person's political diversity and flexibility of thought and action. This theoretical concern is also, of course, of great practical importance, since the degree to which, and the conditions that have to apply when people are prepared to change their minds, is a major influence on the dynamic of political deliberation.

The stress on how beliefs are formed and changed for the Good Tourist at the individual level, is crucial because it gets us away from the fallacy that variations in fundamental beliefs and values are a function of racial, ethnic or gender group identity, away from 'them and us', towards the celebration of individuality. The latter is a major defence against the prejudice that arises from group opposition. To despise a group is easier than to despise individuals who are claimed to belong to that group. When our white, male, fellow passenger on the trip to the river mouth at Kosi Bay made derogatory remarks about the local black women working in the fields as we drove past them and they turned to smile at the visitors on the truck, he did not see them as individuals but perceived them as members of a group of people who did not deserve respect as human beings, because of their ascribed laziness and their sexual immorality and, more generally, because they could not be trusted.

> Intolerant people are uninterested in the individuals who compose despised groups; in fact, they hardly 'see' them as individuals at all. What matters is the constitution of a primal opposition between 'them' and 'us'. Individuality only complicates the picture, indeed makes prejudice more difficult to sustain, since it is at the individual level that empathy often subverts the primal group opposition [Ignatieff, 1998, p.63].

The stress on individuality that determined the way in which the Truth and Reconciliation Commission went about its work was entirely correct. Individuals may be reconciled to other individuals in ways that groups and nation states can never achieve. What we are stressing here is that the political backcloth to tourism development in KwaZulu-Natal reflects and is conditioned by a new agenda of inclusion. Apartheid can be seen as an extreme variant of an ideology that chooses to maintain civil order through a wide variety of disempowering exclusions. The new political correctness stresses inclusion for all and the task is to see whether a civic order of individuals can develop and sustain itself without depending on the domination of elites or on a global rhetoric of human rights or abstract humanism. The latter can co-exist, as it does in present day South Africa, with intolerable intolerance between groups and neighbours (for a short and controversial account of the political struggle between groups in the lead up to the 1994 election, see Shapiro, in Shapiro and Hacker-Gordon, 1999, pp.212–15). Tourism and television, the two main 'windows on the world' have made it harder to maintain indifference or ignorance towards the citizens of other countries and their welfare.

International politics, global economics and the way in which development is funded, based in part on the rhetoric of a gift relationship, has led to the emergence of the evocative term 'compassion fatigue'. This may be something more than boredom with issues of development and something more than resignation to the impotence of individuals, of an acknowledgement that it is impossible 'to make a difference'. It may be also be more than anger and dismay that certain societies seem incapable of improvement, irrespective of the level of support. We mention this point here because international tourists carry with them, to their destination, the baggage of the way in which the holiday has been mediated to them by the tourism press, by others who have visited before, and so on. They also carry back with them the possibility of moral engagement with far away places, but this engagement will be conditional on coming to an understanding of what they have experienced and what they think is going on. More knowledge, of course, can lead to a reversion to disgust, if things turn out to be worse than people imagined they would be (either from a position of relative ignorance, or from mediated knowledge only).

It may be that tourists are capable of resisting travelling to countries with clearly visible poverty and a general lack of basic opportunities for majorities of individuals because the tourist urge is undermined and deflected by a version of compassion fatigue. One British tourist we met returning home declared that, because of a visit made to Kwa Mashu, a township close to Durban, he would not be visiting South Africa again. He could 'not take it any more' because he had no idea what to do about what he had seen and heard. The 'it' here was the experience of poverty and obvious distress among local peoples. This we might call 'empathy fatigue'. The role of compassion fatigue and empathy fatigue in understanding the British tourist experience of South Africa is, of course, speculative, and is not captured in any way by the surveys of international tourists, still largely British, carried out by the South African tourist authorities (Seymour, 1999) wanting to know why people visited and what they made of their visit and, especially, whether they would visit again and/or encourage others to visit.

We are not claiming that international tourism to South Africa should be viewed as part of a global moral education industry, but we are saying that the visit will have moral and political education impacts that may be significant in understanding the experience of tourism for all concerned. Rich tourists visiting poor countries may reinforce or take on the moral rationale of the indivisibility of human needs and interests in an interdependent world, or they may remain convinced that there is a fundamental and welcomed disconnection between themselves and the people they meet, or successfully avoid directly meeting because of the risks involved, when travelling as tourists. When British tourists visit the much marketed battlefield trail in KwaZulu-Natal they can share the facts of the Zulu wars with local peoples; or when they visit the waterfront in Cape Town, they can share the facts of the exploding pipe bombs in Cape Town over a drink with South African friends. But the moral significance of these facts may be closed to them and, as outsiders, they may remain immune to the political impact of moral argument that arises from these occurrences. The truths of crime and violence, for example, may only be fully documented by those who have suffered their direct consequences.

What about the truths of the direct tourism experience? We only want to introduce one line of thought here, that is obvious yet appears to be neglected in the tourism literature. We have already referred to the politics of exclusivity in our brief discussion of the problem of group representation in a democracy, and the influence that the history of apartheid, and its 'separate development' principle, might have on addressing this problem.

There is also an economic dimension to the exclusivity construct, cleverly drawn out by Hirsch (1977), that illuminates the tourist experience. He works though the significance for our thinking about the way the economy works, of a type of good that he calls 'positional goods' that involve 'positional competition'. In game theory language, positional competition is a zero-sum game; what winners win, losers lose. The sense of positional goods that we are interested in here is that the construct may explain some of the tourist inclination to visit far away places and to do things and see things that few others of their acquaintance may have done. This is the inclination that may persuade tourists to break the bonds of Furedi's (2002) precautionary principle (see chapter 6) and to have an expansive rather than impoverished tourist experience. The consumption of positional goods is exclusive in so far as when others also seek to consume them, they destroy or certainly distort the nature of the good. Such goods abound in the tourist industry and are more commonly described, and promised, as a 'unique' experience, and constitute, in part, a form of 'one-up-manship'. British tourists, like us, who wend their way off the luxury of the A2 motorway through Jozini and Sihangwane to Kosi Bay, hope not to find too many, if any at all, other British tourists there. Kosi Bay is 'off the beaten track' and that is part of its attraction. This obscurity is part of the consumption experience, and obscurity is a positional good.

Similarly, when we walked eastwards for five miles along the wonderful beach at St Lucia in search of sand dunes with no footmarks on them, this natural virginity was part of a purposeful ritual of cherry-picking consumption. The decision to consume appears less attractive, and may offer negative utility if others decide to consume the same space as well. Indeed, these others may not be in search of solitude, but simply want to sit on the beach somewhere. This also explains the situation when, to compound the felony, not only does someone else invade 'our' territory but they decide to sit near us when there is a virtually empty beach, each spot apparently otherwise as attractive as the other, so they could sit anywhere.

The link here with our previous discussion of compassion fatigue and its possible significance for the tourist experience is that, taking the risk of getting closer to local populations than others advise, might be something we can do that is exclusive to our experience as tourists, that gives our personal tourist experience individuality. If other tourists plan to do the same, say, to catch a combi from Durban central bus station into Kwa Mashu, the oldest township in South Africa, known for its history of group violence and, as we have said, once the home of Gandhi, we might decide not to go. Their consumption would deny our own because what we are hoping to enjoy is the feeling of uniqueness and perhaps the exclusivity of 'one-up-manship'. We may, as inter-national tourists travelling to 'far away places', want the perceived authenticity of the 'noble savage' to ourselves.

According to Whellan (1999), we owe to Montaigne the idea of the attractive-ness of visiting people who live in a state of innocence or, more generally, the need for rich people to experience 'life in the raw'. This tendency is a significant factor in shaping the South African vacation experience of some international tourists. The recollection stimulated by the treasured unique-ness and the risks involved in the experience, though later shared through digital snapshots with all those who will tolerate the holiday photos, can create the world view that life has been different and therefore can be radically different again, 'The restoration of remembrance to its rights, as a vehicle of liberation, is one of the noblest tasks of thought' (Marcuse, in Dallmayr, 1998, p.155).

This possibility, of course, is more obvious in the experience of people living in developing or transitional economies, since it acts as a potential bulwark against the cultural imperialism of globalisation. The people who travel in elaborate religious uniform by combi or coach from Kwa Mashu to the Durban beaches in order to practise religious rituals that include bathing fully clothed in the water and regular baptism in the sea, may be part of an unconscious cultural resistance movement, closing ranks against the pressures of modernisation and the North, such as the marketing of models of Western-style secularism. Curious international tourists sunbathing on the spectacular Durban beaches gaze in amazement, as we did, at the spectacular sight of dozens of brightly dressed women traversing the steep bank to the beach and making straight for the water in order to roll and loll about in the shallows before gathering to sing and pray together, and to collect sea water to take back to Kwa Mashu. How far this particular ritual is part and parcel of the significance of new indigenous culture resources acting as a buffer against the homogenising effects of 'one-nation' South African democracy and global cosmopolitanism has not yet, to our knowledge, been fully explored.

Certainly no-one can join in with the rituals who is not a member of the group and other beach people, swimmers, surfers, sunbathers, walkers and so on, seemed to allow for the practice of this radical exclusivism or essentialism. In contrast, despite the technical equipment and distinctive and specialised clothing of the surfers, strangers appear to be welcome to 'ride the waves' with them, even if they are clearly not 'surfers'. A politics of difference welded to a politics of recognition of individuality would condition the everyday lives of people in South Africa so as to avoid both essentialism or radical exclusivity and the romanticism of a claim to harmonious convergence. The metaphor of a 'Rainbow Nation' might well represent a vivid and accurate resistance to these polarities in that sense. The challenge for tourism development, mirroring the national political project and its ambitions, is to recognise difference without sanctioning discrimination and individual and group privilege, and to promote universalism without selling out or acquiescing to those global forces that are not in the national interest. The people of Kwa Mashu need to remain autonomous as individuals but be prepared also to be an integral part of society through a process of democratic deliberation. Whether tourists meet the residents of Kwa Mashu on the Durban beaches, on the pavement outside the house where Gandhi once lived, or at the covered Indian market in downtown Durban; or when it is a cleaner from Kwa Mashu, who has caught three buses and travelled for two hours, arriving at the Durban rented beachfront apartment door at eight in the morning, international tourists are meeting citizens bound up in a major national political transformation project.

Developing citizens

A question we have begun to address elsewhere (see chapter 8) is what is meant by the word 'citizen' as applied to globalisation or to a world view? Are the Durban tourists and Kwa Mashu residents bound together by some shared stake in the world? Dower (1998, p.72) distinguishes three senses in which it might be claimed that we are all 'world citizens' now:

> a claim that we are world citizens as members of a world political community, somewhat analogous to being a citizen of a nation-state; a claim that we are world citizens as members of a global community as a social reality in that a significant number of social bonds, background institutions, self-consciously shared values are in place; and a claim that we are world citizens because we belong to a moral domain or sphere of all human beings in that obligations and responsibilities between individuals anywhere exist in principle.

All three may be wishful thinking. On the other hand, any truth in the first claim may lie in the fact that we share the possibility of a common consumer culture, most obvious in the consumption of style, symbols and logos, design and celebrity and sport and music (Ritzer, 1999). For the second, the strength of belief in the nature of fundamental human rights may begin to substantiate this claim, though we are in the early stages yet of the practice of universal human rights. The third claim seems to offer a definition of what it means to be truly human, to be a moral agent, and simply reflects a world view rather than being the basis of it. Dower's brave search for the possibilities of a promise and practice of ethical world citizenry emerging in the near future, necessarily implies the impact of such citizens on the nation state. We have seen the need to avoid the fallacious step of aggregating individual difference to make a social entity but, nonetheless, we can logically argue that the new South Africa may set a development agenda, in terms of its relations with other countries, with future generations and with the environment, that reflects the influence of its citizens' 'world view' on their development preferences. The United kingdom and South Africa share a common development agenda in so far as the three basic elements of their external relations are the same: relations with other countries, with future generations and with the environment. The tourism industry sits amidst the 'clash' (Huntington, 1996) of these shared concerns as citizens of the two countries meet, and is a major institutional means by which the notion of 'world citizen' may be substantiated.

The significance of this discussion for the maturity of tourism theory is that it stresses the overlap between debates concerning identity, and the relative identities and identity shifts of tourists and hosts as a result of tourism, and citizenship. Traditional social scientific research has focussed on whether there are essential attributes that define and distinguish groups and whether, in contrast, there are no durable group qualities at all, leaving only explanatory significance for socially constructed identities. In any case, postmodernism, with its concern with the structural transformations of modern capitalism leading to new forms of production, distribution, regulation and consumption, suggests that identity is thereby fragmented and dynamic and more self-conscious than ever – the 'self' has become a project in its own right. In South Africa, the sociological meta concepts of belonging, recognition and solidarity intersect with their political counterparts, influence or power, rights and equality, leading to tensions between the universal and the particular, between what has been called 'cosmopolitan virtue' (Isin and Wood, 1999, p.157), national and civic virtue and individuality. In everyday life in South Africa, people may experience a growing disparity between a near globally accepted standard for the protection of universal human rights and the daily denial of those basic rights, pushing the possibility of what the critical theorists graphically called 'concrete utopias' (Booth, in Dunne and Wheeler, 1999, p.45) still further away, and sustaining aspects of the former political regime that practised 'Crimes against Humanity' (the title of Geoffrey Robertson's recent book where, in a chapter called 'Slouching towards Nemesis', he has a useful commentary on the significance of and relationships between citizenship, truth commissions and transitional justice).

The vast majority of people in the South remain territorially, linguistically and culturally tied. Those others who are the substance of the intensification of transnational activity, who travel in aeroplanes, communicate through the latest technology, are able to speak some English and have instant spending power wherever they find themselves, have a profound influence on the former group. What tourism can do is to bring the two populations directly in contact with each other (hence the significance of the management of the tourist experience, for example, through 'enclave tourism', that tries to exclude this direct contact) so as to create the possibility of two-way influence, of bringing together different clusters of the cosmopolitan, national and local. Kaldor (in Dunne and Wheeler, 1999) repeats the interesting point that Kant made about travel to other countries: that cosmopolitan right could be confined to the right of hospitality. What Kant meant here was that nationals had a duty to treat foreigners with civility but not to treat them as fellow-nationals; here we have an early and limited account of global citizenship.

We return, finally, to the theme of 'community-led' tourism development, for the strength of this *modus operandi* in South Africa lies in its evocation of the need to ensure that all those people with a stake in the process and outcome of tourism development, need to have a true belief in the appropriateness of what is going on and what is planned – it must accurately feel right to them.

The rhetoric of people 'owning' the process of planned social change fits in with other issues concerning ownership, especially of land and property and people themselves (personal autonomy). Changes in ownership of this type are defended as part of the establishment of a liberal democracy where freedom and equality as principles underwrite the new distributional policies and practices. We have added to this vision the possibility of South Africa achieving a particular form of democracy which it seems it needs and may be ripe for, namely, a deliberative democracy, focussed on the discourse of disagreement and accepting the perpetuation of deep conflicts of interest between individuals. All planned social change, inside such a fully operating democracy replete with disagreement, would indeed be 'community-led' and give definition and meaning to the latter. The involvement of previously 'marginalised groups' and the 'forgotten people', or invisible citizens, would be the acid test for the new politics. It remains to be seen whether poor people are prepared either to buy into the new system, or to free ride on the roller coaster of political struggle, or to embrace the politics of indifference.

The success or otherwise of 'community-led tourism' development in KwaZulu-Natal and in South Africa more generally, will prove an important indicator of progress towards the national political project. International tourists, especially British tourists, may have a particular intentional or inevitable impact on both projects and in so doing, may alter their own world view. We leave the final word in this chapter to one of history's famous marginal men, himself a distinguished traveller, Oscar Wilde (1891) writing in *The Soul of Man under Socialism*, 'A map of the world that does not contain Utopia is not even worth glancing at.'

Chapter 11

Community, conflict and development

At the national level, economic policy has taken a massive swing away from the driving goals of equity and redistribution so eloquently promoted by the leaders of the ANC in 1994. The new president, Thabo Mbeki, in his State of the Union Address at the opening of Parliament in 1999, announced a new austerity programme that was to have enormous repercussions for many of the black population of South Africa. This programme contained plans for large-scale privatisation of state activities, the restructuring of the civil service, cuts in public spending, and the amendment of labour laws that effectively removes protection for workers.

Members of the business sector largely welcomed the new proposals and urged the government to push ahead with the programme. They made clear their feelings that the years since the elections of 1994 had been a tragic waste of opportunities to attract billions of dollars of investment into the South African economy. In November 2000, during a meeting in Pretoria, the government's harsh measures were endorsed by representatives of the IMF and the World Bank, who were pleased with the fiscal progress that had been made since the implementation of the austerity programme. At that meeting, Eduardo Aninat, Deputy Managing Director of the IMF, insisted that further steps to be taken in the near future would be reductions in the wages of the workforce, and major cuts in public spending. Thabo Mbeki expressed his open support for these proposals and stressed their urgency. Economists present called on the government to be more active in attracting foreign capital, citing the car industry as a possible locus for large-scale investment. Earlier in 2000, car workers had already suffered cuts in their wages, and strikers had been sacked.

Millions of workers live in awful poverty. There is a chronic housing shortage, and millions of families, in spite of the pledges made by the ANC in 1994, still lack basic facilities such as a fresh water supply and adequate sanitation. Unemployment runs at 40 per cent, and over half a million jobs have been lost since the ANC first came to power. Large sections of the population who were politicised during the years of struggle against apartheid, have become disillusioned with their leaders and have lost faith in the political process itself. The once strong alliance between the ANC and the Congress of South African Trade Unions (COSATU) is weakening, and some union leaders are even considering the formation of a new party in opposition to Thabo Mbeki, who has shown impatience with the activities of the mass organisations. Several large-scale strikes have been organised in protest against the economic policies of the ANC (February and Jacobs, 2001). While a small elite has been seen to have prospered from the policies of black empowerment, many blacks are now worse off than they were under the National Party. The magic of the Mandela years is fading.

While at the national level hope is dwindling for the poor who had expected so much in 1994, our exposure to eco-tourism in KwaZulu-Natal also poses questions about the faith in democracy automatically delivering development to desperate rural communities. What has become obvious is that the relationships between the state system and civil society are complex, open to abuse, and not as accountable as the RDP required. The system designed to connect the poor to the means of improving their lives is, in fact, unable to deal with the multiple interests and relationships of power within deeply divided communities. The most marginalised continue to be excluded, and do not assume proactive roles in forums and CBOs, and the plurality of their needs is not authentically represented. This suggests that the orthodoxy of democracy and good governance leading to, and being essential for development, has to be re-examined. As it stands, the apparently straightforward paradigm of eco-tourism development based on the seductive notions of good governance, a framework of democratic institutions and community participation, appears unable to match the scale of human needs, and the multiple contests over resources and power in South Africa's agrarian society.

Participation, as we have said earlier, is notoriously difficult to elicit, costly and time-consuming (Glaser, 2001). Further, there is no convincing evidence or argument that it actually comprises an essential ingredient for economic development. Indeed, as the tourist locations we visited show, concern for empowerment through participation may make eco-tourism initiatives vulnerable to the manipulative influences of local elites or powerful institutions. In other words, projects based on particular models of participation, such as direct democracy, may actually hinder plans to overcome structural exclusion through eco-tourism development. The relevant agencies in civil society need to recognise their tendency to forge ahead with worthy goals while failing to understand the changing realities of the impoverished communities they claim to represent. The need to survive will always generate practices among the poor, such as poaching or violent crime, that can appear incomprehensible and subversive to an agency attempting to apply principles of sustainability. Strategies of survival do not fit well with development orthodoxies based on the abstract virtues of democracy and participation. Interpretive skills are needed to understand the realities of life in South Africa's rural communities. Social movements among the poor may not take recognisable forms, and may emerge in efforts to deliberately circumvent the functioning of agencies claiming to act at the grassroots level. People rely on special relationships, and on networks and sources of knowledge to feed themselves and their families. Civil organisations have to formulate business plans to apply for funding. Such agencies have time-frames and budget limitations, they will want to adhere to founding targets, rather than to incorporate the various schemes and changing goals of local people.

Eco-tourism initiatives that involve stated limits to growth to ensure sustainability, can appear irrelevant to the personal immediacies to individuals desperate for relief from the awful poverty that characterises rural society in northern KwaZulu-Natal and the black housing areas of Durban. Without taking into account the resurgence of Zulu chieftainship, the overwhelming desire for land, the continuing marginalisation of women, the fear of violence, the political volatility, the ineffectiveness of sometimes corrupt institutions, and the incommensurate values attributed to place and the environment, eco-tourism initiatives such as those discussed in this book have little hope of delivering benefits on anything like the scale necessary to make genuine improvements in the welfare of poor rural communities in KwaZulu-Natal.

Our central theme has been an exploration of the actual and possible conflicts of interest that arise in societies that emphasise the role that community-led eco-tourism initiatives and international tourists can and should play in reconstruction. In the South Africa context, and, more particularly, in KwaZulu-Natal Province, examples and features of community-based and community-led tourism development were highlighted, exploring the ways in which social change is, or is not, taking place according to planned development. Our journeys took us to northern KwaZulu-Natal, to Phinda Lodge and Game Reserve, to Kosi Bay Lodge, to St Lucia via Dukuduku, and to Durban, all significant tourism resources and destinations in KwaZulu-Natal (Seymour, 1999). The detail of change and the detail of the inhibitors to change are in constant flux, and description and commentary can quickly date. However, an attempt has been made to suggest new ways of building theory that can allow us to identify long-term, culturally specific continuities and discontinuities in planned development.

An argument has been put, gently, that the currently available tourism literature suggests that the sort of theory-building needed to engage with this task is only partially in place. This book is in part an attempt to contribute to tourism theory through drawing on and extending work in development studies, given the structural relationships between South Africa and the majority of its international tourists; in social anthropology, recognising the vital relationships between community, culture and the identification and resolution of conflicts of interest; and through identifying key social scientific concepts and approaches that seem to have suffered from benign neglect as far as the academic study of tourists and tourism is concerned.

The main pressure for what began as an eclectic trawl of mainstream and backwater social scientific concepts was a belief that somewhere out there in the social scientific academic world, were ways of thinking that could and should enable us to have a fresh look at the nature of tourism activity and its impacts. The net result was to focus on the moral and rational bases of politically and economically complex decision choices arising from tourist activity. In particular, emphasis was put on the need to consider the logic of collective action and its explanatory powers in understanding the limits to community-led tourism development and political mobilisation issues in general, that we can now refer to as indicating, for us, the poverty of empowerment theories in tourism planning.

Also, new thinking about the nature and significance of theories of citizenship was drawn on as a way into issues concerning identity and belonging, and concomitant rights and responsibilities, duties and obligations, and offered the tentative view that discussions of heritage and cultural industries, as part of tourism activities, could usefully incorporate a defensible view about the social, political, cultural and legal origins of citizenship. Finally, out of political philosophy, we have used the concept of toleration, to help explore how people do and should behave in the different settings and situations they find themselves in. And all of this has been infused with examples of situations that the writers, as tourists, found themselves in during visits to KwaZulu-Natal between 1995 and 2002, and with a necessarily restricted attempt to map and explain the prevailing political economy and life-situations of KwaZulu-Natal Province and its peoples. In particular, ways of thinking about the triumvirate of crime, violence and corruption, as formidable blocks on tourism development's actual and potential role in promoting the South African government's vision of a reconstructed democracy, were charted.

There are great expectations in South Africa, still, for the economic benefits that tourism development will create in the new millennium. Faith in the capacity of tourism to generate income and wealth is a feature of many societies suffering from relative economic decline or a perceived failure to do as well economically as societies that are salient competitors in the wealth game. The conceptual framework from economics that still dominates our thinking about how well off people are, and how well off we are, is that of rational economic man. That is not to say that there are major attempts to reconceptualise the way in which we should and do, sometimes, value income and welfare in the context of other valued aspects of life, but these attempts remain as alternatives to the dominant orthodoxy that still has a stranglehold on the interpretation of rational behaviour. Rational economic man is culturally bound, of course, and a Zulu may exemplify the concept through actions in a quite different way than a contemporary British tourist. However, the central features of the model, that people always prefer more of the things they value in life, given the choice, and we always seek to obtain these valued things, money, for example, at least cost to themselves, and with no thought to the consequences of their actions for others in so doing, would be recognised by people the world over.

Economists have always known that there are other forms of economic rationality, or motivation, but they have not, until recently, built these alternative rationalities into first principles of model-building. The single strongest influence on this 'new' economics, seen, for example, through the fast growing sub-disciplines of economic psychology and evolutionary economics (Hodgson, 2002), has been the discovery of altruism as a major potential or actual feature of people's economic decision-taking. Altruism we take to be happening when people voluntarily give something of value to themselves to someone else, knowing that there will be a real cost to the transaction. The point here is that when the tourism literature conceptualises people as 'tourists' and 'hosts', these descriptive flags of convenience actually obscure the origins of people's complex economic psyches. Chapter 10 discusses the significance of the stranger both for the South African political project and for the success of the tourism development project that exists, in important ways, as a microcosm of the wider project. The notion of the stranger is an important way of conceptualising trust relationships in a society and, in doing so, follows well-trodden theoretical and empirical work in social theory and anthropology. What is less clear, but will have to be addressed by the 'new' economics, is how the nature of economic transactions between individuals vary according to the nature of the trust relation between them.

The study of tourism is unnecessarily impoverished by a failure to fully make use of some useful social scientific concepts and approaches in order to build a political economy of tourism development. Our selection of concepts and frameworks was guided by the particularities of the South African situation and the demands it makes on the capacity to understand what is going on in terms of the general political economy and tourism development in particular. The book is partly a rehearsal for future work.

The key political feature of tourism development in South Africa is whether the main social and economic impacts of tourism-induced development are congruent with the main structural features of an emerging democratic state. The meanings of democracy are contested, and democratic states take many forms. Nonetheless, claims to democracy normally include two components: 'that people, collectively, are presumed entitled to an equal say in decisions that affect them, and that opposition to currently prevailing policies is always legitimate' (Shapiro, 1999, p.211).

The strong version of democracy advanced in this book as the suitable aspiring model for South Africa, a project to establish a deliberative democracy would still have at its roots the presumption that whatever the procedures by which a decision is arrived at (deliberatively in this preferred case), there must be mechanisms for those people who are dissatisfied with a particular outcome, say the Dukuduku South forest dwellers, to seek to change things in the future. The Good Tourist, as a Good Citizen, will have the knowledge, inclination and capacity to produce social changes when the current social world is perceived to be in need of changing because of unfair distributional impacts from tourism development.

An analysis of the history of recent political change in South Africa, in the context of a discussion of the possibilities of establishing some form of democratic state, is beyond the confines of this book but, as has been argued, cannot be ignored altogether if the current position and future prospects for community-led eco-tourism in KwaZulu-Natal and for urban tourism in Durban are to be understood. Inkatha's foundational and principled opposition to democracy is fundamental to the political discourse of tourism development in the province. The ANC and the National Party now accept democracy as the governing principle of the country but Buthelezi, as a member of the Zulu royal family, is more interested in consolidating the power position of local chiefs than any commitment to electoral politics. Or, more subtly, the IFP's leadership will tolerate democratic discourses and structures as long as it suits their long-term interests. There is no commitment to democracy for its own sake. The participation of the IFP in elections, in 1994, reflected their assessment that electoral processes in South Africa are now here to stay, or can't be cheaply derailed. Similarly, according to Shapiro (1999), they played a cat and mouse game during the negotiations on the permanent constitution, refusing to participate unless the province's independence was guaranteed. The main symbol of the latter was the freedom to establish the province's own army, under Buthelezi's personal command.

The political litmus test for tourism-induced development is whether it supports and promotes democratically defensible claims to self-determination. The political identities of the people who the international tourist to KwaZulu-Natal meets are formed by some as yet unspecified process and mix of basic personal constitutions, limiting the possibilities of socially constructed identities. The latter claim suggests where we are now in the domain of political socialisation studies and theories.

In KwaZulu-Natal, the violence that broke out after 1984 was politically inspired, fuelled by the formation of the United Democratic Front (UDF) and its challenges to the IFP monopolisation of Zulu support. Similarly, some of the highly publicised violence among white nationalists resulted from competition for the nationalist vote. The theoretical point here is to be found in an analysis of the relationships between group aspirations, self-determination claims, the logic of violence, and democracy. In practice, political mechanisms have to evolve that reduce and remove exclusion and domination. 'Group aspirations that by their terms cannot be realised within democratic constraints are to be resisted, but it is better to work for a world in which such aspirations will diminish. Getting rid of institutions that press in the opposite direction seems like a logical place to start' (Shapiro, 1999, p.220).

The problem is one of limited cognitive resources. In South Africa, the discourse of empowerment rests on the presumption that people are able to bridge the unbridgeable. People are limited in their abilities to know and judge the contingencies that bear on their lives. One way in which this intellectual chasm is crossed is through trusting other people, institutions and systems with their future well-being. Complexity is reduced in direct proportion to the degree and forms of trust relations in a society (Giddens, 1999), since certain things can be taken for granted when trust exists. In its most basic and significant form, the lack of trust relations is socially and experientially impoverishing. The impact of the precautionary ideology of the international hotel groups operating in Durban, fuelling a generalised distrust by tourists of local peoples, enhances their profits, by containing tourist expenditure, and simultaneously impoverishes the tourist experience.

This problem of incomplete understanding is one of the circumstances of moral conflict well known to philosophers but not yet called on to examine the tourist experience. We do not know whether, if we enjoyed perfect understanding in social settings, the personal experience of tourism would be different. At any one time and place, such as the Kosi Bay truck drive, we live in conditions of moral conflict. This is well rehearsed by Hume (Gutmann and Thompson, 1996), who offered two principles of moral conflict: scarcity and limited generosity, to which Gutmann and Thompson add two more, incompatible values and incomplete understanding. Each of these four is sufficient to cause moral disagreement.

The moral dilemmas of the relatively rich tourist from the Northern Hemisphere travelling through the South, can be untangled by an accurate and truthful descriptive account of what tourists think and do, combined with an analysis of the explanatory powers of this four-fold paradigm. Visitors to South Africa, and supporters of the South African 'project', may have a utopian view based on the disappearance or resolution of moral conflicts. This may be an element that legitimates the 'new' in the 'new South Africa'. But incompatible values and incomplete understandings may be endemic to politics and, if so, moral disagreement is a condition that we have to expect to live with. In South Africa, as elsewhere: 'the principles and values with which we live are provisional, formed and continually revised in the process of making and responding to moral claims in public life' (Gutmann and Thompson, 1996, p.26).

Some of the NGOs and pressure groups concerned with monitoring tourism impacts, such as the British-based Action for Southern Africa (ACTSA), the former Anti-Apartheid Movement, urges UK tourists now to go to South Africa but to act on their duty to book through a South African-owned company, rather than First Choice. This is part of the ideology of 'reco-tourism', trade that assists in economic and political reconstruction. Philosophically, a distinction should be drawn between what morality (or rationality) requires of us and what goes beyond those requirements. Acts that go 'beyond the call of duty' are said to be 'supererogatory' (Lockhart, 2000, p.8). Driving inland from Durban, the tourist act of buying goods that one does not really need or want from lay-by sellers of beads, may be an example of a supererogation, whereby we tourists maximised or optimised with respect to his small expenditure. We were happy to do this because we guessed our few rand would be a significant boost to the family income of the female bead-sellers. Seeking less than the best, rather than maximising or satisfying, has been coined as 'satisficing'. Here, actions are chosen

> that achieve at least a certain minimum expected degree of moral rightness but leave up to us whether and how far we go beyond that minimum level. Perhaps we are entitled to praise if we go far above the minimum that is required. However, to require maximization as a necessary condition for moral or rational behaviour is to confuse the obligatory with the supererogatory [Lockhart, 2000, p.99].

The point here is that to see tourism as a social process, among all the others, whereby people come together to make decisions that affect each other and do so under conditions of moral uncertainty, leads us to consider the particularities of moral uncertainties that tourism creates. In the South African case, this consideration is overlain with a development or North–South agenda. ACTSA exhorts people in the UK to support South Africa through travelling there as tourists and spending money according to their duty or even beyond their duty to promote the interests of deserving others. This is conceptually similar to the attempts by Comic Relief, through Red Nose Day, to donate money for Comic Relief to spend on their deserving causes. Should we resist such demands on the moral purse? One guiding principle, much debated in moral philosophy, is that if we can prevent anything bad from happening without sacrificing anything of comparable moral significance, we morally ought to do it. In this sense, there are no rational limits to demands on our altruism and on this count, we should go to South Africa, and carefully spend as much as we can. But, as we have seen, the problem of uncertainty created by limited knowledge and competences remains, unless we put our trust in ACTSA's exhortations.

Tourist decisions can be described and analysed in a way complementary to moral philosophy, using game theory. In particular, the tourist faces a special, but common, form of decision problem. These occur in situations where the narrow interests of the tourist is in conflict with the interests of others, say the local sex workers they meet on the Durban beachfront. These types of situations are called prisoner's dilemmas or collective action problems. The classic formulation here is where each individual is better off not co-operating, no matter what others do, but everyone is better off if all co-operate (Goldberg and Markoczy, 1998). The decision that is best for everybody is one type of co-operation. For the individual, what is best in the individual instance is defection. Olson's (1971) free rider, not taking part in community action with the other residents in Dukuduku South, is defecting while also enjoying the benefits of the co-operation of others. Co-operation requires bearing some individual, or private costs, for the common good (social benefit). The free riding person reduces private costs and simultaneously secures private benefits because the public benefits of co-operative behaviour cannot be ring-fenced by those who act collectively. The logic of collective action is not then persuasive.

The 'new economics', incorporating psychological theories of human behaviour, is grappling with the finding that people tend to co-operate more than a rational analysis of the situation would indicate. There are less free riders in the world than we would expect. This may be because of what Nozick has called (1974, p.127) an 'illusion of influence'. When ACTSA asked British people whether they would be willing to pay more for their holidays in South Africa if they thought the 'extra' money would benefit local people, and they said they would, they may have been demonstrating the explanatory force of the 'illusion of influence'. The simplest everyday manifestation of this construct in action is believing that others will follow our example when we act or, when others cannot witness our actions, we do things in the belief that 'like-minded' persons will be doing the same. When we voluntarily paid the Durban beach-front car security guards for looking after our car, we could have been saying: 'If we don't do it, why should anyone?' or, one step beyond this, 'If we don't do it, no-one will'.

Not all collective action problems are prisoner's dilemmas. Goldberg and Markoczy (1998, p.23) discuss the tendency to 'play chicken' through the example of two people driving fast towards each other, 'Alice and Bob have agreed to drive toward each other fast. Whoever swerves out of the way is humiliated, while not swerving indicates courage. If both swerve then the humiliation is less for each. If neither swerves they both suffer injury.'

It is not absolutely clear what the best course of action is. Many commercial situations that people find themselves in, including tourists, are of this nature. 'Haggling' over goods is a classic example. When we stopped to enjoy the view back towards the Indian Ocean and Durban, on the winding road through the Valley of a Thousand Hills, and the lay-by people crept up on us, we did not immediately drive off. Through staying and talking with them, we entered into a game of chicken. Both parties implicitly agreed that something was to be bought and sold; the price was to be more than we would ordinarily pay but how much more? What we could get away with paying in order to carry on with our journey? From the point of view of the women traders and their participating children, how far could they push us into this non-obligatory purchase? Who would call it a day first, and settle on prices, goods and quantities – us or them? Note that the situation, in game theory terms, was anonymous – nobody else need know what we did. This situation, and the reasoning and questioning that arises from it, can be transposed to many of the situations created by tourism in South Africa and elsewhere.

> The sort of reasoning discussed may be involved in daily decisions on whether to practise stewardship of organisational resources, on whether to place the interest of the larger organisation in front of oneself or working group. And on whether to remain loyal to one's organisation in light of better opportunities. The outcome of these daily decisions often remains anonymous and it is up to the individual whether to be a good citizen of the organization or not. A theory of co-operation – of good citizenship – in these situations is vital [Goldberg and Markoczy, 1998, p.28].

This discussion of the individual and the collectivity, and its exemplification through the experiences created by tourism, is but one way in which the touristic phenomenon can be better understood. The selection of perspectives has been selective and is designed to complement the more developed arguments in earlier chapters and to show the rich array of theoretical perspectives that can usefully be applied to the real lives of people engaged in tourism. These people, like ourselves, try to live in ways that they have endorsed and one of the meanings of liberal societies – some would claim, its distinctive value – rests in part on the claim that people are entitled to live their lives in whatever way they think best. In liberal societies, and in countries in transit to the liberal state, as South Africa is, there needs to be a middle way between the recognition of collective identities and an acknowledgement of individuality. This might be found (Mendus, 1999) in drawing a distinction between the values people can appeal to in justifying their own behaviour and thoughts and those they can appeal to in justifying the exercise of political power. It was ironic for us that when we encountered the family of American tourists in Shakaland, and we witnessed what for us was the deplorable behaviour of the 'dad', we tolerated their presence in our touring party because at the political level it is important to respect people's autonomy and difference. The irony came from the construction, by us, of the liberal state inside a reconstruction of a traditional Zulu village, not noted for its liberality.

The search for national unity in South Africa has been built on an amnesty for crimes against humanity. The work of the Truth and Reconciliation Commission suggests that a new civic ethic, based on extended boundaries of toleration, can be founded upon forgiveness and, some would say, without justice (Phillips, 1997). The new political dynamic in South Africa puts more emphasis on reason and facts than on due apology and contrition, but only victims are entitled to forgive. The counter-argument is that the rhetoric of reconciliation tends to equate justice with witch-hunts and people who take this position may think that punishment itself is inhumane. These matters are raised again here to recall the linkage of limited knowledge and moral uncertainty and to suggest that current work in tourism studies (Inglis, 2000) on heritage and the heritage industry, that we have not drawn on, would be particularly helpful in understanding the political, moral and religious contexts of tourism-induced development.

The truth and reconciliation business or bandwagon, as it has been called (Krog, 1999) is drenched in the language of Christian redemption. There was much talk of healing, of cleansing, of bearing witness, and of joining hands across a great divide. A spirit of New Testament forgiveness co-existed with an Old Testament notion of vengeance. People we met spoke of ubuntu, of a human forgiveness. On 14 October 1997, ex-foreign minister Pik Botha appeared before the TRC, asking for 'god's forgiveness for failing to do more to prevent the atrocities committed under the National Party's rule' (O'Hagan, 1997, p.4).

Drawing on Ignatieff's (1999) work, the particular position of the British tourist to South Africa was discussed in terms of the possibility and signi-ficance of the historical transmission of entitlements; in this case, that the British tourist 'owes' something to South Africa and that British tourism can be constructed and analysed as a form of compensation. The general issue of compensation is still very influential in setting the moral climate in South Africa. The relationship between rights, especially property rights, and their stability over time (whether they persist intact through other social changes), and, if they do persist, what degree and form of compensation is due to disposed people, underscores current political protocols and processes concerning the ownership of land in South Africa. Dukuduku is the case in point for us. These matters are discussed in detail by Sher (1997), in a stimulating chapter aptly called 'Ancient Wrongs and Modern Rights'.

The universality of human wrongs is the foundation of any convincing argument to do with claims to universal human rights. Human wrongs are everywhere and societies usually find it easier to recognise and agree these; in this sense, wrongs are universal in ways that rights are not. The Truth and Reconciliation Commission is an explicit recognition of this point since concentration on wrongs shifts the locus of attention to possible victims, and to identifying and identifying with, and thereby humanising, the powerless (Booth, 1999). The relationship between 'facts' and 'values' is at the heart of the tourist response to the historical subjectivity of the new South Africa. 'That it is a bad thing to be tortured and starved, humiliated or hurt is not an opinion: it is a fact. That it is better for people to be loved and attended to, rather than hated or neglected, is again a plain fact, not a matter of opinion.' (Warnock in Booth, 1999, p.63).

This leads us to the Kantian position of the universal nature of wrongs in the world, that are felt everywhere, and that lead to the inevitability of concern by individuals about the condition and experience of others, and to the possibility of moving from concern to intervention. Tourism companies in South Africa, who organise trips into Soweto, put tourists into centre moral stage in these respects.

The ANC's Reconstruction and Development Programme (1994) puts improvements in the social condition of women at the forefront of the political project, not just in terms of improving the well-being of women, a 'welfareist' stance, but through an emphasis on promoting women's political 'agency', on the politicisation of women. The need to realise the possibilities of agency, and to reconstruct, if necessary, the possibilities of political influence, is a major distinguishing feature of the typology of human needs put forward by Doyal and Gough (1991). And it is a moot point, given presumptions about the domination of violence by men as a way of settling conflicts of interest, whether an increasingly influential social, economic and political role played by women in South Africa will impact on the rates of violent crime. This is to argue for a better deal for women because it leads to a better world for all, but of course there are more direct arguments to be made:

> Perhaps the most immediate argument for focusing on women's agency may be precisely the role that such agency can play in removing the iniquities that depress the *well-being* of women. Empirical work in recent years has brought out very clearly how the relative respect and regard for women's well-being is strongly influenced by such variables as women's ability to earn an independent income, to find employment outside the home, to have ownership rights and to have literacy and be educated participants in decisions

within and outside the family. Indeed, even the survival disadvantage of women compared to men seems to go down sharply – and may even get eliminated – as progress is made in these agency aspects...The extensive reach of women's agency is one of the more neglected areas of development studies, and most urgently in need of correction. Nothing, arguably, is as important today in the political economy of development as an adequate recognition of political, economic and social participation and leadership of women [Sen, 1999, pp.191, 203; original italics].

And, it should be added, following O'Riordan (1998), the actual transfer of power and respect from minorities to majorities, an elusive process (Fox Piven and Cloward, 1977), needs to be part and parcel of an equally elusive yet currently impeachable transition to sustainability. This should be an accessible element in the discourses of a deliberative democracy and the words that have to be learnt and used, following Freire (1998) and Chambers (1998, p.120), are 'well-being, livelihood, capability, equity and sustainability', five words that, according to Chambers, capture and express the current normative consensus of 'putting people first'.

The principles of deliberative democracy are crucial to the evolution of the main institutions charged with tourism development in KwaZulu-Natal and South Africa more generally. These institutions must be congruent with and play a part in defining a democracy governed on the basis of values adopted and refined through collective deliberations. All of the makers of public policy can then defend their reasons for doing things based on principles that reflect these values. This fusion of moral reasoning with the skills of political action should be the aim of social education in the schools system, helping to promote civic integrity alongside civic magnanimity as a means to mutual respect. For the latter to survive at least, and flourish at best, as has been argued earlier in the face of fundamental disagreements about the possibility and desirability of alternative forms and impacts of tourism development, the tourism institutions, such as the KNW and the KZNTA (now Tourism KwaZulu-Natal, or TKZN), have to propagate these virtues through example. One possibly valuable step has been the instigation, by the Tourism Business Council of South Africa (www.tbcsa.org.za/intiatives) of an 'Empowerment Transformation Annual Review'. The first of these, released in June 2002, aimed to assess the current state of Black Economic Empowerment (BEE), and suggests high levels of awareness of the transformation needed, but a frustratingly limited ability to translate political aspiration into reality.

The linkages of development, culture, and democracy are intimate. Development questions presuppose reflective judgement and hence their adequate treatment is dependent on a consideration of culture (Dallmayr, 1998) and reflective judgement is one major method congruent with deliberative democracy, with teasing out and monitoring the politics of recognition and identities. One of the more uncomfortable conclusions that this sort of thinking leads to is that it is easier to expose problems than to offer solutions to them.

> There is a diagnostic and a remedial side to our scientific concern with these societies, and the diagnostic seems, in the very nature of the case, to proceed infinitely faster than the remedial. Therefore, one result of very extended, very thorough, periods of careful research is usually a much keener realisation that the new states are indeed in something of a fix [Geertz, 2000, p.24].

The stress in this book has been the personal question of virtue on vacation in South Africa. The central general question for the international tourist is: 'How shall we do right and live well while visiting other countries?' (Inglis, 2000, p.172).

This in the context of critiques of tourists that turn tourists into economic and social terrorists:

> Tourism does not benefit the majority of people. Instead it exploits them, pollutes the environment, destroys the ecosystem, bastardises the culture, robs the people of their traditional values and ways of life and subjugates women and children in the abject slavery of prostitution ... It epitomises the present unjust world economic order where the few who control wealth and power dictate the terms [Secretary to the Ecumenical Coalition on Third World Tourism, quoted in Inglis, 2000, p.172].

The number of UK tourists visiting South Africa in 1999 rose by 4 per cent, to 334,226, according to Satour, compared to 250,000 visitors in 1995. Satour also announced that they were continuing to step up their marketing, advertising and PR campaigns to further increase numbers, and we mentioned examples of these in our introductory 'snapshot' of South African tourism. Between 1985 and 1987, UK tourists to South Africa fell by 20 per cent, then rose by 40 per cent in 1989, levelled out between 1991 and 1995, and since then has risen steeply. The trend reflects the influence of an apartheid effect and a Mandela effect, as in-country influences on the decisions taken by the UK international tourist as to where to go. The tourism attraction research suggests that while 'image' is the most important aspect of tourist attraction, it is reality that determines if they will enjoy themselves and return again (Butler, 1990).

In 1997, the ANC held its 50th conference and Nelson Mandela spoke for over four hours, delivering a speech written by the new president, Thabo Mbeki. The main questions posed by and in the speech concerned the possibility of a black revolutionary movement, forged by 20 years of struggle against white supremacy, being able to transform itself into a multi-racial ruling party competent to run an increasingly complex and problematic economy. And this party has to create simultaneously a tolerant democracy in order to sustain political legitimacy for its economic and social reform programmes. Tourism-induced economic development is seen by Mbeki as a central part of progress, and reflects his conviction that economic growth is the means to racial peace (Sampson, 1999).

The other particularly South African means to progress is the business of forgiveness, discussed in O'Hagan's interview (1997) with Archbishop Desmond Tutu, who led the TRC. Their discussion reminds us to stay focussed on human nature if we are to understand the nature and degree of development-induced conflict:

> We Africans are not like you Europeans. We are a great deal more communal. You are the great individualists. Each has advantages, but we say a person is a person through other persons; the solitary individual is a contradiction in terms. Something that happens here to an individual impacts on the whole community.

Good Tourists visiting KwaZulu-Natal, wallowing, perhaps, in a porridge of hedonism and politeness, will almost certainly want to get in touch with nature. In so doing, they will reflect on the nature in human nature, and on the old social problems, such as income and wealth inequalities, and new problems, such as the spread of HIV/AIDS and the tensions between cultures of violence and aggression, and will therefore join the trek for the holy grail of genuine democracy.

Bibliography

Note: all citations in the text referring to a particular date, for example '9/12/98', are to an interview with the individual cited.

African National Congress (1994) *The Reconstruction and Development Programme*. Johannesburg: Unanyano Publications.

African National Congress (1996) *The Development and Promotion of Tourism* (White Paper). Pretoria: ANC.

Allen, G. (1997) *Education at Risk*. London: Cassell.

Allen, G. (2003) 'Can Universities be Trusted? Academic Capitalism in the Age of Uncertainty'. Unpublished manuscript.

Allen, G., D. Acres and R. Tromans (2001) *The Regional Contribution of Higher Education in the South West Region*. London: Universities UK.

Andriampianam, J. (1985) 'Traditional Land-use and Nature Conservation in Madagascar', in J. McNeely and D. Pitt (eds) (1985) *Culture and Conservation. The Human Dimension in Environmental Planning*. London: Croom Helm.

Anson, C. and Allen, G. (2003) *Sacred Space. The Search for Identity in Disputed Societies*. CSER Working Paper. Plymouth: CSER.

Archer, D. and S. Cottingham (1996) Action Research. 'Report on Reflect'. Serial No 17. Overseas Development Administration.

Argyle, W.J. (1968) 'Faction Fights and the Problem of Explanation in Social Anthropology'. Unpublished paper, University of Natal.

Attfield, R. (1999) *The Ethics of the Global Environment*. Edinburgh: Edinburgh University Press.

Bachrach, P. and M.S. Baratz (1963) 'Decisions and Non-decisions. An Analytical Framework'. *American Political Science Review*, 57, 641–51.

Baden, S., S. Hasim and S. Meintjes (1998) *Country Gender Profile, South Africa*. Prepared for the Swedish Institute of Development Cooperation Agency. Brighton: Institute of Development Studies.

Baden, S., S. Hasim and S. Meintjes (1999) *Country Gender Profile, South Africa*. Pretoria: Swedish International Development Office.

Barker, N. (1997) 'The Battle for St Lucia is Far from Over'. *Mail & Guardian*, 14 November.

Barnes, J. (1995) 'Tourism in KwaZulu-Natal'. Unpublished paper, University of Natal.

Barrett, C.B. and P. Arcese (1995) 'Are Integrated Conservation Development Projects (ICDPs) Sustainable?' *World Development*, Vol. 23, No 7, 1073–84.

Barry, J. (1999) *Rethinking Green Politics*. London: Sage.

Baskin, J. (1995) 'Tourism and Small to Medium Enterprises'. Unpublished paper for Land and Agriculture Policy Centre, Durban.

Baskin, J. and A. Stavrou (October 1995) 'Synthesis Report on the Issues Related to Various Land Use Options in the Greater St Lucia Area'. Land and Agriculture Policy Centre, Durban.

Baudrillard, T. (1983) *Fatal Strategies*. New York: Semiotext(e).

Baumol, W. (1991) *Perfect Markets and Easy Virtue*. Oxford: Basil Blackwell.

Beck, U. (1992) *Risk Society. Towards a Modernity*. London: Sage.

Bekker, S. (1992) 'Conclusion', in S. Bekker (ed.) *Capturing the Event. Conflict Trends in the Natal Region, 1986–92, Indicator SA*, December, 68–71.

Bierstedt, R. (1981) *American Sociological Theory. A Critical History*. New York: Academic Press.

Billy, A. (1996) 'The plight of rural women'. *Natal Witness*, 26 September.

Boo, E. (1990) *Eco-tourism. The Potential and Pitfalls*. Washington: World Wildlife Fund for Nature.

Booth, K. (1999) 'Three Tyrannies', in T. Dunne and N. Wheeler (eds) *Human Rights in Global Politics*. Cambridge: Cambridge University Press.

Boshoff, G.B. (1996) 'Beating the Participation Trap. Ensuring Sustainable Community Development in Marginalised Communities. A South African Perspective'. *Sustainable Development*, Vol. 4, 71–76.

Brennan, F. and G. Allen (2001) 'Community-based Eco-tourism, Social Exclusion and the Changing Political Economy of KwaZulu-Natal, South Africa', in D. Harrison, *Tourism and the Less Developed Countries*. London: C.A.B. International.

Brown, F. (1998) *Tourism Reassessed: Blight or Blessing?* Oxford: Butterworth-Heinemann.

Brown, P. (1996) 'Untangling the land issue'. *Natal Witness*, 26 January.

Butler, R. (1990) 'The Influence of the Media in Shaping International Tourist Patterns'. *Tourism and Recreation Research*, Vol. 15, No 2, 46–53.

Butler, R. (1994) 'Alternative Tourism. The Thin Edge of the Wedge', in V.L. Smith and W.R. Eadington (eds) *Tourism Alternatives*. Chichester: Wiley.

Carlisle, L. (1997) 'An Integrated Approach to Eco-tourism', in G. Creemers (ed.) *Research on Community Involvement in Tourism*. Pietermaritzburg: Natal Parks Board.

Carnie, T. (1991) 'Only Months to Save Dukuduku'. *Natal Mercury*, 1 May.

Carnie, T. (1993a) 'New Home for the Forest People'. *Natal Mercury*, 14 July.

Carnie, T. (1993b) 'Solution Hopes Still Running High'. *Natal Mercury*, 23 May.

Carnie, T. (1996) 'Kosi Patch of Paradise'. *Natal Mercury*, 29 June.

Carnie, T. (1997) 'The Dukuduku Tragedy Gains Momentum'. *Natal Mercury*, 17 January.

Carruthers, E. and A. Zaloumis (eds) (1995) 'People and Parks'. *Parks and People Conference*, Summary Proceedings. Durban.

Carver, R. (1996) *Continued Violence and Displacements*. Durban: Writenet Country Papers.

Cater, E. (April 1993) 'Eco-tourism in the Third World; Problems for Sustainable Tourism Development'. *Tourism Management*, Vol. 14, No 2, 85–90.

Cater, E. (1994) 'Eco-tourism in the Third World; Problems and Prospects for Sustainability', in Cater, E. and G. Lowman (eds) *Eco-tourism*. Chichester: Wiley.

Cater, E, and G. Lowman (eds) (1994) *Eco-tourism*. Chichester: Wiley.

Centre for Community Organisation, Research and Development (CORD)a (no date) 'The Limits of Traditional Ethnic Paradigms in the Explanation of Rural Social Organisation and Survival Strategies'. University of Natal.

Centre for Community Organisation, Research and Development (CORD)b (no date) 'Overcoming Apartheid's Land Legacy in Maputaland'. University of Natal.

Chambers, R. (1983) *Rural Development. Putting the Last First*. Harlow: Longman.

Chambers, R. (1985) *Rural Development: Putting the Last First*. Harlow: Longman.

Chambers, R. (1986) *Normal Professionalism, New Paradigms and Development*. Institute of Development Studies. Discussion Paper 227. University of Sussex.

Chambers, R. (1988) *Sustainable Livelihoods, Environment and Development. Putting the Poor People First*. Institute of Development Studies. Discussion Paper 240. University of Sussex.

Chambers, R. (1998) 'Us and Them. Finding a New Paradigm for Professionals in Sustainable Development', in D. Warburton (ed.) *Community and Sustainable Development*. London: Earthscan.

Christopher, A.J. (1999) 'The South African Census 1996. First Post Apartheid Census', *Geography*, Vol. 84, No 2, 270–75.

Coan, S. (1999) 'Story of an African Landscape'. *Natal Witness*, 10 February.

Coan, S. (1999) 'Taking Land Reform to a Village'. *Natal Witness*, 11 February.

Cioffi-Revilla, C. (1998) *Politics and Uncertainty. Theories, Models and Applications*. Cambridge: Cambridge University Press.

Cokayne, R. (1997) 'Satour Undertakes to Expose Corruption'. *Natal Mercury*, 1 July.

Community Resources Optimisation Programme (CROP) (1995) 'The CROP experience in Maputuland'.

Conservation Corporation (no date). 'Share a Dream'.

Conservation Corporation (no date). 'Tourism. South Africa's Reawakening'. Unpublished paper.

Cook, J. (1995) 'Empowering People for Sustainable Development', in P. FitzGerald et al. (eds) *Managing Sustainable Development in South Africa*. Cape Town: Oxford University Press.

Cox, M. (1999) (ed.) *Remorse and Reparation*. London: Jessica Kingsley.

Crick, B. (1969) *In Defence of Politics*. London: Penguin Books.

Dallmayr, F. (1998) 'Alternative Visions'. *Paths in the Global Village*. New York: Rowman and Littlefield.

Daniels, G. (2001) 'Rural Women to Fight for Their Land'. *Mail & Guardian*, 5 June.

Dann, G. (1996) 'Tourism. The Nostalgia Industry of the Future', in W. Theobold (ed.) *Global Tourism. The Next Decade*. Oxford: Butterworth-Heinemann.

Data Research Africa (1995) 'An Assessment of Alternative Economic Opportunities in the Greater St Lucia Region'. Unpublished paper.

Deininger, K. et al. (1999) *Implementing 'Market Friendly' Land Redistribution in South Africa. Lessons from the First Five Years*. Pretoria: Department of Land Affairs.

Deininger, K. and J. May (2000) *Is There Scope for Growth with Equity? The Case of Land Reform in South Africa*. Durban: University of Natal.

Delaney, G. (2000) *Citizenship in a Global Age*. Buckingham: Open University Press.

Department of Economic Affairs and Tourism, KwaZulu-Natal (1995) 'Annual Report'. Durban: DEAT.

Department of Environmental Affairs and Tourism (1996) 'White Paper on the Development and Promotion of Tourism in South Africa'. Pretoria.

Department of Environmental Affairs and Tourism (1997) 'White Paper on the Conservation and Sustainable Use of South Africa's Biological Diversity'. Pretoria.

Department of Environmental Affairs and Tourism (2000) 'South African Tourism Statistics'. Pretoria.

Department of Environmental Affairs and Tourism (2001) 'Parliament's Meeting in Gugulethu. Taking Tourism to the People'. Pretoria.

Department of Land Affairs (1995) 'Draft Land Policy Principles'. Pretoria.

Derwent, S. (1996) 'Land claim on St Lucia comes to fore'. *Daily News*, 8 March.

Dicken, P. (1998) *Global Shift*. London: Paul Chapman.

Dickson, P. and B. Streek (2000) 'Threat of Zim-style invasions in the Eastern Cape'. *Mail & Guardian*, 28 April.

Dower, N. (1998) *World Ethics. The New Agenda*. Edinburgh: Edinburgh University Press.

Doyal, L. and I. Gough (1991) *A Theory of Human Need*. London: Macmillan.

Duffy, R. (2002) *A Trip Too Far. Eco-tourism. Politics and Exploitation*. London: Earthscan.

Duminy, A. and B. Guest (eds) (1989) *Natal and Zululand. From Earliest Times to 1910*. Durban: University of Natal Press.

Dunkerley, D. et al. (eds) (2002) *Changing Europe. Identities, Nations and Citizens*. London: Routledge.

Dunne, T. and N. Wheeler (eds) (1999) *Human Rights in Global Politics*. Cambridge: Cambridge University Press.

Dunning, J.H. and M. McQueen (1982) 'Multinational Corporations in the International Hotel Industry'. *Annals of Tourism Research*, Vol. 9, No 1, 69–90.

Dworkin, R. (1996) 'Objectivity and Truth. You'd Better Believe It'. *Philosophy and Public Affairs*, 25, 87–139.

Easton, D. (1953) *The Political System. An Inquiry into the State of Political Science*. New York: Knopf.

Economist Intelligence Unit (1995) 'International Tourism Report South Africa, Report 4'.

Economist Intelligence Unit (2000) 'Country Report 2. South Africa'.

Ecoserv (Pty) Ltd (1995a) 'A Review of Eco-tourism Aspects in St Lucia Eastern Shores Mining Impact Assessment'. Land and Agriculture Policy Centre: Durban.

Ecoserv (Pty) Ltd (1995b) 'The Comparative Advantages of Eco-tourism in St Lucia'. Land and Agriculture Policy Centre: Durban.

Ecoserv (Pty) Ltd (1995) 'Minutes of the Workshop on Eco-tourism Opportunities in the St Lucia Region'. Educational Opportunities Council (EOC) (1995) Community Training and Capacity Building Programme: Pretoria.

Ellis, S. (1994) 'Of Elephants and Men. Politics and Nature Conservation in South Africa'. *Journal of Southern African Studies*, Vol. 20, No 1, 53–70.

Evans, M. (1998) 'Behind the Rhetoric. the Institutional Basis of Social Exclusion and Poverty'. *IDS Bulletin*, Vol. 29, No 1, 42–49.

Eveleth, A. (1996) 'Key Figures Named in Funding Row'. *Mail & Guardian*, 2 February.

Fanon, F. (1967) *Black Skin, White Masks*. New York: George Weidenfeld.

Farrell, B.H. and R.W. McClennan (1987) 'Tourism and the Physical Environment'. *Annals of Tourism Research*. Vol. 14, No 1, 1–16.

Farrell, B.H. and D. Runyan (1991) 'Ecology and Tourism'. *Annals of Tourism Research*, Vol. 18, No 1, 26–40.

FitzGerald, P. (1995) 'Towards a Developmental Public Administration' in P. FitzGerald et al. (eds) *Managing Sustainable Development in South Africa*. Cape Town: Oxford University Press.

FitzGerald, P. et al. (eds) (1995) *Managing Sustainable Development in South Africa*. Cape Town: Oxford University Press.

Fox Piven, F. and R. Cloward (1977) *Poor People's Movements. Why They Succeed and How They Fail*. New York: Pantheon Books.

Freie, J.F. (1998) *Counterfeit Community. The Exploitation of Our Longings for Connectedness*. New York: Rowman and Littlefield.

Freire, P. (1972) *Cultural Action for Freedom*. London: Penguin.

Freire, P. (1998) *Pedagogy of Freedom. Ethics, Democracy, and Civic Courage*. Oxford: Rowman and Littlefield.

Fukuyama, F. (1995) *Trust. The Social Virtues and the Creation of Prosperity*. London: Hamish Hamilton.

Furedi, F. (2002) *Culture of Fear: Risk Taking and the Morality of Low Expectation*. London: Continuum.

Furlong, D. (1996) 'The Conceptualisation of "Trust" in Economic Thought'. Institute of Development Studies. Working Paper 35. University of Sussex.

Gamble, W. (1989) *Tourism and Development in Africa*. London: John Murray.

Gaventa, J. (1998) 'Poverty, Participation and Social Exclusion in North and South'. *IDS Bulletin*, Vol. 29, No 1, 50–57.

Geertz, C. (2000) *Available Light. Anthropological Reflections on Philosophical Topics*. Princeton: Princeton University Press.

George, R. (1998) 'Measuring the Effects of the Planet Hollywood Incident on International Tourist Visitors to Cape Town'. Unpublished paper.

Ghai, D. (ed.) (1994) *Development and Environment. Sustaining People and Nature*. Oxford: Basil Blackwell.

Ghimire, K.B. (1994) 'Parks and People. Livelihood Issues in National Park Management in Thailand and Madagascar', in D. Ghai (ed.) *Development and Environment. Sustaining People and Nature*. Oxford: Basil Blackwell.

Ghimire, K.B. (2001) (ed.) *The Native Tourist. Mass Tourism within Developing Countries*. London: Earthscan.

Gibson, H. (1996) 'At last! Land Reform a Reality'. *Sunday Tribune*, 28 July.

Gibson, H. (1997) 'Anger Erupts over Muden Land Sale'. *Sunday Tribune*, 7 September.

Gibson, H. (1997) 'Death for Christmas'. *Sunday Tribune*, 7 December.

Giddens, A. (1999) *The Consequences of Modernity*. Stanford: Stanford University Press.

Glaser, D. (2001) *Politics and Society in South Africa*. London: Sage.

Gluckman, G. (1940) 'The Kingdom of the Zulu in South Africa', in M. Fortes and E.E. Evans-Pritchard (eds) *African Political Systems*. Oxford: Oxford University Press.

Gluckman, G. (1973) *Custom and Conflict in Africa*. Oxford: Blackwell.

Goldberg, J. and L. Markoczy (1998) 'Time Travel, Mind Control, and Other Every Day Phenomena Required for Cooperative Behaviour'. Paper presented at the

ESRC Economic Beliefs and Behaviour Conference on Decision Making in Theory and Practice, 1–2 July, University College, Oxford.

Gosling, J. (1990) *Weakness of the Will*. London: Routledge.

Goulet, D. (1995) *Development Ethics. Theory and Practice*. London: Zed Books.

Government of National Unity (1994) 'Reconstruction and Development Programme'. Pretoria.

Government of National Unity (1995) 'Rural Development Strategy'. Pretoria.

Gowans, J. (1994) 'Sharing the future'. *Focus*, Winter, 14–15.

Gowans, J. (1999) 'Tourism: the key'. *Sunday Tribune*, 22 March.

Green, R. (1979) 'Toward Planning Tourism in African Countries', in de Kadt (ed.) *Tourism. Passport to Development?* Oxford: Oxford University Press.

Grossman, D. and E. Koch (1995) 'Nature Tourism in South Africa. Links with the Reconstruction and Development Programme'. Unpublished paper.

Gunn, C.A. (1994) 'Emergence of Effective Tourism Planning and Development', in A.V. Seaton (ed.) *Tourism. The State of the Art*. Chichester: Wiley, 10–19.

Gutmann, A. and D. Thompson (1996) *Democracy and Disagreement. Why Moral Conflict Cannot Be Avoided in Politics, and What Should Be Done about It*. Cambridge, MA: Harvard University Press.

Guy, J. (1998) 'Battling with Banality. Tourism, Historians, and the Killing Fields of Zululand'. History and African Studies Seminar Series, No 13, University of Natal.

Gwala, Z. (1992) 'Natal Conflict Under the Microscope. A Case Study Approach', in S. Bekker (ed.) *Capturing the Event. Conflict Trends in the Natal Region, 1986–1992. Indicator SA*, December, 55–67.

de Haas, M. (1994) 'Sorrow in Sundumbli'. *Indicator SA*, Vol. 11, No 3, 23–27.

de Haas, M. and P. Zulu (1994) 'Ethnicity and Federalism. The Case of KwaZulu-Natal'. *Journal of Southern African Studies*, Vol. 20, No 3, 433–46.

Habermas, J. (1975) *Moral Consciousness and Communicative Action*. Cambridge, MA: MIT Press.

Hales, D. (1989) 'Changing Concepts of National Parks', in D. Western and M. Pearl (eds) *Conservation for the Twenty-first Century*. Oxford: Oxford University Press.

Hans, B. (2001) 'Benefits in store for reserve community'. *Echo*, 6 April.

Hare, R.M. (1981) *Moral Thinking*. Oxford: Oxford University Press.

Harré, R. and D.N. Robinson (1995) 'On the Primacy of Duty'. *Philosophy*, 70, 513–32.

Harré, R. (1999) 'Trust and its Surrogates. Psychological Foundations of Political Process', in M.E. Warren (ed.) *Democracy and Trust*. Cambridge: Cambridge University Press.

Harris, P. (1990) *On Political Obligation*. London: Routledge.

Harrison, D. (2001) *Tourism and the Less Developed Countries*. London: CAB International.

Hartley, R. (1996) 'The Land Revolution'. *Sunday Times*, 19 May.

Harvey, D. (1973) *Social Justice and the City*. London: Edward Arnold.

Harvey, D. (1996) *Justice, Nature, and the Geography of Difference*. Oxford: Blackwell.

Healy, R. (1994) 'The Role of Tourism in Sustainable Development'. Unpublished paper.

Heath, E. (1994) 'Beyond the New South Africa; Into the New Tourism'. *Satour Quarterly Review*, Vol. 3, No 1, 2–3.

Hirsch, F. (1977) *Social Limits to Growth*. London: RKP.

Hirshleifer, J. (1987) *Economic Behaviour in Adversity*. Brighton: Wheatsheaf.

Hobbes, T. (1962) *Leviathan*. New York: Macmillan.

Hodgson, G. (ed.) (2002) *A Modern Reader in Institutional and Evolutionary Economics*. Cheltenham, UK: Edward Elgar.

Honey, M. (1999) *Eco-tourism and Sustainable Development. Who Owns Paradise?* Washington, DC: Island Press.

Humphrey, J. and H. Schmitz (1996) 'Trust and Economic Development. Institute of Development Studies'. Discussion Paper 355. University of Sussex.

Huntington, S. (1996) *The Clash of Civilisations and the Reworking of the World Order*. New York: Simon and Schuster.

Ignatieff, M. (1998) *The Warrior's Honour. Ethnic War and the Modern Conscience*. London: Chatto and Windus.

Ignatieff, M. (1999) 'Nationalism and Toleration', in S. Mendus (ed.) *The Politics of Toleration*. Edinburgh: Edinburgh University Press.

Inglehart, R. (1999) 'Trust, well-being and democracy'. in M.E. Warren (ed.) *Democracy and Trust*. Cambridge: Cambridge University Press.

Inglis, F. (2000) *The Delicious History of the Holiday*. London: Routledge.

Institute for Public Policy Research (1999) 'Regulating Regulation'. Unpublished paper.

Isin, E.F. and P.K. Wood (1999) *Citizenship and Identity*. London: Sage.

Jenkins, C. (1994) 'Tourism in Developing Countries. The Privatisation Issue', in A.V. Seaton (ed.) *Tourism. The State of the Art*. Chichester: Wiley.

Johnston, A. (1993) 'Zulu Dawn', *Indicator SA*, Vol. 11, No 3, 23–26.

Jones, A. (1992) 'Is there a real "alternative tourism"?'. *Tourism Management*, Vol. 13, 102–3.

de Jouvenal, B. (1958) 'The Efficient Imperative', in D. Wrong (1979) *Power. Its Forms, Bases and Uses*. Oxford: Basil Blackwell.

de Kadt, E. (ed.) (1979) *Tourism. Passport to Development?* Oxford: Oxford University Press.

de Kadt, E. (1990) 'Making the Alternative Sustainable. Lessons from Development for Tourism'. Institute of Development Studies, Discussion Paper 272. University of Sussex.

Kaldor, M. (1999) 'Transnational Civil Society', in T. Dunne and N. Wheeler (eds) *Human Rights in Global Politics*. Cambridge: Cambridge University Press.

Khosa, M. (1994) 'Transport and Popular Struggles in South Africa'. *Antipode*, Vol. 27, No 2, 167–88.

Kidder, R. (1995) *How Good People Make Tough Choices*. New York: Simon and Schuster.

Kitching, G. (1982) *Development and Underdevelopment in Historical Perspective*. London: Methuen.

Koch, E. (1991) 'Rainbow Alliances. Community Struggles Around Ecological Problems', in J. Cook and E. Koch (eds) *Going Green. People, Politics and the Environment in South Africa*. Cape Town: Oxford University Press.

Koch, E. (1994) 'Reality or Rhetoric? Eco-tourism and Rural Reconstruction in South Africa'. United Nations Research Institute for Social Development (UNRISD).

Koch, E. (1997) 'New Culture of Hope in KwaZulu'. *Mail & Guardian*, 18 July.

Koch, E. and P.J. Massyn (2001) 'South Africa's Domestic Tourism Sector. Promises and Problems', in K.B. Ghimire *The Native Tourist*. London: Earthscan.

Koch, E., P. Stober and M. Edmonds (1995) 'Pretoria Fiddles while KwaZulu-Natal Burns'. *Mail & Guardian*, 22 September.

Kothari, S. (1993) *Poverty: Human Consciousness and the Amnesia of Development*. London: Zen Books.

Krippendorf, J. (1987) *The Holiday Makers*. London: Heinemann.

Krog, A. (1997) 'Cry, beloved country', *Guardian*, 18 January.

Krog, A. (1999) *Country of My Skull*. London: Vintage.

Kuhn, T. (1962) *The Structure of Scientific Revolutions*. Chicago: University of Chicago Press.

KwaZulu-Natal Nature Conservation Service (1999) 'St Lucia. A World Heritage Site'. Pietermaritzburg.

KwaZulu-Natal Nature Conservation Service (2000) 'Fees and Charges'. Pietermaritzburg.

KwaZulu-Natal Tourism Authority (1997) 'International Tourism Market Trends with Specific Reference to KwaZulu-Natal'. Durban.

KwaZulu-Natal Tourism Authority (1998) 'KwaZulu-Natal Lubombuo Spatial Development Initiative. Framework Planning for Tourism Development'. Durban.

KwaZulu-Natal Tourism Authority (1999) 'KwaZulu-Natal's Domestic Tourism Market, October 1997–September 1998'. Durban.

KwaZulu-Natal Tourism Authority (2000) 'Annual Report, 1999–2000'. Durban.

KwaZulu-Natal Tourism Authority (2001) 'Our Tourism Industry'. Durban.

Lasswell, H. (1936) *Politics. Who Gets What, When, and How*. New York: McGraw Hill.

Lea, J.P. (1993) 'Tourism Development Ethics in the Third World'. *Annals of Tourism Research*, Vol. 20, No 4, 701–15.

Leftwich, A. (ed.) (1996) *Democracy and Development*. Cambridge: Polity Press.

Leftwich, A. (1996) 'On the Primacy of Politics in Development', in A. Leftwich (ed.) *Democracy and Development*. Cambridge: Polity Press.

Leipitz, A. (1992) *Towards a New Economic Order*. Cambridge: Polity Press.

Leslie, D. (1994) 'Sustainable Tourism or Developing Sustainable Approaches to Lifestyle?' *World Leisure & Recreation*, Vol. 36, No 3, 30–36.

Lessing, D. (1986) *The Good Terrorist*. London: Grafton Books.

Levin, R. and D. Weiner (1996) 'The Politics of Land Reform in South Africa after Apartheid. Perspectives, Problems, Prospects'. *The Journal of Peasant Studies*, 23, 93–119.

Levy, N. (1995) 'Affirmative Action Interventions', in FitzGerald, P. et al. (eds) *Managing Sustainable Development in South Africa*. Cape Town: Oxford University Press.

Liebenberg, L., G. Creemers and P.M. Massyn (1995) 'A New Perspective on the Economic Contribution of Key Conservation Areas in South Africa. A Case Study of St Lucia'. Unpublished paper for presentation to the St Lucia Land Use Options Workshop, 7–8 November.

Lillywhite, M. (1991) *Low Impact Tourism on a Strategy for Sustaining Natural and Cultural Resources in Sub-Sahara Africa*. Washington DC: USAID.

Linscot, G. (1991) 'Game Reserve's Eco-tourism Venture'. *Natal Mercury*, 16 August.

Lipzet, S. (1959) 'Some Social Requisites of Democracy. Economic Development and Political Legitimacy'. *The American Political Science Review*, Vol. 53, No 1, 65–91.

Lockhart, T. (2000) *Moral Uncertainty and its Consequences*. New York: Oxford University Press.

Lodge, T. (1996) 'South Africa. Democracy and Development in a Post-apartheid Society', in A. Leftwich (ed.) *Democracy and Development*. Cambridge: Polity Press.

Lodge, T. (1998) 'Corruption in South Africa'. *African Affairs*, 97, 157–87.

Louw, A. (1994) 'Conflicts of Interest: Overview of Conflict in KwaZulu-Natal from 1989–1993'. *Indicator SA*, Vol. 11, No 2.

Louw, A. and S. Bekker (1992) 'Conflict in the Natal Region. A Database Approach', in S. Bekker (ed.) 'Capturing the Event: Conflict Trends in the Natal Region', 1986–1992. *Indicator SA*, Issue 4, 15–54.

Machiavelli, N. (1998) *The Prince*. Oxford: Oxford University Press.

MacIntyre, A. (1981) *After Virtue. A Study in Moral Theory*. London: Duckworth.

MacIntyre, A. (1999) 'Toleration and the Goods of Conflict' in S. Mendus, *The Politics of Toleration*. Edinburgh: Edinburgh University Press.

Mader, U. (1988) 'Tourism and the Environment.' *Annals of Tourism Research*, Vol. 15, No 2, 274–76.

Mainsbridge, J. (1980) *Beyond Adversary Democracy*. New York: Basic Books.

Mair, L. (1983) *An Introduction to Social Anthropology*. Oxford: Oxford University Press.

Makele, B. (2000) 'Who Rules. Mayor or Chief?' *Sunday Tribune*, 23 September.

Mandela, N. (1999) 'Opening Address in the Special debate on the Report of the Truth and Reconciliation Commission'. 25 February, www.anc.org.za/ancdocs

Mann, M. (1973) *Consciousness and Action Among the Western Working Classes*. London: Macmillan.

Marx, K. and F. Engels (1954) *Manifesto of the Communist Party*. Moscow: Foreign Languages Publishing House.

Mathenjwa, S., C. Poultney and E. Russell (1995) *Greater St Lucia Wetland. Community Based Projects for Conservation and Development*. Durban: Community Resources Optimisation Programme.

Mathieson, A. and G. Wall (1982) *Tourism. Economic, Physical and Social Impacts*. Harlow: Longman.

Matlou, J. (2000) 'A beginner's Guide to Land Matters'. *Mail & Guardian*, 8 May.

May, J. (1995) *An Assessment of Alternative Economic Opportunities for the Greater St Lucia Region*. Durban: Data Research Africa.

May, V. (1991) 'Tourism, Environment and Development, Values, Sustainability'. *Tourism Management*, Vol. 12, No 2, 112–18.

Mbhele, W. (1997) '"Betrayed" Chiefs Cut ANC Ties'. *Mail & Guardian*, 3 October.

McCannell, D. (1976) *The Tourist. A New Theory of the Leisure Class*. New York: Schoken.

McIntosh, M. et al. (1998) *Corporate Citizenship. Successful Strategies for Responsible Companies*. London: Financial Times Publishing.

McLean, L. (1994) 'The Politics of Policing', *Indicator SA*, Vol. 12, No 1.

Meer, S. (1997) 'Gender and Land Rights. The Struggle over Resources in Post-apartheid South Africa'. *IDS Bulletin*, Vol. 28, No 3, 133–44.

Mendus, S. (1988) *Justifying Toleration. Conceptual and Historical Perspectives*. Cambridge: Cambridge University Press.

Mendus, S. (ed.) (1999) *The Politics of Toleration*. Edinburgh: Edinburgh University Press.

Meyer, M. and L. Zucker (1989) *Permanently Failing Organizations*. Newbury Park, CA: Sage.

Midgely, S. (1995) *Social Development*. London: Sage.

Mill, J.S. (1978) 'On Liberty', in J.M. Robson (ed.) *The Collected Works of John Stuart Mill*, Vol. 18. Toronto: the University of Toronto Press.

Ministry for Administration and Tourism (1992) 'White Paper on Tourism'. Pretoria.

Ministry for Economic Affairs and Tourism (1995) 'KwaZulu-Natal Tourism Development Summit'. Durban.

Mishra, R. (1999) *Globalization and the Welfare State*. Cheltenham, UK: Edward Elgar.

Morrison, O. (1997) 'Community Involvement in Tourism near the Hhluhluwe-Umfolozi Park', in G. Creemers (ed.) *Research on Community Involvement in Tourism*. Pietermaritzburg: Natal Parks Board.

Motteux, N. et al. (1999) 'Empowerment for Development. Taking Participatory Appraisal Further in Africa'. *Development in Practice*, Vol. 9 No 3, 261–73.

Munck, R. (1994) 'South Africa. The Great Economic Debate'. *Third World Quarterly*, Vol. 15, No 2, 205–17.

Munnik, V. (1995) 'Turning the tide', *Sunday Tribune*, 12 November.

Munslow, B. and P. FitzGerald (1994) 'South Africa. The Sustainable Development Challenge'. *Third World Quarterly*, Vol. 15, No 2, 227–41.

Munslow, B. et al. (1995) 'Sustainable Development. Turning Vision into Reality', in P. FitzGerald et al. (eds) *Managing Sustainable Development in South Africa*. Capetown: Oxford University Press.

Münster, D. (1996) *Planning with People. A Transactive Planning Case Study*. Pietermaritzburg: Natal Parks Board.

Mutume, G. (1997) 'Protests as World Bank Chief Slips in and out'. *Mail & Guardian*, 18 February.

Nash, D. (1996) *Anthropology of Tourism*. New York: Elsevier Science.

Natal Parks Board (1991) 'Annual Report'. Pietermaritzburg: NPB.

Natal Parks Board (1994) 'Annual Report'. Pietermaritzburg: NPB.

Natal Parks Board (1995a) 'Research Economics Programme'. Pietermaritzburg: NPB.

Natal Parks Board (1995b) 'Annual Report'. Pietermaritzburg: NPB.

Natal Parks Board (1996a) 'A Gateway to the Greater St Lucia Wetland Park'. Pietermaritzburg: NPB.

Natal Parks Board (1996b) 'Land Use Proposals for the Dukuduku Forest'. Pietermaritzburg: NPB.

Natal Parks Board (1997) 'Annual Report 1996/7'. Pietermaritzburg: NPB.

Natal Parks Board (1998) 'Community Levy. People Helping People'. Pietermaritzburg: NPB.

Ndleia, Ntokozo Fortunate (2002) 'Representations of Zulu Cultural Identity in Cultural Tourism. A Case Study of Izintaba Cultural Village'. Unpublished M.A. dissertation, Graduate Programme in Cultural and Media Studies, University of Natal.

Nieuvoudt, L. (1994) 'Wind Through The Whitelands', *Focus*, Winter, 5–6.

Nozick, R. (1974) *Anarchy, State and Utopia*. Oxford: Basil Blackwell.

Nozick, R. (1998) 'Newcomb's Problem and Two Principles of Choice', in J. Goldberg and L. Markoczy 'Time Travel, Mind Control, and Other Every Day Phenomena Required for Cooperative Behaviour'. Paper presented at the ESRC Economic Beliefs and Behaviour Conference on Decision Making in Theory and Practice, 1–2 July, University College, Oxford.

Offe, C. (1999) 'How Can We Trust Our Fellow Citizens?', in M.E. Warren (ed.) *Democracy and Trust*. Cambridge: Cambridge University Press.

O'Hagan, A. (1997) *Guardian*, 26 November.

Olivier, J. (1992) 'Political Conflict in South Africa. A Resource Mobilisation Approach', in S. Bekker (ed.) *Capturing the Event. Conflict Trends in the Natal Region, 1862–1992. Indicator SA*, 1–14.

Olson, M. (1971) *The Logic of Collective Action*. Cambridge, MA: Harvard University Press.

Orams, M, (1995) 'Towards a More Desirable Form of Eco-tourism'. *Tourism Management*, Vol. 16, No 1, 3–8.

O'Riordan, T. (1998) 'Civic Science and Sustainability', in D. Warburton (ed.) *Community and Sustainable Development*. London: Earthscan.

Orwell, G. (1949) *Nineteen Eighty-Four, a Novel*. London: Secker and Warburg.

Parinello, G.L. (1993) 'Motivation and Anticipation in Post-Industrial Tourism'. *Annals of Tourism Research*, Vol. 20, No 2, 223–49.

Parker, D. and R. Stacey (1994) 'Chaos, Management and Economics'. IEA Hobart Paper No 5, London.

Pateman, C. (1970) *Participation and Democratic Theory*. Cambridge: Cambridge University Press.

Paton, C. (1999) 'Gender Laws. In Search of a Kinder Face for Traditional Values'. *Sunday Times*, 19 December.

Pearce, D. (1992) 'Alternative Tourism Concepts, Classifications and Questions', in V.L. Smith and W.R. Eadington (eds) *Tourism Alternatives*. Chichester: Wiley.

Phillips, M. (1997) *Observer*, 30 November.

Picard, L. and M. Garrity (1995) 'Development Management in Africa', in P. FitzGerald et al. (eds) *Managing Sustainable Development In South Africa*. Cape Town: Oxford University Press.

Pleumaron, A. (1994) 'The Political Economy of Tourism'. *Ecologist*, Vol. 24, No 4, 142–48.

Poole, P. (1989) 'Developing a Partnership of Indigenous Peoples, Conservationists and Land Use Planners in Latin America'. Washington DC: World Bank.

Poon, A. (1994) 'The 'New Tourism' Revolution'. *Tourism Management*, Vol. 15, No 2, 91–92.

Preston-Whyte, R. (1995) 'The Politics of Ecology. Dredge Mining in South Africa'. *Environmental Conservation*, Vol. 22, No 2, 151–56.

Preston-Whyte, R. (1997) 'Sustainable Urban Development and the Dynamics of Change. The Case of Durban'. *Urban Forum*, Vol. 8, No 2, 137–52.

Pretty, N. (1995) 'Participatory Learning for Sustainable Agriculture'. *World Development*, Vol. 23, No 8, 1247–63.

Proctor, C. (1995) 'KwaZulu-Natal Sub-Provincial Priority Study. Tourism'. Prepared for the Government of KwaZulu-Natal. Pietermaritzburg.

Province of KwaZulu-Natal (1996) 'The KwaZulu-Natal Tourism Act (as amended)'. Durban: Tourism South Africa.

Rawls, J. (1999) *A Theory of Justice*. Oxford: Oxford University Press.

Ray, M. (1996) 'Struggle for a Place in the Sun'. *Natal Witness*, 7 November.

Redclift, M. (1991) *Sustainable Development. Exploring the Contradictions*. London: Routledge.

Ritchken, E. (1995) 'The RDP, Governance and Rural Development', in P. FitzGerald et al. (eds) *Managing Sustainable Development in South Africa*. Cape Town: Oxford University Press.

Ritzer, G. (1999) *Enchanting a Disenchanted World. Revolutionising the Means of Consumption*. Thousand Oaks: Pine Forge Press.

Roberts, S.E. et al. (1997) 'Report on a boundary survey of the proposed Nature Reserve'. East Griqualand, Pietermaritzburg: Unpublished report, NPB.

Robertson, G. (1999) *Crimes against Humanity. The Struggle for Social Justice*. London: Allen Lane.

Rural Development Task Team and the Department of Land Affairs (1997) 'Rural Development Framework'. Pretoria.

Ryan, R. (1994) *Sustainable Development and the Environment in Chile*. Geneva: UNEP.

Said, E. (1986) 'On Palestine Identity: A Conversation with Salman Rushdie'. *New Left Review*, 160, 63–80.

Sampson, A. (1999) *Mandela: The Authorized Biography*. London: HarperCollins.

Satour (1994) 'Analysis of Arrival Statistics and Trends'. Pretoria: Satour.

Satour (1994) 'International Visitors To South Africa. Market Survey'. Pretoria: Satour.

Satour (1994) *Quarterly*, Vol. 3, No 1. Pretoria: Satour.

Satour (1995a) 'International Visitors To South Africa. Market Survey'. Pretoria: Satour.

Satour (1995b) 'Analysis of Arrival Statistics and Trends'. Pretoria: Satour.

Satour (1995c) 'Eco-tourism. Principles and Practice'. Pretoria: Satour.

Satour (2001) *Tourism in South Africa in the New Millennium*. Pretoria: Satour.

Scarman, Lord (1981) *The Scarman Report*. London: HMSO.

Schattschneider, E.E. (1960) *The Semi-sovereign People*. New York: Holt, Rinehart and Winston.

Schumacher, E.F. (1973) *Small is Beautiful. Economics as if People Mattered*. New York: Harper and Row.

Schutte, L.B. (1995) 'New Training Approaches. Exploring the Paradigm Shift', in P. FitzGerald et al. (eds). *Managing Sustainable Development in South Africa*. Cape Town: Oxford University Press.

Schwartz D. and S. Schwartz (1975) *New Directions in Political Socialization*. New York: The Free Press.

Seabrook, J. (1996) *Travels in the Slave Trade*. London: Pluto Press.

Selwyn, T. (ed.) (1996) *The Tourist Image*. Chichester: Wiley.

Sen, A. (1999) *Development as Freedom*. Oxford: Oxford University Press.

Seymour, J. (1999) *KwaZulu-Natal International Tourism Market: January 1998–December 1998*. Durban: KZNTA.

Shapiro, I. and C. Hacker-Gordon (eds) (1999) *Democracy's Edges*. Cambridge: Cambridge University Press.

Shapiro, I. and C. Jung (1996) 'South African Democracy Revisited. A Reply to Koeble and Reynolds'. *Politics and Society*, Vol. 24, No 3, 237–47.

Shaw, G. and A. Williams (1994) *Critical Issues in Tourism*. Oxford: Blackwell.

Shepherd-Smith, J. (1995) 'Reserve Fence Torn Down'. *Sunday Tribune*, 19 November.

Sher, G. (1997) *Approximate Justice*. Oxford: Rowman and Littlefield.

Simon, H. (1969) 'Notes on the Observation and Measurement of Power', in T. Bell (ed.) *Political Power. A Reader in Theory and Research*. New York: The Free Press.

Smith, D.M. (ed.) (1992) *The Apartheid City and Beyond*. London: Routledge.

Smith, V.L. (1994) 'Privatisation in the Third World. Small-scale Tourism Enterprises', in W. Theobald (ed.) *Global Tourism. The Next Decade*. Oxford: Heinemann.

Smith, V.L. and W.R. Eadington (eds) (1994) *Tourism Alternatives*. Chichester: Wiley.

South African Wetlands Conservation Programme (1999) www.environment.gov.zu

Spivack, S. (1991) 'Foreword'. *World Travel & Tourism Review*, xi.

Stober, P. (1995) 'KwaZulu's Game Park Training Grounds'. *Mail & Guardian*, 22 September.

Streeker, B. (2000) 'Farmland Expropriation Threat Denounced'. *Mail & Guardian*, 23 October.

Swilling, M. and L. Boya (1995) 'Local Governance in Transition', in P. FitzGerald et al. (eds) *Managing Sustainable Development in South Africa*. Cape Town: Oxford University Press.

Taylor, C. (1992) 'The Politics of Recognition', in A. Gutmann (ed.) *Multiculturalism and the Politics of Recognition*. Princeton, NJ: Princeton University Press.

Taylor, G. (1995) 'The Community Approach. Does it Really Work?' *Tourism Management*, Vol. 16, No7, 487–90.

Taylor, R. (1995), *Greater St Lucia Wetland Park*. Cape Town: Struik.

Taylor, S. (1995) *Shaka's Children*. London: HarperCollins.

Taylor-Gooby, P. et al. (1998) 'Risk and the Welfare State'. Paper presented at the ESRC Economic Beliefs and Behaviour Programme Conference, on 'Decision Making in Theory and Practice', University College, Oxford, 1–2 July.

Tearfund (2000) 'Tourism. An ethical issue'. *Guardian*, 15 January.

Theobald, W. (ed.) (1994) *Global Tourism. The Next Decade*. Oxford: Heinemann.

Thomas, A. (1999) 'Remorse and Reparation. A Philosophical Analysis' in M. Cox (ed.) *Remorse and Reparation*. London: Jessica Kingsley.

Titmus, R. (1970) *The Gift Relationship. From Human Blood to Social Policy*. Oxford: George Allen and Unwin.

du Toit, A. (1993) *Understanding South African Political Violence. A New Problematic?* New York: United Nations Research Institute for Social Development.

Ulslaner, E.M. (1999) 'Democracy and Social Capital', in M.E. Warren (ed.) *Democracy and Trust*. Cambridge: Cambridge University Press.

United Nations Development Programme (1999) *Human Development Report*. Oxford: Oxford University Press.

Vanderhaeghen, Y. (1998) 'A War the Government Doesn't Need'. *Natal Witness*, 28, February.

Var, A.P. et al. (1996) 'Tourism and World Peace', in W. Theobold (ed.) *Global Tourism. The Next Decade*. Oxford: Butterworth-Heinemann.

Venter, A. K. (2000) *Community-Based Natural Resource Management in South Africa: Experience from the Greater St Lucia Area*. Burkino Faso: IUCN.

Walle, A. (1995) 'Business Ethics and Tourism. From Micro to Macro Perspectives', *Tourism Management*, Vol. 16, No 4, 263–68.

Wanhill, S. (1994) 'Role of Government Incentives', in W. Theobald (ed.) *Global Tourism. The Next Decade*. Oxford: Heinemann.

Warren, M.E. (ed.) (1999) *Democracy and Trust*. Cambridge: Cambridge University Press.

Wells, M. and K. Brandon (1992) *People and Parks*. Washington: World Bank.

Western D. and M.R. Wright (1994) *Natural Connections. Perspectives in Community-based Conservation*. Washington: Island Press.

Whellan, R. (1999) *Wild in the Woods. The Myth of the Noble Eco-Savage*. London: IEA Studies on the Environment No 14.

Wheeller, B. (1991) 'Tourism's Troubled Times. Responsible Tourism is not the Answer'. *Tourism Management*, Vol. 12, No 2, 91–96.

Wheeller, B. (1992) 'Is Progressive Tourism Appropriate?' *Tourism Management*, Vol. 13, No 1, 104–5.

Whelan, T. (1992) 'Eco-tourism and its Role in Sustainable Development', in T. Whelan (ed.) *Nature Tourism*. Washington: Island Press.

Wilde, O. (1891) 'The Soul of Man under Socialism', in Holland, V. (ed.) (1966) *Complete Works of Oscar Wilde*. London: Collins.

Williams, B. (2002) *Truth and Truthfulness*. Princeton: Princeton University Press.

Williamson, O. and S. Masten (eds) (1999) *The Economics of Transaction Costs*. Cheltenham, UK: Edward Elgar.

Wooldridge, D. and P. Cranko (1995) 'Transforming Public Sector Institutions', in P. FitzGerald et al. (eds) *Sustainable Development in South Africa*. Cape Town: Oxford University Press.

Worden, N. (1994) *The Making of Modern South Africa*. Oxford: Blackwell.

World Bank (1988) 'Madagascar Environmental Action Plan'. Washington DC.

World Bank (1994) 'The World Bank and Participation'. Washington DC.

World Tourism Organisation (1992) 'Guidelines. Development of National Parks and Protected Areas for Tourism'. Madrid.

World Tourism Organisation (1996) 'Educating the Educators in Tourism'. Madrid.

World Tourism Organisation (1997) 'Towards New forms of Public Private Partnership'. Madrid.

World Tourism Organisation (1999a) 'Sustainable Development of Tourism. An Annotated Bibliography'. Madrid.

World Tourism Organisation (1999b) 'Observations on International Tourism'. Madrid.

World Tourism Organisation (2001) 'Agenda 21 for the Travel and Tourism Industry'. Madrid.

Worpole, K. (1998) 'Bottle Banks in Arcadia? Environmental Campaigning and Social Justice', in D. Warburton (ed.) *Community and Sustainable Development*. London: Earthscan.

Wringe, C. (1995) 'Educational Rights in Multicultural Democracies'. *Journal of Philosophy of Education*, Vol. 29, No 2, 285–92.

Wringe, C. (1999) 'The Future of European Citizenship'. Conference paper, Bremen, Germany.

Wrong, D. (1979) *Power. Its Forms, Bases and Uses*. Oxford: Basil Blackwell.

Zondi, D. (1997) 'A Community Torn over Land Issue'. *Natal Mercury*, 26 November.

www.mintel.com/country
www.satour.org
www.tbcsa.org.za/initiatives
www.und.ac.za/und/ccms/intro
www.zulu.org.za

Index